7/15

WITHDRAWN

D0144430

Hebbing

Vintage Game Consoles

Bound to Create

You are a creator.

Whatever your form of expression — photography, filmmaking, animation, games, audio, media communication, web design, or theatre — you simply want to create without limitation. Bound by nothing except your own creativity and determination.

Focal Press can help.

For over 75 years Focal has published books that support your creative goals. Our founder, Andor Kraszna-Krausz, established Focal in 1938 so you could have access to leading-edge expert knowledge, techniques, and tools that allow you to create without constraint. We strive to create exceptional, engaging, and practical content that helps you master your passion.

Focal Press and you.

Bound to create.

We'd love to hear how we've helped you create. Share your experience:

www.focalpress.com/boundtocreate

Focal Press
Taylor & Francis Group

Vintage Game Consoles

AN INSIDE LOOK AT APPLE, ATARI, COMMODORE, NINTENDO, AND THE GREATEST GAMING PLATFORMS OF ALL TIME

Bill Loguidice *and* **Matt Barton**

Focal Press
Taylor & Francis Group

NEW YORK AND LONDON

First published 2014
by Focal Press
70 Blanchard Road, Suite 402, Burlington, MA 01803

and by Focal Press
2 Park Square, Milton Park, Abingdon, Oxon OX14 4RN

Focal Press is an imprint of the Taylor & Francis Group, an informa business

© 2014 Taylor & Francis

The right of Bill Loguidice and Matt Barton to be identified as the authors
of this work has been asserted by them in accordance with sections 77 and
78 of the Copyright, Designs and Patents Act 1988.

All rights reserved. No part of this book may be reprinted or reproduced or
utilised in any form or by any electronic, mechanical, or other means, now
known or hereafter invented, including photocopying and recording, or in
any information storage or retrieval system, without permission in writing
from the publishers.

Notices
Knowledge and best practice in this field are constantly changing. As new
research and experience broaden our understanding, changes in research
methods, professional practices, or medical treatment may become
necessary.

Practitioners and researchers must always rely on their own experience
and knowledge in evaluating and using any information, methods,
compounds, or experiments described herein. In using such information
or methods they should be mindful of their own safety and the safety of
others, including parties for whom they have a professional responsibility.

Product or corporate names may be trademarks or registered trademarks,
and are used only for identification and explanation without intent to
infringe.

Library of Congress Cataloging in Publication Data
Loguidice, Bill.
Vintage game consoles : an inside look at Apple, Atari, Commodore,
Nintendo, and the greatest gaming platforms of all time / Bill Loguidice,
Matt Barton.
    pages cm
Includes bibliographical references.
ISBN 978-0-415-85600-3 (pbk.)
1. Video games—Equipment and supplies—History. 2. Video games—
Equipment and supplies—Collectors and collecting. 3. Video games—
United States—History. I. Barton, Matt. II. Title.
    TK6681.L644 2014
    794.8028'4—dc23
    2013038380

ISBN: 978-0-415-85600-3 (pbk)
ISBN: 978-0-203-72831-4 (ebk)

Typeset by Alex Lazarou

Printed in Canada

Contents

Acknowledgments

We would like to thank our families and the wonderful folks at Focal Press for their help and support with this ambitious project. In particular, we'd like to thank Sean Connelly and Caitlin Murphy. Working with you two has been a rare pleasure. We'd also like to thank our amazing cover artist, Nathan Strum.

Foreword

In the vaults of the videogame industry lie many relics. Some are mere curiosities, obscure and grotesque contraptions that few have seen, and even fewer loved. Is there treasure amongst this labyrinth of cardboard boxes and ceiling-high metal shelves, this jungle of snarled AV cables and piles of AC adapter bricks? The dull fluorescent lights high above you flicker, and for a moment you fear getting lost in this dire place. What was it the old man said about grues?

But suddenly, out of the corner of your eye you see what you have not seen for many years. Those brown keys, that beige box, that bold red LED shining in the darkness! At last, you are reunited with a love you once forsook, but never forgot. Many gamers would argue that the Commodore 64 has not aged gracefully, but to someone who grew up playing and adoring classics like *Forbidden Forest, Archon, Zak McKracken and the Alien Mindbenders*, or *The Bard's Tale*, the Commodore 64 is still a great platform for gaming. But why did the Commodore 64 succeed and remain successful in the face of so much competition, which included heavy-hitters like the Atari 800 and the Apple II? Was it really just a question of value for money, or was there something intangible and unique about the machine, its games, or its fans?

In his foundational book *Diffusion of Innovations*, sociologist Everett M. Rogers wrote about how and why certain inventions—or "innovations," as he called them—catch on while others are either forgotten or ignored altogether. Rogers argued that successful innovations are not necessarily superior to alternatives in any objective sense. Instead, what seems to matter most when deciding whether to adopt an innovation is the opinion of your peers, or at least the peers who are the most like yourself. Despite the huge expenditures lavished on marketing and advertising, it's the ordinary people who enjoy and tell others about their products that determine their fate in the marketplace.

This book is essentially about the diffusion of a certain type of innovation that has become an integral part of our culture: the videogame platform.[1] Over the course of the videogame industry's history, we've seen countless consoles, computers, and programming languages come and go. Some, like the Atari 2600 and the Nintendo Entertainment System, diffused deeply and rapidly into our society, making indelible impressions on millions of gamers. Far more common in the history books than in the wild, however, are contraptions such as Nokia's N-Gage, Smith Engineering's Vectrex, or Nintendo's Virtual Boy, all of which failed to move beyond a niche audience despite their promising innovations. It's not easy to explain these failures, nor pinpoint precisely why other systems like the Sega Genesis or iPad are runaway successes. But it sure is fun to try!

---

[1] In this book, we use the term "console" to refer to a device intended purely for gaming, such as the Atari 2600 or Sega Genesis. "System" may refer to consoles as well as personal computers like the Commodore 64. "Platform" is a broader term that includes any combination of hardware and software that can run the same software. For example, the original Apple II, Apple IIGS, or a Windows PC running an Apple II emulator can all support the Apple II platform. Interestingly enough, "console" was the term used in the title of this book because that's considered more recognizable than "platform" to the average consumer!

Your humble authors, Bill Loguidice and Matt Barton, have always been fascinated by games and gaming machines, and now avidly collect hardware and software for every system we can get our hands on. We are lifelong gamers who began gaming shortly after leaving the womb (nice place, but the Wi-Fi is spotty at best). However, not content to simply play and enjoy games, we also write about them. In 2009, we wrote *Vintage Games: An Insider Look at the History of Grand Theft Auto, Super Mario, and the Most Influential Games of All Time.* We had a great time doing it, but all along we kept running into the "platform issue." While our purpose in that book was to focus entirely on the games—that is, the software—it was difficult to avoid crossing over into hardware. That's because the devices we use to play a game are a huge part of how we experience it.

For instance, if you're playing *Space Invaders* at home on your Atari 2600 instead of an arcade machine—are you truly playing the same game? How about if you're playing *Breakout* with a joystick or mouse instead of a spinner? A large part of the videogame experience is inseparable from the hardware—the peculiarities of the hardware for which it was originally designed and optimized, such as the amount of RAM, processor speed, graphics technology, default controllers, or storage media. In short, hardware is just as important as software when talking about videogames.

It's quite fascinating to see how a single quirk in a system's design can affect its destiny in ways the manufacturer could never imagine—an important process Rogers calls "re-invention." For instance, in deference to controlling costs, the Atari 2600 shipped with only 128 bytes of memory—not enough memory, in fact, for a frame buffer, which would have stored all the information needed to display the screen. As Nick Montfort and Ian Bogost describe in their book *Racing the Beam*, this crippling limitation actually became an asset later, when clever programmers learned to use it to their advantage. While the Atari 2600 was designed to draw only two sprites on the screen, its lack of a frame buffer meant that it could be ingeniously hacked to draw entire rows of sprites, contributing greatly to its longevity and competiveness against rival machines like the Intellivision. It also meant that millions of Atari 2600 owners were spared the indignity of playing a game called *Space Invader.*

In short, a vintage game system is much more than the sum of its parts. There are deep and complex relationships between the aesthetics, capabilities, marketing, regulation, reception, and adoption of a platform that determine not only what type of games get made and sold, but also the type of gamer it attracts. When a system's fan base reaches a critical mass then cliques, clubs, and entire subcultures develop with their own perspectives, tastes, and attitudes about gaming—all of which might clash with the company's own efforts to create a brand image. Knowing something about these subcultures, or "fanboys" as they're often derided, is fundamental to understanding the impact of any game system.

To sum up, your authors have a monumental task ahead of them. Our goal is to discuss each of our chosen platforms in depth, covering not just the machine itself, but also the assumptions behind its manufacture, the ways it was (mis)marketed, received, and developed, and the subcultures it fostered. We'll take you inside the fan bases of each system, many of which are still thriving today in the form of "homebrew" scenes, expos, and online retrogaming communities. We want to situate these systems in their proper social context, and show you, for instance, what it was like as a gamer to own an Apple II in the early 1980s, and how your experience would have been much different with an Atari 800, Commodore 64, or ColecoVision.

Obviously, we cannot talk about every gaming system ever released. If we tried, this book would weigh more than a PS3![2] So, much as we did with *Vintage Games*, we're taking a selection of the 20 systems that we feel are some combination of the most influential, innovative, important, and interesting to read and write about. We also want to feature the systems with the most active homebrew and emulation scenes. It really says something about a vintage system when people are still developing new software for it 30 years later!

Finally, in yet another parallel with *Vintage Games*, and further defining this book as the next entry in our *Vintage* series, we will again be presenting the North American, or, more specifically, the US perspective of our subject. That means that great game systems like the British ZX Spectrum or Japanese MSX platforms were not up for consideration when forming our list, although they may still get a passing mention. Similarly, that is why a platform like the Atari ST, which was a big success in Europe, can lose out in consideration to the relatively similar Commodore Amiga platform, which enjoyed a higher level of North American support. Perhaps future volumes of *Vintage Game Consoles* or entries in the *Vintage* series could rectify such an unintended slight for fans of a specific platform.

The chapters in this book are organized roughly chronologically and grouped into "generations," an industry term that indicates a sort of collective step forward in technology. We'll stop with the third generation, which extends to 2001 and the introduction of the PlayStation 2, Xbox, and GameCube. While each chapter is focused on a single system or platform, expect to find some overlap, especially in situations where two systems competed head-to-head, like the Sega Genesis and Nintendo Super NES. While you may be tempted to jump to your favorite platform, we recommend that you read the book cover-to-cover to get the full picture. Each of the systems we cover here has played an important historical role in the formation of the entire games industry, and you might get inspired to (finally) get around to playing games on computers and consoles you've never owned or even heard of before.

---

[2] Sony's original version of the PlayStation 3 weighed over 11 pounds.

Preface : The Birth of Videogames

Living in a society so dependent on smartphones, laptops, and the Internet, it can be difficult to remember when videogames and computers were pure science fiction. Yet, just over four decades ago, videogames were as futuristic as holodecks and hoverboards are today. Just imagine how miraculous a Wii U would have seemed back in 1952, when one of the world's first videogame players—a group of highly trained engineers—hunched around a room-sized Electronic Delay Storage Automatic Computer (EDSAC) to challenge the lumbering beast to a round of tic-tac-toe. Although no one could have predicted it at the time, these humble videogames were the first glimpses of a phenomenon that would change the way the world played.

The origins of today's digital computing devices can be traced back to World War II. In December 1943, a British engineer named Tommy Flowers and his team secretly unveiled the world's first electronic, digital, programmable computer, the Colossus Mark 1. Operational by early February of the following year, the Colossus and its successors were used by British codebreakers to read encrypted German messages.[1] These codebreakers included the likes of Alan Turing,[2] whose seminal 1936 paper on the notion of a "universal machine" capable of performing the tasks of any other machine showed that anything computable could be represented by 1s and 0s, which proved critical when trying to decipher codes with 15 million million possibilities. The improved Colossus Mark 2 went into operation on June 1, in time for the pivotal Normandy landings. In total, ten Colossus computers were in operation by the war's end. Unfortunately, their strict focus on codebreaking and top secret status—strictly maintained until the 1970s—prevented their diffusion into the marketplace.

Like the armed forces of the other world powers at the time, the US Army was also on a continuous quest to gain an upper hand against its enemies, and several promising—if far-fetched—projects were given funding on the off chance that a few might be successful. One such proposal was to create a high-speed electronic device to calculate ballistics firing tables, a task that was being performed manually by female "computers," a word that meant "one who computes."

As a result of that proposal, development of the Electronic Numerical Integrator and Computer—better known as ENIAC—began on June 5, 1943. It was fully operational by 1946, when it became the first reprogrammable, electronic general-purpose computer. Conceived and designed by John Mauchly and John Eckert, the room-sized ENIAC was a modular computer, composed of individual panels that performed different functions. It weighed over 30 tons, and contained more than 18,000 vacuum tubes that burned 200 kilowatts of power.[3] More flexible than the Colossus and not constrained by the secrecy of the war effort, the ENIAC was

---

[1]   A large number of electromechanical calculating devices known as "bombe" helped decipher encrypted messages specifically from the infamous German Enigma machines.

[2]   Turing contributed several pivotal mathematical and computing ideas in his tragically short life. For instance, in a famous 1950 paper he posed the thought provoking question, "Can machines think?" which led to the famous "Turing test" concept, which is a measure of a machine's ability to exhibit indistinguishably human behavior.

able to more profoundly influence the development of later, increasingly smaller and more powerful computers from a variety of commercial companies. Thus began the transition from centuries-old mechanical and analog paradigms to digital.

The bulky and unreliable vacuum tubes used into the 1950s were phased out by more reliable and less expensive transistors in the 1960s. These transistors were soon incorporated into the Integrated Circuit (IC), where a large number of these semiconductor devices were placed onto small silicon chips. Introduced in the late 1950s by Fairchild Camera and Instrument (later Fairchild Semiconductor), IC was a breakthrough with important implications for both computers and calculators. Compared to the vacuum tube, the IC was faster, smaller, and more energy-efficient. The IC was a huge step forward for the burgeoning computer industry.[4]

Several decades of innovation in circuitry and refinements in operation and utility followed, including a switch to a stored-program methodology that offered a fully reprogrammable environment. Despite these many advancements, large and expensive mainframe computers remained the norm. Fortunately for us, not all programmers were content to slave away on serious applications, and more and more games found their way onto mainframes. As history has shown, any new computing device capable of running a game will, by hook or by crook, soon have them available.[5]

The Nimrod, a single-purpose computer designed to demonstrate the principals of digital computing to the general public by playing the game of Nim, was showcased at the Exhibition of Science during the 1951 Festival of Britain. However, we argue that the grid of light bulbs that passed for its display was too abstract to qualify it as the type of videogame we'll be discussing throughout this book. Nevertheless, it was an important milestone. Interestingly, in that same year and into the next, the UK played host to other innovations, with the Pilot ACE computer simulating draughts (checkers), and the Ferranti Mark 1 computer playing host to the first computer-generated music and one of the earliest attempts at solving chess problems.

The first known instance of an actual recognizable videogame implementation was Alexander Douglas's 1952 creation of *OXO*, a simple graphical single player versus the computer tic-tac-toe game on the EDSAC mainframe at the University of Cambridge. Although more proof of a concept than a compelling gameplay experience, *OXO* nevertheless set the precedent of using a computer to create a virtual representation of a game.

In 1958, for a visitors' day at the Brookhaven National Laboratory in Upton, New York, William Higinbotham and Robert Dvorak created *Tennis for Two*, a small analog computer game that used an oscilloscope for its display. *Tennis for Two* rendered a moving ball in a simplified side view of a tennis court. Each player could rotate a knob to change the angle of the ball, and the press of a button sent the ball toward the opposite side of the court. As with *OXO*, few people had the chance to play *Tennis for Two*, but it can be considered the first dedicated videogame system. Without the benefit of hindsight, this historic milestone was even lost on the game's creators, who, after a second visitors' day one year later, disassembled the machine's components for use in other projects.

It wouldn't be until 1962 that the most famous early computer game, *Spacewar!*, blasted onto the scene. Initially designed by Steve Russell, Martin Graetz, and Wayne Wiitanen, with later contributions from Alan Kotok, Dan Edwards, and Peter Samson, the game was the result of

---

[3] Nobelprize.org, "The History of the Integrated Circuit," www.nobelprize.org/educational/physics/integrated_circuit/history.

[4] And it was becoming a "computer" industry, as the terms "electronic brain" or "mechanical brain" were slowly being phased out in popular usage.

[5] The "Loguidice Law."

brilliant engineering and hundreds of hours of hard work. Developed on the DEC PDP-1 mainframe at MIT, *Spacewar!*'s gameplay was surprisingly sophisticated and ambitious, pitting two spaceships against each other in an armed duel around a star that exhibited gravitational effects on the two craft. Each player controlled a ship via the mainframe's front-panel test switches or optional external control boxes, adjusting each respective craft's rotation, thrust, fire, and hyperspace (a random, evasive screen jump that may cause the user's ship to explode). Over the years, the game was improved many times and inspired countless clones and spiritual successors, including the first arcade videogames in 1971, *Galaxy Game* and *Computer Space*.

It was this ability to inspire that was perhaps *Spacewar!*'s greatest contribution to the future of computing. Even though access to the host hardware severely limited the game's exposure, a few visionaries realized early on that computers had applications that went way beyond the sober needs of businesses, universities, and the government. They could also delight and entertain. At the time, the idea that one day ordinary people would buy computers just to play games on them was absolutely absurd.

Nevertheless, the computer industry was steadily moving away from the corporate model, in which only highly trained experts actually operated computers. With the needs of the individual in mind, Drs. Thomas Kurtz and John Kemeny took the next major step towards computing for the masses at Dartmouth University with the creation of the Beginner's All-purpose Symbolic Instruction Code, or BASIC, programming language, in 1964. While BASIC was not as efficient as "low-level" languages such as machine code and assembly language, it did not require nearly as much skill with math or science to use effectively. For the first time, an ordinary person had a fighting chance of programming a computer.

BASIC emphasized natural language syntax and simple logic, something that enthusiasts of all ages and disciplines could appreciate and more easily work with. In another stroke of genius, Kurtz and Kemeny made their BASIC compiler available free of charge, hoping it would help spread the language far and wide. This altruistic strategy worked, with variations of their original BASIC language becoming a staple on several key computing systems of the time. Their language dominated the first few decades of personal computing, serving as the entry point for countless aspiring programmers.

Throughout the late 1960s and 1970s, breakthrough innovations appeared that we take for granted in our modern computing devices. One of the most notable was Douglas Engelbart's "The Mother of All Demos," in late 1968, which featured a mouse, hyperlinks, and video conferencing. Alan Kay's "Dynabook" concept (1968–1972) predicted form factors and use cases that are realized in today's laptops and tablets. After its founding in 1970, Xerox PARC's stunning working office environment featured locally networked desktop computers with bitmapped graphics, graphical user interfaces, object-oriented programming, and "what you see is what you get" (WYSIWYG) output to high quality laser printers. Still, despite such advancements, computers remained the occupation of a tiny well-trained professional class.

The major roadblock was the standard operating model of the time, which was to leverage a single large computer that needed to be shared and have its time partitioned among many users. This model was certainly effective and a significant improvement over previous decades when a single user's activity would tie up a computer for hours, or even days, but it didn't scale well, and proved costly for the would-be end-user to access. A change was needed. It came from Intel.

By 1971, Intel had developed and released the first mainstream microprocessor, or single-chip Central Processing Unit (CPU). The Intel 4004 became the heart of many small-scale digital computer projects. It offered a clock speed of 740 kHz—less than 3000 times the speed of modern processors. Still, as humble as it might seem today, there would have been no home computer and videogame market without it.

Although microprocessors held great promise for home computer applications, it took another three years before they really caught on with manufacturers and consumers. This meant that "hit" games continued to appear almost exclusively on mainframe systems throughout the 1970s. These included the early dungeon-crawling game *dnd* (1974), by Gary Whisenhunt and Ray Wood for the versatile PLATO computer instruction mainframe system, and Will Crowther's PDP-10 computer game *Adventure* (1975)—the first significant text adventure.

The rise of true home computing began in late 1974 with the release of the MITS Altair 8800 computer kit, based on the Intel 8080 microprocessor released earlier in the year. Advertised in the January 1975 edition of *Popular Electronics* magazine, the kit was an unexpected success, enthusiastically supported by groups of eager hobbyists who had long waited to get their hands on a computer to call their own. While no one would accuse the Altair 8800 of being user-friendly, it was a computer that a hobbyist could actually afford.

The Altair 8800 had a red LED display and several toggle switches to directly program the system. There were no other display or input options, and little could be done with the default configuration. Still, the system was a step up from prior kits and plans that required hobbyists to track down or fabricate their own parts. MITS' designers built most of the machine's intelligence around removable cards, making the motherboard—the heart of the computer that handles system resources—a means to interconnect the components. Since the motherboard accepted 100-pin expansion cards, it eventually became known as the S-100 bus, which became an important industry standard into the early to mid-1980s, often seen in computers paired with the versatile CP/M operating system. In fact, by late 1975, the first of many greatly improved clones appeared in the form of IMS's IMSAI 8080 kit, which ran a modified version of CP/M. The IMSAI 8080 may also mark the first time a real personal computer was the star of a movie—in this case, the 1983 hit *War Games* with Matthew Broderick.

Nowadays, when we think of sharing code and expertise, it's usually in the context of Linux and other open source and free software projects. Computing, however, has rarely been a solo pursuit. In the 1960s, social networks formed between engineers, scientists, and academics, who freely shared their knowledge and code with each other to advance the nascent field. Since the money was assumed to be in the hardware rather than software, programmers seldom took issue with others borrowing and building on their code. This community spirit naturally found its way to the home market after the introduction of the Altair 8800. Enthusiastic groups of hobbyists were allowed to rub elbows with some of the industry's greatest pioneers, spurring progress across the board.

The most famous of these early groups was the Homebrew Computer Club in Silicon Valley, which first met in March 1975. The club's early appeal was the enthusiastic and free exchange of ideas, technology, and information amongst its talented members. Club membership consisted not only of hobbyists, but also engineers and other professionals, like future Apple cofounders Steve Jobs and Steve Wozniak, who, along with many others, would go on to shape the path of the computer industry for the next several decades.

Not everyone liked the idea of free software, however. A young and brash Bill Gates, then of Micro-Soft, wrote an open letter for the Homebrew Computer Club's second newsletter condemning commercial software piracy. His Altair BASIC, cowritten with Paul Allen, was the first language available for the system, and hobbyists were illegally copying the desirable, but expensive, paper tape software in droves. This letter marked the first notable rift between the ideals of free software development and the potential of a retail software market. Gates and the quickly-renamed Microsoft went on to create versions of BASIC, operating systems, and other types of software for nearly every personal computer, creating an important, if infamous, business empire in the process.

With computer user groups and clubs on the rise, specialized retail stores opened to cater to their needs, and publishers churned out in-depth enthusiast magazines like *Byte*. The first major computer fair, the Trenton Computer Festival, took place in April 1976 and featured speakers, forums, user group meetings, exhibitor areas, and an outdoor flea market, setting the template for future trade shows. As computers made the transition from do-it-yourself kits to pre-built systems in 1977, they became more appealing to a wider segment of the population.

Still, home computers were the domain of nerds and professionals; they were much too expensive and complex for the average kid who just wanted to play videogames. Fortunately for them, an engineer named Ralph Baer was already envisioning the videogame console in the 1950s. His work would eventually culminate in the Magnavox Odyssey, a landmark moment for the videogames industry.

We take videogame consoles for granted today, but Baer's concept for a television videogame was so novel that he was unable to garner enough support to build working prototypes until the mid-1960s. His first attempt, *Chase*, was a simple game of tag featuring two squares, which he later expanded into his celebrated "Brown Box" prototype. The prototype included several additional diversions, including paddle and ball as well as target shooting games. After being rejected by several TV manufacturers, Baer finally signed an agreement in 1971 with Magnavox, who released a refined version of the prototype the following year, renaming it the Odyssey Home Entertainment System.

Although relatively limited in its capabilities, requiring considerable manual intervention and imagination from its players, the Odyssey nevertheless boasted several features that became industry standards. These features included detachable controllers, additional controller options (a light rifle/gun), and interchangeable game cartridges. These cartridges appeared to offer players an assortment of different games to play, but were really just plug-in cards that turned the console's built-in features on or off like a complex selector switch. Twelve games were included with the system, with an additional ten eventually released separately.[6] The Odyssey could display only white squares and lines on a black background, so two different sizes of color overlays were provided to enhance gameplay and accommodate different types of televisions. Many games also included external enhancements such as playing cards, maps, dice, and game boards. Much of the system's playability came from these accessories, since the on-screen interaction was so limited. The system only registered object collisions, and there was no sound or score tracking.

Perhaps the Odyssey's most enduring legacy was inspiring Nolan Bushnell at a Magnavox product demonstration in 1972. Later that same year, Bushnell founded Atari and, with engineer Al Alcorn, developed *Pong* for the arcade, the first hit videogame. *Pong* was clearly derivative of

---

6   Like any videogame console worth its salt, the Odyssey has seen additional homebrew games added to its library, starting with *Odball* in 2009. As you'll read throughout this book, dedicated hobbyist have created new games for classic systems that often rival or exceed the best of what was available when these platforms were originally commercially available.

one of the Odyssey's paddle and ball (tennis) games, a design that was unfortunately quite easy for others to copy. Much to Bushnell's chagrin, the success of *Pong* was its own undoing, leading several other companies to copy the game's concept. It also did not sit well with Baer, who was understandably upset that Atari had ignored his patents. Magnavox eventually filed a successful lawsuit against Atari for infringement, forcing the fledgling company to settle for a lump sum and other manufacturers to pay hefty licensing fees.

Pong's simple but compelling gameplay was in stark contrast to Bushnell and Ted Dabney's earlier *Computer Space* for Nutting Associates. Despite its striking cabinet design, relatively large screen, and four control buttons, *Computer Space* was too complex for the general public. Bushnell later admitted that the game appealed mostly to his engineering friends who had enjoyed *Spacewar!*, the even more complicated game that *Computer Space* was based on. Although technologically less impressive, it was *Pong*, not *Computer Space*, that set the foundation for the modern videogame industry.

Although the Odyssey received a small sales boost from the popularity of *Pong* and the various clones that sprung up in the arcade, it never really overcame the limits of its technology or poor marketing. Magnavox's marketing strategy was focused on its television dealerships, which reinforced the unfortunate misperception that it would only work on Magnavox televisions. When Atari created a home version of *Pong*, complete with automatic scoring and sound, dominant retailer Sears agreed in 1975 to distribute it in its sporting goods department[7] under their own brand name, Tele-Games. It was a huge success, and showed that Baer had been right all along about the viability of videogames for the home. Atari released its own branded version of the console starting in 1976, just as an explosion of *Pong* clones saturated the home videogame market. Although these machines were popular and offered increasingly sophisticated feature-sets, there were simply too many systems for the market to bear. They were also soon challenged by fully programmable consoles that used true interchangeable cartridges for more diverse gameplay possibilities, starting with Fairchild's Video Entertainment System (VES) in 1976. This home videogame breakthrough was followed less than a year later on the home computer side with the release of the preassembled and relatively user-friendly Apple II, Commodore PET, and Tandy TRS-80 systems, each of which featured its own interchangeable software, first on cassette tapes and later on disks. The legendary trinity of Apple, Commodore, and Tandy marked the first time fully assembled, programmable computers were readily available and usable by ordinary folks.

With the two markets in place by the late 1970s, it only took until the early 1980s for nearly all of today's familiar videogame and computer elements to take shape. These elements ranged from input devices such as multifunction digital and analog controllers to online services, like the proprietary *CompuServe Information Service* and *The Source*, each of which featured a selection of relatively sophisticated multiplayer games accessible to anyone willing to pay by the hour.

---

[7]   This type of backdoor entry into the marketplace would predict Nintendo's own Trojan Horse, or Trojan Robot, ROB, the Robotic Operating Buddy, which allowed the company to initially push its Nintendo Entertainment System as more of a toy than a console to retailers still wary from the Great Videogame Crash.

Comparing *Pong* and almost any modern game—including those for smartphones—might suggest there are hundreds of years between them, but in fact only a little over 40 years have passed. By contrast, it took Hollywood over 30 years just to introduce sound into their movies! Fortunately for gamers, game developers have enjoyed and continue to enjoy a wide variety of platforms to develop for—each with their own advantages and limitations. The competitive hardware industry has often left software developers struggling to catch up, building increasingly sophisticated games to justify the expensive hardware, much of which is discussed throughout this book.

Part 1
Generation One
(1971–1984)

In 1971, the team at Intel released the first single-chip microprocessor, the Intel 4004, which enabled the production of affordable home computers, or microcomputers. By early 1975, mail-order home computer kits were already popular with do-it-yourselfers. Although preassembled systems remained scarce through 1976, the evolution of the home computer continued with the release of the relatively sophisticated Apple I circuit board. In 1977, this success was followed by Apple with the factory-assembled Apple II, Tandy with the TRS-80, and Commodore with the PET, the first complete system featuring a keyboard, cassette drive, monitor, and power supply in one unit. In 1978, Apple introduced the Disk II, the first truly affordable disk drive peripheral, which surpassed the performance and reliability of the then-standard cassettes to store and retrieve data.

Ralph Baer and Magnavox kicked off the home television videogame revolution in mid-1972 with the release of the Odyssey Home Entertainment System, but Magnavox was never able to properly leverage their running start—except in the courtroom. By late 1975, Atari's *Pong* found its way into many homes, quickly followed by countless clone systems from manufacturers such as APF, First Dimension, and Coleco. However, the 1976 introduction of the Fairchild Video Entertainment System (VES), with its interchangeable game cartridges, signaled the beginning of the end for the fixed game *Pong*-style units, despite game and control variations, including color graphics and enhanced sound. By the beginning of the 1980s, as the era covered in this section of the book came to a close, fixed-game systems were no longer attractive to most consumers. However, the fixed-game concept would return successfully for a time in the early 2000s, starting with devices like Toymax's Activision TV Games, a gamepad controller that ran on batteries, with built-in Atari 2600 games and television output.

With the required technological and marketing groundwork in place, home videogame and computer systems gained serious consumer traction in the 1980s. While still mysterious and intimidating to many people, computers were heavily advertised and received enthusiastic press coverage, including being named TIME Magazine's "Machine (Man) of the Year" for 1982.[1] Home computers were moving out of the hobbyist's workshop and into American living rooms.

Computer and console makers weren't content to rely on the press and enthusiastic owners to generate hype for their products. The early 1980s saw the first signs of aggressive and even hostile competition among different brands, leading to a seemingly endless array of spokespersons from the early to mid-1980s. These celebrity spokespersons included Alan Alda (Atari), William Shatner (Commodore), Isaac Asimov and Bill Bixby (Tandy), Bill Cosby (Texas Instruments), George Plimpton (Mattel), Sarah Purcell (Tomy), and Roger Moore (Spectravideo).[2] In an attempt to one-up the competition, IBM licensed Charlie Chaplin's The Tramp likeness to pitch its PC and PCjr line of computers. At a time when most consumers had never seen a computer before—much less be in a position to compare their hardware specifications—the marketing appeal of charming celebrities was deemed essential.

To distinguish their machines from the competition, marketing and design teams would work to create a unique "personality" for their machines to attract and identify with their owners. An early advertisement for the Apple II, for instance, shows a handsome and stylish young man in a turtleneck creating a graph and sipping from a bright orange cup—while his smiling wife looks on with obvious admiration as she chops tomatoes. An early ad for the Commodore PET, by contrast, shows the computer against the stark backdrop of a college classroom complete with chalkboard, with a stern-looking professor standing at a lectern. Perhaps some early adopters made their decisions based simply on which of these images best suited their personality, although it's more likely they also consulted with salespersons and anyone they knew with a computer.

This era also saw the first memorable videogame system war, fought by the Atari 2600, the Mattel Intellivision, and the Coleco ColecoVision. All three companies created games for each other's systems while loudly declaring their competitors' weaknesses. A typical ad from this era shows an Intellivision screenshot juxtaposed with one from the Atari 2600, with a slightly uncomfortable-looking George Plimpton declaring that these two pictures are worth a thousand words. Naturally, the Intellivision screen is much more visually detailed. Atari could boast that their top-charting system had more games, including best-selling ports of their own arcade hits. Thus, from the very beginning, we see marketers trying to distinguish their platforms in terms of raw power, with consumers usually preferring the system with the largest library of fun games.

While companies battled it out in the mainstream media, the decisive struggle was taking place in thousands of small groups and pockets of fans all over the country. Regardless of a platform's perceived strengths and weaknesses, many consumers who invested in them felt a keen sense of loyalty to their chosen brand, especially if they were part of a group of like-minded

---

[1]   Famously, Apple's Steve Jobs was removed from consideration once the magazine decided to instead run a feature that took a rather harsh look at his life.

[2]   Even software companies got in on the "spokesperson wars" with, for instance, CBS Video Games enlisting the services of a pre-EA Sports John Madden!

enthusiasts. In much the same way that football fans become enamored (and defensive) of their favorite team, computer and console owners can grow downright belligerent if anyone questions their choice. Often derided as "fanboys," these extremely loyal and devoted system owners would literally preach the virtues of their system (and vices of the rest) to anyone who cared to listen, and plenty who didn't. It wasn't all just fanaticism, though. If the kids in your neighborhood owned ColecoVisions, for instance, you could borrow or trade games with them, an important consideration given the high cost of acquiring new cartridges. Likewise, computer owners could copy and swap software, sometimes legally (public domain software or their own programs) and illegally (piracy). If you were the isolated Atari 400 owner in a town full of Commodore VIC-20 fans, you'd miss out on a lot of "free" software—but you might also feel even more pressure to defend and identify with your machine.

As long as there were plenty of first-time computer and console purchasers in the market, the young computer and videogame industries thrived. Once production finally caught up and then wildly surpassed consumer demand, however, the videogame market suffered what became known as the Great Videogame Crash. The industry had become drunk on its own rising sales success between 1980 and the early part of 1983. Arnie Katz best described the crash in a June 1989 article in *Video Games and Computer Entertainment* magazine:

> Companies acted like sales were guaranteed to double every year till the end of time. Publishers stamped out a dizzying array of new cartridges, far more than consumer demand could possibly support. Therefore, retailers dumped the cartridges they couldn't sell at distress prices. The availability of $5 games ruined the market for labels like Activision, Imagic, and Parker Brothers, who wanted to sell titles in the $25 to $40 range.

While fewer systems were sold in 1983 than in the previous year, cartridge sales were up. By mid-1984, however, the industry hit the ceiling, and sales of both consoles and cartridges fell dramatically—followed by a retail backlash against videogames. The mass media turned on the industry, declaring it "dead," and investors pulled out wherever they could. Department stores that had once clamored just to keep games on their shelves were now slashing prices and incurring frightful losses just to get rid of them.[3]

The media consensus at the time was that consumers no longer needed videogame systems because low-cost computers like the Commodore 64 provided the same entertainment value along with all the other benefits of a full-blown computing device. However, news of the videogame console's death was premature. After the supply chain was mostly cleared of the glut of cut-rate videogames and consoles, the Japanese company Nintendo was able to restore consumer confidence. The introduction of the Nintendo Entertainment System at the end of 1985 began the process of salvaging the videogame console from the bargain bin of history, though Nintendo had to use some unusual and downright aggressive initiatives to win over skeptical retailers.

This era was similarly unkind to most computer manufacturers, as what started out as a wide-open field dwindled to a select group. In the lead was Commodore, who had achieved near total dominance of the low-end computer market with unheard-of bargain prices and just enough computing power for both quality games and more serious software applications. For just a bit more money than a dedicated game machine, families could take home a full-fledged computer.

---

[3]   This backlash was mostly isolated to North America. The rest of the world's markets featured different growth trajectories that mostly avoided the highs and lows of the Great Videogame Crash.

The tremendous value of the Commodore 64 led to unrivaled success—indeed, the unit continues to hold the Guinness World Record for the most sales of any single computer system. However, soon after the end of this era would also see the introduction of higher-end, higher-priced systems that would eventually eliminate the demand for relatively underpowered budget systems, particularly when computers based around Microsoft DOS (and eventually Windows) would rise to dominance both in the office and at home.

Arcade (1971)

History

When looking back to the arcade's heyday in the 1970s and 1980s, it's easy to idyllically reminisce about the bustling crowds of eager young players with pockets full of quarters, mixed rows of familiar and newly placed flashing cabinets of every shape, size, and monitor orientation, and the random bleeps, bloops, and musical ditties that somehow came together in a pitch perfect symphony of sights and sounds. Of course, as with all trips of nostalgia, that journey back leaves out the unpleasant bits, like the cigarette smoke, juvenile delinquents and bullies, and occasional sensory overload when that symphony became a crescendo, but the fact remains that the classic arcade was indeed a special time and place, filled more with the positive than the negative.

For the purposes of this chapter, we define an arcade game as a mostly electronic, digital videogame you pay to play in a commercial setting such as a pizza parlor, bowling alley, or dedicated arcade. Typically, these games are designed for quick, but fulfilling play sessions, made to get you to put more money in the machine for just one more try, increasing the venue owner's revenue, who in turn pays the vendor or supplier to get more games from the publisher. Of course, "arcade game" has been co-opted by everything from quick action games on consoles or handhelds to redemption machines, and, these days, you're just as likely to find an arcade machine in a basement rec room as you are at the local restaurant.

The arcade's origins began in the early 1900s at midways, or the area at circuses and fairs where the rides and entertainment booths are concentrated. In addition to the traditional ball tosses and shooting galleries, coin-operated mechanical and electro-mechanical machines began popping up with ever increasing regularity, with everything from automated fortune

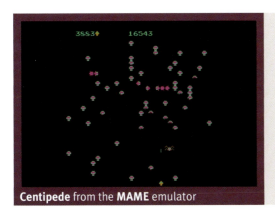

Centipede from the **MAME** emulator

Centipede (1980, Atari, Inc.)

Designed by Ed Logg and Dona Bailey, *Centipede* took the standard space shooter to the garden, placing trippy, regenerating mushrooms as obstacles when trying to blast the enemy spiders, scorpions, fleas, and titular centipede. Although an inherently great game design, play was enhanced tremendously by the use of Atari's trackball, battle tested from their pioneering use in *Atari Football* two years earlier, allowing for the type of lightning quick movements needed to rack up high scores.

tellers to flip movies to bowling games to simple racing games that challenged players to see who could turn a crank the fastest to get their toy car across the finish line. Many of these creations featured beautiful Victorian designs, with specialized wooden cabinets and elaborate ornamentation. With all their moving parts, these mechanical beasts broke down often, but at least were relatively straightforward to fix.

Auto Race, an electro-mechanical game from the Musee Mecanique, located in San Francisco.

By the 1930s, pinball machines were unleashed in force, quickly evolving into star attractions. In 1947, controllable flippers were introduced with Gottlieb's *Humpty Dumpty* machine, an important innovation that is still with us today. Advances in pinball technology continued for several more decades, eventually introducing all of the elements we're familiar with in today's machines, such as solid-state electronic components, microprocessors, and digital sound.

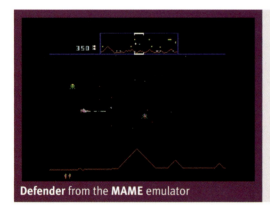

Defender from the **MAME** emulator

Defender (1980, Williams Electronics)

Despite being one of the most notoriously difficult games of all-time, *Defender* embodies everything that made the classic arcade great. It features colorful visuals and great sound, and requires lightning fast reflexes and well-practiced coordination to get a grip on its complex control setup, featuring a two-way joystick and five action buttons. The surprisingly deep play mechanic of destroying alien invaders while simultaneously protecting and rescuing astronauts keeps the quarters coming.

Like today's super competitive MMO and FPS gamers, pinball aficionados took the game very seriously. Even English rock band The Who got into the act, releasing a hit song called "Pinball Wizard" (1969) and later a 1975 companion movie for the album, *Tommy*, where pinball was featured most prominently. Unfortunately for the pinball industry and its legions of fans, they began to be passed over for the far more versatile arcade videogame in the 1970s. The first sign of trouble was Sega's

A series of classic pinball machines featured at Funspot, located in Laconia, New Hampshire.

Periscope in 1966, a smash-hit electro-mechanical light gun target game that was the first to charge a quarter per play. Other electro-mechanical innovations would follow, including rear image projection and electronic sound, but these were evolutionary dead-ends. The games that would finally flip pinball into the drain were being developed by Nolan Bushnell and some talented, visionary engineers.

In the 1960s, Bushnell had been a student at the University of Utah, where he studied electrical engineering and played a lot of *Spacewar!*. He also spent summers working at Lagoon Amusement Park, repairing all those finicky moving parts in pinball and other electro-mechanical games. His time at the park gave him ample opportunity to study hawkers and the gamers they lured to their booths up close, learning the tricks of this unique trade. Bushnell knew that videogames like *Spacewar!* would appeal to the masses just as much (if not more) than tossing ping-pong balls into goldfish bowls, but it just wasn't possible to drag a mainframe computer onto the midway—but perhaps a stripped-down version might still have appeal. He began reducing the game to its core elements, removing all frills to make it practical to produce.

Meanwhile, a similar idea was being formulated by students at Stanford University, only their version would incorporate an actual minicomputer, the DEC PDP-11/20 with vector displays. It was implemented at the Tressider Union at Stanford University in September 1971, at a cost of $20,000, or the equivalent of $100,000 today. It played a ported version of the real *Spacewar!* and was a campus hit at 10 cents a game, or 25 cents for three. Of course, despite its gee-whiz appeal, it was completely impractical for mass production.

Now we return to Bushnell, who by this time teamed up with the brilliant Ted Dabney. By using an array of readily available transistor-transistor logic (TTL) chips and diode arrays placed on three printed circuit boards (PCBs), the duo developed a multidirectional shooter, which, while no match for *Spacewar!*, created a unique, playable videogame experience, which, as Bushnell described in an interview with the authors, "could be built for about $400, and then of course it fit into the regular coin-operated game world, which was about $1000 for a coin-operated game." The display was rendered to a modified General Electric 15-inch black and white

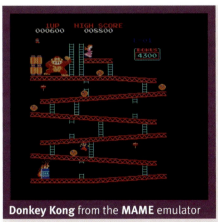

Donkey Kong from the **MAME** emulator

Donkey Kong (1981, Nintendo)

Known as the game that launched Nintendo impresario Shigeru Miyamoto's stellar career after the commercial disappointment that was *Radar Scope* (1980), and being the first appearance of pop culture icon, Mario, then known as Jumpman, *Donkey Kong's* legend has only grown since its original release. Despite being one of the first games with the Japanese preference of the joystick on the left that baffled some of its earliest American players, there was something special about the run and jump platforming and thoughtfully rendered characters that created a charming and competitive atmosphere that endures to this day. The dramatic 2007 documentary *The King of Kong: A Fistful of Quarters* does a good job of capturing the type of competitive spirit the game embodies.

television and placed in a remarkable colored fiberglass cabinet, complete with a control panel seemingly straight out of NASA.[1] Released two months after *Galaxy Game*, *Computer Space* cost 25 cents per single play.

Unfortunately, despite being beautiful enough to serve as a futuristic prop in the 1973 sci-fi film *Soylent Green*, and being cheap enough to mass produce, *Computer Space*'s appeal was mostly limited to those same college campuses that Bushnell and the nascent industry needed to break out of. *Computer Space* was just too sophisticated for its own good. Bushnell, disheartened by the lukewarm response and then unable to come to an agreement on a next game for Nutting Associates, broke ties to form Syzygy Engineering with Dabney.

Because the hottest machine in the arcade at the time was Chicago Coin's electro-mechanical, projection-based racing game *Speedway* (1969), Bushnell wanted Syzygy's first arcade title to be a racer. However, he thought such a task would be too challenging for new engineer Al Alcorn's first game, so he looked for a simpler alternative. Fortuitously, he knew just what that should be after seeing the demo for the Odyssey's *Table Tennis* at a Los Angeles Magnavox dealership in May 1972.

Table Tennis had the now iconic layout pretty much nailed, but also featured the ability to put English (spin) on the ball and had no top or bottom walls, allowing the ball to be knocked off the invisible table. From Bushnell's design and Alcorn's several months of engineering and refinements, *Pong* distilled this crude approximation of table tennis down even further, with a few new innovations. The paddles were elongated, the ball's trajectory was determined only by where it hit the paddle, and sound effects were added for each time the ball hit a paddle or one of the now enclosed top and bottom virtual walls. Perhaps most important, however, was the implementation of automatic scoring, which was perfect for inspiring heated two-player battles.

Golden Tee Golf from the **MAME** emulator

Golden Tee Golf (1989, Incredible Technologies)

The bar scene was always a key barometer for an arcade game's potential for success. If you could foster friendly competition without alienating the inebriated, you knew you had a hit on your hand. *Golden Tee Golf* and its increasingly technologically sophisticated, mostly annual, descendants used the accessibility of the trackball to simulate a golf swing, along with dynamic difficulty and appealing ranking structures that encouraged tournament play. As a testament to *Golden Tee Golf*'s great design, it not only became an arcade mainstay, but also was one of the few games to gain a permanent foothold in bars and restaurants along with casual touchscreen devices like the Midway *Touch Master* (1996).

Their prototype's design proved so compelling that Bushnell and Dabney put the game into production under the Atari Inc. banner (the change in incorporation becoming necessary in June 1972 due to a naming conflict). Using a refined version of the same type of TTL-based technology as

---

[1] Single-players cabinets were available in blue metalflake, red metalflake, white, and yellow, with two-player cabinets featuring larger control panels only coming in green metalflake.

Computer Space, *Pong*'s internals were paired with a small black-and-white television inside a wooden cabinet. This was joined on the front panel by two spinners (rotatable knobs), one for each player, and a coin slot, which, when detecting a quarter, would start the ball's motion. "Avoid Missing Ball for High Score" was all the guidance would-be players needed before pumping quarters into this immediately accessible and compelling creation.

Pong, left, a simple beast, and **Computer Space**, right, a complex beauty. Against all odds, the beast would win the hearts of a generation of gamers and launch an industry. Image courtesy of the Digital Game Museum, taken at the Atari Party 2012 event.

So, it was *Pong*, rather than *Spacewar!* or *Computer Space* that gave birth to the classic arcade—and the inevitable cavalcade of clones. This sea of *Pong* knock-offs, variations, and minor updates became so pervasive so quickly that even Atari themselves got in on the act to help stem some of the losses. In fact, there would be eerie similarities in the consumer market after Sears unleashed Atari's home *Pong* in 1975.[2] In both cases, after the novelty of sometimes interesting competitive variations wore off, the market soon became glutted with too-similar and often cheap products, and consumer demand waned sharply. This was a precarious situation for a fragile, nascent industry, but in both cases, instead of leading to something like the Great Videogame Crash of the mid-1980s, they instead led to depressions, pulled each time from the brink of oblivion by new product and innovations that reinvigorated consumer demand. And for Bushnell, Atari, and fans of the arcade, the innovation didn't stop at the paddle.

Hydro Thunder Hurricane (2010, Microsoft) for the Xbox 360 is one of several quality home translations of the arcade game for home platforms.

Hydro Thunder (1999, Midway Games)

From its clever open cockpit cabinet design, featuring a built-in bass shaking subwoofer, to its full complement of controls with steering wheel, throttle, and foot pedals, it's clear that powerboat racer *Hydro Thunder* was designed to thrill from the start. The crisp, high-speed visuals, which feature an excellent water effect, add to the furious pace of the races, which barely slow even after the most dramatic wipeouts. Excellent home conversions deliver a lot of the fun, but this is definitely an arcade game worth a visit to Chuck E. Cheese to experience in its ideal format.

---

[2] In April 1974 Magnavox filed suit against Atari, Bally Midway, Allied Leisure, and Chicago Dynamics. Bushnell and Atari settled out of court in June 1976, becoming a Magnavox licensee for $700,000 and turning over rights to new products for one year. Thereafter, other companies producing *Pong* clones would have to pay royalties, with Magnavox continuing to pursue legal actions for years to come. All of this worked to Atari's favor, which was able to avoid further litigation and simply delay release of new products for one year.

In 1974, Atari introduced *Gran Trak 10*, a single-player, single-track overhead car race against the clock. It was the first game that stored graphical data (sprites) in a diode-based ROM for the in-game graphics, and also featured a steering wheel, gear shifter, and accelerator, and brake pedals. In that same year, Atari's Kee Games[3] released *Tank*, which improved on *Gran Trak 10*'s technology by storing graphical data in more reliable

A selection of early racing games featured at Funspot, located in Laconia, New Hampshire.

IC-based (solid state) ROMs. *Tank* featured a pair of dual joysticks, offering realistic dueling tank controls. Both games launched many spiritual successors and clones of their own, including Kee Games' oversized *Indy 800* (1975), which cleverly huddled pairs of players around a square tabletop cabinet, where they could look down at the shared color display. Strategically placed mirrors on the cabinet's canopy let spectators keep track of the frenzied competition, as well as get a good look at that first implementation of real color.

Of course, Atari was far from the only game-maker in town by this time. Midway released Taito's influential *Gun Fight* (1975), a western-themed one-on-one duel between two cowboys, which, among its other firsts, included the fact that it was powered by an actual microprocessor. Sega released its early sports title *Heavyweight Champ* in 1976, which, along with its innovative and oversized side-view perspective monochrome visuals, was the first game to feature hand-to-hand fighting and was controlled via unusual boxing glove-like controllers.

Ms. Pac-Man from the **MAME** emulator.

Ms. Pac-Man/Galaga—Class of 1981
(2000, Namco)

Yes, we admit to cheating just a little with this one, as we get two classics for the cost of one entry (three if you count the unlockable *Pac-Man!*), but how could we resist when this is among today's most widely available arcade cabinets. *Ms. Pac-Man* is a dynamic improvement on *Pac-Man*'s already spot-on gameplay, with multiple mazes and fleet-footed bonus items, while *Galaga* one-ups its predecessor *Galaxian* (1979)—which itself was an improvement on *Space Invaders*—by allowing for more than one shot at a time, a hit-to-miss ratio tracker, bonus stages, and an ability to both rescue and then leverage a captured fighter (life) alongside your present ship. The hard part is choosing which game to play first!

---

3   Kee Games was a wholly owned subsidiary of Atari, used to get around the era's distributor-set exclusivity (single vendor) deals. Roughly a decade later, Nintendo would set similar restrictions for its third-party game-makers after the release of the Nintendo Entertainment System, resulting in companies resorting to similar workarounds to release more games.

In 1977, Cinematronics' *Space Wars* had the good fortune of appearing around the same time as George Lucas' blockbuster *Star Wars* movie, which fanned the flames of the space craze sensation lit by the original *Star Trek* television series in syndication. *Space Wars*, which was available in three different cabinet styles, was that long sought-after interpretation of *Spacewar!* for the masses, and featured a clever vector-based graphics engine, forgoing the blocky pixilation of standard raster-based graphics for cleaner and brightly lit points, lines, and curves.

Japan had been a factor in US arcades since Sega's mid-1960s hit *Periscope*, but it was Midway's release of Taito's 100-yen- and quarter-devouring *Space Invaders* that established Japan's reputation for brilliant game designs. The game became so popular that the 1980 release of an official home port for the Atari 2600 quadrupled system sales and jumpstarted the home market. But all those gamers merely wanted to replicate the thrills of the arcade version. Tomohiro Nishikado's offense-oriented and much copied design immediately resonated, with iconic alien graphics and killer, bass-filled sound. As Bethesda's Todd Howard put it in an interview with the authors,

> What was fun about Space Invaders? Here are aliens that are going to kill you. For what it was it became a very, very different kind of shooting gallery that you had never seen before. The primal beat of shooting things in a game, *doot... doot... doot...* that was the first time.

Capping off the decade-ending space craze was perhaps the most famous and influential vector-based arcade game, Atari's *Asteroids*,[4] released in 1979. *Asteroids* was the first arcade game that let you pair initials with your high score, where it stayed until it was beaten by a better player or was anticlimactically lost in a power outage.

Several other key vector-based titles would be released through the 1980s, with color vectors available by the early part of the decade. Unfortunately for fans of the clean and bright vector look, raster-based graphics of ever increasing detail and complexity rendered vectors obsolete by the mid-part of the decade.

In October 1980, a new craze was unleashed: the maze game. While there had been maze games and even dot collecting games before, most notably Sega's *Head On*

A flyer for Deluxe Space Invaders, aka, Space Invaders Part II. The early Space Invaders arcade games used a clever technique to mirror and reflect its display onto cardboard backdrops to create a unique visual experience.

---

[4]   *Lunar Lander*, which came out the same year, was Atari's first use of this vector technology. Though not a commercial success, *Lunar Lander* was an amazing, influential simulation with clever controls. It also predicted other unexpectedly detailed arcade simulations of the future, including full flight and racing simulators.

from the previous year, none had put together that special combination of colorful characters and tight, approachable gameplay of Namco's *Pac-Man*. As game developer John Romero put it in an author interview,

> Everything was shoot the alien. Shoot, shoot, shoot. When *Pac-Man* came out, it was this awesome color game. Funny music. Funny character eating dots. Instead of shooting you are running away from the things, the opposite. What a crazy game idea! *Pac-Man* really stood out. It was the future and the promise of what game design could be.

Instead of simply copying existing paradigms, *Pac-Man*'s designer Tōru Iwatani created something both unique and infinitely playable.

Indeed, soon enough, everyone got *Pac-Man* fever and loved every minute of it. This was the first breakout arcade game since *Pong* that knew no age or gender boundaries. Anyone could grab the joystick, become enchanted by the breakthrough cutscenes, or identify with one of the enemy ghosts, each of whom seemed to exhibit distinct personalities. It was one of the first games that could truly be said to have character(s). Unsurprisingly, ports, clones, and knock-offs, both cheap and inspired, followed in droves, although few were as charming and endearing as *Pac-Man*.

NBA Jam from the **MAME** emulator.

NBA Jam (1993, Midway)

Released in the same competitive era as *Street Fighter II*, *NBA Jam* and its later football-based sibling *NFL Blitz* (1997) brought the same type of intensity featured in the best fighting games to sports videogames. *NBA Jam*'s perfectly distilled two-on-two basketball action appealed to game fans, not just sports fans, which is an amazing accomplishment regardless of era. From its digitized visuals to its pitch perfect sound and upbeat announcer, *NBA Jam* and its sequels remain "on fire" with gamers to this day. Boomshakalaka!

With the cult of personality set by *Pac-Man*, other colorful, character-driven games were soon added to the already stellar mix of driving and shooting titles. These games included Konami's *Frogger* (1981), where the titular amphibian just wants to cross the road and stream; Exidy's *Venture* (1981), where you play Winky, an arrow-slinging, dungeon crawling smiley face; Atari's isometric gem collecting maze game, *Crystal Castles* (1982), starring Bentley Bear; Sega's *Pengo* (1982), where the titular red penguin needs to crush the blob-like Sno-Bees by sliding blocks of ice; Konami's *Pooyan* (1982), where Mama Pig has to protect her piglets by shooting arrows with slabs of meat attached at wolves from her elevator basket; Stern's *Bagman* (1983), where you play a thief collecting bags of gold in an abandoned mine; and Midway's *Mappy* (1983), where the titular police cat is chased by no-good cats. The list goes on and on, culminating in the mascot wars of the Generation Two and Generation Three home systems, where characters like Mario, Sonic,

Bonk, and Crash Bandicoot battled it out for mind and market share.

Although there was the occasional brilliant port, such as *BurgerTime* (1983, Mattel) on the Intellivision, *Satan's Hollow* (1984, Commodore) on the Commodore 64, or *Root Beer Tapper* (1984, Coleco) on the ColecoVision, most arcade translations to Generation One home platforms could only hope at best to capture the feel of the arcade game rather than the complete package.

Arcade cabinet designs, controls, themes, and genres varied greatly at the peak of the classic arcade's popularity throughout the 1970s and 1980s, as this selection of games at Funspot, located in Laconia, New Hampshire, demonstrates.

Arcade hardware still had a clear edge over home platforms, able to throw in more memory, extra hardware like additional sound processors, or fancy controls that could take a beating—simply put, their custom engineering was impractical for the living room.

This arcade advantage was never more apparent than with the 1983 release of the laserdisc classic from Cinemaware, *Dragon's Lair*. Instead of a quarter, it cost 50 cents per play, but it was worth it just to impress the large crowds who gathered around to watch Dirk the Daring rescue the fair Princess Daphne from the clutches of Singe the dragon in the evil wizard Mordroc's castle. It was a rare case in which watching someone else play was almost as fun as playing it yourself!

Robotron: 2084 from the **MAME** emulator.

Robotron: 2084 (1982, Williams Electronics)

What do you do for an encore after the unqualified success that was *Defender*? If you're Eugene Jarvis and Larry DeMar, you simply create *Robotron: 2084*, which is perhaps even more beloved. While just as difficult to advance in many ways as *Defender*, *Robotron: 2084* added a new dimension of accessibility with its dual joystick controls one for movement and one for shooting. Even if first-time players couldn't survive the first frenetic waves of enemy robots, it was a safe bet they'd drop in another quarter to try again and again, getting just a little better each time.

Unfortunately, the feature-film-quality cartoon visuals masked limited interactivity. A surge of laserdisc games followed in the wake of *Dragon's Lair*'s success. Despite the initial enthusiasm,

games that played similarly to *Dragon's Lair*, like *Cliff Hanger* (1983, Stern), *Road Avenger* (1985, Data East), and even Cinematronics' own 1984 encore, *Space Ace*, failed to make anywhere near the same impact. Others still, like shooters *Bega's Battle* (1983, Data East), *Astron Belt* (1983, Bally Midway), *MACH 3* (1983, Mylstar), and *Firefox* (1984, Atari),

A screenshot from the 2009 version of **Dragon's Lair** for the iPhone and iPod Touch. It was not only until relatively recently that it was possible to match or exceed the arcade version's audiovisual quality in the home.

overlaid traditional graphics on top of mostly non-interactive video backgrounds to up the level of interactivity while still keeping the pizazz. These efforts didn't do much to sustain consumer interest and the persnickety nature of the laserdisc players frustrated arcade operators, who had trouble keeping the machines operational.

Years later, for later Generation Two home systems, the introduction of the CD-ROM triggered a similar rush of consumer enthusiasm followed by almost complete disinterest in games with Full-Motion Video (FMV). By the time Generation Three was underway, the shift in favor to far more versatile polygon-based 3D models over live video was all but complete. Nevertheless, more reliable technology did lead to a short-lived renaissance of FMV arcade games in the first half of the 1990s thanks in part to the efforts of American Laser Games and their series of popular light gun shooters, starting with the release of *Mad Dog McCree* in 1990. Stuart Horvath recalled the thrill of having 20 people cheering him on in the arcade as he played. "I used to go back and kill Mad Dog for the 15th time just because I had the reflexes to do it and it made me feel almost like a celebrity," he reminisced.

Despite the sharp shooting, FMV proved that it once again had limited ammunition. Even when the brains behind *Dragon's Lair*, Rick Dyer, teamed up with Sega for a stereoscopic laserdisc game in 1991, *Time Traveler*, which convincingly faked holographic technology, it was still not enough to overcome FMV's ever-present limitations, let alone change the format's ultimate destiny.[5]

With laser-disc's inability to spark long-term relief, the decline in arcade revenue continued apace. A February 3, 1984, article in *The Philadelphia Inquirer* entitled, "Can Lasers Save Video Arcades?" pegged 1983 arcade revenue at $5 billion, compared to a high of $8 billion in 1981. Many of the same problems that were affecting the home market, including a glut of inferior product, were also affecting the arcade. The Great Videogame Crash played no favorites.

Despite the financial gloom and doom, fantastic new arcade games continued to be released throughout the 1980s even as more and more arcade locations closed. These included Namco's action-packed digging game *Dig Dug* (1982); Williams Electronics' flying dueler *Joust* (1982); Namco's high-speed *Pole Position* (1982); Gottlieb's charismatic hopper *Q*bert* (1982); Bally Midway's dazzling movie license *Tron* (1982), and licensed to thrill *Spy Hunter* (1983); Konami's button mashing *Track & Field* (1983); Atari's lushly produced crossbow light gun shooter

---

5   Cecropia's unreleased 2007 interactive cartoon arcade game, *The Act*, was one of the few games to make excellent use of FMV. Rather than worrying about real-time interaction, the game asks players to properly guide the emotions of a bumbling window washer trying to win the heart of a beautiful nurse. Fortunately, Chillingo developed authentic ports of the game for iOS and Macintosh platforms in 2012.

Crossbow (1983) and bicycle handlebar equipped newspaper delivery game *Paperboy* (1984); Capcom's scrolling shoot-'em-up *1942* (1984); and Nintendo's energetic and visually arresting, *Punch-Out!!* (1984). It's little wonder this period is considered the Golden Age of video arcade games.

Many more classics and breakthroughs would follow throughout the 1980s, but it would take Capcom's release of *Street Fighter II: The World Warrior* in 1991 for the fighting games craze to make the arcade truly profitable again. Predated by classics like *Karate Champ* (1984, Data East), and side-scrolling beat-'em-up, *Double Dragon* (1987, Taito), *Street Fighter II* set the standard for competitive fighting games for years to come and is still the primary influence for fighting games today, even as they've moved to advanced 3D engines. Notable games in this vein include *Mortal Kombat* (1992, Midway Games), which thrilled with its over-the-top fatalities; *Virtua Fighter* (1993, Sega), which was the first 3D fighting game; and *Killer Instinct* (1994), which was the first arcade game to incorporate a hard drive, which it leveraged to stream high quality pre-rendered graphics.

By this time, the Generation Two home systems were playing host to far more accurate ports than was previously possible. Conversions such as *Popeye* (1986, Nintendo) on the Nintendo Entertainment System, *Golden Axe* (1990, Sega) on the Sega Genesis, or *Street Fighter II Turbo* (1993, Capcom) on the Super Nintendo, strongly rivaled the audiovisuals and speed of their arcade counterparts. Arcade hardware was starting to lose its edge. Nevertheless, before the 1990s were out, the arcade would influence home videogames greatly one more time, and again briefly make the few arcades that remained the places to be.

Star Wars from the **MAME** emulator.

Star Wars (1983, Atari, Inc.)

Like *Star Trek* before it, the *Star Wars* series inspired a large number of unauthorized videogames, some good, some bad, but never the real thing in the arcade[6] until Atari felt the force in 1983. Combining their dazzling color vector graphics technology, digitized speech straight from the film, and a control yoke that could pass for a movie prop, Atari's *Star Wars* impressed. Whether as an upright cabinet or special sit-down cockpit, both *Star Wars* and videogame fans couldn't have asked for much more as they re-enacted the first film's climactic attack on the Death Star from a thrilling first-person perspective. The slightly improved *Star Wars: The Empire Strikes Back* (1985) was sold as a conversion kit, but few arcade operators, and ultimately, players, bothered to upgrade.

In early 1999, Konami unveiled their *Dance Dance Revolution* (*DDR*) dance and rhythm game in North America. Unlike the American arcade sector, the Japanese arcade scene had remained vibrant, and in fact played host to several earlier and successful music and rhythm

---

6   Parker Brothers had the home rights to the *Star Wars* series license and produced a mix of games from all three original films, primarily for the Atari 2600. The company even ported Atari's arcade *Star Wars* to various home platforms of the era, with mostly positive results considering the inherent technological differences and limitations.

games. Still, there was something special about *DDR* that allowed it to succeed even in the finicky North American arcade market. The premise is simple: play a game of Simon Says with your feet, stepping on the correct arrow or arrows on the dance platform to the beat of eclectic dance music. Two players could dance side-by-side and often did, to the delight of the types of crowds that hadn't gathered since the heights of *Dragon's Lair* and *Street Fighter II*'s popularity. In many ways, it was a return to the exquisite simplicity and fun competition of games like *Pong* and *Pac-Man.*

Generation Three home systems were not content to let the arcades have all the dancing fun, of course. The novelty of the arcade experience again started to wear off as gamers were able to dance to the beat or play on plastic instruments in the comfort (and privacy) of their homes. It also became more common to find the same types of technology found within Generation Three systems powering arcade machines. Further, as online connection speeds improved, so too did the experience of playing multiplayer games long distance. While some players seem to enjoy the spectacle of performing at a crowded arcade, the majority seems to think there's no place like home.

With home systems now firmly in control of the modern gamer, today's arcades are just as likely to play host to prize ticket redemption machines and ride-like simulators than anything of note. In fact, it's often the home systems that influence what few games are released in the arcade the most these days, a trend evidenced by Global VR's ports in the mid-2000s of a series of console favorites like *Madden NFL Football*, *Need for Speed Underground*, *EA Sports PGA*

Tour Golf Challenge Edition, and *Blazing Angels: Squadrons of WWII*. It was clear this trend was going to be the norm when even smartphones and tablets started getting in on the reverse port, as seen with unusual touchscreen translations *Infinity Blade FX* and *Fruit Ninja FX*, both released by Adrenaline Amusements in 2011.

Arcade racing games that border on full-fledged simulations are still popular attractions, often offering expandable networked play and dynamic leaderboards. Image of **EA Sports NASCAR Team Racing** (2007), four player version, from Funspot, located in Laconia, New Hampshire.

The Arcade Community Then and Now

Today's arcades have replaced the simple joys of laying down a quarter for next play with emotion-less swipe cards—which, coincidentally, make it much harder to keep track of how much you're spending. But nothing has swayed the arcade enthusiast's nostalgia for classic arcade games and vintage machines. One of the most popular rallying points is the website for the International Arcade Museum (www.arcade-museum.com), which consists of a database, calendar of events, active discussion forums, and more that cater to the buying, trading, and general enjoyment of everything related to the arcade. However, it's interesting to note that many other videogame websites, whether they're spe-cific to arcade games or not, readily welcome arcade discussions. It seems that, unlike every other platform in this book, which practically encourage an "us versus them" attitude, the love of the arcade knows no borders or divid-ing lines, except maybe when it comes to what the best arcade game of 1987 was.[7]

What was special at the arcade of yesteryear still lives on in the occasional local hole-in-the-wall with limited hours and maybe a dozen classic machines or so. There's also the occasional destination worth a cross-country pilgrimage. A few of these destinations include two New Hampshire arcades, Funspot in Laconia, which was named "Largest Arcade in the World" by Guinness World Records in 2008, and the Pinball Wizard Arcade in Pelham; three Las Vegas strip arcades at the New York-New York,

You'll often find today's popular arcade machines act more like amusement park attractions than the more straightforward classic twitch games of the 1980s. Image of the **TsuMo Deluxe Multi-Game Motion System** (2003) from Funspot, located in Laconia, New Hampshire.

Excalibur, and Circus Circus casinos; and San Francisco's Musee Mecanique, which throws some of the amazing electro-mechanical antiques discussed earlier in this chapter into its mix of playable amusements. It may take a bit of searching, but you should find a decent arcade or two beyond the Dave & Busters or Chuck E. Cheese's chains. At least at Chuck E. Cheese's you can still plunk tokens instead of swiping cards, even if it can be a struggle to find working machines worth playing.

Collecting and Emulating Arcade Games

Used arcade machines are still readily available from the hundreds to the thousands of dollars. There are even new creations that either play one or even multiple, officially licensed games. Arcade cabinets come in a huge range of form factors, be it standard upright, cocktail, candy, deluxe, cockpit and environmental, mini, bartop, and more, so finding some type of solution for your home arcade enjoyment shouldn't be too difficult.

Various standards were introduced starting in the mid-1980s, including JAMMA, and SNK's Neo Geo in 1990, just to name two. This standardization has made it easier than ever to acquire replacement parts and components cheaply and easily. Parts, accessories, and add-ons are

---

[7]　It definitely wasn't Bally Midway's *Spy Hunter II*.

readily available to both restore the classics, as well as create custom computer-based emulation machines. As mentioned earlier, there is a plethora of information online and generally helpful communities that make getting started in any way you choose easy.

MAME, or the *Multiple Arcade Machine Emulator*, is the undisputed king of emulators. It was introduced in 1997 and has enjoyed continuous development and refinement ever since. Originally limited to PCs running the DOS operating system, the emulator has now been ported to every feasible platform, including today's smartphones and tablets. To have the ability to play thousands of classic arcade games in the comfort of your home and with a variety of devices is something that those of us who grew up with a joystick in our hands never could have dreamed possible.

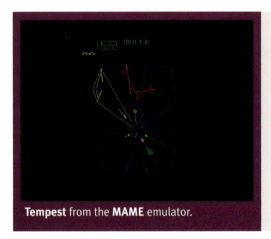

Tempest from the **MAME** emulator.

Tempest (1981, Atari, Inc.)

With 96 different playfields and the breakthrough of a selectable level of difficulty, Atari's first color vector graphics game certainly impressed with its ambition and innovation. What really differentiated this three-dimensional perspective tube shooter from other shoot-'em-up competition was how perfectly mated the game was to its controller. With its spinner, a two-direction rotary dial, players could move their spaceship along the edge of the playfield as slowly or quickly as they desired, while still maintaining an amazing degree of precision.

For those with more limited space or budgets for full-sized machines, solutions like the X-Arcade from Xgaming, Inc., offers arcade quality controls that work with PCs and consoles. With the prevalence of officially licensed emulators and themed game packs for today's platforms, it's easier than to ever to re-experience the classics in just the way you'd like.

Such was the allure of the arcade aura that great pains have been taken to virtually recreate the experience. Some recent examples include Microsoft's mostly failed arcade experiment for the Xbox 360 and Windows PC's, *Game Room*, a sub-set of the wildly successful and somewhat misnamed Xbox Live Arcade, and Sony's *Home* for the PlayStation 3, complete with a misguided recreation of

Microsoft's **Game Room** service was an ill-fated attempt to recreate the arcade and classic home game system experience virtually on the Xbox 360 and Windows PCs. Although still available, it hasn't received new game packs since late 2010, the year of its release.

the arcade experience, which unfortunately included waiting virtually in a line for your turn to play. Concepts like achievements, gamer scores, virtual trophies, and online leaderboards have been far more successful in capturing the elusive competitive spirit of the classic arcade.

Some of the classic arcade manufacturers, or, in many cases, the present rights holders, continue to release new products based on the classics, either direct recreations or emulations, or new games or variations inspired by the well-worn legends. Someone who is rather cynical might say that's because there was more creativity back then. Instead, perhaps there was simply more opportunity to try something new since not that much came before, and, as such, few rules to adhere to. In fact, such pioneering spirit is often seen from today's indie development scene, although it's harder for that group of developers to get the same type of recognition that the past masters did, since the sea of games is now a veritable galaxy, on its way to becoming a seemingly limitless universe. Through all of the industry's ups and downs, now is still the best time to be a gamer.

Apple II (1977)

History

The Apple II is one of the longest lived computing platforms in history, which, when looking at the list, really says something about its remarkable staying power. Along with the Commodore PET and the TRS-80 Model I, the Apple II was part of the original personal computing trinity of 1977, but unlike them retained its powerhouse reputation well into the 1980s. Even when it was overpowered by the Atari 800 and dramatically underpriced by the Commodore 64, the Apple II platform's solid foundation, architectural flexibility, and expandability allowed it to remain commercially viable until production finally stopped in late 1993. In its more than 15 years on the market—a miracle by technological standards—it witnessed the rise and fall of dozens of determined and worthy competitors. In short, the Apple II's impact on the computer and videogame industries is difficult to overstate.

The Apple II commanded such loyalty, in fact, that Apple itself seemed reluctant to tamper much with the formula. The IIGS, for instance, was a more capable, backwards-compatible model introduced in late 1986. Initially a sales success, the IIGS was hamstrung by Apple's decision to limit its technology—ostensibly to avoid competition with their new line of Macintosh computers. Within a few years, enthusiasm for the IIGS waned from both Apple and consumers, and the company's focus shifted back to the original core technology found in the Apple IIe Platinum, the last model off the production line in November 1993. Speaking of the Macintosh, it was the Apple II platform's remarkable consistency that bought Apple the years it needed to build the Macintosh brand, which was in turn the bridge to unprecedented commercial success with the iPod and iOS platforms. Indeed, it's hard to imagine what the tech industry would look like today if the Apple II had remained a "crazy" dream of its eccentric designers.

The tale of the Apple II begins with two Steves from Sunnyvale, California. The first was Steve "Woz" Wozniak, a talented, socially awkward, but unflappably sincere engineer specializing in calculators at Hewlett-Packard (HP). He couldn't have been a starker contrast to the other Steve, Jobs, the quintessential free-spirited hippy with remarkable charisma. Woz, five years older than Jobs, had been introduced to him by a mutual acquaintance, when Jobs was still in high school in Cupertino, California. The two computer wizards became fast, if unlikely friends, engaging in constant pranks and making money selling "blue boxes," illegal devices used by "phreakers"— phone system hackers—to steal free long-distance calls and eavesdrop on private conversations.

Jobs became Atari's 40th employee in 1974, serving the innovative young company as a willful, but unremarkable hourly technician. However, he soon left Atari for a year-long hiatus to India, returning to work with a shaved head and traditional Indian garb. It was the type of wild, ballsy, and utterly unpredictable behavior that would help cement Jobs' reputation as a true

Airheart (1986, Broderbund)

After several unfinished attempts at creating a worthy follow-up to *Choplifter*, Dan Gorlin finally completed *Airheart*, which put the player in control of a jet-propelled circular raft in order to gather items and battle water-born obstacles and enemies. Gorlin leveraged the Apple IIe Enhanced's double hi-res graphics and 128K of memory to deliver a high-speed, visually rich arcade adventure.

Airheart from the **AppleWin** emulator.

eccentric. Whenever Jobs took into his head to do something, he'd do it—regardless of the consequences or what other people thought.

Atari had scored big with its arcade version of *Pong*, and was soon to repeat its success with its famous play-at-home version. Jobs, hired back on at Atari as a night-shift engineer, was asked to create a prototype for a single-player, vertical *Pong* variant called *Breakout*.

The goal of *Breakout* is to clear rows of blocks at the top of the screen by bouncing a ball off a small, movable paddle at the bottom. It's a fun game that many people still enjoy in various incarnations today. However, at the time, the technology required to create a *Breakout* machine was too costly to make it profitable to manufacture, so Atari needed a seriously streamlined design. Faced with this daunting engineering challenge, Jobs sought the help of his old friend Woz.

Rumor has it that this is exactly what some combination of Nolan Bushnell, Steve Bristow, and Al Alcorn wanted Jobs to do. The team at Atari had witnessed Woz's impressive self-built home *Pong* clone, but failed to woo him away from HP. Nevertheless, Woz was a fan of both Atari arcade games and engineering challenges, so he came to his friend's rescue. He completed the bulk of the work in only four days, with an efficient design that used far fewer chips than any other Atari arcade game at the time. Atari's engineers were pleased and gave Jobs a nice payout and bonus—most of which he famously kept for himself.[1] *Breakout* become another smash hit for Atari, even though the company had to compromise somewhat on Woz's design by adding more chips (Woz's design was actually more efficient than the company could successfully manufacture).

After years of hardware hacking and his two dalliances in videogames, Woz was inspired by Don Lancaster's TV Typewriter design and the recent availability of the inexpensive MOS 6502 microprocessor to begin work on a television computer terminal. He realized that one major stumbling block for the nascent home computer industry was the lack of a cheap and effective means of displaying output. Computer hobbyists could either content themselves with a row of flashing LEDs or ante up the big bucks for a video or text terminal. Neither solution was particularly desirable.

Woz had been attending regular meetings at the legendary Homebrew Computer Club, where many of the industry's pioneers shared their ideas and passions. Inspired by this creative and highly motivated group, Woz soon demonstrated a prototype that would ultimately become the Apple

---

[1] According to the book *iWoz*, Jobs only gave Woz $375, claiming Atari had only given him $750. In reality, he'd received $5,000.

Captain Goodnight from the **AppleWin** emulator.

Captain Goodnight and the Islands of Fear
(1985, Broderbund)

On a platform not known for its audiovisual prowess, *Captain Goodnight and the Islands of Fear* impressed with its richly cinematic, multistage gameplay. Large, detailed sprites scroll smoothly as the player attempts to guide Captain Roscoe "Buzz" Goodnight through Fear Islands' challenging scrolling stages to destroy Doctor Maybe's doomsday machine before it can be activated. Battle enemies on foot and from a wide variety of transports, including diverse types of aircraft, ships, vehicles, and even a tram, to achieve your ultimate goal.

Computer, known later as the Apple I, or Apple-1. Really nothing more than an elegantly-designed circuit board with a low-cost MOS 6502 microprocessor, 4KB RAM, and expansion connectors, the Apple I nevertheless laid the foundation for the juggernaut Apple II. Unfortunately for them, nei-

ther Atari, who couldn't justify the diversion of funds, nor HP, who didn't see the value in personal computers, showed any interest in the prototype. Nonplussed by this rejection, the two Steves formed their own company, Apple Computer, on April 1, 1976.

Working out of Woz's bedroom and Jobs' garage, the two soon began production of the Apple I. The ever-persuasive Jobs negotiated with a local hobbyist computer store, the Byte Shop, for an order worth $50,000. Credit, time, and supply constraints were tight, but the Byte Shop order was met, and the computer store provided full-stroke keyboards and wooden cases to its customers to complement the circuit board. Through the Byte Shop, as well as magazine coverage and advertisements, Apple had slow, but steady growth from sales of its first computer. It was a promising start, but it's doubtful that even Jobs predicted the scale of the success just around the corner.

The October 1976 issue of **Interface Age** featured the second ever magazine advertisement for the Apple I, starting prices of $666.66, which, as the story goes, was due to Woz's fondness for repeating digits, as well as representing a one-third markup on what the Byte Shop bought each unit for. According to Woz, Apple only sold a few hundred units in its first year, but, critically, got the company's name out there to the day's computer clubs and magazines.

Even before they officially released the Apple I, Jobs and Woz were thinking up new features. They frequently updated the design and shared their progress with their fellow enthusiasts at the Homebrew Computer Club. The eventual result was the Apple II. Even though little time had passed since the first Apple, the new unit improved on it in nearly every way. It sported a complete molded plastic enclosure with full-stroke keyboard, external peripheral ports, and eight easily accessible internal expansion slots. Even if some might look at it today and find it clunky, at the time it was the sleekest home computer anyone had ever seen; the Ferrari of the industry.

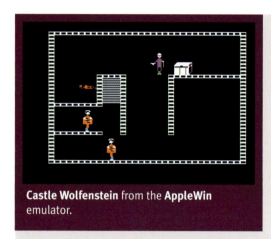

Castle Wolfenstein from the **AppleWin** emulator.

Castle Wolfenstein (1981, Muse Software)

Silas Warner had a stellar year in 1981 on the Apple II, with the release of both the popular programmable robot battle game *RobotWar*, as well as the even more remarkable *Castle Wolfenstein*, which successfully merged the best of action and adventure games to create the industry's first stealth-centric videogame classic. Set in World War II, your mission is to escape from a Nazi prison complex by sneaking past and impersonating guards, searching for critical equipment, and carefully employing lethal force (when necessary). The sophisticated control schemes and ahead-of-its-time software-based speech synthesis heighten the already intense gameplay. Its high concept sequel, *Beyond Castle Wolfenstein* (1984)— where you break into a secret Berlin bunker to retrieve a bomb to place near Hitler during a meeting with his senior staff—is also worth a look. Amazingly, after a long and storied development cycle, the series' spiritual successor, id Software's classic first-person shooter *Wolfenstein 3D* (1992) was successfully ported to the Apple IIGS in 1998.[2]

An original Apple II computer, courtesy of Jonathan Zufi, **Shrine of Apple,** http://shrineofapple.com.

Appropriately enough, the Apple II owes many of its innovations to the *Breakout* game. The Apple II was clearly designed to be something special, and, as Woz recalled in the October 1986 issue of *Call-APPLE Magazine,* "a lot of these features that really made the Apple II stand out in its day came from a game, and the fun features that were built in were only to do one pet project, which was to program a BASIC version of *Breakout* and

---

2   For the full story, see http://apple2history.org/spotlight/the-long-strange-saga-of-wolfenstein-3d-on-the-apple-iigs.

show it off at the club." As a result of his *Breakout* ambitions, Woz's design for the Apple II came to incorporate color graphics commands, circuitry for paddle controllers, and a speaker for sound. With these standard features in place, the Apple II offered technology that its rivals in 1977, the Commodore PET and Tandy TRS-80, simply couldn't match.

As impressive as it was, however, the Apple did suffer one very noticeable limitation: it relied on the ubiquitous but cumbersome cassette tape for data storage. The Apple II's built-in cassette port could read and write data using any decent off-the-shelf cassette recorder, matching most other computers' storage abilities at the time. Although cassette recorders were slow and unreliable for storing computer data, they were cheap, which made them the early standard over more reliable disk-based systems that could cost more than a computer.

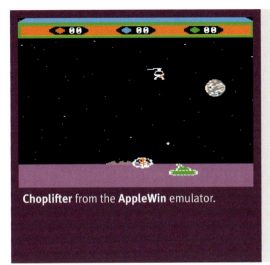

Choplifter from the **AppleWin** emulator.

Choplifter (1982, Broderbund)

Among the most ported games of the 1980s, *Choplifter* first appeared on the Apple II and took optional advantage of the platform's paddle controllers to offer what was arguably the smoothest control experience for the in-game helicopter. However you played it, *Choplifter* offered up the intensity and compelling rescue mechanic from Williams Electronics' arcade classic *Defender* (1980) and grounded it in the reality of the days' hostage crisis scenarios. If you like this, you may wish to try an even more sophisticated take on helicopter action with the prototypical real-time strategy (RTS) game, *Rescue Raiders* (1986, Sir-Tech).

Luckily for Apple, Woz had more tricks up his sleeve. His next act was a design for an efficient, speedy, and relatively inexpensive 5.25-inch floppy disk drive called the Disk II, which was released in 1978 to instant and near-universal acclaim. Disks soon ejected cassettes as the storage medium of choice on Apple systems, and it would take competitors years to catch up to Apple's decisive lead with this important storage technology.

The early disk standardization complemented the platform's color graphics and sound, as well as its well documented and versatile architecture, making the Apple II series the preferred target of both application and game developers well into the 1980s. As a result, even though other platforms easily outsold and eventually outperformed the Apple II series, fans of these rival systems often had to settle for quick and dirty ports of games originally designed on and for the Apple II.

By 1980, the company boasted nearly 1000 employees and had outgrown several office spaces. In December, Apple Computer, Inc., successfully went public, with a valuation close to $2 billion. Several millionaires were created in the process, Jobs and Woz among them. In 1981, after an injury received in a plane crash, Woz took a leave of absence and returned only briefly

An early ad from the September 1979 issue of **BYTE,** which demonstrates Apple's expectation of a Disk II purchase with every Apple II.

before departing for good to explore educational, charitable, and other business ventures. Meanwhile, Jobs became chairman of Apple.

In 1983, Jobs appointed John Sculley, then president of Pepsi-Cola, to become president and CEO of Apple. By 1985, significant differences between Sculley and Jobs led to Jobs' resignation. He didn't lose much sleep over it, founding both Pixar Animation Studios and NeXT Computer shortly after. He didn't return to Apple until 1997, when, older and wiser but still indefatigable, he began the remarkable turnaround of what had become an ailing and financially weakened company in his absence.

Model Highlights

What follows are some highlights of the major Apple II and related systems released in the United States:

An original Apple II+ computer, courtesy of Jonathan Zufi, **Shrine of Apple,** http://shrineofapple.com.

- **1977–1980:** The Apple II initially included 4KB RAM, a four-color (later six-color) display, built-in Integer BASIC, two game paddles, and one demo cassette. It was available preassembled or in kit form.

- **1979–1983:** The Apple II+ (aka, II Plus) included 16–48KB RAM, six-color display, and a new BASIC from Microsoft, which established critical new base specifications for the computer line. It was also at this time that Apple allowed media equipment specialist Bell & Howell to make the only authorized clone, a black Apple II+ with special audio/video ports and a case accessible only with a screwdriver. This special Apple II+ was targeted at schools, where Apple hoped to firmly establish their platform. The strategy worked, and countless American school children received their first exposure to home computers courtesy of the Apple II+.

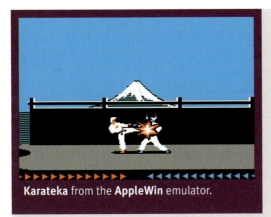

Karateka from the **AppleWin** emulator.

Karateka (1984, Broderbund)

With few words and even less button mashing, *Karateka* makes you the star of your own dramatic martial arts epic. Amazingly, even though he did it as a side project while a student at Yale University, Jordan Mechner was still able to maximize the Apple II's modest audiovisual capabilities and required just 48K of memory and 140K of disk space to do it. To rescue the Princess Mariko from the clutches of Akuma and his evil henchman—including a trained hawk—requires well-timed punches, kicks, and blocks. Combined with Mechner's pioneering use of rotoscoping motion capture techniques, *Kareteka* creates a gameplay experience quite unlike any other before or since. Avoiding the few traps and pitfalls, including showing the proper respect to the princess if you're ever able to reach her, requires the deftness of a true master. Finally, if you're lucky enough to play from a real disk, be sure to boot from side 2 to experience one of the greatest Easter Eggs[3] in videogame history.

- **1983–1993:** The Apple IIe, Apple's most successful II-series system, helped the company capture over 15 percent of the computer market in 1984, its highest ever percentage.[4] The IIe included 64KB RAM and the important capability to display both upper and lowercase characters. It eventually shipped with both DOS 3.3 and the newer ProDOS. The Enhanced IIe

The inside of an Apple IIe, with several of its expansion slots populated.

---

3   Usually intentional hidden messages, secrets, or extra features in a videogame or other computer software. Although first popularized by Warren Robinett's *Adventure* (1979) on the Atari VCS, Easter Eggs have been a part of computer history's earliest days.

4   http://jeremyreimer.com/m-item.lsp?i=137. In contrast, the Atari 8-bit platform would have over 3 percent of the market, down from a high of almost 28 percent in 1980, while the Commodore 64 would also have its best year ever, with almost 40 percent market share.

was released in 1985 and included many of the improvements found in the IIc. The last IIe variation, known as the Platinum because of the color of its case, included a numeric keypad and several additional minor enhancements, and was manufactured from 1987 to 1993. In the same year as the first IIe, the $10,000 (more than $22,000 in today's dollars) next-generation Apple Lisa business system was introduced, but was unsuccessful and ultimately deprecated in favor of the Macintosh.

- **1984–1990:** The compact Apple IIc was introduced with 128KB RAM and a built-in 5.25-inch floppy drive. The IIc+, whose production replaced the IIc's, was introduced in 1988 with a faster 4 MHz processor, high-capacity RAM expansion option, and a 3.5-inch internal disk drive, which had the same 800KB capacity as the drive for the Apple IIGS. The first Apple Macintosh was released the same year for just under $2000, though the price was soon raised to just under $2500 (about $5400, adjusted).

An Apple IIc computer, shown for its size comparison with the 5.25-inch floppy disk for SSI's real-time strategy game **Cytron Masters** (1981).

- **1986–1992:** Apple released the 16-bit Apple IIGS, the true backwards compatible successor to the original 8-bit II-series of computers. Although Apple was built on the back of the II-series, within a few years the Macintosh began to receive most of the company's attention and resources, and by 1987 was consistently outselling its brethren.

Apple II Forever

Despite the famous proclamation of "Apple II Forever" during a 1984 event to unveil the Apple IIc, "forever" ended about ten years later when Apple committed themselves exclusively to the Macintosh. Nevertheless, for technology with roots as far back as 1976, the Apple II series of computers had an amazing run. Indeed, it still enjoyed a remarkably devoted fan base, and if Apple had continued to fully support it instead of lavishing its energies on the Macintosh, who knows, maybe the Apple II series would still be in production today.

One of the reasons the Apple II was so successful was that the inner workings of the hardware was made public, whereas other manufacturers treated such things as trade secrets. Another key factor was being one of the first systems for which a disk drive was an expected end-user accessory. Developers took advantage of the Disk II standard, and within a few years there was an explosion of disk software. As stated in the December 1983 issue of *Electronic Games* magazine, "Just about anything the acquisitive computerist might want for his or her system is available to the Apple II owner." This was no exaggeration.

The Apple II had two major disk operating systems, DOS 3.x and ProDOS, each of which might be needed to run specific software that didn't automatically boot. DOS 3.1 (not 1.0 due to internal versioning) was released along with the original Disk II. In 1980, DOS 3.3 was the last new version of the original DOS released. It supported increased disk capacities and a new sector format. The new format required a conversion before old disks could be used on the newer disk drive, which had an updated ROM.

Since the original Apple DOS was designed exclusively for Disk II, ProDOS was released in 1984 to make mixed disk formats and hard drives more accessible, as well as faster and more flexible. Based on the Apple III's versatile Sophisticated Operating System (SOS), ProDOS was able to support the II-series for the entire original run of the systems and through to the present day. In 1986, with the release of ProDOS 16 1.0 on the 16-bit Apple IIGS, the original 8-bit ProDOS software's name was changed to ProDOS 8 with the release of version 1.2. The last version of ProDOS 8, version 1.9, was released in 1990.

Dan Bricklin and Bob Frankston created the first "killer app" for the business world with their *VisiCalc* spreadsheet software in 1979, but the II-series was not destined to rule the office. That honor, of course, would go to the IBM PC and its endless clones, which are discussed later in Chapter 1.6. However, Apple still enjoyed a lucrative slice of the business market well into the 1990s, with plenty of software for both professionals and casual users. If the Commodore 64 (released in 1982) was the low-cost computer for the masses, the Apple II was the more refined and tasteful computer for the classes.

The Apple II platform was ideal for the classroom because its solid Woz-constructed design elements encouraged expansion, extension, and experimentation. Its audiovisual demands were also relatively modest and it had a wide range of software development tools, which further aided the development of massive amounts of educational software. Apple would continue this tradition with the Macintosh. Even though the Mac failed to garner the market share of its older

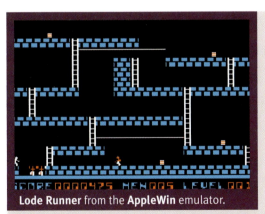

Lode Runner from the **AppleWin** emulator.

Lode Runner (1984, Broderbund)

Another of the many games from Broderbund worth checking out, for many gamers, *Lode Runner* is without peer. A brilliant combination of arcade action and puzzle-solving, *Lode Runner* was one of the first games to include a level editor, which added even more value to a game that already featured 150 levels. Each multiplatform level challenges the player to collect all the gold, while either avoiding or trapping pursuing guards in temporary holes. Part of the fun comes from placing said holes in just the right place at just the right time, while avoiding falling into them yourself. For an even greater challenge, check out the game's first of many offshoots, sequels, and successors, *Championship Lode Runner* (1985).

brother at its best, peaking at 12 percent in 1992, it has still enjoyed a decidedly disproportionate presence in education.

However, Apple's versatile computers were as good for gaming as productivity and educational programs. Since the Apple II was a prime platform for more than a decade, it's hardly surprising that thousands of games were produced for it. Although a haven for strategy, role-playing, and adventure software, the Apple II's massive game library was hardly limited to these categories. Genre-defining releases came from a full range of famous developers and publishers, including Broderbund, Electronic Arts, Infocom, Interplay, Origin, and SSI. In short, the Apple II's influence on the videogame industry is tremendous. What these games may have lacked in audiovisual wizardry were more than made up for by their originality and innovativeness.

Mystery House (1980) by On-Line Systems (later, Sierra) was the first commercial text adventure with graphics. The company's later *Time Zone* (1982) was one of the first truly epic games, spanning six double-sided disks and featuring 1500 screens to explore. Although Richard Garriott released his *Akalabeth: World of Doom* (1980) first, his second role-playing game, *Ultima* (1981), set the stage for one of the most storied franchises in gaming.

Penguin Software's *The Graphics Magician* (1982), although not technically a game, was a popular graphics and animation-creation package that joined a mass of other programs helpful in making them, improving the Apple II's cachet as a development platform. Electronic Arts' *Music Construction Set* and *Pinball Construction Set* were both released in 1983, and brought creative development to the masses. The latter let the user create unique virtual pinball machines with drag-and-drop simplicity, and the former did the same for music composition. Also in 1983, The Learning Company produced *Rocky's Boots*, an award-winning example of "edutainment" software, which combined educational and instructional content with gaming, a hallmark of the Apple II series, which was led by MECC's legendary *The Oregon Trail* (various editions throughout the 1980s) and continued with the likes of Broderbund's *Where in the World is Carmen San Diego?* (1985), a series that thrives to this day.

As *Electronic Games* magazine so aptly put it in their 1983 Buyer's Guide, "It would be impossible to mention more than a small fraction of the hundreds of interesting games available for the Apple II computer system." This pattern of firsts and trendsetters continued through to the end of the 1980s, and included the first ever appearances of *John Madden Football* (1989) from Electronic Arts and Broderbund's action adventure *Prince of Persia* (1990), which was one of several games released after 1984 that took full advantage of the double hi-res graphics features available with 128KB enhanced Apple IIes, IIcs, and IIGSs, which allowed for 16 on-screen colors instead of six, as well as increased pixel density.

The IIGS Detour

By 1986, Apple's Macintosh computer had been on the market for about two years, but its high price and monochrome graphics had so far limited its appeal to mostly professionals and a few technology enthusiasts. Meanwhile, there was still a large base of Apple II users, with the IIc and especially the IIe helping to keep the platform active and thriving. However, the new Commodore Amiga (see Chapter 2.2) and Atari ST systems far surpassed these earlier systems in many areas, including graphics and sound capabilities. Rather than introduce a low-end Macintosh into the fray, Apple decided to revitalize the II series with the IIGS, releasing it in 1986.

The IIGS was Apple's fifth computer in the II series, and it brought significant enhancements to the standard set by the best-selling IIe, particularly in the realms of graphics and sound, with the GS in the name indeed standing for graphics and sound. Expectations were high. Michael Malone in the October 13, 1986, edition of the *San Francisco Chronicle*, stated, "The Apple IIGS might be called the great rec-

An Apple IIGS with a full complement of disk drives and third party trackball. The IIGS was the first Apple II series computer with a detachable keyboard.

onciler, for it begins to rejoin the halves of Apple that Jobs tore apart." And indeed, at first, the unit enjoyed good sales and seemed to be holding its own against the slightly more powerful and less expensive next-generation machines from Atari and Commodore, but it soon began to lose momentum as Apple never fully committed itself to the platform's success. By 1992, Apple had stopped manufacturing the IIGS to concentrate solely on its Macintosh line for its future market ambitions.

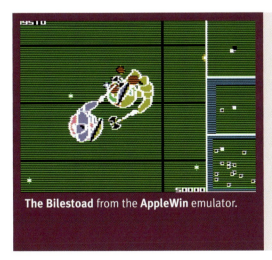

The Bilestoad from the **AppleWin** emulator.

The Bilestoad (1982, Datamost)

Marc Goodman's *The Bilestoad* is a one-on-one arena fighting game known for two things. The first, was the game's amazingly sophisticated and violent combat, which allowed players to strategically target and lop off limbs. The other was the fact that this was the game nearly everyone seemed to have and love, but precious few actually bought.[5] The result of this rampant piracy was Goodman's unfortunate decision to never make another game. Controversy aside, few fighting games since have managed to capture the same type of intensity or realism, so it is a title that should still be on any videogame fan's radar.

The IIGS debuted on September 1986 for Apple's 10th anniversary as a company and sold for $999 without a monitor. For an extra $500, users received an analog 12-inch RGB color monitor with a built-in speaker and support for up to 640 × 400 resolution. At these prices, the IIGS's audience was limited mostly to existing Apple fans; Atari's and Commodore's new systems offered more power for less money. Nevertheless, there was no shortage of loyal Apple users willing to

---

[5]   Goodman himself puts the estimate at around 5000 copies sold. See www.dadgum.com/halcyon/BOOK/GOODMAN.HTM.

purchase the system, and it is arguable that the platform could have remained commercially viable for several more years after it was discontinued had Apple continued to actively support it.

To help celebrate the new system, Apple shipped the first 10,000 units with Steve Wozniak's trademark signature ("Woz") on the front. Commodore had tried something similar with its Amiga 1000, but there the pressed-in signatures of the Amiga designers (and a paw print) were hidden under the case. The Woz signature on the IIGS illustrated just how closely Apple users associated Steve Wozniak with their favorite platform, in much the same way guitar manufacturers occasionally release signed versions of guitars designed by recognized masters such as Les Paul. Indeed, although there are certainly cheaper guitars that arguably play just as well, the raw social capital of owning a true Les Paul, like that of an Apple computer, are enough to keep demand high among certain sectors of society. There is just something unique and intangible about these products that makes them worthy of their money and affection; they are more than the sum of their parts.

Internally, the Apple IIGS is by far the most advanced of the II series, yet backward compatibility with older Apple II computers is possible thanks to a special Mega II custom chip, a variant of which was also used in the Apple IIe Card for the Macintosh LC computer. The system's main processor, a 16-bit chip from Western Design, the 65C816,[6] runs at 2.8MHz and allows the IIGS to handle up to 8MB of RAM (although most games required only 256K to 768K). The system originally shipped with 256K of RAM, although later systems came with 1MB. The graphics hardware is capable of simultaneously displaying up to 16 colors from a palette of 4096 in a resolution of 320 × 200. Other, seldom-used graphics modes allowed the IIGS to display more colors at higher resolutions, such as 16 dithered colors at 640 × 200. The sound hardware featured an Ensoniq

Ultima IV: Quest of the Avatar from the **AppleWin** emulator.

Ultima IV: Quest of the Avatar
(1985, Origin Systems)

Arguably the height of 8-bit computer role playing, Richard Garriott's first entry in the "Age of Enlightenment" trilogy lived up to its own hype and the high expectations set by its earlier, more traditional predecessors that comprised the "Age of Darkness" trilogy. Unlike most role playing games that task the player with simply killing a master bad guy or collecting prized artifacts, *Ultima IV*'s ultimate goal is to become the people's spiritual leader and role model by living a virtuous in-game life as various obstacles are overcome. Each in-game action contributes to the player's character development, either positively or negatively. For those users lucky enough to own a Mockingboard, even Ultima IV's musical score delights. Three years later, the last Ultima series game for the Apple II was released, *Ultima V: Warriors of Destiny*, which pushed the platform hard, improving both the graphics and sophistication of the game world, but also clearly demonstrated that the Apple II's time as the primary development platform had reached its useful limits.

---

[6] Since it utilized the same processor, this design made the Apple IIGS the ideal development platform for Super Nintendo (SNES) games, which are discussed in Chapter 2.5.

5503, a powerful synthesizer chip designed by Robert Yannes, the same engineer responsible for the Commodore 64's famous SID chip.

Unfortunately for Apple Computer, the musical abilities of the 5503 chip led to a long and costly lawsuit with Apple Corps, owner of Apple Records (the Beatles' recording company). Apple Corps had settled out of court with Apple Computer back in 1978 over a trademark infringement case regarding the name. Apple Computer had then promised to stay out of the music industry, but the IIGS's synthesizer chip seemed like a violation of that agreement to Apple Corps. The suit dragged on for years, and some historians cite it as another reason Apple decided to drop support for the platform and concentrate on the Macintosh. Regardless, these legal battles with Apple Corps over the name and market encroachment would continue to plague Apple Computer, particularly after the introduction of the iPod and iTunes in 2001, but they were finally resolved. In January 2007, Apple Computer officially changed its name to Apple Inc., then confidentially settled the trademark dispute with Apple Corps the following month.

Owners of Apple's earlier IIe computer were offered a $500 upgrade option for their system to convert it to a IIGS. However, the IIe's keyboard had a slightly different layout and the trade-in did not include the all-important mouse and 3.5-inch floppy drive. By the time all of these add-ons were added to the bill, it made more sense just to buy a stand-alone IIGS. Needless to say, not many IIe users took up the option to upgrade and either lived with the legacy platform's limitations or purchased new stand-alone systems.

Like the Commodore 128 (C-128) and Radio Shack Color Computer 3 (CoCo3), the Apple IIGS is an intriguing mix of old and new. On the one hand, there was much more power at the disposal of users and developers, and the path was laid for games that were much better-looking than any previously available on the Apple II platform. On the other hand, software developers faced a quandary over whether to target the new and better system or continue to cater to the well-established body of Apple II owners.

The IIGS's excellent backward compatibility with the earlier Apple II family ensured access to a massive software library right from the beginning, especially since adding a 5.25-inch disk drive or two was a common practice in typical setups. However, with this compatibility came an inherited liability: only

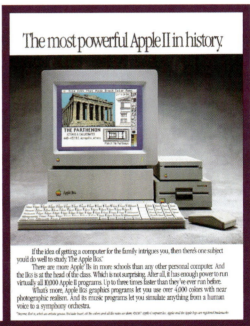

The most powerful Apple II in history.

THE PARTHENON

If the idea of getting a computer for the family intrigues you, then there's one subject you'd do well to study: The Apple IIGS.

There are more Apple IIs in more schools than any other personal computer. And the IIGS is at the head of the class. Which is not surprising. After all, it has enough power to run virtually all 10,000 Apple II programs. Up to three times faster than they've ever run before.

What's more, Apple IIGS graphics programs let you use over 4,000 colors with near photographic realism. And its music programs let you simulate anything from a human voice to a symphony orchestra.

Anyone that is, who's an article genius. But take heart, all the colors and all the notes are there. ©1987 Apple Computer Inc. Apple and the Apple logo are registered trademarks.

An early Apple IIGS ad from **Apple IIGS: The Buyer's Guide,** Fall 1987 issue, which emphasized Apple's dominance in the education sector.

one two-button analog joystick was supported by default. For two-player games, a keyboard or mouse had to be used by the second player.

There were some 200 commercial titles released for the IIGS that took advantage of its improved graphics and sound capabilities. Many of these games were ports of popular Amiga or Atari ST titles, such as Cinemaware's *King of Chicago* (1988) and *Defender of the Crown* (1988), and FTL's *Dungeon Master* (1989). Sports games were well represented by Epyx (*Winter Games*, 1987; *World Games*, 1987), Accolade (*Hardball!*, 1987; *Fast Break*, 1989), Electronic Arts (*Skate or Die!*, 1988), and Melbourne House (*John Elway's Quarterback*, 1990). Both Sierra On-Line (*King's Quest I*, 1987; *Space Quest II*, 1988) and ICOM Simulations (*Shadowgate*, 1989; *Uninvited*, 1989; *Deja Vu II*, 1989) offered their successful graphical adventure games for the platform. There were also many arcade ports, such as Taito's *Arkanoid II* (1988), and Mindscape's *Gauntlet* (1988) and *Paperboy* (1988). Suffice it to say, even though it didn't have the software depth of other computers, all the common genres of videogames were well represented on the system.

Compared to the original Apple II, there are precious few games that help define the capabilities of the IIGS. Some of the best known are Electronic Arts' *The Immortal* (1990), PBI Software's platform exclusive *Tower of Myraglen* (1987) and *Alien Mind* (1988), Sandcastle Productions' *Zany Golf* (1988), California Dreams' *Tunnels of Armageddon* (1989), and Naughty Dog's *Dream Zone* (1988), which was similar to *Tass Times in Tonetown*, a popular hybrid adventure game published in 1986 by Activision, who was also the first major publisher to debut its titles on the platform, including *Paintworks Plus*, *The Music Studio*, the classic tile-matching game *Shanghai*, and the suspenseful *Hacker II: The Doomsday Papers*. By 1990, third-party software support dwindled down to a trickle in favor of Amiga and PC compatible EGA formats.

The Apple II Community Then and Now

The Apple II platform has a rich and unparalleled history of magazine and newsletter support, with everything from classic multiplatform publications, like *Byte* and *Interface Age*, to Apple-specific titles, like *Call-APPLE* and *Nibble*. Apple fans loved reading about their favorite platforms and supported the best magazines and newsletters well into the 1990s. In fact, one such publication, *Juiced.GS*, which was launched in 1999, continues publishing new issues to this day!

There are a wide variety of websites where fans of the platform congregate and share information, which, besides the usual multi-platform sites, includes the Apple II-specific *Apple II History* (http://apple2history.org), *Applefritter* (www.applefritter.com) and *What*

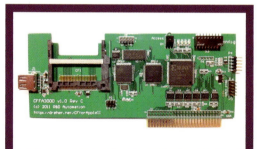

The popular CFFA3000 CompactFlash/USB flash drive interface plugs into slot-based Apple II systems to provide a modern-day alternative to traditional floppy disks.

is the Apple IIGS? (www.whatisthe2gs.apple2.org.za). Similarly, Apple II fans regularly meet in person at local and international events, including the popular KansasFest (KFest), which has been held annually in Missouri since 1989, and features keynotes from platform luminaries, and new homebrew product unveilings.

While the Apple II platform does not receive the same type of homebrew software support, particularly games, that many of the other platforms do, it does receive regular new hardware releases. These include plug-in Apple II cards from Briel Computers, like the Replica 1, which is one of many clones of the Apple I, and A2MP3, which features a USB interface and allows the playing of MP3 audio files, as well as R&D Automation's best-selling CFFA3000, with support for CompactFlash and USB flash media instead of floppy disks. These cards join a host of other newly produced memory expander, accelerator, and networking devices.

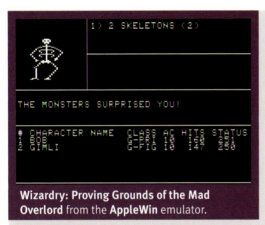

Wizardry: Proving Grounds of the Mad Overlord from the **AppleWin** emulator.

Wizardry: Proving Grounds of the Mad Overlord (1981, Sir-Tech Software)

While visually primitive and shockingly hard by today's standards, the core turn-based dungeon crawling and combat mechanics of the first *Wizardry* game were so good that they're still being mimicked to this day. Recreating the intense role-playing experience and sophistication from the pen and paper version of TSR's *Dungeons & Dragons* was a task that most developers shied away from, for obvious reasons. Nevertheless, from its multicharacter, multiclass party members whose strengths and weaknesses were statistics-driven, to the monsters, magic, and treasures straight out of Fantasy 101, *Wizardry* proved it could be done, and done well. Just make sure you're armed with graph paper so you can map your own progress—*Wizardry* offered few concessions to accessibility, just the way role-playing fans back in the day liked it.

Collecting Apple II Systems

One of the major problems facing a modern would-be Apple enthusiast is the compatibility (or rather the lack thereof) among all the various models. Many of these models have different ROM variations and other differences ranging from keyboard layout and configuration to standard RAM and expansion options. These differences range from the subtle to the extreme, so it's worth doing some preliminary research to determine which model is right for you.

On a related note, despite aggressive legal action by Apple against unauthorized manufacturers, dozens of clone systems were produced, with varying degrees of compatibility with the original Apple II. One example is the Franklin Ace 1000, released in 1982. Annoyingly, the reset button is so poorly positioned on the keyboard that it is easy to press it accidentally—seldom a pleasant occurrence. The best clones are VTech's Laser models. These systems are the general size of an Apple IIc, but have many of the Apple IIe's standard expansion options and are overall highly compatible. Surprisingly, the relative obscurity of some of these clones makes them more valuable to collectors than many of the more common genuine Apple computers, so don't expect a great value.

The Apple IIGS offers some intriguing pluses, but might not be as much fun for those that like older system styling or have no interest in IIGS-specific software. An Apple IIe Card was even released for the Macintosh LC in 1990, but that hardware configuration is a difficult mix to pull together and has its own set of disadvantages.

Luckily, the popularity of Apple II systems in both homes and schools makes it easy to find genuine Apple hardware at reasonable prices today. Nostalgic users may prefer standard Apple II systems for their highly collectible status, but the most popular choice for casual users is the Apple IIe. The popular IIe offers the best mix of compatibility and expandability, regardless of variation. Likewise, the "Enhanced" and "Platinum" were the last models based on the Apple IIe and make excellent choices. The former is closer in design to the original IIe, whereas the latter features a keyboard and styling more consistent with early Macintosh systems and the Apple IIGS.

Anyone purchasing an Apple computer should take a moment to consider memory: 48KB of RAM is sufficient for a great deal of software, but 64KB minimum is better; 128KB is optimal, since certain later games require it. Disk II and compatible disk drives are easy to come by, and unlike competing systems, a relatively high percentage of software supports the concurrent use of two. This feature eliminates much of the tedious disk swapping so common on other machines of this era.

Although some software can be found on 3.5-inch disks, 5.25-inch disks remained the standard for the life of the system. It is best to have a copy of the latest versions possible of both DOS 3.x and ProDOS, since not all software booted on its own. Another useful program, *DOS.MASTER*, was created in the late 1980s by Glen Bredon. *DOS.MASTER* enables the large base of previously ProDOS-incompatible programs written for DOS 3.3 to run under the more versatile format.

Originally, many users owned monochrome monitors, usually with green tubes. Monochrome displays are not necessarily a bad thing, since the color palette was fairly limited and could be a bit garish if the software didn't support a favorable resolution and color depth. Many games used the Apple II's original color scheme of purple, green, black, and white, although later games support blue and orange. Some users claim that monochrome displays make reading text easier, so if your primary interest is text adventure games, they could be a nice fit.

An even smaller percentage of games supported the higher resolutions and 16-color options available on expanded and late model systems. Despite the limited color range of most software, the II-series outputs a standard composite video signal, which allows direct connection to just about any modern TV.

Sound is generated internally from a small speaker, and there's no way to physically control the volume level on many models. Despite the relatively primitive one-channel sound, brilliant programming techniques enabled everything from music to speech, although nothing that could match the quality of later competitive systems in either performance or range.

On II-series systems with the standard expansion slots, countless programming language and feature upgrade cards were developed, including sound boards. The most popular and best supported of these sound boards was the six-channel Mockingboard series by Sweet Micro Systems,

```
OPENING THE MAILBOX REVEALS A LEAFLET.
>READ LEAFLET
(TAKEN)
WELCOME TO ZORK!
     ZORK IS A GAME OF ADVENTURE,
DANGER, AND LOW CUNNING.  IN IT YOU WILL
EXPLORE SOME OF THE MOST AMAZING
TERRITORY EVER SEEN BY MORTALS.

   NO COMPUTER SHOULD BE WITHOUT ONE!

   THE ORIGINAL ZORK WAS CREATED BY TIM
ANDERSON, MARC BLANK, BRUCE DANIELS, AND
DAVE LEBLING.  IT WAS INSPIRED BY THE
ADVENTURE GAME OF CROWTHER AND WOODS.
THIS VERSION WAS CREATED BY MARC BLANK,
DAVE LEBLING, JOEL BEREZ, AND SCOTT
CUTLER.

   (C) COPYRIGHT 1979 & 1980 INFOCOM,
INC. ALL RIGHTS RESERVED.
>
```

Zork: The Great Underground Empire—Part I
from the **AppleWin** emulator.

Zork: The Great Underground Empire—Part I
(1980, Personal Software/Infocom)

While today's smartphones and tablets are finally taking natural language processing mainstream, allowing us to ask our devices such profound questions as "Is that rain?," those in the know were enjoying a surprisingly sophisticated form of the technology more than 30 years ago on their modest personal computers. In *Zork*, when the game displayed, "There is a small mailbox here," you could type as one of many possible responses, "Open the mailbox," and the game's parser would interpret exactly what you meant, displaying: "Opening the small mailbox reveals a leaflet." While the game was purely text-based and had a rather mundane goal of "collect the 20 treasures of Zork and install them in the trophy case," the possibilities for creating a vivid, interactive world that had the quality of a good novel were clear. Just like with subLOGIC's *Flight Simulator* (A2-FS1) from the same year, the oft-ported *Zork* demonstrated very early on that personal computers could be used for more than just simple videogames. While nearly all of the classic Infocom text adventures are worth checking out, their first commercial product, *Zork*, remains one of the best gateways to the world of interactive fiction.[7]

which are coveted by today's collectors, and could be used in pairs for a total of 12 voices, and expanded with the addition of speech chips. A few of the games that take advantage of the Mockingboard include Progame's *Lady Tut* (1984) and Electronic Arts' *Adventure Construction Set* (1985), each of which features enhanced music, as well as Penguin Software's *Crime Wave* (1983) and Sir-Tech's *Crypt of Medea* (1984), each of which make use of the optional speech chips.

Finding boxed software is easy. Prices vary from a few dollars for arcade-style games to triple digits for the rarest and oldest role-playing games. The analog, two-button joysticks are easy to locate, with paddles less so, but both are still generally available. Except under specific circumstances, most games support only one player with a controller, so a second player must use the keyboard. In any case, most games do not assume a player has access to anything other than a keyboard, so external controls are not required.

There is one critical factor to consider when purchasing a IIGS: its ROM version. Early IIGS computers shipped with a bug-ridden ROM (ROM version 00) that renders them incompatible with most IIGS software released after 1987. Apple released a new ROM in September 1987 (ROM version 01) that fixed these problems and offered free upgrades to all current owners of existing IIGS systems. In 1989, Apple began producing IIGS systems with ROM version 3, which increased system performance, allowed for more RAM, and added several new features. However, the company did not offer free upgrades from ROM 1 to ROM 3 since doing so would have required an expensive motherboard replacement. Collectors who intend to run software on their IIGS should seek out a system equipped with ROM 1 for maximum compatibility or ROM 3 for maximum performance.

---

[7]   "Zork" was originally MIT hacker slang for an unfinished program. The term appeared as one of the sayings after a car crash in the 1976 Midway arcade game known as *Datsun 280 Zzzap*, or simply, *280-Zzzap*. A port for the Bally Home Library Computer/Professional Arcade (aka, Astrocade) *280 ZZZAP/DODGEM 2001* appeared in 1981, which also featured the saying.

Emulating the Apple II

Emulation is well implemented and supported on a variety of modern platforms, including smartphones and tablets. Standouts include *AppleWin* and *Virtual II*. There are even web-browser-based emulators, such as the one at *Virtual Apple* (www.virtualapple.org), with a ready selection of games to try on demand for both the Apple II and IIGS.

No matter whether you choose real hardware or emulation, there are tons of classics to try out, regardless of interest or age group. As "mmphosis" related on the Applefritter website:

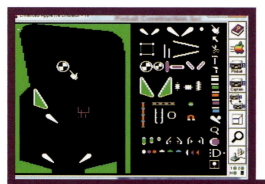

I recently loaded *Oregon Trail* using Blurry's *JACE* (Apple II emulator) on my Mac. This old game entertained a ten year old for way longer than I thought they would want to be into playing a 25+ year old game when they have handheld game consoles, iPhones, a PC, a Mac... but they played the Apple II version of *Oregon Trail* through to the end. Go figure.

Screenshot from the **AppleWin** emulator, running **Pinball Construction Set.**

Atari 2600 VCS (1977)

History

1977 was a big year for American nerd culture. One of the biggest events happened in May, when George Lucas' *Star Wars* blasted onto the big screen. *Star Wars* thrilled audiences with unprecedented special effects, unforgettable action sequences, and a fascinating new mythos. *Star Wars* was much more than just another hit movie, of course. Lucas shrewdly negotiated with the studio for rights to merchandise toys and other products based on the film. After watching the movie for perhaps the hundredth time, kids could go home and set up confrontations between the Empire and the Rebellion with their own action figures and play sets.

Four months after Luke Skywalker destroyed the first Death Star, Atari released the Video Computer System (VCS). If *Star Wars* redefined the Hollywood blockbuster, the VCS redefined the videogame, firmly moving the industry away from units with built-in games like *Pong* to a world of interchangeable cartridges and peripherals. As with *Pong* and the founders' earlier game, *Computer Space*, Atari wasn't the first company to introduce these innovations, but they were the first to successfully diffuse them to the American public. However, the glorious future of the VCS was anything but evident in 1977.

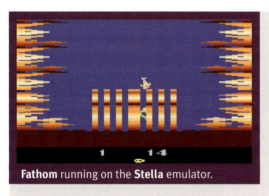

Fathom running on the **Stella** emulator.

Fathom (1982, Imagic)

While not nearly as successful or prolific as Activision, Imagic made its case for best third-party Atari 2600 publisher with games like *Fathom*. Rob Fulop's classic is a multiscreen action adventure that alternates play as a dolphin or seagull in your quest to find a starfish that will give you a piece of Neptune's trident. Once the trident is assembled, you can then free Neptune's mermaid daughter from her sea prison. In true competitive fashion, be sure to check out Activision's similarly water-themed *Dolphin* (1983), where you play the titular mammal in a race from a pursuing squid, using audio cues to avoid obstacles.

Like its rival systems at the time, the Fairchild Video Entertainment System (VES), which was released in August 1976, and the obsolete-at-launch RCA Studio II, which was released in January 1977, the VCS sold only a few hundred thousand units in its early months. All three systems suffered from competition from bargain bins full of *Pong*-clones, which had oversaturated the market after the introduction of General Instruments' AY-3-8500 "Pong-on-a-chip." These systems often advertised four to six games that were usually just subtle variations of the same basic tennis game—all for $100 or less. The VCS's initial price of $199 (over $700 in today's money) was a substantial investment, and the modest library of game cartridges certainly didn't help the launch. However, an influx of funds from parent company Warner Communications supported Atari during these years and a growing supply of quality game cartridges, advertisements, and positive press helped Atari sell millions of VCS consoles by 1980.

The first VCS units shipped with two joysticks,[1] a single pair of paddles, and the two-player *Combat* cartridge, which contained several tank and plane action games inspired by Atari arcade games. The eight other game titles, several of which were also loose interpretations of Atari's popular arcade games, were *Air-Sea Battle*, *Basic Math*, *Blackjack*, *Indy 500*, *Star Ship*, *Street Racer*, *Surround*, and *Video Olympics*. Although these games were relatively simplistic and not much better than games for rival systems, their variety hinted at what was to come. As an increasing number of rival manufacturers would come to tout their systems' technological superiority, Atari could boast of a substantially larger variety of games and ways to play them. Ed Riddle's *Indy 500*, for instance, came packaged with two steering (driving) controllers, an early addition to the soon-to-be massive array of VCS controller types. Unlike the paddle controllers they resemble, these "driving" controllers did not have stops and could rotate continuously.

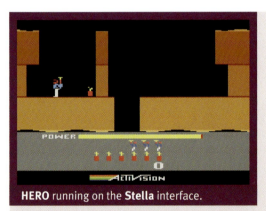

HERO running on the **Stella** interface.

HERO (1984, Activision)

John Van Ryzin's *HERO* (Helicopter Emergency Rescue Operation) is an imaginative game in which the protagonist, Roderick Hero, must descend into a mineshaft using his convenient (if physically impossible) prop pack—think *Inspector Gadget*. Roderick must avoid or blast a variety of dangerous creatures such as bats and spiders, blow up walls with his sticks of dynamite, and eventually rescue a trapped miner before the time limit expires. All in all, it's a very challenging, fun game with audiovisuals that wouldn't look out of place on an Atari 5200 or ColecoVision cartridge. Did we forget to mention the rising lava? Dedicated players who sent a photo of their screen with 75,000 points on the score could receive an official "Order of the HERO" badge from Activision.

As celebrated Atari designer Howard Scott Warshaw and others have pointed out, despite the massive research and development budget in comparison to its peers, the VCS was primarily built to play two games: *Pong* and *Tank* (a popular arcade game that was incorporated into *Combat*): "That was it. You had two players, two missiles, one ball, and a playfield." It definitely didn't seem like a huge leap from the aforementioned *Pong* consoles. For many gamers, the Atari VCS just didn't seem like a good way to spend two hundred bucks.

---

[1] The initial models were the CX-10, which were had slight cosmetic differences and were better constructed than the far more common CX-40 models paired with all later Atari systems.

All this changed in 1980, but it wasn't one of Atari's own games that made the difference. Instead, it was a licensed conversion of a game that had swept across Japan and was now taking America by storm: Taito's arcade blockbuster *Space Invaders*. Designed by Tomohiro Nishikado and adapted for the VCS by ex-Fairchild employee Rick Mauer, *Space Invaders* was the first non-Atari licensed game—and what a license it was! The game grossed over $100 million and caused a tremendous surge in system sales as well.[2] Mauer, however, reportedly received a measly $11,000 in compensation for all his hard work and genius.[3]

AtariAge forum member, Ken Netzel describes the appeal of the *Space Invaders* VCS cartridge:

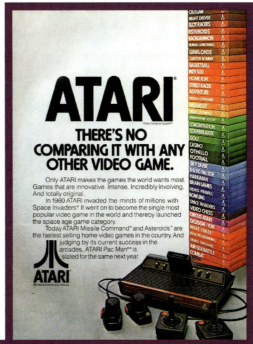

As this ad from the Winter 1981 debut issue of **Electronic Games** magazine makes clear, Atari was positioned to dominate with its VCS since it was the only system that could boast of so many big name titles.

I heard Atari was going to have a *Space Invaders* cartridge come out. I decided right then that I would HAVE to have an Atari VCS. My wife and I just got married and got our first credit card. And the first charge on the card was the Atari VCS my wife bought me for my birthday that year (1980) and the *Space Invaders* cartridge. Back in the day, that was a pretty hefty investment, but we took the plunge. I was hooked playing *Space Invaders* all hours of my free time.

Mauer wasn't the only programmer at Atari gifted at adapting high-end arcade games to the limited capabilities of the 2600. *Asteroids,* ported to the VCS by Brad Stewart,

Space Invaders running on the **Stella** emulator. Although it didn't look quite like the arcade game, gamers everywhere were still thrilled by the 112 available play variations, a hallmark of early Atari 2600 titles.

---

2   Mark J.P. Wolf, *Encyclopedia of Games: The Culture, Technology, and Art of Gaming*, Greenwood, 2012.

3   Steve Bloom, "30 Secrets of Atari," www.atarimuseum.com/articles/30secrets.html.

introduced bank-switching, a technique invented by Carl Nielsen that allowed access to cartridge memory beyond the prior 4KB limit. Although the earliest VCS cartridges were generally 2KB–4KB in size, greater memory sizes—including modern homebrews at 32KB and beyond—allowed for increased depth and complexity, contributing to the system's impressive longevity. *Asteroids* was another big hit for the VCS.

Another notable early title was Warren Robinett's *Adventure* (1979), a pioneering graphical action adventure. It was also among the first games with a notable Easter Egg. Gamers who found or knew the secret could find the name of the game's programmer. Robinett included the Easter Egg to protest Atari's policy of keeping programmers out of the spotlight and thus immune to better offers from rival companies. The policy might have

As this August 4, 1980, news item from **InfoWorld** shows, the future of third-party software development for consoles was in immediate legal jeopardy.

made sense to Atari's management at the time, but it ultimately led to an exodus of top star talent and subsequent rise of third-party software houses whose often excellent products would compete directly with Atari's own lineup.

It all began with the departure of four prolific and talented programmers—David Crane, Larry Kaplan, Alan Miller, and Bob Whitehead. They founded Activision in 1979, one of the earliest and best of the third-party software developers. Activision raised the bar on VCS game quality. Their landmark titles include *Pitfall* (1982), one of the first running and jumping multiscreen games; *Space Shuttle—A Journey into Space* (1983), a surprisingly sophisticated flight and mission simulator; and *Private Eye* (1984), a multiscreen action adventure game. Grossing over $70 million in their first year, the founders of Activision must have felt quite justified in leaving behind their meager salaries at Atari.[4]

Atari was no stranger to litigation, although courts seldom ruled in its favor. It did score a minor victory in 1972, however, by settling a dispute with Magnavox over arcade *Pong* by paying a small one-time licensing fee. This arrangement was much more favorable than those Magnavox reached with Atari's rivals. Magnavox, with the engineering expertise of Ralph Baer, won videogame patent court cases for many years to come. However, when Atari tried to shutdown Activision, their complaint was eventually thrown out. This did lead, however, to a licensing arrangement in which Atari would receive a royalty for each VCS cartridge sold. Other companies took Activision's lead, leading to the industry-standard licensing model

---

4   Joe Grand and Kevin Mitnick, *Hardware Hacking: Have Fun While Voiding Your Warranty*, Syngress, 2004.

Missile Command running on the **Stella** emulator.

Missile Command (1981, Atari)

Before leaving Atari, Inc., to join Imagic, Rob Fulop programmed this well-wrought conversion of the popular arcade game by Dave Theurer. While the arcade version suggests a nuclear confrontation on Earth, Fulop opted for a sci-fi story between the Zardonians and the Krytolians. He also snuck in an Easter Egg with his initials. Fulop adapted the arcade's control scheme—which utilized a trackball and three separate fire buttons—for a standard Atari joystick with a single button. Regardless of these and other differences from the arcade version, gamers loved the sound effects and fast-paced action of Fulop's game. AtariAge forum member "Serious" recalls playing marathon sessions of *Missile Command* with his father, who would yell, "If it flies, it dies!" when the action got intense.

between console maker and software houses still in use today.

The success of third-party software companies, especially those composed of their own ex-employees, was bittersweet for the managers at Atari. While companies like Imagic made small fortunes with well-crafted games like the shooters *Demon Attack* (1982) and *Cosmic Ark* (1982)—fortunes that formerly would have flowed directly to Atari and Warner—there's no denying that they also contributed to greater system sales and market penetration, keeping the VCS dominant even in the face of technologically superior competition.

Of course, not every third-party game maker was an Activision or Imagic. There were also companies like Ultravision, whose clunky one-on-one fighting game *Karate* (1983) and copycat shooter *Condor Attack*

As this Xonox ad for one of their double-sided cartridges demonstrates, third parties would often go to extraordinary lengths to try to distinguish their games from the competition.

(1983) are rightfully forgotten. Incidentally, *Condor Attack* was a clone of *Demon Attack*, which itself was inspired by yet another game, Centuri's 1980 arcade game *Phoenix*. Atari officially converted that game in 1982 and tried to force Imagic to remove their version from the shelf. Atari lost yet again. Eventually their inability to prevent third-party companies from saturating the market with cheaply made "shovelware" would damage not just Atari's reputation, but also that of stellar publishers like Activision and Imagic.

Rival system manufacturers, of course, went to great lengths to knock Atari off its throne. Competing systems such as Coleco's ColecoVision and Mattel's Intellivision II offered external expansion modules that allowed their system to play VCS cartridges. Naturally, Atari sued, but Coleco countered that they were protected by antitrust laws. Again, Atari settled out of court, settling for a royalty for each adapter unit and clone console sold.

In 1983, Atari launched the "Atarisoft" brand, which published Atari games for rival consoles and home computers. Mostly produced by third parties, these games varied wildly in accuracy and quality, much like Coleco's and Mattel's (M Network) similar efforts for the VCS and other competing platforms. The end result of all this sharing and cross-licensing was an unusual type of hardware and software quid pro quo that would be all but unimaginable today—imagine, for instance, if Sony's PS4 received conversions of Nintendo's latest *Mario* and *Zelda* games instead of just the Wii U.

Montezuma's Revenge running on the **Stella** emulator.

Montezuma's Revenge (1983, Parker Brothers)

The name of this game might conjure up images of tourists racing for the bathroom, but Robert Jaeger's platform game is anything but crap. The challenging game puts players in the boots of one Panama Joe, an Indiana Jones type out to plunder a deadly Aztec pyramid loaded with traps. Panama Joe must face everything from deadly snakes to creepy "headbones" as he searches for keys, amulets, and, of course, treasure. It's a stunning achievement for Jaeger, who was only 16 when he created and showed his first prototype of the game to Parker Brothers.

As you can see, Atari's experiment with the VCS provided many lessons for future console makers such as Nintendo. While they certainly stumbled at times, some of their greatest "mistakes" led to dramatic and far-reaching changes in the industry as a whole. It's fun to ponder, for instance, what the market would look like today if Atari had simply placated its best programmers, giving them sufficient rewards and recognition to keep them in-house—or succeeded in shuttering their operations through litigation. It might seem a given today, but the current system of publishers and manufacturers we currently enjoy was anything but inevitable.

Technical Specifications

The first system, known today as the "heavy sixer," featured dense internal RF shielding (giving it its considerable weight) and six chrome selector switches for power on/off, color/black and white, player A difficulty, player B difficulty, select, and reset. The design featured sharp angles with black plastic and wood-grain styling that gives it a distinctively 1970s aesthetic.

With miniscule system memory of 128 bytes of RAM and Motorola's 8-bit 6507 microprocessor running just over 1 MHz, the VCS seems at first glance anything but a powerhouse. Sound was limited to two channels, but, if thoughtfully programmed, could support decent sound effects and music. Graphics, while displayed at a fairly low resolution and with limitations on the number of flicker-free objects per line, could

An Atari "light sixer," which lightened up on the shielding found in the original model. This would be the first of several redesigns.

draw from an impressive 128-color palette. In fact, the platform's use of colors and color cycling became the VCS's signature feature, enabling interesting effects that helped extend the effective life of the console far beyond what could have ever been imagined during its development.

Later Models

In 1978, Atari released a revised model with lighter RF shielding and a slightly streamlined case. The last VCS revision, released in 1980, moved two of the six switches to the top of the unit. In 1982, Atari released the Atari 5200 SuperSystem. To standardize the product line, the VCS officially became the Atari 2600 Video Computer System, or simply Atari 2600. This design was streamlined like the previous revision, but with an entirely black exterior.

Oddly, when Atari released the 5200, no backward compatibility option was offered, confusing some consumers and hurting system sales. Atari tried making amends with a smaller 5200 system redesign and an awkward add-on module that enabled the backwards-compatibility gamers demanded. Unfortunately, this add-on was incompatible with the earlier, larger 5200 consoles without modification at a service center.

Pitfall II: Lost Caverns running on the **Stella** emulator.

Pitfall II: Lost Caverns (1984, Activision)

Pitfall Harry, the character in David Crane's *Pitfall* series, may not be as famous as Nintendo's Mario or Sega's Sonic, but for VCS owners in 1984, he was the man. While the first game, released in 1982, was a smash hit and remains a fan favorite, the sequel is more expansive, allowing Harry to descend deeply into the titular caverns in the Andes. To win, players must help Harry collect his pet mountain lion, Quickclaw, his niece, Rhonda,[5] and a diamond ring. The game also features a soundtrack with a four-part harmony, a trick enabled by an innovative custom chip in the cartridge, which would become a common technique on the NES. In short, David Crane really outdid himself with this magnificent achievement. To get your official Activision "Cliff Hangers" badge, all you needed to do was reach 99,000 points and send a photo of the screen.

The impressively small Atari 2600 Jr. shown below the next generation 7800. Both systems could have seen wide release as early as 1984, but corporate and market upheaval meant a critical two-year delay.

After the NES revived America's passion for videogames, Atari reestablished its presence in 1986 with the long-awaited wide releases of a mothballed Atari 2600 redesign, which was unofficially referred to as the Jr., and 7800 ProSystem, which, in addition to playing its own advanced games that could utilize its extra memory, higher resolution, and greater color palette, was almost completely compatible with its older sibling's games and accessories. The Jr. was Atari's most significant design departure from the original heavy sixer, featuring a small and thin, black and silver enclosure, which mimicked the styling of the larger 7800. Pushed as a budget-friendly option in comparison with other systems, the 2600 continued to sell fairly well in what had become a very different market.

---

[5] Both Quickclaw and Rhonda were Pitfall Harry's co-stars on the 1983 cartoon, *Pitfall!*, which was part of the *Saturday Supercade* that ran on CBS from 1983 to 1985, and featured a lineup of other popular videogame cartoons, including *Frogger*, *Donkey Kong*, and *Q*bert*.

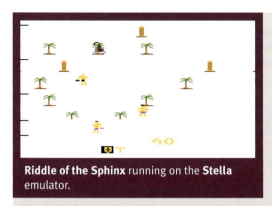

Riddle of the Sphinx running on the **Stella** emulator.

Riddle of the Sphinx (1982, Activision)

Bob Smith programmed several Atari 2600 games, including *Dragonfire* (1982, Imagic), *Moonsweeper* (1983, Imagic), *Star Voyager* (1982, Imagic), and *Star Wars: The Arcade Game* (1984, Parker Brothers), but perhaps his most interesting creation was *Riddle of the Sphinx*. With its well-chosen colors for its in-game objects set against a stark white background, this surprisingly complex adventure game doesn't look quite like anything else on the platform. You play the son of a pharaoh who must traverse the Egyptian desert in search of treasures that must be offered at various temples in order to appease the ancient gods and lift a curse. In order to check how much time has elapsed, check various player statistics, and perform other key in-game functions, you need to make use of not only the joystick, but also all of the console's color and difficulty switches. It's a handful, but the payoff is a rich play experience not often seen on the platform.

The End of the Atari 2600 Line

Atari's console sales peaked in 1982, after which a glut of poor third-party game titles and bad licensing decisions caused heavy losses throughout the industry. Product dumping, with high volumes of poor-quality games sold at or below cost, caused full-priced, high-quality game sales to suffer. However, two games in particular released that year are always brought up when discussing the fall of the Atari VCS: *Pac-Man* and *ET the Extra-Terrestrial*.

In what should have been the deal of the year, if not the decade, Atari got sole rights to Namco's arcade smash-hit *Pac-Man* (1980) in 1981. While Atari aggressively promoted and protected their exclusive right to produce *Pac-Man* and any derivative works, they apparently didn't bother to actually play their programmer Todd Frye's rushed conversion. With poor graphics, bad sound, and awkward controls, *Pac-Man* for the VCS was a travesty of a game and a devastating blow to Atari's reputation. It seemed to prove that the VCS paled in comparison to the thrills of the arcade. However, it's not necessarily fair to blame Frye for the disaster. After all, his original design was intended for an 8KB ROM, but he was forced to cram it into a 4KB ROM instead. Atari wrongly guessed that the name alone would generate enough interest to sell the dismal product. Their hubris was so great that they actually manufactured more *Pac-Man* cartridges than there were VCS systems!

According to AtariAge forum member "Serious,"

Pac-Man was such a terrible game, and such a huge disappointment. I remember feeling like Atari ripped me off (even though my family didn't buy the game). All of my friends and other families we knew felt the same, and the enthusiasm that everyone seemed to have for Atari games never seemed to be the same after that.

As for *ET the Extra-Terrestrial*, lead programmer Howard Scott Warshaw seemed like a logical choice for the project. He had impressed Steven Spielberg with his work on the translation of another popular film by the famous director, *Raiders of the Lost Ark*, which, in 1982, was successfully released as a sophisticated, if obtuse, two-joystick action-adventure. He was also the developer behind *Yars' Revenge,* an action game widely considered among the best games on the platform, and was one of Atari's best sellers.

The story goes that Atari CEO Ray Kassar paid $20 million for the *ET* license, but the negotiations took so long that in order to make a holiday release, the entire game had to be programmed in six weeks, several months short of a typical development cycle at that time. Warshaw liked both the programming challenge and the money he was able to negotiate for the task, so he began the project in earnest.

Although Spielberg would have been happy with a copycat of *Pac-Man*, Warshaw insisted on something more original. Miraculously, he managed to meet the deadline, and Atari rushed the cartridge into production with a blitz of advertising. Unfortunately, the end result confused and frustrated many players; guiding the slow ET creature through a seemingly endless series of nearly inescapable pits did not have wide appeal. Although the popularity of the license alone ensured over a million sales of the game, Atari suffered another huge financial loss because of returns and millions more unsold cartridges. Legend has it that Atari ended up burying most of the unsold inventory in a New Mexico landfill.[6] All of the millions Atari had spent on licensing and advertising could not compensate for the fact that these were terrible, almost unplayable, games.

River Raid running on the **Stella** emulator.

River Raid (1982, Activision)

One of the few Atari VCS games designed by a woman, Carol Shaw's *River Raid* is a fast, vertical-scrolling shoot-'em-up with dynamically generated terrain. The game puts players in the cockpit of a fighter plane soaring over the River of No Return, destroying enemy tanks, copters, and jets, all the while avoiding contact with the river's borders. As if that wasn't already enough challenge, the plane's fuel must be regularly replenished by flying over a depot. Players who were able to reach 15,000 points—and snap a photo of their achievement—could receive an official River Raider badge.

By 1984, the Great Videogame Crash had taken a lot of companies out of business, due in no small part to Atari's own inflexible inventory requirements at retail outlets the year before. These requirements demanded that retail outlets had to stock more product than consumer demand could support. In that same year, Warner Communications sold a large portion of their interests in Atari to ex-Commodore executive and founder, Jack Tramiel, who seemed to have little desire to aggressively pursue the stagnant console market.

While trying to get a grip on the state of the company, Tramiel shelved both the unreleased 2600 redesign and its backward-compatible next-generation successor, the 7800, in favor of new

---

6   In the 2012 book by Marty Goldberg and Curt Vendel, *Atari Inc.: Business is Fun*, this has since been clarified to unsold inventory being sent to a dump in Sunnyvale, California.

Atari computers (see Chapter 1.4). While a few new 2600 cartridges were made available in 1985 by Activision and other companies, there were no new Atari systems to go with them.

Existing 2600 and 5200 inventory remained in the various sales channels and continued to sell, but almost two years passed before Atari attempted to reclaim their dominance in the home videogame market. By this time, the Nintendo Entertainment System (NES) had established itself in America, and Atari was left playing catch-up. Ironically, in 1983 Atari had turned down a chance to distribute an early version of the NES. Once established in the United States, Nintendo would prove a deadly adversary, quickly cornering the market with a series of killer games, in combination with price fixing and monopolistic retail policies. As a result, like Sega with the Master System, Atari didn't stand a chance against the NES, even with a multiconsole strategy.

The Jr., with cosmetic revisions, continued to represent the VCS line until production was stopped completely by the early 1990s. Atari itself ceased to exist as a company in 1996. The name and intellectual assets have been sold and bought countless times since.

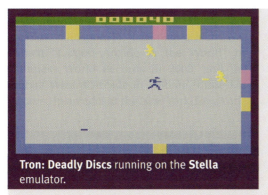

Tron: Deadly Discs running on the **Stella** emulator.

Tron: Deadly Discs (1982, M Network)

While Mattel created several quality officially licensed games based on the cult favorite Disney sci-fi film *Tron* (1982) for their own Intellivision and Aquarius platforms, it's arguable that one of the two M Network releases they created for the Atari 2600, *Tron: Deadly Discs*, was the best of them all. The basic premise is ripped straight from the film: throw your "identity disc" at your enemies before they hit you with their own discs. Once you throw your disc, if it doesn't hit an enemy, you can either call for its return or wait for it to bounce off a wall and come back. Once the discs start flying, the action heats up fast, making for an incredibly intense experience. For you collectors out there, be sure to also keep an eye out for the special blue *Tron*-themed joystick Mattel produced for its Atari *Tron* games. If you like *Tron: Deadly Discs*, be sure to check out Atari's stellar conversion of Stern's arcade classic *Berzerk* (1982), which features similarly intense gameplay.

The Atari VCS Community Then and Now

The Atari VCS was the first console to enjoy a vibrant, thriving community during its original production run and, as a result, still enjoys a tremendous amount of support today. Countless sites like *AtariAge* (www.atariage.com) and *Atarimania* (www.atarimania.com) continue to provide quality information and centralized meeting places for devoted fans and hobbyist programmers alike.

From the mid-1990s through today, homebrew authors emerged to produce a wide range of often high-quality hacks, conversions, and new original games. These include Ed Federmeyer's groundbreaking *SoundX* (1995) sound demo program and *Tetris* clone *Edtris 2600* (1995), which got the modern homebrew ball rolling; Ebivision's platformer *Alfred Challenge* (1998), which

was compatible with multiple worldwide television standards; Xype's *Thrust+ Platinum* (2003) by Thomas Jentzsch, which supports a wide range and combination of control options; AtariAge's *Fall Down* (2005), which is a competitive twist on the standard platform game by Aaron Curtis that supports Richard Hutchinson's 2004 AtariVox add-on for in-game speech and high-score saves; Spice-

Both the Atari 2600 and 7800 continue to receive impressive new homebrew releases, consisting of a combination of previously unreleased prototypes, hacks of existing games, and entirely new creations.

Ware's AtariAge-published *Warlords* reimagining, *Medieval Mayhem* (2006); Bob Montgomery's hectic platformer *Elevator's Amiss* (2007), which was coded in the BASIC-like programming language, batari Basic; and the AtariAge-published, officially licensed port of the First Star Software action puzzler classic *Boulder Dash* (2012).

Collecting Atari VCS Systems

Because there were over 30 million Atari VCS units sold, working machines are still relatively easy to come by. The four-switch model with the famous wood veneer panels are usually the easiest to find. The Atari 7800 is nearly 100 percent compatible with VCS software and most add-ons, making it a great choice for collectors who want to play both platforms' games.

Besides all the variations Atari itself produced, there have been many clones and add-ons for other systems, most commonly from Sears and Coleco. Sears rebranded Atari hardware from the original heavy sixer right through to a sleek custom unit with a unique case, and combination joystick and paddle controllers. The famous retailer sold them under the Video Arcade name, also

rebranding games: *Indy 500* became *Race*, for instance. The only cartridges released with the Sears branding that didn't also have an Atari counterpart were *Steeplechase* (1980), a paddle controller-based horse racing game, *Stellar Track* (1980), a strategy game set in space, and *Submarine Commander* (1982), an undersea target game.

Coleco released both the stand-alone Gemini console, which also featured a single joystick and paddle combination (one above

The Sears version of the heavy sixer and a few of the Sears-branded games.

the other) and its popular Expansion Module #1 for the ColecoVision console and Adam computer. Each allowed for high VCS game compatibility, as did the Mattel System Changer for the Intellivision II.

Warlords running on the **Stella** emulator.

Warlords (1981, Atari)

This conversion of the Atari arcade game by the same name allows up to four players—armed with paddle controllers—to battle for supremacy against other warlords, *Breakout* style. Occupying each corner of the screen, the warlords are armed only with a shield (rotated by the paddle) to bounce the ball away from their castle walls and into those of an enemy. An engineer named Carla Meninsky did the conversion. A full-on four player competitive game of *Warlords* is still a great way to liven up a party.

Games range in value depending on whether they are sold as loose cartridges or complete in boxes or sealed, but a decent collection can still be assembled for a reasonable amount. Rarer games can cost into the tens of dollars or even hundreds, with titles such as the first voice-enabled VCS game *Quadrun* (Atari, 1983), the double-sided cartridge *Tomarc the Barbarian/ Motocross Racer* (Xonox, 1983), and the jumping and matching game *Q*Bert's Qubes* (Parker Brothers, 1984), selling for far more than their more plentiful counterparts. Collectors should also consider that many games were released in different styled boxes and cartridges.

Like nearly every system, there are prototype games that were either finished and not released or only partially completed. However, because of the popularity of the system and the timing of the Great Videogame Crash, the 2600 has a particularly large collection of unreleased games, and new prototypes are still being uncovered. Once recovered, the homebrew community often makes these lost titles available for purchase on cartridge or as a download for emulators.

Because the VCS was the first breakout success in home videogames, there was little precedent for developers and publishers to learn from when designing and manufacturing products for it. This led to some pretty novel experimentation, particularly with add-ons, such as the limited release CompuMate from Spectravideo, which consisted of a flat membrane keyboard, additional memory, and the ability to load and save from cassette. In effect, CompuMate turned the VCS into a simple computer system. Some peripherals were tied to their time period, such as GameLine, which featured an oversized cartridge hooked into a phone line that allowed the user to download games for short-term use from a subscription service. Countless others, however, are still quite useful today, such as the Starplex Game-Selex, an external expansion box that allowed instant switchable access to multiple cartridges.

What also helped in this area was that the joystick ports on the VCS were what many other companies such as Commodore and Sega standardized on for their systems. In fact, although

it usually wasn't practical to use single-button joysticks on later systems such as Sega's Master System or Genesis, multibutton gamepads from those consoles often work just fine when used on the VCS.

Besides the standard joysticks, paddles, and other controllers already mentioned, a few others are worth pointing out as well. Obscure releases such as the Foot Craz from Exus, which was a foot mat with five colored buttons that came packaged with *Video Jog-*

Both Atari and third-party manufacturers created a seemingly endless supply of controller types and add-ons.

ger (1983) and *Video Reflex* (1983), contrasted with the more pedestrian options such as the Booster Grip from CBS Electronics, which added extra fire buttons to a standard joystick (a stock ColecoVision controller is also a suitable alternative).

Yars' Revenge running on the **Stella** emulator.

Yars' Revenge (1981, Atari)

Howard Scott Warshaw is often paradoxically called the best and worst game developer on the Atari VCS for his work on both this game and *ET*, respectively. Whether or not you agree with this claim, there's no denying that *Yars' Revenge* is a remarkable technical achievement and definitely among the best games the platform has to offer. *Yars' Revenge* began as an effort to convert the arcade hit *Star Castle* to the VCS, but Warshaw eventually gave up on that idea.[7] However, in the process he'd developed a prototype that was quite fun in its own right. The game offers clever graphic hacks, exotic sound effects, and compelling gameplay, but that's not all—Warshaw went a step further and helped create a comic book (included in the box), *The Qotile Ultimatum!*, to explain the backstory.

Atari released wireless controllers that looked similar to their standard joysticks, just with thick antennas and much larger bases. Atari also released different variations on their keypad controllers, which supported overlays and were originally for *BASIC Programming* (1978) and *Codebreaker* (1978), but were later restyled and repackaged for use as the Video Touch Pad for *Star Raiders* (1982), and as the Kid's Controller for educational games such as *Big Bird's Egg Catch* (1983). Suffice it to say, the VCS boasts an amazing range of software and peripherals.

---

7   There have since been two recent homebrew ports of *Star Castle*, both of which are well worth checking out.

Emulating the Atari VCS

Gamers who choose the emulation route have plenty of great options to choose from. Websites such as *Virtual Atari* (www.virtualatari.org) offer hundreds of Atari 2600 games playable within a web browser. Software options include *Stella*, a GPL-licensed product by Bradley W. Mott and Stephen Anthony, *z26* by John Saeger, and *PC Atari* by John Dullea. Almost every modern system also has official compilations of Atari classics available, such as the *Atari's Greatest Hits* series for the Nintendo DS, iOS, and Android platforms, among others.

Of course, many gamers will not be satisfied playing these games with their keyboard, touchscreen, or modern gamepad. Gamers longing for a traditional Atari-like joystick experience should check out the Atari Flashback line of TV game consoles. Pre-programmed with many classic Atari games, these units ship with joysticks inspired by the originals, which are also available separately, along with new sets of paddle controllers.

The **Stella** emulator running Data Age's excellent platform game **Frankenstein's Monster** (1983).

Other alternatives include Atari to PC USB adapters, which allow gamers to connect many 2600 controllers to modern computers and other devices for a more authentic experience. Finally, for the ultimate combination of modern day convenience with the simple pleasures of vintage technology, Fred Quimby's *Harmony Cartridge*, distributed through AtariAge, allows game ROMs to be placed on an SD card and then played on any Atari 2600-compatible console with a cartridge port.

Atari 8-bit (1979)

History

As we saw in Chapter 1.3, Nolan Bushnell's Atari company was almost single-handedly responsible for bringing videogames to the masses. Throughout the 1970s, Atari scored hit after hit in the arcades, and their *Pong* consoles—followed closely by the much more versatile VCS (or 2600)—had made them the undisputed king of the videogame industry. Unfortunately for Bushnell, his decision to sell his company to Warner Communications to fund development of the VCS ended in his departure soon after.

Bushnell, an engineer infused with an entrepreneur's spirit, constantly butted heads with Ray Kassar, the no-nonsense businessman Warner had appointed president of Atari's Consumer Division. Under Kassar's direction, the creative and relaxed hacker culture of the company was transformed into an *Office Space*-like atmosphere[1] of disgruntled nerds and humorless men in suits. According to Howard Scott Warshaw, the designer of *Yar's Revenge* and *ET*, Kassar insisted on treating his game developers like blue-collar workers, refusing even to speak to anyone too low on the org chart. In Kassar's mind, it took no more raw talent to make a game than it did to make towels or bars of soap. Whereas Bushnell's Atari had been run by and for engineers, Kassar valued marketing experience, hiring managers from Polaroid and a tin can manufacturer. While Atari would have its greatest financial success in the years leading up to the Great Videogame Crash, this attitude would have obvious repercussions for the future of the company.

Shortly before Atari's new computer line hit the shelves, Bushnell was forced out, turning his attention to his fledgling Chuck E. Cheese's Pizza Time Theatre family restaurant company.

Alternate Reality: The City.

Alternate Reality: The City
(1985, Datasoft, Inc.)

This unique first-person perspective role-playing game, designed by Philip Price, offered a number of innovative features such as an environment that responds to the player's ethical decisions. The colorful graphics and effects are among the best on any 8-bit computer system. Feel free to sing along with the intro music; the lyrics are displayed karaoke-style! Also be sure to check out its 1987 sequel, *Alternate Reality: The Dungeon*.

---

[1] The cult favorite 1999 film from Mike Judge satirizing work life at an American software company in the 1990s.

Atari's foray into home computers had been stymied by their strong relationship with Sears, who insisted on FCC Type 1 compliance. That meant strict limits on radio interference—a high standard that Apple and other home computer makers didn't bother with. According to Bushnell, these regulations "turned out to have no teeth at all," but time and money had been wasted trying to meet them.[2]

With Bushnell gone, Warner promoted Kassar to CEO of the entire Atari Corporation. Kassar saw the future of Atari in home computers, and promptly launched and segregated a separate division to focus on their development.

Unlike their competition in the home computer market, which loudly touted their productivity and educational applications, Atari could also play to their strengths in the entertainment sector. Their "Candy" and "Colleen" 8-bit computer projects (it was an open secret that Atari engineers would code-name projects after attractive female employees) combined the proven game technology of the VCS and excellent computing capabilities with plug-and-play ease of use. Indeed, members of the VCS engineering team played a key role in its design, including industry legend Jay Miner, who had designed the innovative display hardware of Atari's game console and led the development of what became the Commodore Amiga, which is discussed in Chapter 2.2.

The Atari 400.

In late 1979, Atari released the Atari 400 ("Candy") and the Atari 800 ("Colleen"). The 400 was intended as a starter computer, while the 800 was a higher-end alternative for more sophisticated users with deeper pockets. By 1980, Atari formed a large portion of Warner Communications' total revenue and became the fastest growing company in US history, mirroring Apple's own meteoric success and

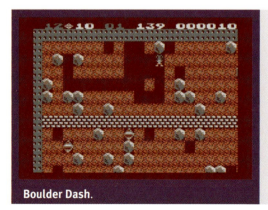

Boulder Dash.

Boulder Dash
(1984, First Star Software, Inc.)

This classic third-person perspective puzzle-solving game was loosely based on an earlier 1982 arcade game by Taito called *The Pit*. *Boulder Dash*, developed by Peter Liepa and Chris Gray, brought the addictive concept to the home computer scene and is still ported to new platforms to this day. The player guides the spelunker Rockford through a series of caves, collecting treasures while avoiding monsters and falling boulders.

---

2   See Benj Edwards' "VC&G Interview: Nolan Bushnell, Founder of Atari," www.vintagecomputing.com/index.php/archives/404.

preceding Commodore's ascension by several years. Their rapid gains in the home computer sector were due in part to their relatively low cost. For just a few hundred dollars more than an Atari VCS, you could afford a home computer without missing out on the games. As it was said in *Electronic Games* magazine in their 1983 Buyer's Guide,

> The Atari 400 is a microcomputer that was designed with game-players firmly in mind. Using a 6502 microprocessor combined with 128-color capability and four, independent sound synthesizers, gaming comes quite naturally to this budget-priced home computer.

Unfortunately for Atari, there would soon be fierce competition from Texas Instruments and Commodore for the budget-minded home computer buyer.

Technical Specifications

The Atari 400, which used the MOS 6502B microprocessor, came with 8KB RAM (later 16KB), a cartridge port, four controller ports, television output, and a membrane keyboard. This keyboard, which featured slightly indented keys on its plastic sheet-like surface, was intended to be "childproof." While it was easy to keep clean and was resistant to the occasional splash of Kool-Aid, it was painful to type on. With some technical effort, the memory could eventually be expanded to 48KB and the keyboard replaced. Even with those improvements in place, however, the 400 was a poor substitute for the 800. However, by 1982 it was possible to buy a new 400 for under $200, quite a reduction from its original sticker price of $549.95.[3]

The Atari 800 offered 16KB RAM (later 48KB), full-stroke keyboard, monitor output, expansion slots, and two cartridge ports (marked Left Cartridge and Right Cartridge). This dual-cartridge slot would remain unique to the system. The expansion slots were most often used for memory expansion, but also supported display adapters and other devices. Most expansion modules came in long plastic cases and snapped in like cartridges. Later releases were just boards without an enclosure, a utilitarian design that improved internal air flow. Most users outfitted the four slots with a 10KB ROM and three 16KB RAM modules to achieve the maximum standard 48KB system. The Atari 800 cost twice as much as a 400, originally retailing just shy of $1000. By 1983, the price had fallen to $400.

The **Atari 800** with its cartridge door open and a BASIC cartridge inserted in the Left Cartridge slot.

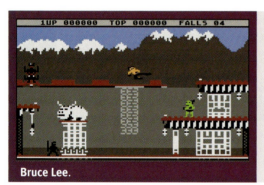

```
READY
10 PRINT"ATARI ROCKS!"
20 FOR I = 0 TO 5
30 PRINT"OH, YEAH!"
40 NEXT I

RUN
ATARI ROCKS!
OH, YEAH!
OH, YEAH!
OH, YEAH!
OH, YEAH!
OH, YEAH!
OH, YEAH!

READY
```

Atari basic.

With no cartridge inserted, both the 400 and 800 booted into a simple Notepad application. BASIC had to be loaded from cartridge, which was inserted into the Left Cartridge slot on the 800, allowing another cartridge to be used in the Right Cartridge slot, if needed. Because the Right Cartridge slot was rarely used, later Atari systems omitted this promising, but costly, feature.

The Atari computers were pin compatible with VCS controllers, providing an excellent range of single-button digital control options. The four controller ports would not be repeated on another Atari system until the Atari 5200 SuperSystem in 1982, which was a videogame console based on the Atari 400, though it was not directly compatible.[4]

Bruce Lee.

Bruce Lee
(1984, Datasoft, Inc.)

Designed by Ron J. Fortier, *Bruce Lee* is a combination of platformer and beat-'em-up gameplay. It features 20 challenging single-screen levels, tight controls, and puzzles to balance the intense arcade-style gameplay. In an innovative twist, a second player can control the Green Yamo, either helping or hindering Lee's progress.

A small selection of games supported the additional controller ports. The most famous of these are Electronic Arts' classic multiplayer strategy game by Dani Bunten, *MULE* (1983) and Atari's own *Super Breakout* (1981), which accommodated up to an amazing eight players using four sets of paddle controllers. As with later versions of the Atari 5200, new entries in the 8-bit computer line would forego the extra pair of controller ports.

The sound of the Atari computers was generated by the versatile POKEY chip, which was a favorite for use in arcade machines, and would also influence the development of Atari's later 7800 ProSystem console. The POKEY, which also read input from the keyboard and helped with serial communication, generated an impressive four channels (voices) of sound (the Commodore 64 had three). Thus, the Atari 8-bit computers offered the best potential audio performance for years. A simple internal speaker similar to the one in the Apple II emitted clicks when a key on the keyboard was pressed. This speaker was sometimes used as a fifth voice.

The original graphics chip, the CTIA, was an improved version of the VCS's flexible TIA chip and was capable of an impressive range of color and resolution modes. In 1981, Atari upgraded

---

4   Thanks to clever hacks, fans of the Atari 5200 have seen many conversions of classic Atari 8-bit games over the years.

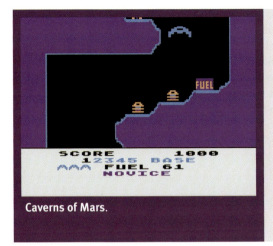

Caverns of Mars.

Caverns of Mars (1981, Atari Program Exchange)

This fun and fast-paced variation on the 1981 arcade game *Scramble* lets you go where no rover has gone before: a heavily armed cavern of Mars! Programmed and designed by a high school student named Greg Christensen, *Caverns of Mars* became the best-selling APX title of all time and was made an official Atari release in 1983. We're not quite sure how destroying fuel tanks refuels your ship, but you'll be too busy dodging walls and missiles to ponder such things. If you like *Caverns of Mars*, be sure to check out the tweaked 1982 update *Phobos*, as well as the sequel, *Caverns of Mars II*, also from 1982.

the 400 and 800 with a new graphics chip, the GTIA, which was even more powerful. Both graphics chips worked with the ANTIC microprocessor to help balance the display workload for superior performance. This arrangement allowed for 12 different display mode combinations with the CTIA and 16 with the GTIA. All future Atari 8-bit systems would come standard with the GTIA.

As David Fox, former Lucasfilm Games Developer put it in an author interview,

When the Atari 400 and 800 came out, we were running the Marin Computer Center, the first public access microcomputer center. Most of our computers relied on a cassette player to load in games or programs (i.e., Apple II, TRS-80, Commodore PET, and our nine Processor Technology Sol 20s). Being able to load games via cartridges, and expand RAM with another cartridge, was a revolution in user friendliness to us. But then I learned about the special graphics and sound chip hidden in the Atari's guts. I fell in love with its power (compared to everything else on the market) and decided to make it the focus of my Computer Animation Primer.[5] Even just using the BASIC cartridge that came with these computers, it was easy to do some very cool tricks. And with a few assembly language helper routines, you could access smooth scrolling and player missile graphics. I was really sorry when the Commodore 64, which I considered to be an inferior computer, passed up the Atari's in sales and popularity. Never could figure that out.

Peripherals such as printers, cassette recorders, and disk drives attached to the SIO port and could be daisy-chained. Although easy for the end-user and extremely versatile, this proprietary port required an adapter for use of third-party devices based on more typical industry standards.

---

[5]   www.atariarchives.org/cap.

From top to bottom, the Atari 410 Program Recorder (tape drive), the Atari 850 Interface module (showing two SIO ports), and the Atari 1050 disk drive.

Eastern Front.

Eastern Front (1981, Atari Program Exchange)

Initially turned down by Atari because they thought a war game wouldn't sell, Chris Crawford instead submitted his creation to the APX, where it became a great success. *Eastern Front* was noted for its accessible strategic gameplay and smooth scrolling. Perhaps its most innovative feature, however, was an AI that "thought" while the player was taking a turn, planning better moves the longer the player took. Like *Caverns of Mars*, *Eastern Front* was picked up by Atari for an official release in 1982, where Crawford took the time to make several improvements, including a move from disk to cartridge.

Later Models

What follows are some of the highlights of the major Atari 8-bit systems released in the United States after the 400 and 800:

- **1982:** With a consolidated number of chips, the Atari 1200XL, a sleek silver and black machine, was designed as a replacement for both the 400 and 800. When released, however, it was buggy, and the operating system sometimes rendered it incompatible with older software. The number of controller and cartridge ports was cut in half, and the internal speaker was removed, with the "fifth" channel of sound now routed in the same way as the POKEY's audio. These changes would become standard in later models.

    Interestingly, it's been said that instead of replacing the aging 400 and 800 line, the Atari 1200XL actually increased sales of those systems when news of its issues spread. Whether actually true or not, the clumsy launch of the 1200XL did nothing to slow Commodore's success with its low-priced VIC-20 and announcement of the powerful, and soon to be priced to move, Commodore 64.

- **1983:** The Atari 600XL and 800XL were meant as replacements for the failed 1200XL. They had better backward compatibility and a tiered system approach similar to that of the 400/800. Both new systems had BASIC built in, and the 600XL shipped with 16KB RAM, while the 800XL featured 64KB. Despite the relative inconvenience, translator software addressed most of the remaining compatibility problems with older software. Unfortunately for Atari, by this time, the Commodore 64 was already establishing itself as the dominant 8-bit computer.

An Atari 800XL with Thorn Emi's **Jumbo Jet Pilot** (1982) cartridge inserted.

- **1985:** The Atari 65XE/130XE replaced the black and silver XL line. These units were cheaper to manufacture and sell and had gray cases and keyboards that matched Atari's new 16-bit ST line of systems. The 65XE came with 64KB RAM, while the 130XE contained an extra memory management unit, bringing its total to 128KB.

The box for the Atari 130XE.

- **1987:** After the Great Videogame Crash and Atari's more aggressive return to the videogame market in 1986 with the reintroduction of the 7800 and the 2600 Jr., the company decided it was time to introduce a third console into the mix the following year. This unit was the XEGS (XE Game System). To fans, the XEGS could be seen as a complete, back-to-the-roots, reimagining of the 8-bit computer line based on the 65XE, with detachable keyboard, light gun, and built-in *Missile Command*. A skeptic might instead say it was an attempt by Atari to clear out old 8-bit computer software and accessories.

An Atari XEGS with matching joystick and light gun.

Fort Apocalypse.

Fort Apocalypse
(1982, Synapse Software Corporation)

This fantastic helicopter-extraction game by Steve Hales has players coaxing a "Rocket Copter" into the heavily guarded bowels of a massive underground prison. Pay attention to your radar—the blips that follow you are probably enemy helicopters. You'll also need precision bombing and piloting skills to blast through barricades and evade traps—oh, and there are people you should rescue, too. Heck, just refueling your chopper at the beginning of the game is a challenge!

Whatever the motives behind its creation and release, the XEGS represented a solid value at just $199.99, as it also came bundled with *Flight Simulator II* and *Bug Hunt* on separate cartridges. The latter supported the included light gun, while the former, which was previously an expensive disk game, represented the first of several such conversions to the more convenient form factor. Although the release of the XEGS brought an influx of re-released and new software for Atari 8-bit computers on cartridge (some not compatible with the older systems featuring less than 64KB), the three-console approach against the single Nintendo Entertainment System was ultimately ineffective.

The End of the Atari 8-Bit Line

So, with all the custom chips and comparatively impressive performance, what went wrong for Atari? The most likely answer is that the company couldn't recover from the disappointment it caused with the highly anticipated 1200XL. Its efforts to atone for this mistake were too late and

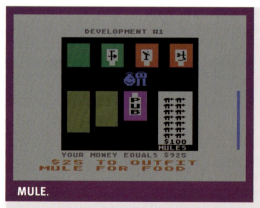

MULE.

MULE (1983, Electronic Arts)

Danielle Berry's classic action strategy game pits up to four players in an intense race to settle a colony on Planet Irata (Atari spelled backward). *MULE* was part of EA's early lineup and received the classic "rock album" style packaging that defined the publisher's first years. A fan favorite despite so-so sales at the time, *MULE* is saturated with geeky insider-jokes and radiates with personality. Play against the AI, but it's more fun with the family. If you have time left after assigning your MULEs to your plots, head to the mountains to hunt for the wampus. The instantly-recognizable theme music by Roy Glover is one of our favorite game tunes.

expensive to win back consumers, particularly when competitive price-cutting became downright cutthroat.

Unlike Apple, Atari was initially secretive about the inner workings of their systems. Often, no one would know something was even possible until Atari itself used the technique in a game or grudgingly divulged the information. This "trade secret" approach sometimes left a quality gap between first-party and third-party games. Nevertheless, clever programmers eventually found ways around Atari's corporate policies to make impressive games of their own. Some critics point to On-Line Systems' 1981 maze game *Jawbreaker* as a turning point for technically sound third-party titles on the platform, but it took another year before the system truly had a library of games that were a match for other 8-bit systems of the era. Certainly games from one Atari 8-bit maestro, Bill Wil-

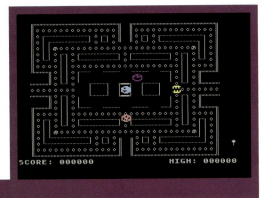

Jawbreaker.

liams, provides a clear example of this, as his Synapse-published games, *Alley Cat* (1982), an eclectic multiscreen action platformer, and *Necromancer* (1983), where you plant, defend, and control trees in a brilliant take-off on *Robotron: 2084*, were obvious stand-outs.

Even though Atari was not very forthcoming about revealing technical information about the systems' internals, the company nevertheless took a positive step towards fostering a strong user community with the creation of a new division, the Atari Program Exchange (APX). The APX featured a free quarterly mail order catalog of user-written software that went to all Atari computer owners who opted into the program. Users could both submit their own programs and purchase the programs of others, who would receive a small royalty from each sale, as well as occasional prize money.

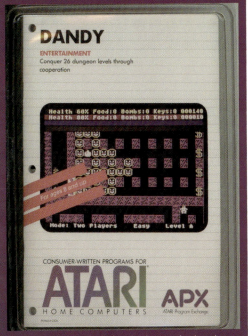

An APX package for the four player action dungeon-crawler, **Dandy** (1983), which was the inspiration for Atari's arcade classic, **Gauntlet** (1985) and the later two-player only **Dark Chambers** (1988) for the Atari 8-bit, Atari 2600, and Atari 7800 platforms.

As a company known mostly for games, Atari never achieved the legitimacy of an Apple on the high end and was unable to sustain momentum or reduce prices in the low-end market, particularly after the Commodore 64 became dominant. In 1984, in the face of declining sales, Atari's home computer and videogame divisions were bought from Warner Communications by former Commodore founder Jack Tramiel.

Tramiel formed Atari Corporation, and his leadership changed the course of both divisions after the Great Videogame Crash of 1984. He steered the company away from its focus on the videogame market and turned to the development of a new 16-bit line of computers. Atari staked its future on its 16-bit Atari ST systems, which launched in 1985.

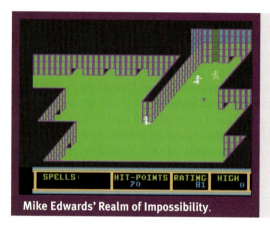

Mike Edwards' Realm of Impossibility.

Mike Edwards' Realm of Impossibility
(1983, Electronic Arts, Inc.)

An improved version of Mike Edwards' earlier self-published *Zombies*, this isometric puzzle-solving action maze game puts players through 13 M.C. Escher-inspired dungeon levels in a quest to defeat an evil cleric. Be sure to try out the acclaimed two-player mode, which allows for coordinated strategies that really lets the game design shine.

However, the company began to place greater focus on videogames again in 1986, leaving even fewer resources for properly supporting the 8-bit computers. Still, even as "third choice" systems for a good portion of their initial run, the Atari 8-bit computers were a success, especially considering the early exits of many competitors. Atari Corporation dropped its support for the 8-bit computer line on January 1, 1992, formally ending an eventful 12-year odyssey. Unofficially, of course, the creative energy around the platform wouldn't be quite so easy to extinguish.

The Atari 8-Bit Community Then and Now

Like most of the early computer game communities, fans of the Atari 8-bit were usually interested in playing games and learning how to program. They were also ferociously defensive of their chosen brand, despising the growing legions of Commodore fans.

As "Magic Knight" commented on the AtariAge forums,

I'm glad my dad picked up an Atari 800XL instead of a Commodore 64. It opened my eye to all aspects of computers and how they worked—if I'd had a C64 I would have just played games instead of exploring behind the scenes, as the magazines for the C64 didn't give enough balance to programming and hardware like the Atari's.

Today, Atari 8-bit fans can easily find like-minded people on online forums such as *AtariAge*, which boasts a very active and supportive base of dedicated users. Another good resource is Bostjan Gorisek's *Atari 8-Bit Forever* site (http://gury.atari8.info), which contains a massive amount of information on games, hardware, books, and more.

As Mike Vox commented on the *Armchair Arcade* website,

> The original Atari 800 is unique in the history of home computers. It has four built-in joystick ports, all easily accessible from the front of the unit (early games like *MULE* and *Survivor* took advantage of the four joystick ports). It has two heavy-duty cartridge slots. The top hatch also flips open to easily plug in expandable memory cards. The Atari 800 was built like a tank with a very robust keyboard. Unfortunately, these unique features are missing on all later models where the design was streamlined.

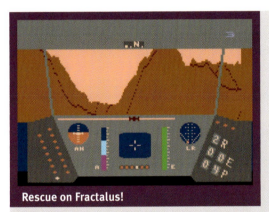
Rescue on Fractalus!

Rescue on Fractalus!
(1984, Lucasfilm Games LLC)

Loosely inspired by *Star Wars*, this 3D flight simulation game puts players in the cockpit of a search-and-rescue aircraft. The innovative fractal-based routines for generating randomized terrain, created by Loren Carpenter, give it its title and tremendous replay-value. What most gamers remember, though, is that guy with the green helmet... For other titles from Lucasfilm Games that leveraged the same innovative fractal-based technology, be sure to check out first-person shooter and adventure game *The Eidolon* and action strategy game *Koronis Rift*, both from 1985.

Since the end of its commercial lifecycle, new homebrew games have been regularly released both commercially on cartridge, tape, and disk, as well as for free as images to play on your favorite emulator or to transfer for use on a real Atari computer. In recent years, there have been on average as many as a dozen quality new releases annually. Some highlights include arcade conversion *Bomb Jack* (2008), which requires a full 320KB of RAM, platformer *Mighty Jill Off* (2011), and action puzzler *Ridiculous Reality* (2012). These and a large database of other games, both new and old, are cataloged and usually available for download from the excellent *Atarimania* website.

Collecting Atari 8-Bit Systems

Obviously, new Atari 8-bit collectors have many things to consider when making their first system purchase. There are several different models and configurations available, as *Electronic Games* magazine editorialized as early as December 1983:

The overnight switch from the 400 and 800 to the XL series may confuse some potential buyers. It isn't always easy to figure out which machines have which features—and Atari's dismal naming system doesn't exactly endow each model with a distinctive personality.

Optimally, a hardcore collector would have both a 48KB 800 with GTIA and a minimum 64KB XL or XE system, for the full spectrum of native compatibility. If you're just going to get one, however, go for an XL or XE. Today, most of the various Atari 8-bit computer variations are available for around the same price, with the final choice often coming down to a buyer's preference for a particular system style and class.

The XEGS came with both a light gun and a classic Atari-style joystick with gray styling instead of the usual all black. The joystick functioned as expected, but the light gun was generally inaccurate in comparison to the equivalent on the Nintendo Entertainment System or Sega Master System.

The classic 48KB 800 had four controller ports and a second cartridge slot—features that no other Atari 8-bit could match. Although not without its quirks, Atari's 1200XL is generally considered to have the best keyboard and styling of any model in the line. The 64KB XEGS is the only Atari 8-bit with a detachable keyboard and functions like a videogame console without one. The 130XE is the only Atari 8-bit with 128KB of standard memory, though most of the other models are expandable well beyond that amount.

Star Raiders.

Star Raiders (1979, Atari, Inc.)

Doug Neubauer's *Star Raiders*[6] is a massively influential dogfighting game set in space. Its fully-navigable 3D environment all the more impressive when one considers it required only 8K of RAM and 8K of ROM. Modern developers use more resources than that for a single letter! Despite the game's popularity and technical innovations, Atari's miserly policies prevented Neubauer from collecting royalties on his masterpiece. Perhaps that's why the Zylons got so riled up against the Atarian Federation.

Software on cartridges, cassettes, and disks are also easy to locate, with a range of online stores and auction websites still catering to the platform. Since Atari 8-bit computers used the same controller connection standard as the VCS, any compatible joystick, paddle, or other controller will work fine. Many Sega Master System and Sega Genesis gamepads are also compatible.

The XG-1 light gun that came with the XEGS (also available separately) is unique to the Atari 8-bit line. It's the only light gun Atari ever released and is used by a small number of games on both the VCS and Atari 7800. Collectors of those systems are often on the lookout for one as well.

Peripherals are nearly as plentiful as the systems themselves, with a good range of compatible cassette recorders, disk drives, and printers still available at reasonable prices. If you don't wish to deal with the quirks of classic tape drives, disk drives, or even cartridges, though, there

---

6   For an in-depth look at the game, see "The History of *Star Raiders*: Taking Command" on *Gamasutra*, www.gamasutra.com/view/feature/132516/the_history_of_star_raiders_.php?page=1.

are many modern options available to make using the classic Atari 8-bit computers far more enjoyable. Atarimax offers several great options, including the Maxflash USB Cartridge System, which lets you store multiple programs on a cartridge for quick access from your Atari computer, and the Universal SIO2PC/ProSystem interface, which works with *APE for Windows* to allow bi-directional control of both PC and Atari peripherals for the ultimate in flexibility. Lotharek.pl offers a product called Sio2sd, which lets you easily load programs into your Atari computer via its SIO interface directly from an SD or MMC flash card.

Emulating the Atari 8-bit

There are several unauthorized emulators available for the Atari 8-bit. Perhaps the most popular is *Atari800Win PLus*, a free and versatile emulator for Microsoft Windows. Other popular options include *Atari800MacX* for Macintosh computers, and *Atari++*, which works on Linux, Unix, and Windows systems, and offers cycle-precise emulation. If you own an Android smartphone or tablet, one of the better options is *Colleen*.

Emulation is often hampered by the need for system ROM BIOS images, which are still under copyright and thus illegal to host. While it is possible to extract the ROM information from an actual Atari 8-bit computer, this procedure is likely too complex and involved for a casual user. Despite the threat of litigation, however, there are several websites that make the system ROMs available for use in any emulator. Google is your friend.

Atari800Win Plus 4.0 running the action strategy classic **Archon: The Light and the Dark** (1983, Electronic Arts).

Mattel Intellivision (1979)

History

When reflecting back on the storied career of George Plimpton, the celebrated editor, journalist, writer, actor, and gamesman, there are few among us who would think first and foremost of his stint as official pitchman for the Mattel Intellivision. Still, while his tenure as the face of Mattel's console will likely be relegated to the footnotes section of his official biographies, for Mattel, the hiring of Plimpton proved an insightful and apropos choice. Along with Bill Cosby for Texas Instruments and Alan Alda for Atari, Plimpton was one of the most prominent and memorable personalities used as weapons in the "spokesperson wars" of the 1980s. While not as well-known among the general public as Cosby or Alda, Plimpton was nevertheless well-suited to the role. Primarily a well-regarded journalist, the versatile Plimpton was perhaps most famous for competing in various pro sporting events and then writing about the details of his often humbling experiences from his uniquely novice perspective.[1] Even if you didn't get the clever connection when he endorsed Mattel's superior sports games in television commercials, Plimpton's droll and pitch-perfect delivery of the technical merits of the Intellivision over its biggest rival, the Atari 2600 VCS, helped Mattel's marketing department position their product as the intelligent choice for the sophisticated, informed consumer.

The story of the Intellivision's unusually long 12-year run begins even further back, with the founding of Mattel in 1945. Mattel was then primarily a manufacturer of picture frames and dollhouse accessories. After the wildly successful introduction of the Barbie doll line in 1959, however, the company made the obvious decision to focus entirely on toys.

Much to the delight of Mattel and little girls everywhere, the Barbie franchise had great legs, and the greatly expanded profits allowed the company to diversify with a talking doll (Chatty Cathy) in 1960 and the See 'n Say educational toys in 1965.[2] The Hot Wheels line, unveiled in 1968, drove the company to the top of the American toy industry.

An early two-page Plimpton ad from the March 1982 issue of **Electronic Games** touting the Intellivision's comparative sophistication.

---

[1] Fun fact: Plimpton's 1966 non-fiction book *Paper Lion*, where he recounted his experiences trying out as the third-string quarterback for the 1963 Detroit Lions, was dramatized in a 1968 film of the same name. The star of that film? Alan Alda, of course.

[2] The See 'n Say toys allowed children to choose the item they wanted to hear. The Farmer edition allowed even the most urban of children to hear what a duck or cow sounded like. Instead of batteries, the units were powered by a metal coil, wound manually by pulling on a string.

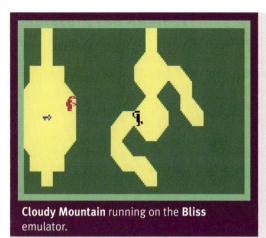

Cloudy Mountain running on the **Bliss** emulator.

ADVANCED DUNGEONS & DRAGONS Cartridge (1982, Mattel)

Also known as *ADVANCED DUNGEONS & DRAGONS Cloudy Mountain Cartridge*[3] to distinguish it from the later games, Mattel was the first videogame company to get the coveted TSR license.[4] While *Cloudy Mountain* didn't necessarily capture the more cerebral elements of TSR's pen-and-paper role-playing classic, it was still a smashing action-adventure. The goal is simple: guide your archer through randomly generated, scrolling mazes in search of treasures and weapons in your quest to recover the two pieces of the Crown of Kings. The game was later referred to as *Adventure* or *Crown of Kings* after the license expired, so you may need to track it down under one of those names.

Today, Mattel is one of the world's largest toy-makers, but a series of disasters in the 1970s made this destiny anything but certain. After losing one of their largest toy plants in a fire, a 1971 dock workers' strike ruined their crucial Christmas season. Another misstep included a toy World War II-era German airplane complete with swastika decals, which unsurprisingly offended the American Jewish Congress. On top of all these woes, the SEC was investigating them for lying on their financial reports, further tarnishing their image. Mattel needed something drastic to recover its reputation as well as its finances, and by the late 1970s made the fateful decision to gamble on the videogame market.

In 1977, Mattel, under its Mattel Electronics line, produced the seminal *Auto Race*, the first all-electronic handheld game. Crude by today's standards, with visuals represented by red LED lights and sound consisting of simple beeps, *Auto Race* nevertheless showed the entertainment potential of a portable electronic game. The novel product was a huge success, spawning several other handheld games such as *Football* and *Battlestar Galactica*, the latter being the first of many examples of Mattel Electronics' deep-pocketed licensing prowess.[5] These games sold millions and gave Mattel the confidence to move into the fledgling videogame console market in 1978. Development on the Intellivision Master Component began.

Mattel successfully test marketed the Intellivision in Fresno, California, in 1979, along with four games: *Las Vegas Poker & Blackjack*, *The Electric Company: Math Fun*, *Armor Battle*, and *Backgammon*. The following year, Mattel went national, and quickly sold out the first year's production run of the popular systems. The new electronic games sent the company's reputation flying high again, and accounted for a full quarter of their sales by the end of the year.

---

[3]   TSR was particular about use of their license and making a clear distinction with their other products, which is why there's the capitalization and "Cartridge" in the games they allowed Mattel to produce.

[4]   TSR themselves produced and published two mediocre computer games for the Apple II in 1982, *Dungeon!* and *Theseus and the Minotaur*. Outside of Mattel's 1983 port of *ADVANCED DUNGEONS & DRAGONS Treasure Of Tarmin Cartridge* for the Aquarius, those would be the last official TSR games on a computer until SSI's triumphant 1988 release of the first "Gold Box" role-playing classic, *Pool of Radiance*.

[5]   Sadly, Mattel's other *Battlestar Galactica* licensed products did not prove as successful for the company. After a four-year-old tragically choked to death after swallowing a missile part from one of the toys, Mattel spent half a million dollars recalling the line.

The Master Component was a large, flat rectangular box with stylish brown-and-gold detailing. Unlike the Atari 2600, this system's two controllers were attached to the system and could not be removed. They had unique thumb-operated control discs with 16 possible movement directions, which was twice the number of a typical digital joystick.

The controllers also had 12-button keypads with two action buttons on each side. The top two action buttons were wired together, so only three unique functions could be performed by the four action buttons. Since the control disc and action buttons registered as the same inputs, they could not be used simultaneously with the keypad buttons. On the plus side, simultaneously pressing the 1 and 9 keys would pause any game, an unusual feature for the time.

The Master Component
   Mattel Electronics has designed a number of features into the Master Component, making it one of the most versatile video game units available.

Our exclusive overlay system makes it easy
   Every game cartridge comes with two durable overlays which fit directly over the hand controller for easy and simple game play decisions. No additional controllers are needed.

Input keys call the play
   Special input keys allow each player to select different game functions and maneuvers, enabling them to choose the exact kind of programming each situation requires.

Side-mounted action buttons make it come alive
   Four buttons, two on either side of each hand controller, send action commands to the Master Component and make right or left handed use equally easy.

Object control disc keeps it moving
   Objects on the screen can be maneuvered with accuracy in 16 different directions, which provides a realistic simulation of life-like movement.

Entertainment Networks
   26 different game cartridges (6 of them new for this year!) put a world of challenging excitement at your fingertips. From home runs to space battles, Intellivision game cartridges deliver an unprecedented level of player involvement. All of the entertainment networks encourage both physical and mental dexterity while bringing a totally unique game experience. Each cartridge sold separately.

Sports • Strategy • Children's Learning
Action • Gaming

A page from an early 1981 Mattel Electronics dealer catalog enumerating the many benefits of the Intellivision Master Component. Dealer pricing was $210 each for a package of six consoles.

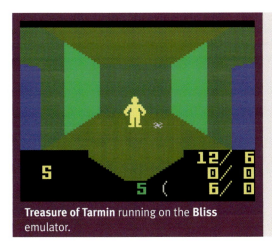

Treasure of Tarmin running on the **Bliss** emulator.

ADVANCED DUNGEONS & DRAGONS *Treasure of Tarmin* Cartridge (1983, Mattel)

Unlike *Cloudy Mountain*'s modified top-down perspective, *Treasure of Tarmin* went for a more traditional first-person dungeon view and placed less emphasis on action and more on strategy. The objective is still simple: slay the minotaur who guards the treasure, but the turn-based battles, stats, and enemy types are more faithful to the type of role-playing elements found in the source material and make for a unique play experience from the time period. Post-license, the game has been referred to as *Minotaur*.

Because of its design quirks, Intellivision controllers were notoriously difficult to use. Although the multifunction controllers worked well for games requiring complex input, such as the genre-defining *Major League Baseball* (1980) and other sports games, they proved sluggish for titles that required precise directional movement or timely button presses, such as the Nintendo arcade port *Popeye* (Parker Brothers, 1983). Regardless of their usability, it's not hyperbole to say that they stand today as the single most divisive and controversial—as well as hardest to reproduce or emulate—of the stock console controllers.

The heart of the Intellivision was a 16-bit microprocessor from General Instruments, quite a step up from most other videogame and computer systems at the time, which still relied on the cheaper 8-bit microprocessors. The Intellivision's sound chip, the General Instrument AY-3-

8910, was also notable, outputting three 8-bit sound channels and a noise generator. By contrast, the Atari 2600 had only two one-bit channels. The AY-3-8910 was also a popular choice for arcade machines, allowing Intellivision arcade ports to sound more authentic.

The machine boasted a 16-color palette, but games with more than eight sprites (called "moving objects") would cause the screen to flicker—something the company's marketing team would not allow. Fortunately, Mattel's programming team devised a clever method

Screenshot from the **Bliss** emulator showing **NFL Football** (1980), one of many great Intellivision sports games that benefited from its unique controller.

Astrosmash running on the **Bliss** emulator.

Astrosmash (1981, Mattel)

For a platform that emphasized its sophistication, John Sohl's *Astrosmash* was anything but. The game's premise was simple: shoot or avoid the falling asteroids, spinners (bombs), homing missiles, and patrolling flying saucers. Part *Space Invaders*, part *Asteroids*, *Astrosmash* was exactly the type of non-stop action that videogame players of the day craved, proving, when programmed correctly, how versatile the Intellivision's hardware really was in delivering the goods. Perhaps *Astrosmash*'s most innovative and welcome feature is that as the game gets faster and harder at higher levels, as you start to lose lives, the pace and difficulty starts to scale back down again. This makes long play sessions and big scores a real possibility for players of even modest abilities.[6] Along with Don Daglow and Ji-Wen Tsao's widely imitated big fish-eat-smaller fish game *Shark! Shark!*, Astrosmash helped define action gaming on the Intellevision.

called "GRAM sequencing" to work around this issue. The technique can be seen in games such as *Space Armada* (1981) and *Star Strike* (1982).

At first, Mattel farmed out game programming duties to a company named APh Technological Consulting. In 1980, however, they decided to form their own in-house team, which

---

[6]   Easter Egg: If you own an Intellivision and a copy of this game on cartridge, you can rapidly press the console's reset button to unlock the original *Asteroids*-inspired variation of the game that was unintentionally left in. Unfortunately, there's no way to reliably access this variation other than trying to glitch the console with the reset button.

became known as the Blue Sky Rangers. These nine programming gurus became intimately familiar with and passionate about the hardware, innovating impressive software tricks, such as the GRAM sequencing technique mentioned above. Several of the team's members would continue to produce software that pushed the platform's hardware long after Mattel officially dropped support. They took their name from their division's formal brainstorming meetings, which were called "blue-skying" sessions. Howard Polskin, a writer for *TV Guide* who interviewed the group in 1982, describes them as eccentric math wizards whose eyes were "sunken and hollow from countless hours spent toiling indoors in front of computer terminals." Like other software companies at the time, their management preferred to keep their identities secret to prevent their being lured away by the competition. Still, the team managed to have a lot of fun playing each other's games, hanging out at the local arcade, and throwing Frisbees at the park.

Although an unthinkable practice today, Mattel followed Atari's example with its VCS, and sublicensed the rights to distribute the Intellivision Master Component under different brand names, including the Sears Tele-Games Super Video Arcade, Radio Shack Tandyvision One, and GTE Intellivision. Except for cosmetic differences, most of these systems were identical to the original Master Component. However, the Sears version offered detachable controllers, which were a welcome improvement over the original model, as well as a different default title screen. In addition, as it did with the Atari VCS, for a time, Sears rebranded Mattel games under its own label.

A page from the 1982 Sears holiday catalog showing the rebranded Tele-Games Super Video Arcade console.

The Keyboard Component

Despite the success and sophistication of the Intellivision, Mattel didn't always deliver on its promises. The most infamous of these is the Keyboard Component, an add-on that would turn the console into a full home computer system. The idea had been around for a while, and other consoles already had their own computing add-ons, including the Bally Home Library Computer (aka Bally Astrocade), APF M-1000, Magnavox Odyssey2, and Atari 2600. However, these were either poorly marketed and distributed or simply not useful enough to resonate with consumers. Mattel was in a position to change all of that.

Mattel told consumers they would have the Intellivision Keyboard Component by 1981. Despite that promise, ambitious technical specifications, production delays, and manufacturing issues made the Keyboard Component's timely release impractical. Internally known as the "Blue Whale," the component was being developed by Dave Chandler and his team of engineers, the same group who had finalized the Intellivision's design. Unfortunately for Chandler and Mattel, the team simply could not find a way to make the component cheap enough for release.

Comedian Jay Leno perhaps summed it up best at the 1981 Mattel Electronics Christmas party, "You know what the three big lies are, don't you? 'The check is in the mail,' 'I'll still respect you in the morning,' and 'The Keyboard will be out in the spring.'" To Mattel's detriment, the Federal Trade Commission (FTC) was not as amused by the delay, and

Mattel was promising "Intelligent Television" from as far back as its original creation in 1978, as this title screen screenshot from a dealer demo cartridge via the **Bliss** emulator demonstrates.

Beauty and the Beast running on the **Bliss** emulator.

Beauty and the Beast (1982, Imagic)

Coleco's *Donkey Kong* (1982) arcade conversion for the Intellivision was the definition of mediocre, with grating sound, odd looking graphics, and sluggish play. Adding insult to injury was the fact that it was one of the three Coleco Intellivision releases that, thanks to Mattel's hardware tweaks, didn't work on the Intellivision II. While Intellivision fans would finally receive a brilliant new homebrew conversion of the arcade game as *DK Arcade* in 2012, courtesy of Carl Mueller, Jr., the wait wasn't quite as bad as it could have been thanks to Wendell Brown's *Beauty and the Beast*. The premise was to rescue the girl from the boulder-hurling bully at the top of the high rise building. What the game lacked in originality by cribbing from Nintendo's *Donkey Kong*, it made up for in masterful execution. With fully animated graphics, lots of sound effects, intermissions, multiple levels, and many other little flourishes that kept the gameplay fresh, even without a compelling license, this was the type of platforming action that Intellivision gamers craved. Although not a direct sequel, Steve DeFrisco's island-based platformer *Tropical Trouble* (1983) uses a similar premise and graphics, just with more innovative side-scrolling gameplay.

the US agency for consumer protection became involved after receiving a series of complaints. Once again, Mattel was under federal scrutiny, casting a cloud of doubt over investors.

Although Mattel was eventually able to release a few units to test market and to those consumers who complained the loudest, the Keyboard Component proved too costly for Mattel to reliably mass produce on a large scale at a competitive price. It certainly wasn't for lack of effort, though.

The Keyboard Component added an 8-bit 6502 microprocessor, expandable RAM, full keyboard, digitally controlled cassette drive for both data and audio content, expansion ports, and a printer port. All of its features, in addition to the Master Component's own capabilities, made it more than a match for nearly any other stand-alone computer of the day. However, each setback and delay reduced this advantage until, finally, it was a case of too little, too late.

The roughly 4000 Keyboard Components that were eventually produced were not enough to appease the FTC. The agency imposed daily fines, which prompted Mattel to move to an alternate plan with a much lower priced, but far less capable, computer expansion, the Enhanced Computer System (ECS). Even this unit was not released until 1983.

The Keyboard Component was extensively advertised for a number of years in Mattel catalogs, including this example from 1982, which alludes to its availability in "test markets."

Despite its problems with the Keyboard Component, the Intellivision and its software continued to sell, capturing nearly 25 percent of the home videogame market at its peak. With its growing success, Mattel Electronics was spun off as a separate company under the Mattel banner in 1982. In that same year, the company introduced the Intellivoice Speech Synthesis Module, which, after the Magnavox Odyssey2's The Voice, was the second such device of its kind for a videogame console—and this time, kids would not need to pull a string to hear it.

Through clever use of the built-in prerecorded sound samples and custom recordings loaded on demand for each game, every Intellivoice title had its own unique identity. Although impressive even at the necessarily low sample rates, only five speech games were released. Poor sales of the Intellivoice spurred Mattel to provide a voucher for the module free by mail with the purchase of a Master Component.

That wasn't all Mattel was doing to make 1982 the year of the Intellivision, however. They also released a new version of the console, the sleeker and much smaller Intellivision II Master Component, a white and black unit with removable controllers and external power supply. So why a new Intellivision? Michael Blanchet quipped in the April 1983 issue of *Electronic Fun with Computers and Games,*

> For one thing, it's spiffier than the original. For another, what better way to entice owners of other systems—and those who don't own any system at all—to switch to Mattel than by offering something new? Here's your chance to be first on the block all over again!

The real reason wasn't simply refreshing the line for marketing purposes, however. It was also a bid to reduce production costs and add some highly desirable features. A special video input was added to the cartridge port to make the System Changer possible, which allowed the Intellivision II to play Atari 2600 games. This refresh also gave Mattel Electronics an excuse to introduce another "feature," a secret validation check in the hardware that made third-party software inoperable. This check affected Coleco's 1982 arcade conversions—*Donkey Kong, Mouse Trap,* and *Carnival*—and inadvertently rendered Mattel's own *Electric Company Word Fun* (1980) unplayable. Fortunately, for the health of the console's game library, internal and external development groups soon figured out how to bypass the check.

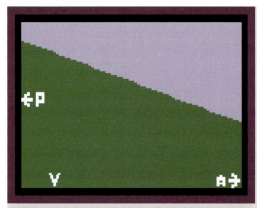

B-17 Bomber running on the **Bliss** emulator.

B-17 Bomber
(1982, Mattel)

While it's arguable if *B-17 Bomber* is a particularly great game, or even the best of the games that require the Intellivoice module, there's no denying the appeal of its total package. It's an intense, but approachable first-person perspective flight simulation with some pretty memorable speech effects. As you fly your bomber on its missions to attack strategic map targets throughout Europe, your crewmate warns you of everything from impending attacks ("Fighter, six o'clock") to when an objective is in range ("Target in sight!")—complete with charming southern accent. This ability to add some personality to its speech effects gave the Intellivoice a leg up on most other speech solutions of the era, and one that in this case added tremendously to the personality and appeal of the core game. It was indeed a rare feat for the time. If you'd like to experience an equally intense, but rather more unusual speech game, check out Mattel's *Bomb Squad* (1982), which tasks you with diffusing bombs with four different tools in the right order, all within tight time constraints.

The following year, Mattel released the ECS, which retailed for under $150. The ECS, like the System Changer, matched the styling of the Intellivision II, though it was compatible with all Intellivision models and the Intellivoice. The computer add-on featured a detachable chiclet keyboard, an expansion box, and power supply. It also added an extra 2KB of memory, three extra channels of sound, two additional controller ports, and the ability to accept a standard tape recorder and a printer, the latter being the same as the one for the original Keyboard Component and Mattel Aquarius computer. A simplified version of BASIC was built in along with the ability to play musical tones.

Despite this flurry of activity, however, the future of the Intellivision's add-ons was anything but certain. Mattel Electronics had a management shake-up in mid-1983 and shifted its focus to software for its own as well as competing videogame and computer systems. This shake-up took priority away from initiatives such as the ECS and Intellivoice; only the Intellivision consoles would continue to receive advertising and software support. In the end, the ECS was only supported with a music keyboard add-on and five cartridges.

An Intellivision II with Intellivoice, ECS, and music keyboard. Also pictured are the printer and standard cassette recorder from the Mattel Aquarius, both of which were compatible with the ECS.

The End of the Line

Following industry-wide losses from the Great Videogame Crash and too many costly dalliances in hardware development, Mattel Electronics was closed in January 1984, and its assets sold to a liquidation company owned by Terry Valeski, who was previously Mattel Electronics' senior vice-president of marketing and sales.

In addition to handling old inventory, Intellivision, Inc., sold some complete, but previously unreleased cartridges. Once most of the old Mattel Electronics inventory was sold, Valeski bought out Intellivision Inc.'s remaining assets from the other investors and formed INTV Corporation.

INTV Corporation hired former Mattel Electronics programmers to produce new Intellivision games. The company also released the INTV Master Component (called INTV System III and INTV Super Pro System, among other names), which was based on the easier to reproduce Intellivision Master Component with only minor cosmetic changes.

Like Atari's 2600 Jr., INTV's system was marketed as a low-cost alternative to the newer and more powerful systems of the day. The main console sold for less than $60 and many of the games were less than $20. INTV continued to produce new products up to 1990, when the company filed for bankruptcy protection, closing its doors for good in 1991.[7]

Today, several of the original Blue Sky Rangers run Intellivision Productions, Inc., which now owns the Intellivision branding and rights to most of the technology and games. This group regularly releases TV Games and compilation software packs for modern videogame consoles, computer systems, and portable devices based on the Intellivision line of products.

---

[7] During INTV's operation, Mattel did not remain idle. The toy company became involved in the videogame industry again by affiliating with Nintendo in 1986. Mattel not only produced new software and peripherals for the Nintendo Entertainment System, but also handled distribution throughout Europe in 1987 and Canada from 1986 to 1990 on Nintendo's behalf.

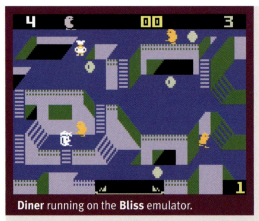

Diner running on the **Bliss** emulator.

Diner (1987, INTV Corporation)

Ray Kaestner's *Diner* was an unlikely sequel to his earlier Data East coin-op conversion of *BurgerTime*, among the Intellivision's best titles. Much like Data East's own attempt at a second game, *BurgerTime*'s sequel was originally going to be *PizzaTime*, with development starting but never finishing at Mattel's French offices. Instead, what originally started out life as a *Masters of the Universe II* prototype in Mattel's California office, was finished by Kaestner years later for INTV Corporation as *Diner*. Kaestner's creation, while officially licensed, was still considered an unofficial sequel, subordinated by the growing number of Data East's own arcade follow-ups. For a game with such a tortured history, you'd be forgiven for thinking *Diner* would turn out to be something of a dog's dinner. Luckily, for Intellivision fans, this isometric platform game was anything but. Kaestner crafted a wholly original game for chef Peter Pepper to star in, with old favorite bad guys, the hot dogs, joining new villains, bananas, cherries, and their leader, Mugsy the Mug o' Root Beer, for fun on the run. *Diner* is among the best original titles unique to the Intellivision and still holds a great deal of appeal today.

The Software

There were 125 cartridge games released for the Intellivision between 1979 and 1990. Several additional homebrew cartridges, including both original creations and previously unreleased prototypes, have been released since 2000.

In general, these games featured some of the best graphics and sound for any early videogame system, at least before Coleco released its more powerful ColecoVision. Still, gameplay speed often seemed a bit slower on an Intellivision than on rival machines.

Mattel generally grouped the games of its first software releases into categories called "networks," including Sports Network, Action Network, Gaming Network, Space Action Network, Strategy Network, Children's Learning Network, and Arcade Network, each with its own distinctive box color. However, Mattel's marketing discontinued the concept in late 1982 since most games were falling into the Action Network category (mostly at their request).

For the Intellivision Master Component's first two years, the system came packaged with *Las Vegas Poker & Blackjack* (1979), which played great one- or two-player versions of the title games, complete with an animated dealer. This was followed by a newer pack-in, *Astrosmash* (1981), one of the system's more popular action titles. Shortly after the release of the Intellivision II, a coupon for the excellent conversion of Data East's popular arcade game, *BurgerTime* (1983), was included as well.

The Intellivision is most famous for its extensive range of quality sports games, including Mattel's own *Major League Baseball*, *NFL Football*, *NBA Basketball*, *NHL Hockey*, and *PGA Golf*, all released in 1980 and among the first games licensed from professional sports

Microsurgeon running on the **Bliss** emulator.

Microsurgeon (1982, Imagic)

At a time when most games featured blocky, barely recognizable visuals, Rick Levine's *Microsurgeon* upped the ante with its bold, colorful maze-like presentation of an internal view of a critically ill patient's head and body. Reminiscent of the 1966 sci-fi movie classic *Fantastic Voyage*, the player navigates a miniature robot probe through the patient's blood stream, removing everything from brain tumors to blood clots near the heart, all while avoiding attacks from white blood cells. Dave Durran's sparse, but effective sound design, helps ratchet up the tension. For more *Microsurgeon*, be sure to check out the later ports for the Texas Instruments TI-99/4A and IBM PCjr, each of which features a slightly different take on the Intellivision original.

associations. Most of these titles were the best sports games of their time on any platform. They made great use of helpful overlays on the keypad for more sophisticated in-game options. The overlay for *Major League Baseball,* for instance, shows a baseball field with the various fielders in position. Players would press the player they wanted to go after the ball and who should receive it when it was caught. It was a great system in an era before modern touchscreens. INTV would later commission renamed updates for many of these games that introduced enhanced features and support for single players, although without the expensive licenses.

Besides sports and arcade licenses, Mattel gained the rights to many other types of properties, including TSR's *Advanced Dungeons & Dragons* pen-and-paper role-playing games, Disney's *Tron* (1982) science fiction film, *The Electric Company* kids' television series, and Hanna-Barbera cartoons, including *Scooby-Doo* and *The Jetsons*. Although the strategy was to gain market share by leveraging familiar brands, Mattel's talented developers weren't content to follow the familiar precedent of making lousy games that relied on brand recognition alone to appeal to gamers. This is particularly true of the ambitious TSR-licensed role-playing games, which many fans consider among the best on the platform.

While Mattel eventually shifted its development focus to mainly action games, for a time, the Intellivision did get some excellent games that required cunning, rather than quick reflexes. These titles included *ABPA Backgammon* (1979), *Horse Racing* (1980), *Reversi* (1982), and *USCF Chess* (1983), the first and last of which were licensed from their respective associations. The chess game is particularly remarkable since it was assumed that the AI for a chess game was well beyond the capabilities of the consoles of the day. Mattel felt, however, that such a product would bolster their claim that the Intellivision was indeed "intelligent television," and gave the project extra funding. The result was a cartridge with a full 2K of RAM, a luxury no other Mattel cartridges enjoyed. Although the complexity of the programming delayed its release, when it was finally rolled out in 1983, reviewers praised it.

Most of the games set for release in 1983 were advertised as having "SuperGraphics." The label was intended to help shield the Intellivision against marketing attacks from the newer and more advanced ColecoVision and Atari 5200 SuperSystem. However, in reality, "SuperGraphics" was just a marketing ploy, much like Sega's later use of "blast processing" to describe games on the Genesis. Though these later Intellivision games did tend to feature better graphics and smoother gameplay than many of the system's previous titles, there was nothing more to it than increasingly experienced developers using more sophisticated programming routines.

Despite there being only five games released for the Intellivoice, they were some of the system's most innovative titles. These included *Space Spartans* (1982), in which aliens relentlessly attack the player's spaceship and starbases; *Bomb Squad* (1982), in which the player must follow voice prompts to disarm a terrorist bomb; *B-17 Bomber* (1982), which simulates a World War II bombing run; and *Tron Solar Sailer* (1983), in which the goal is to decode an evil computer program.

There was also the ECS-based *World Series Major League Baseball* (1983), which was one of the first multiangle baseball games, with its fast-paced gameplay based on real statistics, play-by-play with the Intellivoice, and the ability to load and save games and lineups from cassette. Unfortunately, the rarity of the hardware combination allowed only a few gamers to experience programmer Eddie Dombrower's simulation of the Major League Baseball experience—at least until the release of his popular *Earl Weaver Baseball* for PC DOS and Commodore Amiga computers four years later.

In 1983, the remaining ECS cartridge lineup was released. These titles included *Mind Strike*, a challenging, feature-rich board game for one or two players; *Mr. BASIC Meets Bits 'N Bytes*,

Thin Ice running on the **Bliss** emulator.

Thin Ice (1986, INTV Corporation)

While Mattel Electronics didn't have many arcade exclusives in comparison to competitors like Atari or Coleco, they did have a first look deal for many Data East arcade properties, which is why they got top notch titles like *Lock 'n' Chase* and *BurgerTime*. Occasionally, however, some questionable titles would be offered by Data East to Mattel, like *Disco No. 1* (1982), where the player controlled Disco Boy, who skated around a dance floor to trap Disco Girls in squares. The game was fun, but the theme dated. Julie Hoshizaki, who had done a stellar job on the earlier *Lock 'n' Chase* conversion, took Keith Robinson's proposal for a revision to the arcade game called *Thin Ice*, and ran with it, with help from Monique Lujan-Bakerink's graphic designs and George "The Fat Man" Sanger's[8] musical theme, "Carnival of the Penguins." In the new interpretation, Duncan dunks his fellow penguins when he encloses them on the thin ice, which he loves skating on. After a brief flirtation with changing the character to the official Olympic mascot, Voochko the Wolf, and the further distraction of Mattel Electronics closing down in January 1984, it would take INTV Corporation until 1986 to release the game as originally envisioned.

---

[8]   This was George Alistair Sanger's first videogame soundtrack, which lasted all of 15 seconds. Under his nickname, The Fat Man, he has gone on to produce a long list of increasingly complex videogame soundtracks. See author Barton's series of interviews with Sanger here: http://www.armchairarcade.com/neo/taxonomy/term/2979.

which taught computer programming basics through three games and an illustrated 72-page manual; and *Melody Blaster*, a musical version of *Astrosmash* and the only other title besides the built-in music program that made use of the music keyboard add-on. Unfortunately, while additional titles were in development before Mattel stopped supporting the ECS, no software took advantage of the additional controller ports for four-player gaming.[9]

Even with Mattel's attempts to lock out third-party developers through the release of the Intellivision II, external software support soon picked up anyway. Besides Coleco, top publishers like Activision, Atarisoft, Imagic, Interphase, Parker Brothers, and Sega all released cartridges for the system after 1982. Although many of these were ports from other systems (mostly the Atari VCS), console exclusives found their way to Mattel's platform as well. These exclusives included Activision's *Happy Trails* (1983), which required a player to create new trail pathways by sliding jumbled pieces into place, and Imagic's *Dracula* (1983), which cast the player in the title role as both vampire and bat. In fact, Imagic was particularly prolific on the platform, releasing an additional seven exclusives, bringing its final total to 14 titles.

After Mattel Electronics closed in January 1984, the newly formed Intellivision, Inc., bought all remaining inventory for major toy store and mail order liquidation, including the remaining supply of cartridges from the Intellivision's third-party software providers. With sales going well for the streamlined company, Valeski decided to try marketing new games. These games included *World Series Baseball* (now supporting one or two players), *Thunder Castle* (action role-playing), *World Cup Soccer* (one or two players), and *Championship Tennis* (one or two players).

The first two games were completed at Mattel Electronics but never released, and the last two were completed by a former Mattel Electronics office in France and originally saw release in Europe through Dextell Ltd. The success of these new games spurred Valeski to buy out Intellivision Inc.'s assets and form INTV Corp., to more aggressively pursue new Intellivision releases and reprints.

To save money, the company's new releases and reprints were produced with thinner boxes, contained no controller overlays (or, when absolutely necessary, reduced-quality overlays), featured cartridge labels and instructions that were printed in black and white, and often failed to renew licenses, necessitating a name change for the affected titles.

Despite intense competition in the reinvigorated videogame market, INTV held its own until 1990, releasing 21 additional games in total, six of which were coded from scratch rather than built off pre-existing code. These six originals included sports games *Chip Shot Super Pro Golf* (1987), *Super Pro Decathlon* (1988), *Body Slam! Super Pro Wrestling* (1988), and *Spiker! Super Pro Volleyball*

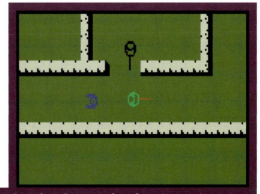

A screenshot from the **Bliss** emulator for Imagic's **Swords & Serpents** (1982), an impressive action dungeon-crawler featuring one- or two-player simultaneous gameplay as a warrior and wizard.

---

[9] The last game finished at Mattel Electronics - the day before the final layoff - was Dave Stifel's innovative *Game Factory* (aka, *Game Maker*) for the ECS, which let you create your own games from a library of components, including being able to borrow characters from other cartridges! It was yet another example of a potential pre-Crash game changer that was sadly never released.

Tower of Doom running on the **Bliss** emulator.

Tower of Doom (1987, INTV Corporation)

After the release of the sophisticated role-playing game, *Treasure of Tarmin*, Mattel Electronics' marketing arm wanted a less complex, more action-oriented Dungeons & Dragons title as its follow-up. Dan Bass took the lead on *ADVANCED DUNGEONS & DRAGONS Revenge of the Master Cartridge*, with graphics by Monique Lujan-Bakerink and Karl Morris, and music and sound effects by Dave Warhol and Joshua Jeffe. After being renamed *ADVANCED DUNGEONS & DRAGONS Tower of Mystery Cartridge*, the game ended up only half complete when Mattel Electronics closed its doors. INTV Corporation commissioned John Tomlinson to finish the rest of the game, along with Connie Goldman, who provided additional graphics. Avoiding the expensive TSR license, the game was released in 1987 as simply *Tower of Doom*. Even released as late as it was, the game was a triumph for the platform, with a selection of ten different characters of varying abilities, and ten different adventures with either more of a puzzle or action orientation to choose from. Furthering the innovation were a mix of predetermined and random mazes, along with close-up battle scenes whenever a monster was encountered.

(1989), as well as arcade translations *Commando* (1987) and *Pole Position* (1988). This spirited post-Crash effort helped get approximately 500,000 additional Intellivision consoles into homes, adding to the approximately 3 million units already sold during the platform's original commercial run.

The Intellivision Community Then and Now

Despite its quality, the Intellivision was always just a step behind the type of community, third-party, and advertising support that first the Atari VCS and then Coleco's ColecoVision received. In spite of its underdog status in comparison to those two systems, the Intellivision platform still received more mindshare and support in those critical areas than any of the other contenders for top dog in videogame consoles by a wide margin. The fact that the Intellivision was the only other console of its generation besides the VCS to continue to receive significant support well after the Great Videogame Crash, including prime shelf space at retailers like Toys R Us, speaks volumes to the enthusiasm exhibited by both the platform's creators and its fans.

Besides Intellivision Productions, Inc.'s own website (www.intellivisionlives.com), there are a wide range of other sites that today's fans rally around. These include the *INTV Funhouse* (www.intvfunhouse.com), *IntelliWiki* (wiki.intellivision.us), *Intellivision* (www.intellivision.us), and *Intellivision Revolution* (http://intellivisionrevolution.com). Of course, general sites like *AtariAge* (www.atariage.com) and *Digital Press* (www.digitpress.com) have regular discussions about the platform, or even dedicated forums. Of course, many of the users on these forums were active Intellivision fans back in the day, with stories like Graydingo's:

My dad picked up an Intellivision circa 1980. I became so good at *Snafu* that no one wanted to play me. Still to this day I love the 'SNAP, PEWWWW' sound FX of that game. I played a lot of *Astrosmash* as well. It started a lifelong love of games and consoles.

In short, today there's no lack of information or community surrounding the Intellivision. If you're interested in collecting, emulating, or just learning more about the system, joining one of these forums and introducing yourself is a great way to get started.

One major factor for the resilience of the community today is due to Intellivision Productions' continued licensing and release of their own products, including the *Intellivision Lives!* game collection, which was first released for Window-based computers in 1999, and was followed by versions for Sony's PlayStation 2, Microsoft's Xbox, and Nintendo's GameCube and DS platforms, as well as the similar *Intellivision* for iOS devices. Another major factor is the growing collection of quality homebrew software releases that has really been kicked into high gear in recent years.

With a combination of previously unreleased prototypes, like the 2011 IntelligentVision releases of the James Bond-themed action game *Scarfinger* and the ECS-based *Flintstones' Keyboard Fun*, and original creations like the incredible *Moon Patrol*-inspired ECS-enhanced *Space Patrol* (2007, Left Turn Only Productions), the combined ports of *Donkey Kong* and *D2K: Jumpman Returns!* as *D2K Arcade* (2012, Elektronite), and the polished maze game, *Christmas Carol vs. The Ghost of Christmas Presents* (2012, Left Turn Only Productions), there are no shortage of quality new cartridge releases for the active fan to plug into their console.

A collection of modern-day homebrew releases. Many of these titles match or exceed the packaging quality found in the boxed games from the Intellivision's heyday.

Collecting for and Emulating the Intellivision

With a decade of releases in its mass market prime, Intellivision systems and variations are easy to find and relatively inexpensive, often selling in cost-effective bundles with many loose games and an Intellivoice, although care must be taken that the controllers are in good working condition since they're difficult to replace. The ECS add-on is rarer and often goes for quite a bit more than the console with some games. The music keyboard add-on often goes for a little more than the ECS alone.

Since the Intellivision Keyboard Component had such a limited production run and many were recalled, that particular add-on is among the rarest items for any system. When a Keyboard Component becomes available, even if it's not fully functional, it will sell for well into the thousands of dollars. As expected, the software is even rarer and comprises the *BASIC Programming Language* cartridge and the *Conversational French, Crosswords (I-III), Family Budgeting,*

Utopia running on the **Bliss** emulator.

Utopia (1981, Mattel)

Having already won countless industry awards and accolades, it's little wonder that *Utopia* was chosen as just one of 80 videogames to appear in the Smithsonian Institution's *The Art of Video Games* exhibition that took place March 16–September 30, 2012. Don Daglow's breakthrough simulation helped set the template for the popular real-time strategy (RTS) genre, requiring the planning and thinking ahead of a game of chess with the reflexes of an action videogame to set the strategies in motion. Tasked with ruling one of two opposing islands, players could play competitively or cooperatively to increase the welfare of their respective peoples and their need for food, housing, and other essentials in the face of natural disasters, and even rebels. For the only official port of the game, check out the Mattel Aquarius version, which retains the original's charms, while taking into account its target platform's relative strengths and weaknesses.

Geography Challenge, Jack LaLanne's Physical Conditioning, and *Spelling Challenge* cassettes.

New hardware has thus far been mostly limited to low production run cartridges that allow loading of ROM images and assist with programming, such as Chad Schell's *Intellicart* and *Cuttle Cart 3*. Other devices, like the *Ultima PC Interface for the Intellivision* from Hafner Enterprises, allow connection of real Intellivision controllers, as well as the ECS keyboard and music synthesizer, making emulating the console on a computer all the more authentic.

Besides the official Intellivision emulation compilations released by Intellivision Productions for modern platforms, a variety of other unofficial emulators are available that can deliver a good approximation of the real system experience. These emulators include Kyle Davis' *Bliss* for Windows and Joes Zbiciak's *jzIntv* for Windows, Macintosh, and Linux, with many of the better ones also doing a good job of emulating the functionality of the ECS and other add-ons.

For a nice compromise between the authenticity of the actual console and emulation, inquisitive fans would do well to check out AtGames' officially licensed digital apps and Intellivision Flashback TV Game system, which were released in 2014. While the console can only play the selection of Intellivision games it has built-in, it's an inexpensive, low hassle way to experience the platform on a dedicated device.

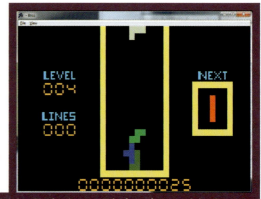

The **Bliss** Windows emulator running Joseph Zbiciak's **Tetris** clone **4-Tris** (2000), one of the first cartridge homebrew releases for the platform.

PC DOS Computers (1981)

History

Before the "IBM PC compatible" dominated the market, a trip to the local computer retailer was like a night at the casino. With a roulette wheel of incompatible platforms to choose from, consumers risked wasting hundreds, if not thousands, of dollars on a machine that could very well be extinct within a few months. Naturally, the stakes were also high for software developers, who had to take on the financial burden and risk of building and porting software for all of these different systems.

Companies such as Apple, Commodore, Tandy, Texas Instruments, and Atari (just to name a few!) struggled mightily to eliminate their rivals and become the standard home computing platform. Some succeeded in dominating for a time, but it was not their destiny to produce the computing platform synonymous with the term "Personal Computer." IBM would claim the victory, but not the spoils, of the home computer war, introducing and then losing control of what would become a truly ubiquitous home computing platform.

No other computer manufacturer had the corporate clout and deep pockets of IBM. For generations of professional businesspeople, the word "computer" meant a mainframe; anything else was just a gadget or—worse, in their eyes—a videogame system masquerading as a computer

Doom running on the **DOSBox** emulator.

Doom (1993, id Software)

Designed primarily by John Carmack and John Romero, *Doom* introduced millions of gamers to the joys of the now ubiquitous first-person shooter. Featuring blazing speed and some of the most polished gameplay the genre has to offer, *Doom* is still on many lists of the best games of all time. Originally released as shareware, the game showcased the latent power of the IBM PC as a gaming machine, making even the best games on other computer platforms seem primitive by comparison. As a gift to their many fans, id released the source code for *Doom* in 1997. *Doom* and its various sequels and add-ons are available to download or purchase on the Steam store (http://store.steampowered.com) and id Software (www.idsoftware.com) websites. If you like this game, check out 3D Realms' *Duke Nukem 3D* (1996), which was another early high point for the genre, offering a bit more freedom and personality than *Doom*.

(consider how Atari marketed its 2600 console as the "Video Computer System"). Indeed, the very idea of a "personal computer" was suspect; the term "computer" meant a refrigerator-sized machine and a bevy of professionals to operate it (ordinary mortals never touched the actual computer). The old way of doing computing had worked well for IBM in the past, but it was becoming increasingly clear that the future was in personal computers, not mainframes.

As told in Emerson W. Pugh's 2009 book, *Building IBM: Shaping an Industry and Its Technology*, IBM can trace its roots back to 1890, when inventor Herman Hollerith developed a punched-card machine used by the US Census bureau. Later, Hollerith merged his company

with two others to form International Business Machines, hiring Thomas J. Watson in 1914 to manage the combined operation. Watson (1874–1956) and, later his son, Tom Jr. (1914–1993), were the brilliant capitalists at the helm who literally changed the way the world does business. In 1964, IBM introduced the System/360, a "family" of versatile mainframe computers that became the industry standard, remaining in production until 1978.

The original 360 was the IBM System/360, a highly successful mainframe computer "family" produced from 1965 to 1978. Shown here is a unit installed for the Volkswagen automobile company. Source: German Federal Archive.

Watson Jr. had retired in 1971 after suffering a heart attack, and the company went through a series of less effective CEOs. Although there were many at IBM who wanted to move into the personal computer sector, the lack of decisive leadership to deal with the endless internal office politics stymied the process. By that point, technological advances such as integrated circuits (ICs) and Intel's "computer-on-a-chip," the microprocessor, were not only shrinking the size, but also lowering the cost of computer hardware.

Tellingly, the IBM PC (later known commonly by its 5150 model name) was developed at a skunk works in Boca Raton, Florida, far away from the company's bureaucracy. It was designed by Philip "Don" Estridge (1937–1985), an employee at IBM's Entry Level Systems Division. As a former systems programmer for the Apollo moon mission and engineer on project SAGE, Estridge was no stranger to challenging assignments. Estridge and his team of 12 fellow engineers wanted to build a home computer out of commonly available parts and then publish the design specifications. The idea was that "open architecture" would offer third-party hardware and software developers an advantage in developing products for the platform. It was a critical design decision that would have ramifications undreamt of by the team and their company.

Furthermore, rather than develop its own operating system, IBM approached Digital Research, whose CP/M software (Control Program for Microcomputers) seemed like a great fit for the new machine. Developed by Gary Kildall (1942–1994) in 1974, CP/M was a highly portable system that allowed programmers to write software that could run on a variety of different hardware standards. It was the dominant 8-bit operating system for professional applications, boasting powerful software like the *WordStar* (1978, MicroPro International) word processor, the *dBASE* (1980, Ashton-Tate) database, and the *SuperCalc* (1980, Sorcim) spreadsheet. Fortuitously, CP/M had recently been ported to work on Intel's 16-bit 8086 as CP/M-86.

The inside of a fairly well-equipped original IBM PC, model number 5150. It was built like a tank and highly expandable. The standards it introduced were so influential that 30 years later, modern PCs can trace much of their inspiration back to its design.

Day of the Tentacle running on the free **SCUMMVM** emulator, which makes running old Lucasfilm adventures a snap in modern Windows.

Maniac Mansion: Day of the Tentacle (1993, LucasArts)

Dave Grossman and Tim Schafer's *Day of the Tentacle* is a point-and-click graphical adventure game that features zany, irreverent humor, a marvelously outrageous story, and some of the funniest and wittiest gags the genre has to offer. Perhaps *Day of the Tentacle*'s best feature, however, is that it will not allow players to die or get the game into an unwinnable state, unlike its prequel, *Maniac Mansion*, and many of the other games in the genre. This more relaxed approach encouraged exploration and avoided much of the frustration associated with Sierra's classics such as *King's Quest*. The game's enduring legacy is seen by the rapid success of Schafer's crowd-funded *Double Fine Adventure*, which raised over $3.3 million by March 2012 to fund a new point-and-click adventure in a similar style.

A deal between IBM and Digital Research made perfect sense, but the companies famously failed to reach an agreement. There are varying accounts as to what happened when IBM's representatives met with Kildall's wife, Dorothy, who handled her husband's business matters. The usual story goes that she refused to sign a non-disclosure agreement, a matter that the representatives considered a routine bit of paperwork that certainly wasn't worth holding up the process for. The "pointless" delay angered them, so they left in a huff. A more likely scenario is that Dorothy didn't want to sell CP/M for a lump sum with no option for royalties. In any case, the fateful decision led to IBM pursuing other options, and CP/M was soon replaced as the industry standard operating system by Microsoft's MS-DOS.

IBM had already established relations with Bill Gates' fledgling Microsoft company in 1980, requesting a version of the company's popular BASIC interpreter. During the talks, when the 25-year-old Gates heard that IBM hadn't decided on the far more important issue of the operating system, he referred them to Digital Research. Only after the negotiations with the Kildalls had fallen through did he propose his own solution. Acting quickly, Gates purchased the rights to Tim Paterson's QDOS (Quick and Dirty DOS) for $50,000, and repurposed it for IBM's needs. He called that version PC-DOS, but he'd make much more money selling the rebranded MS-DOS to IBM's rival manufacturers. Cleverly, Gates had insisted on a non-exclusive arrangement with IBM, guessing correctly that great hordes of other computer manufacturers would seize the opportunity to license his operating system and use it to create cheaper and/or superior versions of the IBM PC. The insight paid off mightily for Gates, of course, eventually making him the richest man in the world.

Even the system's BIOS, the part of a computer responsible for "booting up" the computer before loading the operating system, was made publicly available. This decision allowed companies such as Columbia Data Products, who introduced the first IBM PC compatible desktop in June 1982, and Compaq, who introduced the first IBM PC compatible transportable in November 1982, to easily reverse-engineer it, thereby legally circumventing IBM's patents.

Shown here is the imposing all-in-one Zenith Z-120, which contained dual microprocessors, allowing it to run both the classic 8-bit version of CP/M (on its 8085 CPU) and the newer 16-bit MS-DOS (on its 8088 CPU). The Z-120 was one of many transitional CP/M-based systems that could also run versions of MS-DOS, but, much to their detriment, were not otherwise hardware or software compatible with IBM's PC.

MechWarrior running on the **DOSBox** emulator.

MechWarrior (1989, Dynamix)

MechWarrior finally gave would-be *BattleTech* fans the chance to pilot their own Mech. Utilizing a first-person perspective with flat-shaded 3D graphics, *MechWarrior* was much more than just a combat game. The story focuses on Gideon Braver Vandenburg, who must raise a force of mechs to avenge his murdered family and take his rightful place on the throne of Ander's Moon. The story and role-playing elements make this title stand out compared to other games in the robot fighting genre. Flex your myomer muscle and prove you have what it takes to take on Dark Wing.

It took Estridge and his team only 30 days to complete a working model and a little over a year to get the IBM PC ready for production. The 16-bit IBM PC made its debut on August 12, 1981, and retailed for $1565 in its most basic configuration, although it would take at least double that amount to get something usable. Despite a price point that limited its appeal more to large businesses than consumers, there was enough demand to make the IBM PC the most profitable computer IBM ever produced. By 1984, IBM had sold more than 750,000 IBM PCs. Tragically, Philip Estridge and his wife Mary Ann died in a plane crash at Dallas-Fort Worth International Airport in 1985. Philip and his wife were only 48 and 46 years old, respectively.

Estridge and his team's vision and commitment to expansion and versatility are evident in their design of the IBM PC. It was based on an Intel 8088 processor and shipped with anywhere from 16KB to 64KB of RAM, a cassette-oriented form of BASIC in ROM, and five expansion slots. Complementing the system's sleek, heavy-duty industrial design was a weighted keyboard with highly responsive "clicky" keys that serious typists greatly appreciated and whose design is still admired today. It was exactly the kind of efficient, no-nonsense personal computer that you'd expect from the company that brought you the Selectric typewriter.

Customers could choose from a low-cost Monochrome Display Adapter (MDA) card or spring for the Color Graphics Adapter (CGA). An IBM PC equipped with a CGA card could display a maximum of four colors (from a palette of eight) in 320 × 200 resolution. The CGA card also enabled a monochrome resolution

How to change a forecast.

To help weather the storm of economic variables, a person could use the IBM Personal Computer.

With software like VisiCalc* (really an "electronic worksheet") you can calculate up to 63 columns and 254 rows of numbers — implementing formulas and changing labels as you go.

You can also plan on the IBM Personal Computer to help create a sales forecast. Spot a trend. Test a budget. And aid you on the quest for the right answer to "what if?"

Now, don't wait for a rainy day to visit an authorized IBM Personal Computer dealer.

You'll learn that the quality, power and performance of this tool is what you'd expect from IBM. The price isn't. **IBM***

**The IBM Personal Computer
A tool for modern times**

For a store near you (or information from IBM about quantity purchases) call (800) 447-4700. In Illinois, (800) 322-4400. In Alaska or Hawaii, (800) 447-0890.   * VisiCalc is a trademark of VisiCorp

10 July 1982 Popular Computing   Circle 44 on Inquiry card

An ad from the July 1982 issue of **Popular Computing** featuring Charlie Chaplin's Little Tramp likeness, and a play on words for his famous 1936 movie **Modern Times**. Despite the inference of its spokesperson's ad copy, IBM's PC was far from the most powerful tool of its era, but its open architecture meant that vital components, like graphical display adapters, sound cards, and many other types of expansions could easily be swapped in and out, greatly expanding its capabilities.

of 640 × 200. Hercules Computer Technology released a more sophisticated monochrome card called the Hercules Graphics Card in 1982, which soon became a competing standard to the MDA. The Hercules displayed much sharper text and higher resolution (720 × 348) than the MDA, and, more important, could render graphics. In "text mode," the IBM PC could display 25 lines of as many as 80 characters.

Sound hardware, unfortunately, was more whimper than bang, limited to the computer's internal "PC Speaker." The PC Speaker could produce only one tone at a time, with waveforms generated by a Programmable Interval Timer. Because of its simplicity and rather unimpressive abilities, many users referred to it as a beeper, squawker, or buzzer. Cards to enhance the sound of the IBM PC would remain scarce until the late 1980s, when support for AdLib, Sound Blaster, and other add-ons became more common in computer games. In the meantime, however, gamers on these systems would suffer severe audio envy.

Data storage was initially delegated to cassette tapes, but floppy drives were also available. The all-important hard drives arrived later via expansion cards, and became standard on later models for internal storage.

IBM sold plenty of its own PCs and offered several more innovations, but Estridge's decision to make the system open was great for the platform, not for the company. Essentially, Estridge and Gates had opened the door to rival manufacturers, who could "clone" the IBM PC and compete directly for its share of the market.

Within a few years of its introduction, hundreds of other companies hawking IBM compatibles would soon appear on the market, and so began the famous "clone wars" that continue to this day. Although at the time some manufacturers preferred to offer more feature-rich, proprietary configurations at the expense of compatibility, the clone wars eventually drove down the cost of these systems and fostered massive third-party development to a merged standard. Although it's obviously evolved since then, that same standard is more or less what we find in today's PCs.

Indeed, the advanced graphics, sound, and 3D acceleration that distinguish the modern PC are the result of a long history of third-party manufacturers one-upping one another to sell more expansion cards, or boards designed to enhance the base system, as well as more central components such as motherboards and CPUs. The horde of third-party hardware and computer developers gave the IBM compatible platform a huge advantage over closed, proprietary, and more legally defendable systems, such as those from Commodore, Apple, or Tandy, which tried to block outside competition and cloning. Gradually, and perhaps inevitably, these strategies lost out. The IBM compatible eventually reigned supreme, even as IBM itself gradually faded from the scene.

Because the early MS-DOS systems lacked sophisticated graphics and sound capabilities, most users sought them out for serious business applications rather than games. After all, IBM was legendary for its suit-and-tie, no-nonsense corporate culture, and the idea that their PCs would eventually dominate the computer games industry would have seemed ludicrous. The IBM PC was intended to boost a company's bottom line, not provide the latest arcade thrills. Furthermore, since almost all business applications at this time were text-based, there was little need for fancy graphics, and even less for quality sound. This situation would change, albeit slowly and grudgingly, as more consumers purchased these relatively expensive machines they were using in the office for home use. Of course, the multimedia explosion of the 1990s proved

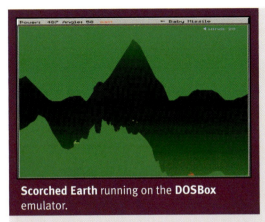

Scorched Earth running on the **DOSBox** emulator.

Scorched Earth (1991, Wendell T. Hicken)

Like the original version of *Doom*, *Scorched Earth* was not a commercial release, but was rather published and distributed as shareware, giving gamer's a nice sampling of the game before potential purchase. Based on the "artillery" genre, players take turns firing at each other's tanks, inputting angle and power. What really sets the game apart, though, is the myriad of weapons of mass destruction at your disposal. The game's small footprint also made it easy to install on your school's PCs, leading to plenty of lunchtime gaming fun with your friends. Who could forget the first time they took out their enemies (along with themselves!) in a MIRV gone horribly wrong? If you like this game, check out the far simpler, turn-based artillery game, *Gorillas* (1991), which was written in the *QBasic* BASIC programming language, both of which were first included with MS-DOS 5. In *Gorillas*, two of the title creatures hurl explosive bananas at each other from the top of skyscrapers.

decisive in this regard, quickly bringing the audiovisual capabilities of DOS-based machines up to snuff with their more game-centric competition.

Despite (or perhaps because of) their buttoned-down reputation, IBM unrolled a humorous and lighthearted marketing campaign for its Personal Computer, featuring a Charlie Chaplain impersonator trying to buy a personal computer. Their television commercials stressed the urgency of buying a personal computer and the ensuing customer confusion—perhaps a stab at the company's many rivals, many of whose MS-DOS-based machines were not entirely compatible with IBM's. IBM assured customers that its computers were the safest bet in the midst of so much upheaval and uncertainty. Another noteworthy IBM television spot of this era features the members of Spinal Tap, the satirical and fictitious heavy metal band. Clearly, IBM was targeting a wide and diverse demographic!

Although the IBM PC was ostensibly a machine designed purely for business, commercial games for the IBM PC and, by extension, the IBM Compatible, were becoming increasingly available.[1] However, since the majority of these computers offered graphics and sound shamed by even the cheapest videogame console, most of these games seem primitive compared to those on contemporary systems. The games that thrived on the system were those that took best advantage of what the platform did have to offer—raw 16-bit processing power. Like most computer manufacturers of the time, IBM published a variety of its own software, including games. One such disk was the text-based *Zyll* (1984), which was an innovative one- or two-player simultaneous game that combined some of the best elements from the adventure and role-playing genres in one seamless experience.

Although the same sorts of ASCII and text-only games available for the CP/M platform were also available for MDA-equipped PCs, anyone who was remotely serious about gaming on the platform purchased a CGA card. The CGA card had two palette options: black, white, cyan, and

---

[1]   As we'd expect given the Loguidice Law. It takes much more than crummy audiovisuals and a reputation for serious business to keep gamers off a platform.

magenta; or black, red, green, and yellow. With palettes intended for bar graphs and pie charts rather than arcade games, they certainly give CGA games a distinctive, if garish, look.

One of the most popular (and arguably best) of the CGA games was *Microsoft Flight Simulator* 1.00 (1982), which offered smoother animation and finer detail on the PC than on any other machine. For the time, it was a highly realistic virtual experience, offering a fully rendered three-dimensional environment and even weather and day/night simulation.

In 1983, SSI released its strategy games *The Warp Factor*, *The Battle of the Bulge: Tigers in the Snow*, and *Epidemic!* for CGA-equipped systems. Broderbund supported the platform in 1985 with the first game in its *The Ancient Art of War* strategy series and Spectrum Holobyte with the popular submarine simulator *Gato*.

Microsoft Flight Simulator on the IBM PC offered an unprecedented level of realism and sold well on the platform. Along with **Lotus 1-2-3,** Microsoft's game was one of the best ways to torture test a clone's true level of compatibility with the PC standard. Shown here is the second version of the game running in the **DOSBox** emulator.

Adventure games were also well represented on the platform. Sierra released many of its highly popular graphical adventure games for the system, including *King's Quest* (1984) and *Leisure Suit Larry* (1987). Fans of role-playing games had plenty to keep them busy, too,

Sid Meier's Civilization running on the **DOS-Box** emulator.

Sid Meier's Civilization (1991, MPS Labs)

This turn-based strategy game boasts one of the most impressive scopes in the history of the genre, allowing players to guide a civilization's development from the Stone Age to the Space Age and beyond. *Civilization* has received an ongoing series of official sequels and several spinoffs, but the original game still has its charms. How many of us learned what we know of history and geography by playing *Civilization*? The game won countless awards and is widely considered one of the most influential and important computer games of all time. For a variation on the theme, check out *Sid Meier's Colonization* (1994), a turn-based strategy game based around the early European colonization of the New World, where the player is tasked with establishing a self-sufficient colony.

including such hits as Interplay's *The Bard's Tale* (1987) and Sir-Tech's *The Wizardry Trilogy* (1987). Arcade-style games, although painfully primitive-looking compared with their counterparts on other platforms, were nevertheless abundant on CGA-era IBM PCs and compatibles. By 1982, a 15-year-old named Gary Kuperberg had cloned *Pac-Man* for the system, calling his game *PC-MAN.* Kuperberg also ported a game called *Paratrooper*, a game reminiscent of Atari's classic arcade *Missile Command.* By 1984, many arcade or action games had been officially ported to the IBM PC from other platforms. Some of the better known titles include the popular martial arts game *Karateka* (1986) by Jordan Mechner. Other notable ports include Sega's isometric arcade shooter *Zaxxon* (1984), Muse Software's stealth game *Castle Wolfenstein* (1984), and Atari's *Marble Madness*, which was ported from the arcade in 1986. In each case, the audiovisuals were vastly inferior to those available in the arcade or more arcade-friendly home computers such as the Commodore 64.

Later Models and the Attack of the Clones

IBM followed up the IBM PC with the IBM Personal Computer XT (model 5160) in 1983 and the AT (model 5170) in 1984. The XT was a high-powered computer designed for business professionals. It shipped with 128KB of RAM, a 5.25-inch floppy disk drive, and a 10MB hard drive. The XT also offered three more expansion slots than its older brother. The AT was built on Intel's 80286 (286) microprocessor, which allowed the AT to run at 6MHz (later models ran at 8MHz). The AT also featured a 20MB hard drive, albeit one that was initially buggy and prone to error (the drives had a 25–35 percent failure rate), and a high-density floppy disk drive that could store as much as 1.2MB on a 5.25-inch disk. Unfortunately, using standard low-density disks in the high-density drive led to all sorts of problems, and the floppy disks themselves were hard to tell apart. Eminently expandable, the AT could handle as much as 16MB of RAM. According to popular legend, IBM purposefully slowed down the AT to 6MHz to stay consistent with their release cycle of planned obsolescence.

The IBM PCjr is another one of those quirky entries in the history of computers that almost defies explanation. Introduced in November 1983, but not released until March of 1984, the PCjr was IBM's attempt to market a more game-friendly home computer, one that would defy the stereotype that IBM could only produce boring and expensive business machines. Although IBM had enjoyed tremendous success with its high-end business computer, the IBM PC, its PCjr (nicknamed "Peanut" by IBM engineers) would face much tougher competition. The life of the IBM PCjr was short-lived,

Left: The PCjr seemed like a good idea on paper, but was a miserable, mismanaged flop. Right: The Tandy 1000, which implemented many of the same features but was able to avoid many of the missteps, enjoyed a much greater level of success, soon becoming its own standard.

particularly after the introduction of similarly capable Enhanced Graphics Adapter (EGA) graph-ics and the arrival of cheap IBM compatibles that could not only match, but exceed most of the PCjr's capabilities.

On one level, the PCjr had much in common with the best-selling and revolutionary IBM PC. Both were based on Intel's 8088 microprocessor and ran versions of PC-DOS. Accordingly, some of the software written for the IBM PC would run on the PCjr. However, the differences between the two machines are more significant than the similarities. For instance, its unusual "user-friendly" design required users to install expansion packs, or "sidecars," on the side of the machine rather than internally, a fact that rendered it incompatible with the vast array of popular add-ons for the IBM PC.

While these expansions could be daisy-chained, the end result was a fairly wide and cumber-some machine, similar to what Texas Instruments users had to endure on the TI-99/4 and 4A before the introduction of the Peripheral Expansion Box (PEB). In addition, the more sidecars added to the formerly svelte system, the more likely a power sidecar would be needed, creating the need for additional outlets since the PCjr's own power supply was not designed to handle excessive loads.

Star Control II running on the **DOSBox** emulator.

Star Control II (1992, Toys for Bob)

Paul Reiche III and Fred Ford's epic *Star Control II* improved upon its predecessor with a story-driven campaign and resource-gathering elements inspired by Binary Systems' 1986 masterpiece *Starflight*. With some of the most creative and memorable alien races you'll ever meet, *Star Control II* showcases its designers unique personalities and humor with fun 2D space dogfighting. Watch out for the Spathi Eluder's Backward Utilized Tracking Torpedo (BUTT) missiles! For an earlier game with similar gameplay, but with more of a focus on role-playing, be sure to check out Karl Buiter's *Sentinal World I: Future Magic* (1989, Electronic Arts).

Perhaps IBM's most infamous innovation with the PCjr was the choice to ship the unit with a wireless, infrared chiclet keyboard with widely separated and raised keys. While the thinking behind this move might have been reasonable and even progressive—the keys were fully pro-grammable and would allow software makers to include useful keyboard templates—it was a fiasco. Besides being difficult to type on, the AA-battery-powered wireless keyboard had a very limited range (IBM claimed it was 6 feet, but users discovered it was more like 2 or 3 feet). Reviewers and users alike slammed it. Although IBM soon issued a conventional (full-stroke) version of the keyboard for the PCjr, the affair no doubt cost the computer significant credibility in a competitive marketplace.

Nonetheless, the PCjr had several advantages for gamers over the IBM PC. Most importantly, it had better graphics and sound. It was capable of displaying 16 colors in a typical resolution of 160 × 200, and its audio chip, designed by Texas Instruments, was capable of three channels of mono sound. The PCjr also had two cartridge slots and two joystick ports. The cartridge slots not only allowed the PCjr to instantly load games, it also helped it run powerful productivity applications—like *Lotus 1-2-3*, a best-selling spreadsheet program—in less memory by using both of these ports simultaneously.

The PCjr was offered in two packages. For $669, purchasers got the 4860-004, which included 64K of RAM. For $600 more, they could get a PCjr with 128K of RAM and an internal 360K 5.25-inch floppy disk drive. At these prices, the PCjr was simply not as competitive as it needed to be to achieve dominance in the home computer market. A complete Commodore 64 or Atari 8-bit computer system could be had for half the price. In fact, even contemporary sources were ambivalent about IBM's chances, with David Kay, marketing product manager for Kaypro, for instance, making the following statement in the March 1984 issue of *Creative Computing*: "Frankly, the Commodore 64 is a far better computer, but the PCjr is slick looking and has IBM's name on it. Even so, I don't think there's a market for it."

Furthermore, Apple had built up quite a bit of marketing momentum with its sleek and recently introduced Apple IIc, and IBM was slow to catch up. Charles Eicher, an employee at a ComputerLand store in Los Angeles, explained that at one point the Apple IIc store displays were running a colorful and attractive demo to lure customers, but the IBM PCjr models were switched off. Apple had shipped its demo on a floppy disk, which could be easily backed up, but IBM's demo for the PCjr was on a proprietary ROM cartridge. Since the store was far more concerned about someone stealing a ROM cartridge than an easily replaced floppy disk, the staff demonstrated the computer only by request. IBM eventually discovered this problem and rushed out a demonstration disk just before Christmas 1984, but it was just one more example of the megacorporation's failure to understand the market it was trying to enter.

IBM's advertising campaign for the PCjr focused on the simplicity of the setup, suggesting that even a small child would have no problem setting it up and operating it. It was the computer that was "easy for everyone." An IBM booklet from late 1983 describes "junior" as a "tireless worker and playmate," a "bright little addition to the family" of IBM home computers. A television spot had the familiar Little Tramp character pushing a PCjr in a baby stroller. This cutesy approach seemed pandering to some critics. As Steve Jobs remarked at the time (quoted in Owen Linzmeyer's 1994 *The Mac Bathroom Reader*), "I expected the computer to wet all over the television set."

Several interesting products were eventually released that improved the PCjr's usefulness after IBM ceased production and more specific support began to dry up. For instance, Racor Computer Products, Inc.'s PCID cartridge fools software into identifying the PCjr as a standard IBM PC, increasing compatibility, and a motherboard modification makes the PCjr compatible with the software, particularly many of the games, designed for the Tandy 1000 series of computers. Other aftermarket products gave the PCjr access to additional memory, disk drives, and even hard drives, making the system a more professional PC compatible.

The most historically important game released for the PCjr was Sierra On-Line's famous *King's Quest* (1984), published by IBM. It was a game that single-handedly redefined the graphical adventure game and helped spawn several megafranchises that still endure today. Indeed, the paradigm Sierra set with this game was essentially unchallenged until Trilobyte's *The 7th Guest* (1993) and Cyan's *Myst* (1994) conclusively demonstrated the startling potential of CD-ROM technology to make expansive, photo-realistic games. With full 16-color animated graphics and three-channel sound, *King's Quest* demonstrated the PCjr's superiority over CGA-equipped IBM PCs and compatibles, setting a high standard that few other systems of the day could match.

There were several games released on cartridge for the PCjr, including Gibelli Software's *Mouser* (1983), a *Pac-Man*-like multiscreen game in which players manipulate the walls of the maze; Sierra On-Line's *Crossfire* (1983), a hybrid maze and shooter game; and Activision's conversions of its popular *Pitfall II* (1983) and *River Raid* (1983) games. Imagic, another big supporter of the platform, released its most graphically lush version of *Demon Attack* (1984) for the system.

On disk, Imagic offered *Touchdown Football* (1984), a highly playable arcade football game that was notable for its use of digitized sound. Sierra On-Line released *Championship Boxing* (1984), a sports game known for its detailed simulation of its subject matter.

Tandy Corporation offered a clone of the PCjr (sans cartridge ports) called the Tandy 1000, which was released in late 1984, not too long before IBM officially pulled the plug on the PCjr in early 1985. Fortunately, in addition to taking steps to improve compatibility with the IBM PC, Tandy proved much more successful than IBM in executing and marketing its system, creating its own "Tandy compatible" standard in the process. Ironically, Tandy was better able to fulfill the potential of the PCjr's technology than IBM itself, mirroring how IBM's main PC series would also eventually lose out to clone systems. In fact, a forward-looking statement by industry analyst Barbara Isgur, in the March 1984 issue of *Creative Computing*, predicted a variation on just such a possibility: "The IBM home computer will probably establish the standard operating system for the home market as it has in business. So even if the PCjrs have gone into the closet, I think that as the software continues to evolve and increase, they will be brought out."

Why was Tandy able to succeed where IBM had failed? There are several possible explanations. First, Tandy was able to lean on the thousands of Radio Shack stores all over the country to help promote, support, and sell the computers. Second, Tandy already had a large and loyal user base for its TRS-80 and Color Computer (CoCo) computers who were willing and able to upgrade. Third, the 1000 corrected two of the worst problems of the PCjr: it had a full-travel keyboard and internal expansion. Last, and perhaps most important, Tandy was able to respond quickly and effectively to the demise of the PCjr, quietly removing all references to the doomed computer in its marketing materials while playing up its compatibility with the IBM PC.

TIE Fighter running on the **DOSBox** emulator.

Star Wars: TIE Fighter
(1994, LucasArts)

This popular space combat simulator puts you in the cockpit of the famous *TIE Fighter* and other craft from the Imperial Navy. A tour de force in graphics and gameplay, *TIE Fighter* is still considered among the best *Star Wars* games ever made and simply a must-have for any DOS games collection. May the dark side of the force be with you!

Tandy's built-in graphics and sound capabilities offered a standard that competed successfully with IBM's AT and IBM compatibles equipped with EGA cards. Once IBM released its VGA card in 1987, and Ad Lib's and Creative's sound cards became more commonplace, Tandy lost its edge and finally gave in to other standards, becoming just another clone until the line was ultimately discontinued.

Like the PCjr, the Tandy 1000 was based on Intel's 8088 processor with 128K of expandable RAM. It featured 16 on-screen colors, with most games displaying in 160 × 200 resolution. Sound was output over three channels in mono. The unit had a built-in 5.25-inch 360K floppy disk drive and an extra bay for a second. Software was offered on 5.25-inch floppy disks, although by 1987 Tandy was offering systems with 3.5-inch drives. Its built-in game ports were compatible with controllers for the CoCo line. The Tandy 1000 enjoyed fairly good compatibility with most MS-DOS software, though the enhanced graphics and sound technology worked only when specifically targeted by developers.

Tandy packaged a proprietary menu-based application suite with the 1000 called *Deskmate*. This surprisingly useful integrated package included a word processor, spreadsheet, calendar, and database application. Everything fit on a single 360KB floppy disk. Some Tandy 1000-series computers even had *DeskMate* (and DOS) built into ROM for faster access, much like the far less useful *3 Plus 1* suite in the failed Commodore Plus/4.

Later models include the EX, a compact 1000 with built-in keyboard, and the HX, with built-in keyboard and 3.5-inch floppy drive. The TX, released in August 1987, featured Intel's 16-bit 80286 CPU and came standard with 640K of RAM, while the SX was a cheaper model based on the 8088 that came with dual 5.25-inch floppy drives. After the TX, models (SL and TL) became increasingly incompatible with the original PCjr-like specifications and more like regular IBM compatibles, culminating in the R-series, which, of all the original features, still only supported the Tandy sound standard.

The Tandy 1000 benefited from its compatibility with the IBM PC and XT and the swathe of titles for these systems. However, these machines were limited to CGA graphics and the PC speaker and thus couldn't take advantage of the 1000's more sophisticated sound and display capabilities. Once the Tandy computers proved themselves a sales success within a few short years, an increasing number of top game publishers made sure to include specific support for the platform when creating their PC games, including Sierra On-Line, Broderbund, Electronic Arts, Epyx, and Microprose.

Since Sierra was familiar with the 1000's technology from its pioneering work on the PCjr, the company naturally started supporting the platform beginning in 1985, releasing its classic graphical adventure game series like *King's Quest*, *Space Quest*, and *Leisure Suit Larry*, among many of its other titles. Broderbund offered the platform hit *Lode Runner* (1984), its popular *Carmen Sandiego* edutainment games (first release, 1985), and the city-planning classic *SimCity* (1989). Electronic Arts offered sports titles (*John Madden Football II*, 1991), strategy role-playing games (*Starflight*, 1986), and flight simulators (*Chuck Yeager's Air Combat*, 1991), to name just a few. In short, with its standard audiovisual prowess and direct joystick support, Tandy's systems offered the best overall gaming experience for IBM compatible users until VGA and sound cards became industry standards in the 1990s.

Nevertheless, with the arrival of the Enhanced Graphics Adapter, or the EGA card, things began to look brighter for gamers on the IBM PC line and their compatibles. The EGA card,

designed for the IBM PC AT, was capable of displaying up to 16 colors at a relatively high resolution (as well as the modes available to the older CGA and MDA cards). No longer were PC users getting mostly ports from other systems as they did with CGA, but were actually becoming a primary platform. Furthermore, the slow emergence of industry standards for sound with the arrival of the

Where in the World is Carmen Sandiego?, shown here running on **DOSBox,** is one of the most successful edutainment titles of all time, spawning a multimedia franchise. The game shipped with a copy of **The World Almanac and Book of Facts,** which contained useful clues for getting through the game. While the Apple II version was the original, like many other games series, **Carmen** saw its greatest success on the PC platform.

AdLib Music Synthesizer Card promised liberation from the PC's seriously inadequate internal speaker. Meanwhile, Intel had released the 80386, a 32-bit processor eventually capable of speeds of up to 40MHz. In short, a perfect storm was forming that would soon alter the face of computer gaming forever, and the very name "PC" would come to mean an IBM compatible computer running MS-DOS (or a compatible variant) and later Microsoft Windows, which, although the first version was released relatively quietly in November 1985, would come to face down a multitude of competitors over the years. Ultimately, by 1990, the oft-cloned PC platform had taken over 80 percent of the market on its relentless march toward ubiquity.

Perhaps the best place to start is by revisiting IBM's PC AT and PCjr. As noted earlier, the PCjr had quickly become an albatross around IBM's neck and dropped out of production—although Tandy resurrected the unit's advanced graphics and audio standards in its Tandy 1000 series of computers. However, IBM's AT equipped with an EGA

There were literally hundreds of different IBM compatibles to choose from in all shapes, sizes, and levels of compatibility. Shown here is a 1984 ad for the interesting looking NCR PC 4, which boasted of its gold standard level of compatibility with programs like **Lotus 1-2-3.** Even NCR spokesperson Dom DeLuise looks amazed!

card promised users a serious computer with serious graphics—better graphics (higher resolution), in fact, than the PCjr. However, by 1986, IBM had begun to lose its edge, gradually falling behind the many companies manufacturing PC clones. Compaq, ever on the forefront of the "clone wars," released a PC based on Intel's new 80386 in 1986, beating even IBM to the powerful new processor. Other PC manufacturers would follow, gradually lowering the price and bringing these systems within reach of a slowly expanding user community. These machines tended to be referred to by the last three digits of their processor; that is, a 286 or 386 computer meant PC models based on Intel's 80286 and 80386, respectively. Eventually, other manufacturers began cloning the EGA card, and some, like ATI Technologies and Paradise, even improved upon them. Although the price of a high-end PC was still more than twice the price of Commodore's Amiga or Atari's ST, the gap was steadily closing. Thus, even as early as 1986, the PC and compatibles constituted the largest single portion—greater than 55 percent—of the home computer market, before the year was out.[2]

Ultima VII running on the DOSBox emulator.

Ultima VII: The Black Gate
(1992, ORIGIN Systems)

Richard Garriott's *Ultima* series may have debuted on the Apple II platform, but it arguably reached its zenith on DOS with this seminal title. Known for its highly detailed isometric graphics and amazing depth of interactivity, *Ultima VII* is also a collector's dream, with a cloth map and triangular trinket called the Fellowship medallion. *Ultima VII* is available from *Good Old Games* (www. gog.com), which includes PDF versions of the manuals, guides, maps, and cluebooks. If you're a fan of *Ultima* or just role-playing games in general, it's impossible to go wrong with this 1992 classic.

The Decline of the IBM PC

IBM's own role in the story begins to peter off in April 1987, with the release of its Personal System/2 (PS/2) line of computers. Essentially, the PS/2 was IBM's effort to repeat the coup it had undertaken with the original IBM PC, but this time keeping things proprietary, or closed, rather than open, to prevent cloning. For years, IBM had steadily been losing market share to clone makers, who were spared the need to expend expensive research and development efforts; they would merely wait until IBM had released a new product, copy it, and offer it for a cut rate. The loopholes that allowed such rampant cloning were the open nature of the architecture (made up of off-the-shelf components) and IBM's non-exclusive license with Microsoft for its operating system (which allowed Microsoft to license the de facto OS to rival manufacturers). To combat this trend, IBM introduced its own OS/2 operating system, which began as a collaboration between Microsoft and IBM, but later became exclusive to the latter when the former decided to focus on refining a resurgent Windows. In any case, the new proprietary hardware and operating

---

2   http://jeremyreimer.com/m-item.lsp?i=137.

system was far more expensive than many other capable MS-DOS-compatible machines, and the bulk of users decided not to migrate. Although the powerful OS/2 operating system received updates for several more years before being discontinued, the lack of specific commercial game development and the rise of Microsoft's Windows never allowed the operating system to gain critical mass acceptance.

Suffice it to say, once IBM let the genie out of the bottle with its original IBM PC, there was no stuffing him back in. The market now belonged to the clone makers—a fact that was being grasped not only by IBM, but also Commodore and Atari, who would release a short-lived run of clones of their own, as well as see a steady release of compatibility options for their proprietary systems. In the words of Charlie Chaplin, "I suppose that's one of the ironies of life—doing the wrong thing at the right moment."

AdLib and SoundBlaster Sound Cards

Although the PCjr and Tandy's 1000 had featured good standard sound capabilities (three mono voices), the typical PC was still limited to the tinny internal speaker, which, despite the occasional clever workarounds, was good for little more than shrill beeps. This situation began to change when a Canadian company called Ad Lib began manufacturing expansion cards that would enhance the computer's sound output. The AdLib Music Synthesizer Card, released in 1987, was built from off-the-shelf parts. It was based on Yamaha's YM3812 sound chip, which allowed the PC to output tunes via FM Synthesis. This technique was optimal from a memory-conservation perspective but inadequate for making realistic sound effects for games. It was only after Creative Labs launched its first Sound Blaster card in November 1989 that such effects were possible. The Sound Blaster was based on the same Yamaha chip, but it also featured a Digital Sound Processor (DSP) that could play back mono sound samples. In addition, the card featured a combined joystick port and MIDI interface. Although there were always competitors offering their own formats, each with varying degrees of official support, both Ad Lib and Creative Labs set industry standards (that others would try to clone) for PC sound that would enable game developers to realistically incorporate music and sound effects into their games.

Wing Commander running on the **DOSBox** emulator.

Wing Commander (1990, ORIGIN Systems)

Chris Roberts' *Wing Commander* is widely considered among the best DOS games, if not one of the best games, period. While everyone marveled at the excellent action during the first-person space combat sequences, they also lauded the award-winning storyline. Later episodes in the series would feature full-motion video, with Mark Hamill of *Star Wars* fame appearing in the third iteration. Fans will want to check out Chris Roberts' *Star Citizen* (2014) game, a crowd-funded spiritual successor to these hits.

As was typically the case, Sierra On-Line was on the cutting edge of PC technology and was one of the first companies to support and recommend that gamers purchase a sound card to get the most out of their games. Other companies soon followed: Interplay with its *Bard's Tale III: Thief of Fate*, Lucasfilm with *Loom*, and Origin Systems with *Times of Lore* (all 1988). However, most early adopters of these sound cards were primarily interested in music composition; it took a few more years before developers and gamers really started taking the cards seriously.

Of course, the product that would eventually tie all of this advanced graphics and sound hardware together was Microsoft's Windows, released in 1985. Originally little more than a graphical front end for MS-DOS, Windows nevertheless boasted simple multitasking capability and, along with competing operating systems (environments) at the time, helped introduce PC users to the mouse. Version 2.0, released in 1987, offered better support for the faster 286 processors and windows that could overlap each other. However, it wasn't until 1990, with the release of Windows 3.0, that the product began to catch on. This third version was optimized for the 386 processor and included a software development kit (SDK) for programmers that made it much easier for them to code for the platform. Computer manufacturers began pre-installing it on their machines, helping to entrench it. Nevertheless, the platform would not become a truly viable choice for gamers or game developers until the release of Microsoft's Windows 95 and companion DirectX standards in 1995, which greatly simplified Windows game programming and efficiency (for more on Windows, see Chapter 3.1).

Although EGA games with PC speaker or even AdLib sound were distinctly inferior in most ways to contemporary games on Commodore's Amiga or Atari's ST platform, the sheer size of the user base was motivation enough for game developers to offer games for the platform. Since the requirements for fast action did not always favor the strengths of the PC at the time, many of the best games continued to be either adventure or role-playing games. For instance, in 1986, Sierra On-Line released *Space Quest I* with support for EGA, and if there had been any doubt before, it disappeared after gamers saw the new card's superiority over CGA. The extra colors and higher resolution made for much sharper detail, a critical feature in a graphical adventure game. Origin Systems also supported EGA with a rerelease of its popular *Ultima I: The First Age of Darkness*. The next year saw four new EGA games, including Interplay's *Bard's Tale* (with the game's sequels supporting it as well). One of the earliest arcade game conversions released with the card in mind was Taito's popular *Arkanoid*, debuting for the EGA specification in 1988.

In 1987 when IBM introduced the backward-compatible VGA card, which allowed games to display 256 colors on-screen in 320 × 200 resolution, the EGA's 16 colors and relatively limited palette seemed rather dated and was slowly phased out as a primary specification. However, even after VGA's establishment as the new standard in the early 1990s, many commercial games still also supported EGA.

The way a game looked on a DOS-based computer varied with the type of graphics card installed. Shown here, left to right, is **Battle Chess** in CGA and EGA running on **DOSBox**. Although no match for the total audiovisual package of the Amiga original, games like **Battle Chess** proved more popular on the PC because of the amazing range of machine configurations supported.

The DOS Community Then and Now

As the dominant platform of the pre-Windows era, naturally there were plenty of user groups, online bulletin board systems (BBSs), clubs, organizations, magazines, and expos dedicated to the IBM PC and compatibles. However, the open nature of the platform meant that no particular hardware manufacturer united the community as a whole. IBM faded relatively quickly from the scene. Indeed, the only glue that really held the sprawling assembly of "IBM compatibles" together was the operating system, MS-DOS.

Relatively few of the millions of purchasers of these machines, however, bought them for gaming purposes—you could get a much better gaming rig from Commodore or Atari for a fraction of the price. As we saw above, IBM's attempt at a more gaming-centric machine, the PCjr, was a fiasco, although Tandy had much more luck with the concept. Of course, these machines also benefited from their association with and presence in thousands of Radio Shack stores, which provided users with a hub for purchasing more hardware and software, as well as meeting fellow enthusiasts.

After the introduction of EGA and then VGA graphics standards, however—and innovative games to showcase their power—the PC seized the computer gaming crown, which it held until well into the Windows era. It was the living embodiment of the idiom, "slow and steady wins the race." Indeed, if anything, PC DOS computers destroyed communities, since eventually all but the most diehard of Atari, Commodore, and Apple fans had abandoned their beloved old machines for a shiny new PC. By the late 1980s, most games were being developed (at least initially) for DOS machines, and by the 1990s, even quality ports for other computers were becoming a rarity.

Collecting for the PC DOS Platform

Collecting old DOS-based machines might seem pointless given the ubiquity of "obsolete" models that were dumped on the market in the wake of Microsoft Windows. There are no doubt still plenty of corporate warehouses stacked floor-to-ceiling with crates of compatibles and all the

X-Com running on the **DOSBox** emulator.

X-Com: UFO Defense (1994, Microprose)

Known as *UFO: Enemy Unknown* in Europe, this 1994 classic by Julian and Nick Gollop puts players at the helm of an organization called X-COM. X-COM has been tasked with countering a massive invasion from outer space, and the player's job is to make the big decisions at X-COM HQ as well as guide individual units in turn-based tactical combat. The challenging and intricately detailed gameplay may make for a steep learning curve, but the fun and addictive gameplay will have you wanting to believe. The game received several sequels and a remake in 2012.

copies of *WordPerfect* and *Lotus 1-2-3* you could ever want. An original IBM PC can, of course, command a higher price than a clone, but even these can be found for a few hundred dollars. An IBM PCjr in good condition can get close to that amount. Tandy 1000-series computers also remain popular, both for the benefits of their own standard and overall compatibility with other classes of PC.

Where the complexity comes in is in building the ideal DOS-based "gaming rig," a machine that can run the broadest range of DOS-games at their best possible specifications. This includes getting just the right type of video or sound card, and maximizing as many of the other specs as possible, without breaking compatibility or era-specific authenticity. It's like a game in and of itself.

Speaking of games, PC DOS game software is among the easiest and cheapest to find on various auction sites, however, as usual, certain deluxe packages and software genres like CRPGs tend to command more of a premium. The earliest games, some of which came in plastic zip bags or demanded very specific PC configurations, also tend to have greater value than when the PC compatible standard exploded in popularity.

Emulating DOS

The best place to start with emulating DOS is *DOSBox*, a free emulator originally developed by Peter Veenstra and Sjoerd van der Berg, and released in 2002. Regularly updated, *DOSBox* is probably the only DOS emulator you're likely to need, and is available for Windows, Mac, Linux, and other platforms. The website www.dosbox.com features downloads and a wiki with all the information you'll need to setup and run the program.

Many users will prefer to use a "frontend" for *DOSBox*. A frontend such as *D-Fend Reloaded* provides a useful GUI to simplify installing and playing games. If you are unfamiliar with DOS's somewhat esoteric command-line interface, you will most likely want to go this route.

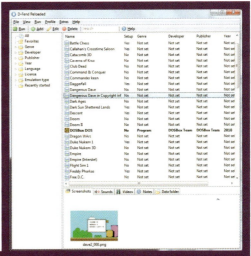

Finding and downloading DOS-era games from the Internet can be tricky. While "abandonware" sites are plentiful, many are ambivalent toward copyright laws and should never be trusted blindly. Thoughtful gamers try to make sure that the game is not legally available from a site like *Good Old Games* (www.gog.com) before hitting the download button on one of those other sites.

DOSBox is a free, full-featured emulator for running old DOS games and applications. It is available for a broad range of systems. Shown here is **DOSBox** running the **D-Fend Reloaded** frontend.

Commodore 64 (1982)

History

There are few vintage home computers as beloved and recognizable as the Commodore 64 (C-64), the best-selling personal computer of all time according to *The Guinness Book of World Records*.[1] Debuting in 1982, the C-64 soon dominated the low-end computer market, enjoying robust support from third-party software and hardware developers into the 1990s. Although the C-64 was no programmer's dream, its low cost and functionality made it a fantastic bargain for consumers. Even at its introductory price of $595, it was still cheaper than the equivalent Apple IIe ($1400) or Atari 1200XL ($599). Furthermore, the C-64's availability at major retail outlets such as Kmart and Sears gave it broad exposure to its target demographic—working-class families who liked the idea of an affordable computer that could also play the latest games and (hopefully) help the kids somehow with their homework. Although the C-64 was finally discontinued in 1994, it still enjoys among the most active and devoted fan communities of all vintage home computers, with dozens of websites catering to the needs of C-64 collectors, retrogamers, and nostalgic fans.

The C-64 is by far Commodore's most famous machine, but it wasn't their first. Indeed, the Commodore PET, introduced in 1977, was part of the original trinity of machines released that year (along with the Apple II and the TRS-80). The PET featured an all-in-one design that included a built-in monitor, keyboard, and cassette drive (called the Datassette). The sturdy, sheet-metal housing made it a popular choice for schools, where it competed squarely with Apple, whose founders had approached Commodore earlier with their prototype. Commodore's infamously cost-conscious founder, Jack Tramiel, however, declined Jobs' offer, then challenged his own engineers to create a cheaper machine along the same lines. The result was the PET.

The Commodore 64 is the best-selling single home computer of all time.

---

[1] Unfortunately, various factors have contributed to the official number being difficult for historians to determine. Sales have been reported by various sources as anywhere between 12 and 30 million. Even taking the lowest number, it's still more than any other single computer.

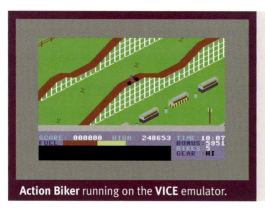

Action Biker running on the **VICE** emulator.

Action Biker (Mastertronic, 1985)

This isometric motorcycle action/adventure game stars "Clumsy Colin," a mascot for a tapioca snack Skips, popular in the UK (but unknown in the US!). Licensing aside, anyone can have fun driving the motorcycle around the map, collecting upgrades while avoiding obstacles, ramping, and even scaling up roller coaster tracks. Legendary C-64 SID composer Rob Hubbard did the music, an earworm that will haunt you for weeks on end. Who needs tapioca?

The PET line was followed by the VIC-20 in 1981. The direct ancestor of the C-64, the VIC-20 was a smashing success, selling millions of units and establishing Commodore's reputation for cheap but versatile home computers. Several ads for the system starred *Star Trek*'s Captain Kirk (William Shatner), who beamed in to ask consumers why they'd buy a "videogame system" when they could have a computer for the same price. Obviously, Shatner wasn't talking about the Atari VCS, which was at least a hundred bucks cheaper, but the Atari 400, the "kid friendly" home computer that would compete directly with the VIC at the major retailers. Despite Atari's own desire to distance its home computer line from its videogame consoles (see Chapter 1.4), Commodore was all too happy to exploit the ambiguity.

However, despite the VIC's enormous success, Commodore was just getting started. Work soon began on the "VIC-40," the machine that would become the C-64. It was designed by several of the same engineers who'd worked on the VIC-20, and even used the same case from when the now-famous beige "breadbox" version was introduced. Although the early models closely resembled their predecessor, the C-64 differed where it mattered, with 64K of RAM (as opposed to the VIC's 5K), a MOS 6510 processor, and the ability to display up to 40 columns and 25 lines of text in 16 on-screen colors (though it was capable of higher resolution, almost all of the games for the C-64 ran at 320 × 200 resolution). The C-64's designers carefully studied and borrowed ideas

freely from rival machines, which included Mattel's Intellivision, the Atari 800, and the Texas Instruments 99/4A. "We tried to get a feel for what these companies could do in the future by extrapolating from their current technology," Charles Winterble said in a March 1985 article for *IEEE Spectrum* magazine. "That made it clear what the graphics capabilities of *our* machine had to be."

The Commodore VIC-20 was a great bargain machine that helped pave the way for the Commodore 64, and provided "inspiration" for everything from its case to its power supply to its interactions with peripherals.

While no one disputes the brilliance of its designers, the C-64 owes much of its success to company founder Tramiel, a Holocaust survivor. Tramiel founded the company back in 1954 to make typewriters, then adding machines. After a trip to Japan, however, he switched to electronic calculators, eventually rising to the top of that market before Texas Instruments took over with cheaper devices. Tramiel would learn from the experience, though, recognizing how "vertical integration," or owning the companies that make the various components of a single product, can keep costs low and competitors at bay.

In 1976 he purchased MOS Technologies, a prominent chip manufacturer. This acquisition gave Commodore a decisive edge in the home computer business, since they now had an in-house chip-fabrication capability that allowed them to design and debug circuitry rapidly and with great precision. They could also avoid the markup suffered by their competition, who had to rely on other companies for their chips. Tramiel also guessed correctly that the cost of memory (DRAM) would drop substantially by the time the C-64 was ready for production, and insisted that it ship with 64K standard. Tramiel also knew how to work the Consumer Electronics Show (CES) circuit, wooing journalists and software publishers to support the platform.

Mail Order Monsters running on the **VICE** emulator.

Mail Order Monsters (Electronic Arts, 1985)

Evan Robinson, Paul Reiche III, and Nicky Robinson are the brains behind this wonderful monster combat game. Long before *Pokémon*, *Mail Order Monsters* let players breed and genetically modify ferocious beasts and then use them to battle it out against the AI or another player in three different modes. As with all of Electronic Arts' early publications, the packaging for the game is also a treat, featuring photos of plastic models built specifically for the purpose. Paul Reiche III would go to design *Skylanders: Spyro's Adventure*, a best-selling game and toy system that can trace a lot of its inspiration back to this 1985 classic. If you enjoy this game, check out Rick Koenig's *Racing Destruction Set*, which came out the same year and lets you create your own tracks and battle against another player in heated, highly configurable split screen, isometric races.

Perhaps Tramiel's key contribution, however, was insisting that the C-64 be made as cheaply as possible. Wherever possible, he ordered his engineers to cut corners, especially when dealing with issues that would never be encountered by the majority of owners. The cost-cutting was especially evident to anyone trying to program using the built-in BASIC, which lacks commands for directly controlling the graphic and sound chips. According to Robert Yannes, one of the C-64's designers, "That was an obvious part of the Commodore philosophy: you don't waste money on things that make the product more expensive and that the majority of buyers aren't going to use."[2] Unlike Steve Wozniak, who built the Apple II with programmers firmly in mind, Tramiel barely gave them a second thought. The upshot was that even after the C-64 had become

---

[2]   See Tekla S. Perry and Paul Wallich, "Design Case History: The Commodore 64," *IEEE Spectrum*, March 1985.

the dominant platform, many game designers did their work on an Apple II, leaving the cumbersome task of adapting their code for the C-64 to other programmers.

A key factor in the C-64's success was their availability alongside Atari's computers in retail outlets like Kmart and Sears. Tramiel tended to put the needs of major retailers first, even when it meant screwing over "mom and pop" Commodore dealers. As Brian Bagnall recounts in his book *Commodore: A Company on the Edge* (2010), Tramiel had a habit of dropping prices suddenly without warning his specialty dealers, forcing them to sell off their inventories at a grievous loss. Still, the terrific exposure offered by these big retailers gave Commodore a huge advantage over many of its rivals like Apple, whose hardware and software were only available at computer stores. The strategy also reveals Tramiel's determination to truly make a computer for the masses—you didn't need to go to a special store and talk to a certified dealer to buy a C-64 or software to run it.

Although the C-64 was equipped with a cartridge slot, most early adopters loaded and saved data from cassette. Although cassettes remained popular in Europe and other countries, by the mid-1980s most C-64 owners in North America had adopted the 1541 floppy disk drive. Notoriously slow, loud, and unreliable, the 1541 was nevertheless much faster than loading programs from cassette tapes. In any case, many users also purchased acceler-

Shown here is the Commodore 1530 Datasette (left) and Commodore 1541 floppy drive (right). The floppy drive was larger, louder, and more expensive than the tape drive, but also faster. Unfortunately for Commodore fans, due to a poorly implemented serial bus, the 1541 was still far slower than disk drives for competing systems, creating a whole aftermarket of "speed up" solutions.

ators like Epyx's *Fast Load Cartridge*, which sped up the loading of some software by many factors. Again, Commodore competed aggressively in the price war, offering the 1541 for $400. Thus, a would-be home computer owner could purchase a computer with a disk drive from Commodore for half the price of an Apple IIe without a drive. For millions of consumers, the choice was obvious.

Indeed, Commodore's ferocious campaign to keep costs low may have played a role in the Great Videogame Crash, especially after the company introduced a $100 rebate to anyone willing to trade in their old computer or console for the purchase of a C-64.[3] A later price drop to $200 drove their rival Texas Instruments (TI-99/4A) clean out of the market segment, providing sweet revenge for Tramiel. Ironically, Texas Instruments had failed to leverage their own chip facilities to drive down costs as they did during the calculator wars, instead buying off-the-shelf parts at great expense. It was an inexplicable mistake that Tramiel was all too happy to exploit.

In any case, even if your primary interest was gaming, it was hard to argue that the C-64 wasn't a better value than a dedicated game console such as the Atari 2600 or Mattel Intellivision.

Naturally, software and hardware developers were eager to support the platform. The website *Lemon 64* (www.lemon64.com), which caters to the C-64 emulation crowd, offers over 4000

---

[3] The most popular trade-in was the Timex Sinclair 1000, an underpowered budget computer, which by that time could be found for $50 or less!

games for download. Compare that to the *Virtual Apple II* site, whose fairly comprehensive selection of Apple II games is limited to around 1500 disk images. It's really no wonder that the C-64 remained the dominant home computing platform for so long, even after rival machines (including Commodore's own Amiga systems) far surpassed its audiovisual and processing capabilities.

Mancopter running on the **VICE** emulator.

Mancopter
(Datasoft, 1984)

Mancopter was programmed by Scott Spanburg, who had earlier ported the arcade game *Pooyan* to the C-64. *Mancopter* puts players behind the pedals of a self-propelled helicopter, in which they compete in a heated race across the ocean. While speed is key, players can also get ahead by crashing into the other racers *Joust*-style. The catchy soundtrack by John A. Fitzpatrick will stick in your head for weeks.

Of course, another hurdle for C-64 game developers was the rampant piracy on the system. Unlike cartridge-based systems, the floppy disks preferred by C-64 owners could be easily copied and distributed among friends, at computer clubs, and eventually over online bulletin board systems. Naturally, publishers introduced a variety of schemes to thwart the illegal practice, but none proved effective against the armies of "cracking" groups. While many if not most C-64 owners purchased all of their software legally, it was all too common for gamers to have dozens of boxes full of hand-labeled floppy disks packed with pirated software. In many cases, the cracking group would place an audiovisual "cracktro" or "demo" that would load before the game. Since this demo had to fit into the often-tiny space left on the floppy disk after the game data was installed, the demo code had to be exceptionally compact, a feat that required considerable talent. This practice was the roots of the modern "demoscene" subculture, in which some of the world's most tech-savvy coders, artists, and musicians compete to make the most impressive audiovisual displays using the smallest possible amounts of computer resources.

Although the C-64 supported a wide variety of business and productivity software, such as Broderbund's *The Print Shop* (1984) desktop publishing package and Microsoft's *Multiplan* (1983) spreadsheet program, the games brought most users to the system. With

While most people associate the C-64 with games, there were also productivity software. Shown here is **Vizawrite 64** (1983), a word processor.

such a huge library of commercial and public domain games available, C-64 owners had access to every conceivable genre. Even when games originated on other systems, the C-64 ports often had enhanced graphics and sound.

The C-64's games library is immense and reveals the extent to which, given enough time, programmers can optimize their code to take full advantage of a system's latent capabilities. This is clearly seen when comparing C-64 games from the early 1980s like *Wizard*, *The Blade of Blackpoole,* and *Choplifter!* with those from the early 1990s like *Chuck Rock* and *Creatures 2: Torture Trouble*. Perhaps the most visually stunning of all C-64 games, however, is 1993's *Mayhem in Monsterland*, designed by brothers Steve and John Rowlands, which could almost pass for a Super NES or Sega Genesis game. This feat was made possible by exploiting a bug in the C-64's graphic chip, a technique pioneered by the demo programmers mentioned above. Undoubtedly, all game platforms have similarly unknown capabilities that could take even the best programmers years, if not decades, to find and exploit. The longevity of a platform like the C-64 gave it a chance to realize feats like this within its commercial lifetime.

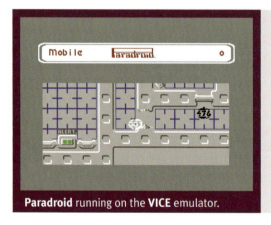

Paradroid running on the **VICE** emulator.

Paradroid (Hewson Consultants, 1985)

This game by Andrew Braybrook is a shoot-'em-up game with a top-down perspective of a space freighter. The crew was killed by berserk droids, and it's your job to take them over and annihilate them with their own weapons. This is possible thanks to the "Influence Device," which allows you to control a droid (temporarily, of course) and start blasting his buddies—assuming you can crack the circuit diagram puzzles before the timer runs out. Just remember to swap to another droid before yours is destroyed!

Some of the most popular games for the C-64 were published by Trip Hawkins' Electronic Arts company, which was founded just a few months before the release of the C-64. In 1983, they ported Bill Budge's *Pinball Construction Set*, Free Fall Associates' *Archon: The Light and the Dark*, Danielle Berry's *MULE*, and Eric Hammond's *Julius Erving and Larry Bird Go One on One*, quickly bringing the fledging platform to parity with the competing Apple II and Atari 8-bit computers. All of these games became smash hits on the C-64, and demonstrate the wide variety of game types that soon became available. Epyx was another prominent C-64 games publisher, with hit titles ranging from the popular Olympics-themed *Games* series to Dennis Caswell's *Impossible Mission* (1984) puzzle platform game, which featured the now-iconic digitized voice sample: "Another visitor! Stay awhile; stay forever!"

The Commodore 64's popularity among mainstream gamers began to decline after the release of the Nintendo Entertainment System in late 1985. Although the C-64 had several technical advantages over it, the NES's full screen hardware scrolling was difficult to match on the C-64, and the NES's processor was nearly twice as fast. These facts didn't stop talented developers from trying to bring *Super Mario Bros.*-style gameplay to the C-64, of course. In 1987, a German company named Rainbow Arts published *Great Giana Sisters,* a remarkable clone of *Super Mario Bros.* programmed by Armin Gessert (with graphics by Manfred Trenz and music by Chris Hulsbeck). Nintendo's response was swift, and the game was promptly removed from the shelves, making boxed copies into very desirable collectibles.

Electronic Arts rode to prominence largely on the back of their many hits for the C-64. Their games were known for their "rock star" album packaging.

Despite the obvious similarities to *Super Mario Bros.*, *Great Giana Sisters* has plenty of innovations, including a variety of hilarious power-ups (punk rock girl!), a wonderful soundtrack, and far freakier-looking monsters, with new, less obvious entries in the series continuing to be released today, even on Nintendo platforms.

Although many of its hit games originated on other platforms, several important and influential games debuted on the C-64. These include Will Wright's *SimCity* (1989), which can trace its development back to Wright's 1984 action-strategy game, *Raid on Bungeling Bay.* When Wright was designing this game, he had so much fun making maps for it that he felt that concept alone might make for a fun game. *SimCity* on the C-64 lacks many of the features of other versions, but C-64 fans still take pride that such a hit franchise began on their favorite platform and theirs was the only version to come bundled with the construction set. Other notable games originating on the C-64 include Lucasfilm Games' *Maniac Mansion* (1987), SSI's *Pool of Radiance* (1988), System 3's *The Last Ninja* (1987), Rainbow Arts' *Turrican* (1990), and *Sid Meier's Pirates!* (1987). *Habitat,* released by Lucasfilm Games on Quantum Link in 1986, was one of the first online role-playing games. However, most of the hit games for the C-64 were ports of games developed on other systems or from the arcade. These include such hits as Firebird's *Elite* (1985), an early sandbox space combat and trading game; Broderbund's *Lode Runner* (1983), a platform game with a level editor; and Origin's *Ultima IV: Quest of the Avatar* (1985), Richard "Lord British" Garriott's RPG masterpiece. Naturally, for countless gamers, the C-64 adaptations of these games are what most people played in the 1980s and remember today.

Since the C-64 used the same joystick ports as the Atari 2600, finding gaming hardware was seldom an issue. Many gamers chose a standard Atari-style joystick with the familiar square bottom and fire button in the corner, but others opted for a specialty controller. Some of the more popular options included the 500XJ joystick from Epyx, which offered a molded grip for more ergonomic gameplay, Suncom's Slik Stik and TAC-2, and Spectravideo's Quickshot II Turbo.

Although much is often made of the C-64's relative graphical capabilities, others point out that SID, the system's powerful sound chip, was even more impressive for its time. Indeed, the C-64 was where "chiptune" maestros like Rob Hubbard, Jeroen Tel, Martin Galway, David Whittaker, Ben Daglish, and so many others got their start. Rob Hubbard's music in the

otherwise-forgettable shooter game *Sanxion*, released in 1986 by Thalamus, caused the game to be praised for its distinctive loading music. At a time when most computer games contained no music or, at best, a melodic sequence of beeps and bloops, Hubbard's tunes demonstrated the potential of the C-64 as a truly musical instrument. The work of Hubbard and many of his contemporary SID composers has been remixed and updated for

Since the C-64 had the same joystick ports as Atari systems, there were a multitude of controllers available, including some from Commodore themselves.

modern audiences, though the original tunes are available on any number of fans' websites. Just like any other musical instrument, the SID chip can sound slightly different depending upon the system model from which it is used and the version.[4]

Project Firestart running on the **VICE** emulator.

Project Firestart (Electronic Arts, 1989)

Jeff Tunnell and Damon Slye's *Project Firestart* is an ambitious action and adventure game hybrid that is remarkably ahead of its time. The production qualities are so high that it could easily be mistaken for a 16-bit title. There's also no mistaking its status as a progenitor of the survival horror genre, with all of the trappings of that style of game—weak main character, limited ammo, graphic violence, and so on. The cut scenes and music are some of the best you'll see and hear on the platform.

Another benefit of the SID was that quality speech synthesis was a possibility without external add-ons (although both those and speech input devices were readily available), found in many popular games such as the aforementioned *Impossible Mission*, *Kennedy Approach* (Microprose, 1985) air traffic control simulator, *Beach-Head II: The Dictator Strikes Back* (Access, 1985) multi-screen action game, *Jump Jet* (Anirog Software, 1985) flight simulator, *Ghostbusters* (Activision, 1984) movie translation, and *Transformers: Battle to Save the Earth* (Activision, 1986) platformer, which filled the entire side of a game disk with a fully narrated introductory story. *SAM* (Software Automatic Mouth), a speech synthesis program from Don't Ask Computer Software, put the SID chip to good use, and let kids have their C-64 utter as many profanities as they wished.

Commodore produced its last C-64 in April 1994, when the company filed for bankruptcy. By that point, of course, DOS-based computers were the industry standard in the US, though the C-64 had continued to sell overseas, especially in Eastern Europe. Indeed, European companies

---

4   The early 6581 and late model 6582 and 8580 revisions of the SID chips generate sound slightly differently from each other. Many enthusiasts prefer the nuances and improvements found in the 8580. Even chips in the same series, however, can produce subtle differences in sound output.

were still releasing major commercial games for the C-64 as late as 1993, including the afore-mentioned *Mayhem in Monsterland* from Apex Computer Productions, and *Lemmings* from Psygnosis, and are at the forefront of the homebrew scene today.

Later Models

- **1984:** Commodore released a C-64 in a briefcase-style case, the SX-64. Powered by AC rather than batteries, the SX-64 was an interpretation of the popular transportable CP/M computer designs from Osborne and Kaypro. It has the distinction of being the first full-color transportable computer, though its small 5-inch screen, heavy weight (23 pounds), and lack of focus on serious business software may have contributed to its lackluster sales (the sticker price was relatively competitive at $995). The SX-64 featured a built-in 1541 floppy drive and a sturdy handle, which doubled as an adjustable stand. The only standard C-64 feature missing from the SX-64 is the datasette port.

Raid on Bungeling Bay running on the **VICE** emulator.

Raid on Bungeling Bay (Broderbund, 1984)

The inspiration for *SimCity*, which also debuted on the C-64, *Raid on Bungeling Bay* was the first videogame by celebrated game designer Will Wright. Anyone who played *SimCity* on the C-64 will instantly notice the similarities in the graphics, but this game is an overhead shoot-'em-up with surprising strategic depth. Players pilot a helicopter around a battlefield, dropping bombs onto factories while evading tanks, anti-air guns, and ships. Meanwhile, the Bungeling Empire has another trick—robots will steadily repair the factories you've managed to bomb. As if that's not enough to ratchet up the tension, the robots are also building a giant battleship in the shipyard. It's not easy to earn the animated ticker tape parade at the end if you ultimately defeat the empire, but it sure is fun trying.

- **1985:** Commodore released the Commodore 128 (C-128), which also failed to perform as commercially well as its predecessor. The C-128 featured 128K of RAM, a MOS 8502 processor clocked at 2MHz, and a Zilog Z80 clocked at 4MHz. It also boasted an updated operating system, Commodore BASIC V7.0, which addressed many of the deficiencies of the earlier C-64 version. While the system was almost entirely C-64 compatible, it did receive a new, higher-speed, higher-capacity disk drive called the 1571, which was also necessary for CP/M compatibility (CP/M was an optional and underpowered cartridge add-on on the original C-64). A sleeker and more professional-looking model, the C-128D, was released soon after and featured a built-in 1571 and external keyboard. These multiprocessor systems could be switched among three different operational modes—C-128, C-64, and CP/M. In short, it was three computers in one but, unfortunately for Commodore, most gamers were happy enough with the one.

In C-128 mode, the computer made up for most of its older brother's technical short-comings—it had the ability, for instance, to display 80 instead of 40 columns of text on a monitor thanks to 16KB of dedicated video RAM (64K of VRAM in the 128D). These enhancements, along with a new numeric keypad, made it far more useful for business and productivity applications. Unfortunately, few games were ever developed specifically for the C-128, although it was highly useful for running an enhanced version of *GEOS*, a Macintosh-like graphical operating system originally released in 1986 by Berkeley Softworks.

The CP/M mode suffered from occasional sluggishness, but made up for it with versatility; the 1571 could access a variety of otherwise incompatible read/write formats. Unfortunately, by the time the C-128 was released, the CP/M operating system was already on its way out, replaced by IBM PCs and compatibles running Microsoft's DOS (see Chapter 1.6).

The Commodore 128 was more powerful and versatile than the C-64, but it floundered in the market relative to its predecessor.

- **1986:** Commodore released the C-64c, which was basically a C-64 system with more modern styling, matching the sleeker lines of the C-128. The C-64c was bundled with its own version of the *GEOS* operating system.

The C-64c offered more modern styling and minor internal tweaks, but was otherwise identical to the original breadbox model.

Seven Cities of Gold running on the **VICE** emulator.

Seven Cities of Gold (Electronic arts, 1984)

Danielle Berry's *Seven Cities of Gold* is set in the fifteenth century and puts players in the boots of an explorer of the New World. Players can choose whether to maintain peaceful relations with the natives or try to conquer them. The political and social commentary aspects of the game were not lost on gamers or critics, who often point to this game as a textbook example of how videogames can do more than simply entertain. Its unofficial sequel *Heart of Africa* (1985) moved the setting to Africa, but was criticized for its less thoughtful, more Hollywood-movie-like interpretation of the continent and its people.

The Commodore Community

Considering the number of C-64s sold over the course of its 12-year production run, it's not surprising that a large and vibrant user community developed around the platform. Commodore-focused user groups and bulletin board systems (BBSs) were common across North America and Europe. Quantum Link (Q-Link) was an online commercial service that ran from 1985 to 1994, catering to C-64 and C-128 users before shifting to the PC market and changing its name to America Online. Amazingly, several Commodore computer clubs formed in the 1980s are still active today. One example is the Fresno Commodore User Group (FCUG), which still meets monthly and even publishes a regular newsletter.

Attending a computer club or logging onto a BBS was a good way to get help and discover the large library of public domain and shareware software available for the platform.

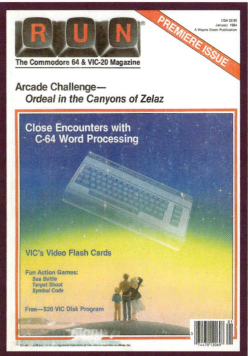

RUN magazine whose premiere issue, shown here, was dated January 1984, provided a key resource for fans of the Commodore 64 series right up until its 94th and final issue, dated November/December 1992. **RUN** was just one of the countless great magazines that catered to Commodore 64 fans.

Wizball running on the VICE emulator.

Wizball (Ocean, 1987)

This bizarre game from Sensible Software has the player controlling a green bouncing ball, who is actually the wizard (named Wiz), who must defeat the Zark, vile creatures determined to suck the light and color from Wizworld. A large assortment of upgrades will make controlling the ball and defeating enemies much easier, but, more importantly, allow you to conjure up your cat to catch the color droplets. If you have a friend weird enough to play the game with you, he or she can plug in a second joystick and control the cat for you.

Many C-64 owners enjoyed writing their own games and software for the system, or typing them in from magazines. Collections of such programs were often compiled on a single floppy disk and distributed to members of a club or subscribers to a magazine. Commodore offered bundles of public domain software as well, which included many educational games for children.

After the introduction of the Commodore Amiga in 1985, some C-64 owners made the move to the new platform, but most eventually switched to PC DOS or Macintosh computers instead. Sadly, no single computer model would ever again enjoy the market share of the C-64 in its heyday. In hindsight, there was simply no way to replicate that special combination of power and price that the C-64 embodied. This was evident by the long list of failed competitors in its class, including Commodore's own C-16 and Plus/4, or with enhanced variations like the C-128 or unreleased C-65 prototype, which promised to be the ultimate 8-bit computer. The problem for these wannabes, however, was that for millions of fans, they already owned the "ultimate" 8-bit computer and would accept no substitutes.

World Karate Championship running on the **VICE** emulator.

World Karate Championship (Epyx, 1985)

Released as *International Karate* in Europe, this two-player beat-'em-up let players fight each other or kick and punch their way through a series of computer-controlled martial artists. In a famous court dispute, Data East attempted to sue the publisher for infringing on its arcade game *Karate Champ*. The judge ruled in Epyx's favor, which is a good thing considering how many rank *World Karate Championship* as one of the best games for the C-64. The distinctive music by Rob Hubbard has become a staple on C-64 music and remix stations.

Collecting Commodore 64 Systems and Software

Because the C-64 was such a ubiquitous and durable platform, finding a unit in working or even mint condition is seldom difficult. Obviously, since so much software was released in disk form, a collector will also want to add a disk drive, most likely a Commodore 1571, which is more versatile and quiet than the 1541. Collectors who aren't nostalgic for the old breadbox styling of the early C-64 may well prefer a C-64c.

The much rarer portable SX-64 is often hard to find in decent condition, but its relative portability makes it desirable to try. The C-128 is fairly easy to find, but the more versatile C-128D represents more of a challenge. The C-128 line is preferred by some C-64 enthusiasts for their more reliable and capable power supplies (which readily support memory expansion cartridges) and greater overall capabilities, but the trade-offs in extra bulk, complexity, and compatibility may not be worth it to most gamers.

Software is easy to find for the C-64, although prices range widely depending on the obscurity and desirability of the individual game. Because of its relative ubiquity, however, many games can be had for a song, with plenty of opportunities to purchase large collections of diverse titles for very reasonable prices on auction websites.

A stunning range of homebrew games continue to be produced on cassette, disk, and cartridge, as well as digital image for use in emulators. The most prolific publisher and distributor of such games today is RGCD, whose 2011 releases included endless runner *C64anabalt* and strategic battle game *Not Even Human—Inhumane Edition*, 2012 releases included action combo *Greenrunner/Redrunner/Retroskoi+* and platformer *UWOL: Quest For Money*, and 2013 releases included platformer *Sir Ababol/Nanako In Classic Japanese Monster Castle* and Vectrex conversions *Spike/MineStorm*.

The Commodore SX-64 is a collector's item, especially if found in mint condition. Designed for executives, it's sure to make a memorable impression at your next business meeting.

Like many of the other platforms from the 1980s, the C-64 has a variety of newly created multicarts, flash memory, and drive emulators available, as well as a host of other interesting add-ons and accessories. These devices include the 1541 Ultimate-II, which can emulate everything from utility cartridges to expansion memory to every type of software format, the EasyFlash 3, which can emulate a variety of cartridge formats, individual Computers' Micromys V4, which connects PC mice to the C-64, and Protovision's 4 Player Interface, which allows the use of four simultaneous joysticks for great multiplayer gaming.

Emulating the Commodore 64

C-64 emulation is mature and well implemented on a variety of platforms. Several online software repositories are readily accessible, and it's easy to get support from the large community of enthusiasts that still exist for the platform. The most popular emulation software is *VICE*, which also works well for other Commodore 8-bit platforms, like the PET and VIC-20.

Cloanto's *C-64 Forever* emulator is a 100 percent legal emulation package available for under $20. It features a well-designed and intuitive graphical user interface for loading and installing games, and includes over 200 demos, games, and applications. If you're new to C-64 emulation, this is by far the best way to start.

Interestingly, the C-64 is the only classic computer to have its games featured on the Nintendo's eShop, though the selection is not particularly robust. Fully featured emulators are also available on iOS and Android devices.

Zak McKracken and the Alien Mindbenders running on the **VICE** emulator.

Zak McKracken and the Alien Mindbenders (Lucasfilm Games, 1988)

This point-and-click adventure designed by David Fox debuted on the Commodore 64 and was only the second to use SCUMM, the engine developed for *Maniac Mansion*. With a story inspired by mysticism and *Weekly World News*-style tabloids, it's definitely among the wackiest games you'll ever play. Can you stop the spread of stupidity before it's too late?

Coleco ColecoVision (1982)

History

In the midst of intense competition from Atari and Mattel, Coleco's ColecoVision tried to distinguish itself with "arcade-quality" graphics and ports. This was 1982, and the arcade was the place to go if you wanted to play state-of-the-art-games. Conversions of hit arcade games like *Pac-Man* for home consoles usually meant a severe reduction in graphical detail and animation, especially in the case of the Atari 2600. Coleco realized a market existed for a higher-end console that could do a better job of bringing the arcade experience home, but the competition would be ferocious. The Atari 2600 had an all-you-care-to-play buffet of great games and accessories, and the Intellivision was the undisputed champion of sports games and had great marketing. For the ColecoVision to succeed, it really would need to stand head and shoulders above these giants.

"Graphic superiority, that's the basis of our faith in Colecovision," declared Arnold C. Greenberg, president of Coleco during this period.[1] Greenberg also stressed the system's expandability—eventually into a full home computer—and his commitment to licensing hit arcade games. He was described as a serious, quiet man who "preaches toys as if they were a form of salvation."[2] He was a graduate of Harvard Law School, a background that would serve him well in the years to come.

Greenberg's ambition was admirable, but the ColecoVision wasn't really the technological powerhouse the company promoted in its advertising. In reality, it had an anemic 1K of memory and no special hardware for scrolling—a vital aspect of arcade games like *Zaxxon* and *Time Pilot*. No doubt, both Atari and Mattel (as well as many gamers!) were rightly skeptical of Coleco's promise to bring home the "arcade quality experience." Despite the odds, however, the ColecoVision was a success, though it owes much of it to clever branding and Greenberg's lucrative licensing deals.

Like Mattel, Coleco was an old, well-established company that was no stranger to competition. The company was founded in 1932 by Maurice Greenberg, a Russian immigrant. At that time, it was called the Connecticut Leather Company and sold leather for shoes. In the early 1950s, the company expanded into leather craft kits and plastic molding. By the end of the 1960s, having long since sold off their leather business and becoming a publicly traded company, Coleco became the premier manufacturer of above-ground swimming pools. After failed attempts to expand into other areas such as motorbikes and snowmobiles, Coleco ventured into consumer electronics in 1976 with one of the first Atari *Pong* clones, called the Telstar.

In 1975, chip-maker General Instrument was looking to develop a low-cost "Pong-on-a-chip" as an answer to Atari and Magnavox's proprietary *Pong* and *Pong*-like systems. The result

---

[1] "Coleco's New Video Challenge," *New York Times*, November 11, 1982.

[2] N.R. Kleinfield, "Coleco Moves out of the Cabbage Patch," *New York Times*, July 21, 1985.

BC's Quest for Tires (1983, Sierra On-Line)

Sydney Development's side scrolling platformer, *BC's Quest for Tires*[3] (although oddly, simply *BC's Quest* on the in-game title screen), is based on the iconic Johnny Hart *BC* comic strip. It is one of the early triumphs of licensing,[4] winning numerous awards in its day. It was also one of the earliest examples of what today is known as an "endless runner," a type of game genre where your avatar is constantly in motion. Unusually colorful, large, and expressive character sprites capture the key comic elements as Thor, riding a stone wheel, tries to rescue Cute Chick from a dinosaur, avoiding all types of prehistoric obstacles and

BC's Quest for Tires running on the **blueMSX** emulator.

enemies along the way, including Fat Broad. Unfortunately, the game's sequel, *BC II: Grog's Revenge* (1984), isn't as good, but is still worth checking out. You can find both games on the commercially unreleased *Best of BC* data pack for the Coleco Adam, which was made available through alternative channels shortly after the computer's commercial demise.

was the AY-3-8500 chip, which could play as many as six paddle and target games, depending on how vendors set it up. Industry pioneer Ralph Baer received early information on the chip's development and contacted Coleco's president, Arnold Greenberg, about the possibilities. This led to Coleco's preferred vendor status for the first and largest supply of chips and to their suc-

cess developing and marketing the Telstar. After supply caught up to demand, a wide range of companies produced hundreds of variant clone systems from the original General Instrument chip and future incarnations. Coleco, however, along with rivals such as Atari and APF, had the greatest success in the fixed-game videogame market. Coleco ended up producing many *Pong*-like games, but none more unusual than the Telstar Arcade, which accepted cartridges with custom microcontrollers.

Coleco's little known first console, the Telstar Arcade. Instead of the Telstar Arcade's "kitchen sink" approach to including most add-ons in-the-box, Coleco wisely decoupled all their add-on ideas for the ColecoVision. While only the Telstar Arcade's steering wheel concept made it as one of the add-ons for the ColecoVision, it's reasonable to speculate that if Coleco's popular console had lasted past the Great Videogame Crash, a light gun would have likely joined the collection as well.

---

3   A play on Thor's main mode of transportation in the game, as well as the title of the popular 1981 film *Quest for Fire*, which itself was based on the classic 1911 Belgian novel of the same name.

4   In another example of the era's "spokesperson wars," Hart's comic creation was also used extensively in the print advertising for the failed Timex Sinclair 2068 computer, a modified version of the UK's popular ZX Spectrum.

Unfortunately, the Fairchild Video Entertainment System's introduction in 1976, followed by Atari's VCS in 1977, signaled the beginning of the end of the fixed-game era, and even though the Telstar Arcade was built for interchangeable cartridges, there were only four to choose from, and its technology was not competitive. Another issue was a second East Coast dock workers' strike that caused them to miss the critical Christmas season. The system was a dismal failure, promptly making its way to retailers' bargain bins and forcing Coleco to absorb $20 million in losses.[5] It was a huge blow, but Arnold C. Greenberg, who had taken the reins of the company after his father's departure, wasn't ready to bow out of the videogames industry.

While the era of the Telstar was behind them, Coleco managed to establish a growing presence at retail with handheld and tabletop electronic games, board games, and other toys. These included the ever-popular *Electronic Quarterback* (1978) handheld and a series of arcade ports designed to look like miniature arcade cabinets, such as *Coleco Pac Man* (1981) and *Coleco Frogger* (1981). By 1982, Coleco was ready to re-enter the console videogame market with a powerful next generation system.

To help make this re-entry a success, Coleco made a key strategic decision to negotiate exclusive licenses for new arcade games before Atari or Mattel got their hands on them. The most coveted of these deals was an agreement with Nintendo in late 1981 for the exclusive console rights to *Donkey Kong*. Coleco soon realized that *Donkey Kong* was the next big thing. Their tabletop version was met with enthusiasm, but they had bigger plans. Since they had the exclusive license, they could prevent Atari and Mattel from offering it on their systems, giving their upcoming

Destructor running on the **blueMSX** emulator.

Destructor (1984, Coleco)

There are precious few games as divisive as *Destructor*. Most who have played this steering wheel controller-based game either love it or hate it. The premise is simple enough. Your starcruiser lands in the island city of Araknid on the planet Arthros to collect precious crystals needed to save Earth. To accomplish this task, you drive a type of armored tractor, the Ramcar, which you use to crash into the Krystaloid insects to form the crystals, which you then have to carry back to the starcruiser. Evading the enemies in the maze-like city requires deft maneuvering of the steering wheel and other controls as you try to gather enough crystals in a particular level to return to Earth, before repeating the process on a harder level. Unfortunately, for some players, the fetch-quest nature of the core gameplay, overly aggressive enemies, jerky scrolling, and occasional programming bugs really hamper the experience. For the rest of us, the tense gameplay, unusual control scheme, and the fact that its high concept theme is quite unlike any other game from its era, more than make up for any of its missteps. For those who don't have or can't properly emulate the steering wheel controller, Team PixelBoy published Stephen Seehorn's 2010 standard controller hack as *Destructor SCE* (Standard Controller Edition), allowing a greater number of people to see if the game falls into the "love it" or "hate it" category.

---

5   R.P. Carlisle (ed.), *Encyclopedia of Play in Today's Society*, SAGE Publications, 2009.

ColecoVision a major advantage in the market. *Donkey Kong* would become the pack-in cartridge for the ColecoVision, and Coleco held off another six months before releasing mediocre ports for the Atari 2600 and Mattel Intellivision. Coleco also made profitable licensing deals with other popular arcade game makers, like Sega and Exidy, who contributed to the strong mix of a dozen titles available for the system's launch.

When the system launched, the main competition was the Atari 2600 and the Mattel Intellivision. The ColecoVision was more than a match for these machines. However, Atari's 5200, which launched three months later, was a much stronger competitor. Unfortunately for both companies, the Great Videogame Crash was just a year away.

It's said that the Atari 5200 SuperSystem was developed mostly in response to the Intellivision. This seems plausible given the design of the 5200's unusual analog joystick. Although its analog design trumped the Intellivision controller's 16 digital directions, it also suffered its poor usability. However, Atari soon found it was the ColecoVision, not the Intellivision, which posed the gravest threat to its shiny new 5200. Compared to that system, the 5200's advantages were far less obvious. In

An early two-page ColecoVision advertisement from the November 1982 issue of **Electronic Games** magazine, emphasizing three key features: arcade quality gaming, Atari 2600 compatibility, and computer expandability. What sealed the deal for many gamers, however, was the **Donkey Kong** pack-in game, shown on the TV screen.

fact, Coleco's masterful launch made Atari's new system seem almost comically inept.

The ColecoVision launched in August 1982 at a retail price of just $199.99, while the 5200, despite its reliance on pre-existing Atari 400 technology, didn't come out until November 1982. Worse, it was saddled with a retail price of $269.99, due in part to its reliance on that same expensive technology. The real clincher, though, was that the 5200 wasn't backwards-compatible with the 2600. Until the release of an adapter cartridge and a two-slot revised design in 1983, the 5200 couldn't play any of the 2600's huge library of games, and games designed for the 5200 were far from plentiful. This was all made worse by the fact that both the ColecoVision and the Intellivision offered adapters that allowed gamers to play 2600 games in addition to their own libraries.

Of course, the real trump card in Coleco's hand was that it came bundled with a colorful interpretation of Nintendo's scalding hot 1981 arcade property *Donkey Kong*. Atari pathetically countered by bundling a colorful arcade interpretation of their *Super Breakout*, a title whose popularity had cooled since its debut in 1978. Furthermore, *Super Breakout* could easily be replicated by any number of other systems, including the Atari 2600. Indeed, it's arguable that the Atari 2600 version was superior since it used paddle controllers instead of the 5200's terrible joysticks. So far, the 5200's response to the Coleco threat was about as sloppy and non-responsive as its controllers.

Fortune Builder running on the **blueMSX** emulator.

Fortune Builder (1984, Coleco)

Just like with Intellivision's *Utopia*, the ColecoVision had a breakthrough console strategy game of its own in *Fortune Builder*, a surprisingly sophisticated real estate planning simulation. *Fortune Builder* challenges one or two simultaneous players to construct a community on a map of undeveloped land, consisting of a seacoast with beachfront, two mountain ranges, midlands, a river and a lake, and a main highway running north and south. Each player starts with a fixed amount of cash to buy and build a large variety of strategically placed properties, including hotels, condos, marinas, factories, malls, and gas stations. The challenge comes from drawing the most profit increasing traffic to these locations, watching out for everything from changing consumer trends and bad weather to worker strikes and sabotage, which can all have adverse effects on profitability. For a less sophisticated, but more accessible simulation grounded in action, check out *Campaign '84* (1983, Sunrise Software), which tasks one or two players with traveling around the United States to literally collect the most electoral votes and become president.

To add insult to injury, Coleco's launch line-up was a sensational mix of fresh arcade conversions as well as some great originals: *Carnival, Cosmic Avenger, Ken Uston's Blackjack/Poker, Lady Bug, Mouse Trap, Smurf: Rescue in Gargamel's Castle, Space Fury, Space Panic, Venture,* and *Zaxxon*. Atari 5200 owners did have *Galaxian, Pac-Man,* and *Space Invaders,* but these were all available elsewhere. The 800-pound gorilla was *Donkey Kong,* and he was sitting at Coleco's table.

"Coleco strong in marketing," ran as a headline in the August 1, 1983 edition of *The New York Times.* In the second quarter of the year, Coleco earned $9.1 million—and was the only one of the major console manufacturers to post a profit. The upstart videogame company had already sold 1.4 million units.[6] While this figure still left them far behind the huge customer base of the Atari 2600, that wasn't necessarily a problem for the ColecoVision's momentum. In their early marketing materials, Coleco emphasized the expandability of their new console, and they delivered on this promise quickly and decisively.

First up was the aforementioned add-on unit to play Atari 2600 games: Expansion Module #1.[7] Next, came Expansion Module #2, which was a new type of steering wheel controller, bundled with a superb conversion of Sega's *Turbo* arcade game. Even though in the coming year Atari would eventually use *Pac-Man* as a pack-in, release a cost reduced Atari 5200 with an Atari 2600 add-on of their own, and demonstrate that they still had strong controller design skills with the release of the high quality Pro-Line Trak-Ball controller, the damage was already done. Heading into 1983, the ColecoVision was the hot property.

---

[6]   K.J., "Coleco Strong in Marketing," *New York Times,* August 1, 1983.

[7]   Coleco would also release a stand-alone Atari 2600 compatible console, the Gemini. Atari would sue Coleco over both the add-on and the console. The two companies eventually settled, with Coleco paying Atari royalties on each compatible unit sold. Litigation was not Coleco's strong suit, as they also agreed to pay Universal 3 percent royalties from *Donkey Kong*'s net sale price for alleged infringement of the *King Kong* character. When Universal eventually went after Nintendo, all judgments eventually fell in the *Donkey Kong* creator's favor.

Compared to the other successful consoles, which were released in the late 1970s, the ColecoVision was clearly a product of the early 1980s. Its black and silver styling was in stark contrast to the Intellivision, with its faux woodgrain plastic panels and brown accents. There wasn't really a huge technological divide between the capabilities of the Intellivision and ColecoVision, but the latter's brighter in-game colors and better ports of arcade games made it seem like a quan-

tum leap. This attention to design extended to packaging. Game boxes sported vibrant colors, screenshots, and photos of arcade machines, whereas the 5200 boxes were mostly gray, sporting painted covers similar to those found on the 2600. All this came together to form the message to gamers that a ColecoVision-powered home was the place to be when the lights were off at the arcade.

The steering wheel controller (Expansion Module #2) came packaged with a great port of Sega's **Turbo** arcade game.

Frenzy running on the **blueMSX** emulator.

Frenzy (1983, Coleco)

Like most of Coleco's arcade ports for the ColecoVision, the home translation of Stern's 1982 arcade sequel to *Berzerk* (1980), *Frenzy*, was more interpretation than direct clone. Unlike most of those other arcade ports, however, Coleco's *Frenzy* featured several enhancements that arguably made it superior to its inspiration. More than a simple upgrade to *Berzerk*'s classic and often cloned shoot-the-robots-in-a-tight-electrified-maze gameplay, *Frenzy* added several new features, including walls that are no longer simply electrified, but can also reflect shots and be shot through to create new escape routes, a greater variety of robot enemies that are both more intelligent and more susceptible to self-inflicted destruction, random mazes, a boss (Evil Otto) who can now be temporarily killed before coming back and attacking with greater speed, and interactive in-room elements (example: a power plant) that affect the game world when attacked. Outside of its lack of speech, Coleco's version improves on the original in nearly every way, featuring better graphics, music, and sound effects, along with slight tweaks to the gameplay.

Technical Specifications

For many gamers of the era, the ColecoVision represented the best of what a console could be. It had the bright colors and speed of an Atari 2600, with the increased graphical and audio fidelity of an Intellivision. This was thanks to Coleco's use of a Zilog Z80A microprocessor, which clocked at 3.58 MHz, and Texas Instruments TMS9928A video processor that allowed for an impressive 256x192 display resolution with 16 colors and 32 simultaneous sprites. The SN76489A sound chip, also designed by Texas Instruments, had three tone and one noise generators.[8]

As with the Intellivision and the Atari 5200, the ColecoVision's controllers were the source of much consternation. For the most part, players took little issue with the two side-mounted action buttons and bottom mounted numeric keypad, which could hold useful overlays to help players remember what button did what. Once players got to the joystick, however, there was plenty to complain about, from its cramp inducing stubbiness, to its tendency to make creaking noises. The latter issue was one of many indicators of Coleco's toy company roots and cost-cutting practices that would come to tarnish the company's reputation.

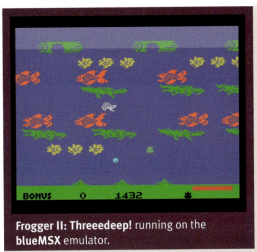

Frogger II: Threeedeep! running on the **blueMSX** emulator.

Frogger II: Threeedeep! (1984, Parker Brothers)

Konami's *Frogger* (1981) arcade game, which was distributed by Sega/Gremlin, was already a well-established classic in both its original version and the countless home ports for seemingly every possible platform,[9] including the ColecoVision, by the time *Frogger II: Threeedeep!* was released. While Parker Brothers got the license to do the sequel from Sega rather than Konami, who never recognized the game as an official sequel, this new title would nevertheless prove a worthy attempt at improving upon the original's depth, in more ways than one. While the original game was limited to one screen consisting of a busy highway and pond with five home berths (goals), this sequel tripled the challenge. As the extra "e"s in "Threee" imply, there are three different screens—Underwater, Surface, and Airborne—for Frogger to move between. While there are still five home berths that need to be filled in order to reach the next difficulty level, these are now spread across the screens, with three in Underwater, and one each in Surface and Airborne. A wide variety of enemies within each of the levels, including Joe the diving turtle, hippos, and a stork, add to the nicely polished hopping action.

The ColecoVision console itself was not without its own flaws and compromises, either, not the least of which was the poor scrolling capability of the TMS9928A, and the miniscule main 1KB of system RAM. Coleco planned to address the memory limitation with the unreleased Super Game

---

8   The same or similar sound chips were also used in arcade machines and other platforms, like the Texas Instruments TI-99/4a, IBM PCjr, and Acorn BBC Master computers.

9   Two of the more unlikely of the many official *Frogger* home ports were the relatively excellent conversions for the TRS-80 and Timex Sinclair 1000, both black and white computer platforms with extremely blocky graphics. Like the version for the colorful, but similarly low resolution Magnavox Odyssey2 console, the playfields for those ports were split between the highway and the pond, creating two distinct play screens. Was this the possible inspiration for *Frogger II: Threeedeep!*? The world may never know.

A page from the short-lived official **ColecoVision Experience** magazine, Volume 1, Number 1, discussing one of the potential release candidates for the Super Game Module, then known as Expansion Module #3. Note the incorrect information about Expansion Module #2 plugging into the expansion port (instead, it used controller port 1 and required four "C" batteries). Coleco was one of many companies at the time to demonstrate and distribute images of early prototypes and mock-ups of accessories and games that, if released at all, ended up looking quite different in their final forms.

Module (SGM) and, later, the Adam computer. Another issue with the ColecoVision was an intentional 12-second delay as the cartridges displayed the Coleco branding before going to the startup or menu screen. Some third-party titles avoided this intentional delay by bypassing the system's normal startup routine, but at the expense of available program space. In any case, most gamers forgot their annoyance once they started playing.

Originally intended as Expansion Module #3, the heavily advertised SGM went through various iterations before Coleco finally gave up and pulled the plug on the idea in late 1983. The core concept of the SGM was to provide extra system RAM, utilize a less expensive but higher capacity storage format, and save high scores. Unfortunately, Coleco could never settle on a reliable storage format and finally gave the Expansion Module #3 designation to the add-on version of the Adam computer,

The Super Action Controllers were imposing beasts, mostly designed for Coleco's sports games, like **Super Action Baseball**, which it came packaged with. Coleco's port of Taito's **Front Line** arcade game did make excellent use of the controller's extra features, however.

which duplicated and surpassed the SGM's intended functionality anyway. In fact, many of the games featured in SGM advertisements would be repurposed and released as "Super" games for the Adam.

Coleco, not one to shy away from hyperbole, also used the "Super" designation for its Super Action Controllers, which were sold in the fall of 1983 as a pair bundled with *Super Action Baseball.* Thoughtfully, the controllers included two snap-on pistol grips to accommodate larger hands. The oversized controller was compatible with any game that supported the regular controller, though there were select games expressly designed for its extra features, which included two extra action buttons and a "Speed Roller." Because of its unique design, its higher quality keypad required a different type of overlay.

Around the same time, Coleco released their best designed add-on, the Roller Controller, which came bundled with *Slither*. This trackball controller allowed for high-speed movement and featured four action buttons. The standard player one and two controllers would plug into the side cradles to the left and right of the unit for joystick and keypad

Coleco's Roller Controller was the least supported of the controller options, but came packaged with a superb port of the arcade game **Slither**, a surprisingly good enhancement of the gameplay found in Atari's classic **Centipede**. Though any game could make use of the Roller Controller's joystick emulation mode, the arcade ports of Exidy's **Victory** and Midway's **Omega Race** were the only other contemporary games to provide full-featured, native support.

Tarzan running on the **blueMSX** emulator.

Tarzan (1984, Coleco)

In the late 1970s through early 1980s, there was renewed interest in vintage pulp characters like Flash Gordon, Buck Rogers, and Tarzan. Newly reimagined movies, television series, books, and comics joined the onslaught of television broadcasts—as well as fancy new videotape sales and rentals—of the vintage movie serials. Videogames were not immune to this pulp fiction multimedia onslaught either, with each of the three characters receiving genre appropriate digital interpretations. For Flash Gordon and Buck Rogers, this meant shooting things from their respective spaceships, but for Coleco's *Tarzan*, this meant a more refreshing platformer. The player, as Tarzan, must run, swim, climb, and punch his way through the jungle to rescue his ape friends from evil hunters and the Beastmen of Opar. While a bit sluggish to control, *Tarzan* is nevertheless lushly illustrated and provides a wide variety of activities to perform throughout its many scenes. The best part? Press any keypad button for the ColecoVision's best impression of the famous "Tarzan yell." If you like this game, check out Atarisoft's excellent 1983 conversion of the faster paced *Jungle Hunt* (1982, Taito) arcade game, which was originally titled *Jungle King* before its titular character's uncanny resemblance to Tarzan necessitated a change to a pith helmet- and safari-suit-equipped explorer.

access, offering even more in-game options, while the Roller Controller itself would plug into both of the console's controller ports, as well as piggyback onto its power supply socket. This latter requirement meant that the stand-alone Adam computer, which had a different power connector, needed an adapter.

Although it never actually released one, Coleco stirred rumors about a laserdisc, CED video disc, or equivalent add-on for the ColecoVision. These rumors gained credence when Coleco acquired the rights to make a home version of the hit laserdisc arcade game *Dragon's Lair* for $2 million. The add-on was technically possible because the console's graphics chip could accept external composite video input and overlay it with its own text or graphics. Sadly, the high costs of such technology at the time made it commercially impractical.[10]

In the 1980s, gamers would carefully analyze every difference between an arcade version and its home ports, considering any deviation a fault of the game, system, or both. Today, however, arcade fidelity is of less concern than whether variations enhance or modify the original in interesting or innovative ways. Indeed, fans may well prefer a ColecoVision port to a more technically accurate MAME installation or even an actual arcade machine! In short, the ColecoVision's library, while never truly bringing the arcade experience home, did live up to its promise to deliver great fun.

The Adam and the Eve of the End

Today, console-makers like Microsoft and Sony work hard to distinguish their consoles from home computers, even if there are no real technical barriers separating them. By contrast, in the early 1980s, a console that could fully function as a computer was a marketer's dream. From the beginning, Greenberg had promised that the ColecoVision would eventually be expandable into a full home computer. That promise turned out to be much more difficult, and costly, than Greenberg thought, however. Indeed, the company was forced to temporarily suspend production of its hot-selling ColecoVision consoles to dedicate more resources for producing the expansion.

By October 1983, ColecoVision owners could finally bridge the gap with Expansion Module #3, which upgraded their console into a home computer. The Adam had 64K RAM, a high-speed proprietary tape drive (Digital Data Pack), a well-built 75-key keyboard, daisy-wheel printer, and built-in typewriter application and *SmartWriter* word processor. Also included were two data packs, *SmartBASIC* and *Buck Rogers: Planet of Zoom Super Game* (aka *Super Buck Rogers*). *SmartBASIC* was based on the Apple II's Applesoft BASIC and mostly source compatible. *Buck Rogers: Planet of Zoom Super Game* featured extra scenes and high score saves versus the standard cartridge version. It seemed as though Adam owners had a lot to look forward to!

Coleco also offered the Adam as a stand-alone unit. Naturally, it had full ColecoVision compatibility. It also had additional video output options for connection to higher quality displays. Sadly, both the add-on and the stand-alone unit were simply too expensive to represent a good value. Production problems and quality control issues made the average price for the stand-alone unit hit $700, while the add-on retailed for around $500. At these prices, it just made more sense to buy a Commodore 64 or Atari 800XL, each of which offered larger software libraries. There was also a great buzz around IBM's upcoming "Peanut," a cheaper, more games-friendly home computer called the PCjr, which would finally launch in March 1984 (see Chapter 1.6).

---

[10]   There were, however, three major attempts at laserdisc-based home systems: RDI Video Systems Halcyon (1985) console, the Pioneer Palcom PX-7 (1985) MSX computer, and the Pioneer LaserActive (1993) media center, whose optional add-on modules could play native or enhanced Sega Mega Drive/Genesis and NEC PC Engine/TurboGrafx-16 titles. All three attempts were doomed to failure due to exorbitant pricing and many of the same limitations that plagued laserdisc games in the arcade.

War Room running on the **blueMSX** emulator.

War Room (1983, Probe 2000)

Robert Harris's *WarGames*-inspired *War Room* barely beat Coleco's official movie adaptation to market, but even if it hadn't, it still had the goods to stand on its own merits, with smooth scrolling gameplay and plenty of depth. The premise was simple: defend the United States from a Russian nuclear attack while maintaining the production of goods and services necessary to keep going. Using only a laser equipped hunter-killer satellite, players must knock out enemy missiles before they destroy a targeted city, which supplies either food, raw materials, machinery, or laser fuel. Using an Uncle Sam avatar to battle against Soviet hammer and sickle symbols, you also had to zoom into the cities to gather resources to supply your satellite or other cities, e.g., a city that produces machinery must be provided food and raw materials. Although labeled "A Probe 2000 Video Game," this was actually produced under the Odyssey Consumer Electronics Corp. label, which fell under North American Philips Consumer Electronics Corp., and was a way for the company behind the Magnavox Odyssey2 console to join the likes of Atari, Mattel, and Coleco in releasing titles for platforms other than their own. Unfortunately, the Crash cut Magnavox's promising third-party ambitions short, which left several other potential releases, like *Pink Panther* and *Power Lords*, targeted to the ColecoVision and other platforms, unreleased. Among these casualties was *Lord of the Dungeon*, which was a hardcore role-playing game similar in design to Sir-Tech's computer classic, *Wizardry*, only this time for the ColecoVision console. Had *Lord of the Dungeon* been released on schedule, it would have been the first cartridge to save games to a battery backup, a feature that wouldn't be common until the late 1980s. To date, two separate homebrew releases of the ambitious role-playing game, one in 2000 and another in 2010, have rectified its unreleased status for the small number of fans able to get in on the limited production runs.

Asked about the high price of his system, Greenberg was undeterred. "Anything under $1,000 that is a complete computer system like Adam is an easy value," he boldly declared.[11]

Perhaps if the Adam had lived up to the hype, Greenberg may have had a point. But the Adam had more problems than a high sticker price. In addition to a standard cartridge input, the Adam came with the aforementioned internal high-speed digital "data pack" tape cassette drive with 256K capacity (another could be added internally for around $150). A low-density 160K 5.25-inch external floppy disk drive was not available until later in the Adam's life. Both options had drawbacks. The tapes were noisy and highly unreliable, and even if you added the second drive, the lack of a copy command prevented making backups. This "feature" might have been less irritating if the tapes weren't so prone to corruption by exposure to pretty much any magnetic field, including the ones generated by televisions. The disk drive, on the other hand, was remarkably quiet, but the disks had a lower capacity than the tapes, which made some software impractical for the format. The printer was loud, slow (ten characters per second), and limited to the

---

11   Eric N. Berg, Special to *The New York Times*, September 7, 1983.

ADAM™
HELPS PREPARE KIDS FOR COLLEGE,
AND HELPS PAY FOR IT TOO.

ADAM
The ADAM Family Computer Scholarship Program

Michael Mitchell
A $500 SCHOLARSHIP

Buy an ADAM Family Computer System
between September 1 and December 31, 1984 and Coleco will provide
a $500 college scholarship for your child.

ADAM
It's the smartest gift you
can give your family.
COLECO

One of the later scholarship ads for Coleco's Adam computer from the December 1984 issue of **Family Computing**. The popular magazine was one of a handful of publications that included a variety of BASIC program listings for a wide range of computers, including the Adam, to type in each month.

characters on its interchangeable wheels. It did, however, provide true typewriter quality output, something that the graphics-friendly dot matrix printers of the day were unable to achieve. A 300-baud internal modem named ADAMLink was also released, as well as a 128K memory expansion option.

Coleco's advertising campaign for the Adam took a rather dull and unimaginative educational approach, stressing the machine's alleged ability to prepare children for jobs in an increasingly computerized world. A later, rather desperate sales strategy involved offering a voucher for a future $500 college scholarship with every purchase. While we can't really judge the effectiveness of these ads for good or ill, they definitely did little to actually demonstrate the system's full potential—or to distinguish it from the competition. Still, by most accounts, early sales were brisk.

Unfortunately, poor quality control at the factory led to a plethora of technical problems and production delays, and Coleco's tech support hotlines were soon buzzing with irritated Adam owners. Some figures cite that nearly 60 percent of Adam systems were returned as defective. An unusual design decision to daisy-chain the system's components meant that a problem with the

printer—where the power supply resided—could prevent the entire system from working. Furthermore, the Adam emitted a powerful magnetic pulse when powering up, which could erase the magnetic information stored on a tape left in a drive. It's almost as if the Adam were designed to fail.

Coleco tried to address these issues through an agonizing and costly series of hardware and software revisions that, combined with the effects of the Great Videogame

Coleco's two systems shared much of the same packaging types, though as was typical for a computer, the Adam featured a bit more variety.

Crash, cost the company $258 million dollars.[12] Even after a price cut brought the price of a stand-alone Adam down to $300, little hope remained for the future of the platform.

Indeed, Coleco was having unbelievable success with its popular Cabbage Patch Kids toys and had little incentive to continue promoting the Adam in the face of such devastating losses. Ultimately, the "byte" that Coleco thought its Adam would take out of Apple turned out to be little more than a "nybble."[13] Coleco officially discontinued its computer in January 1985, with the ColecoVision following in its wake in October.

Given the short life of the system, several unfinished or unreleased Adam games were later made available in the public domain. These titles included unreleased Super Games like *Super Subroc*, as well as quality game show translations like *Jeopardy* and *Family Feud*. These game show translations, along with other games, like *Dragon's Lair*, were quite successful when ported to the Commodore 64 and other platforms, making the Adam's quick demise all the more unfortunate.

While the Adam's public domain library was bolstered by many unreleased commercial titles, independent authors and small companies also took up the development cause to help fill the need for new software.

The Coleco Adam's version of **Dragon's Lair**, shown here running on the real hardware, is a surprisingly good interpretation of the arcade game given the platform's limitations versus the arcade machine. It was also far more interactive!

Much of these consisted of relatively unpolished BASIC software and lots of text adventures. Over time, however, the sophistication of Adam's independent titles grew, with many of the new programming languages, operating systems, utilities, and games equal in quality to commercial releases, like Digital Adventures' *Temple of the Snow Dragon* (1988) or Steve Pitman's *ADAM Bomb II* (1996), and often taking advantage of add-ons like the expanded memory adapters. Despite these labors of love, in total, the Adam's software library remains quite small, only hinting at what might have been possible with greater success.

After abandoning the Adam and then the ColecoVision, Greenberg turned his back on high risk electronic devices and focused on the company's toy line, especially the Cabbage Patch Kids dolls that had sold so far beyond anyone's expectations. It must have seemed like a sensible move now that the videogame "fad" was over. Of course, the real fad turned out to be the Cabbage Patch Kids dolls. In 1985, the frenzy over the dolls allowed Coleco to post record sales of $600 million. Unfortunately, the craze was short-lived, and in 1986, sales were down to $250 million, and the following year to $125 million, with no bottom in sight as supply far outstripped ever weakening demand for the dolls. To add insult to injury, the company also lost the rights to make Trivial Pursuit board games, which were another big profit center. Coleco was doomed.

---

[12]   R.P. Carlisle (ed.), *Encyclopedia of Play in Today's Society*, SAGE Publications, 2009.

[13]   A "nybble" is a spelling variant of "nibble," an information storage unit. It takes two nybbles to make a byte.

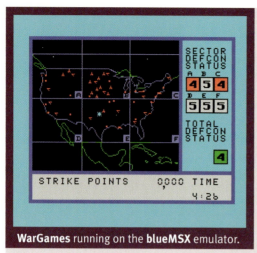

SECTOR
DEFCON
STATUS
A B C
4 5 4
D E F
5 5 5
TOTAL
DEFCON
STATUS
4

STRIKE POINTS   0000 TIME
4:26

WarGames running on the **blueMSX** emulator.

WarGames (1984, Coleco)

Filed under "rare movie license done right," instead of having a pixelated Matthew Broderick running and jumping through lame platforming stages, Coleco's *WarGames* distills John Badham's 1983 film down to its most dramatic element in this inspired variation on Atari's arcade classic, *Missile Command*. While Coleco's *WarGames* has the same basic defense premise and US map as *War Room*, there's no scrolling, zooming, or resource management. Further, instead of just controlling a satellite's laser sites, you also need to take control of subs, jets, and anti-ballistic missiles. The keypad is put to good use as you quickly move to defend each of the six map quadrants and choose the best weapon for the different types of enemies. If you like this game, be sure to also check out Coleco's faithful ports to the Atari 8-bit and Commodore 64 computers.

It's always fun to think about what might have been. If Coleco had toughed it out with the ColecoVision, it would have had a better balanced portfolio of products when the Cabbage Patch Kids died on the vine. Even though the videogame business was shrinking, at less than 10 percent of sales in 1985,[14] it was still a viable source of income. Coleco could then have been a small part of the industry recovery in 1986, along with Nintendo, Sega, Atari, and even INTV, which provided an example of a lean, but sustainable business operation. Instead, with declining interest in its toys, huge amounts of debt, and nothing else to fall back on, Coleco filed for bankruptcy in 1988.

Even the ColecoVision's core technology, despite inadequate amounts of RAM and limited scrolling capabilities, would have been competitive through at least the mid-1980s, particularly with increased cartridge ROM sizes. In fact, using nothing more than intelligent programming techniques and higher capacity cartridges, today's homebrew programmers have fulfilled Coleco's "arcade at home" promise in ways previously thought impossible. Thanks to its expansion port, modern add-ons like the officially licensed Super Game Module from Opcode Games point to one possible avenue that Coleco could have pursued to keep the ColecoVision competitive even long-term, perhaps then selling a combined unit as a ColecoVision II. Unfortunately, the ColecoVision's history played out far differently.

The ColecoVision Community Then and Now

The ColecoVision's post-Crash fate was far more tragic than the Intellivision's. By 1986, Texas-based Telegames picked up most of the remaining Coleco and CBS Electronics (distributors of the system and its games outside of the US) stock, as well as the rights to reproduce a selection of third-party software from companies like Activision, Imagic, and Xonox. Like INTV, some of this

---

third party software was stripped of any licensing, e.g., *Chuck Norris Superkicks*[15] (1983, Xonox) becoming *Kung Fu Superkicks*, and placed in budget packaging.

In that same year, the DINA two-in-one from Taiwan-based Bit Corporation was released, which was rebranded in the US by Telegames as the Personal Arcade. Besides its streamlined appearance and Nintendo Entertainment System-like gamepad, the Personal Arcade contained two cartridge ports, one for the ColecoVision, and another for the Sega SG-1000. This latter fact was downplayed since the SG-1000, the predecessor of the Sega Master System, was never released in the US. The simple *Galaga*-like shooting game *Meteoric Shower* was built-in, rounding out the basic feature set of this reasonably compatible, though mostly mediocre, clone system.[16] No attempt was made to clone the Adam, of course, although Telegames did carry some of the software.

Unfortunately, the Telegames warehouse was in the middle of tornado country, and much of its inventory was damaged or destroyed in 1994. After that tragic event, Telegames focused mostly on developing software for newer systems, though they did go on to produce ColecoVision emulation-based game packages for Windows-based PCs, like the *Personal Arcade* (1997) and *Classic Gamer: ColecoVision Hits Volume I* (1998). Since 2005, brand acquisition and enterprise development company River West Brands has had the rights to the Coleco toys and games branding, and continues to work with interested companies in producing products related to the ColecoVision.

As for the Adam, most of its post-Crash support was limited to newsletters. Two of the most popular of these publications were *ECN* (Expandable Computer News), which ran from 1984 to 1988, and *NIAD* (Northern Illiana ADAM Users), which ran from 1985 to 1994. Newsletters like those provided an important lifeline for the thousands of Adam loyalists and handful of pro and semi-pro developers still creating new hardware and software for the platform in earnest.

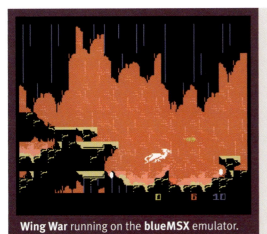

Wing War running on the **blueMSX** emulator.

Wing War (1983, Imagic)

Like *Destructor*, *Wing War* is another of those highly divisive titles of the love-it-or-hate-it variety. The love-it part is the premise and scope, where you control a fire breathing dragon in a multiscreen action adventure to bring a fire, water, and air crystal back to your cave to form a super crystal that unlocks a secret passage containing a diamond. The hate-it part is the controls, where you press the right side button to flap your dragon's wings to gain altitude while carefully maneuvering the joystick so that the momentum-based controls don't inadvertently catapult your avatar between screens or into enemies.

One thing is for sure, *Wing War* is an original and shows yet again why up until their unfortunate dissolution in the mid-1980s, Imagic had some of the most talented developers in their stable. For the adventurous, be sure to check out Imagic's unreleased port of the game for the TI-99/4a, which supported the speech synthesizer, and Europe-only release for the Atari 2600, which looks and plays a bit differently from the other two versions.

---

[15] Chuck Norris fact: The release of *Chuck Norris Superkicks* immediately made all other videogames irrelevant, leading to the Great Videogame Crash.

[16] Fun fact: Unlike most RF-based systems, instead of tuning to VHF channels 3 or 4, Bit Corporation's system needed to be on channel 13 to see its picture!

While outside of annual ADAMCON and other conventions, the Adam is mostly ignored today, the ColecoVision is among the best supported of the classic consoles in terms of new cartridge game releases. These releases include the usual assortment of prototypes and hacks,

but also a large number of new creations. Opcode Games (*Pac-Man Collection*, *Space Invaders Collection*), Team Pixelboy (*Girl's Garden*, *Golgo 13*), CollectorVision (*Armageddon*, *Burn Rubber*), Good Deal Games (*Monster Masher*, *Schlange CV*), AtariAge (*Spectar*, *Astro Invader*), and others regularly publish these great titles from this small, but dedicated population of developers.

The ColecoVision has a large, ever expanding library of homebrew releases.

This abundance of homebrew games is thanks in part to the ColecoVision's shared CPU and graphics chip with MSX computers, which were primarily found in Japan and parts of Europe, as well as Sega's SG-1000 console and SG-3000 computer series, which were primarily found in Japan, New Zealand, Australia, and parts of Europe. Similarly, the Sega Master System shared the same CPU, and (unlike the MSX) sound chip of the ColecoVision, but not its graphics hardware.[17] Not only did the longer commercial life of these architecturally similar systems point the way to how the ColecoVision and Adam platforms might have evolved had Coleco lasted through the Crash, but also provide a ready source of pre-existing software for today's homebrew programmers to leverage for relatively straightforward ports.

In terms of new hardware, there are two recent items of particular interest. The first of these is the Atarimax ColecoVision Ultimate SD Multi-Cart, which, among its other features, runs all standard 32K or smaller ROM images, as well as the new MEGA-CART bank-switch ROM images up to 512K, making it a simple way to experience a huge variety of games from one cartridge. The second of these is the aforementioned Super Game Module from Opcode Games, which plugs into the ColecoVision's or Adam's expansion port to finally enable the platform to truly mirror the technical capabilities of the era's arcade machines. As with the creation of new games for the base consoles, new games for the Super Game Module, like a nearly arcade perfect recreation of *Donkey Kong*, are being regularly produced.

Collecting for and Emulating the ColecoVision

Thanks to the ColecoVision's popularity, original consoles are still readily available today from various auction sites for reasonable prices. Popular tweaks from skilled modders include audio-video modifications for easier and cleaner connections to modern displays, as well as controller knob replacements and cord straightening, which make for more precise control. Further, most Atari or Sega Master System/Genesis controllers can also be substituted for those games that don't make use of the second action button or keypad.

---

17   Another similar platform and source of new homebrew ports was Memotech's MTX computer series, first released in 1983. Likewise, Texas Instruments' TI-99/4 and 4a computers, as well as the Tomy Pyuuta/Tutor computers, shared many of the same audio-visual traits. Only those computers' radically different 16-bit TMS 999x series microprocessors impede the cross-porting process.

GAME 8   AGI   0   FACES 4

0 P1 :17   0 P2

Zenji running on the **blueMSX** emulator.

Zenji (1984, Activision)

Matthew Hubbard's sliding puzzle game *Zenji* was proof that even without an original concept, the right developer can still make a stand-out creation. Variations on the sliding puzzle theme have been an electronic gaming staple since the 1970s, with refinements to the concept ever since, including Konami's 1982 arcade game *Loco-Motion* and, as mentioned in Chapter 1.5, Activision's own *Happy Trails* (1983) for the Intellivision, which also received a port of Konami's game. Hubbard's twist on this subgenre was that instead of sliding pieces of the maze to form complete portions of track for the main character to move through, *Zenji*'s happy face avatar could rotate the section of maze that he rolled onto. The difference seems subtle, but this variation allowed for a quicker pace of play well suited to the platform and mazes that got larger, faster.

Adam computers are also readily available, though the stand-alone form is more common than the expansion module, which also critically forgoes the upgraded video output. If you don't want to use the Adam's enormous printer, you can remove its power supply and place it into a case, or get a somewhat hard-to-find pre-modded stand-alone power supply.

Cartridge software is easy to find loose, while boxed games command more of a price premium. Third-party ColecoVision titles are the most valuable. Due to its rarity, most boxed Adam software is usually a great collector's item.

There were a handful of ColecoVision compatibles released, as well. One example was for an optional add-on for use of ColecoVision cartridges on Spectravideo's SV-318/328 computers, which were the prototypes for the MSX computer standard. Unfortunately, ColecoVision compatibles such as this are quite rare, and add-ons for Spectravideo's computers are seldom available for any price. Other options like the Bit Corporation systems suffer from frustrating design quirks and low reliability.

ColecoVision emulation is fairly mature, with software like *ColEM*, *KOLEKO*, *MESS*, and *blueMSX* (which, as the name implies also emulates the MSX platform) available for a variety of computers and mobile platforms. Some of these programs also emulate the Adam, but it's generally not a priority. Most new commercial homebrew software and add-ons predominantly target the ColecoVision rather than the Adam.

As with the Intellivision, for a nice compromise between the authenticity of the actual Coleco console and emulation, fans would do well to check out AtGames' ColecoVision Flashback TV Game system, which was released in 2014 and officially licensed from River West Brands. The two companies also worked together on a similarly official digital collection of ColecoVision games for Android, iOS, and PC platforms.

Part 2
Generation Two (1985–1994)

As the 1980s wore on, the industry stabilized into its present model of strong first-party hardware and software supplemented with key—usually officially licensed—third-party support. While competition was still fierce among platforms, this consolidation allowed all parties involved with a particular system to both have a stake in and benefit from its success. It allowed the industry to move past the Great Videogame Crash, ensuring a smoother, more sustainable growth curve, and preventing future bubbles from popping.

The old guard of Atari and Commodore would soon lose relevance, vanishing completely at the start of Generation Three. In the computer market, only Apple's Macintosh could withstand Microsoft's DOS and later Windows onslaught. The rise of Linux and other free operating systems in the 1990s seemed to pose a grave threat to both, but never managed to reach beyond niche communities and, more substantially, the server market, although it would eventually see mass adoption in the form of Google's Android operating system. In the console world, newcomers Nintendo and Sega would quickly usurp Atari as the king of videogames. The vicious marketing campaigns between these Japanese giants dominated the fanboy battles in American popular culture and playgrounds everywhere.

Other parts of the world evolved more slowly, with England and other European countries still favoring price over performance. In particular, this meant more sustained competition within the personal computer scene, and Atari and Commodore remained active there far longer than in North America. The vibrancy of the European market in this generation also birthed a whole army of "bedroom coders" whose skills would soon be appreciated the world over, giving the Americans a run for their money as the crème de la crème programmers.

It was also during this time that Japan asserted its own homegrown engineering and programming talents, eventually coming to supplant the US as the world leader in videogames. This prominence was thanks in part to Nintendo's release of the Game Boy. This release kicked off a series of Nintendo systems that continue to dominate the portable videogame market it established, despite facing an ever increasing amount of more technologically advanced competition.

While the Japanese market continued to support its own platforms, some of which were commercially irrelevant or unavailable outside their home country, markets started to merge by the end of this generation. Indeed, by Generation Three, platforms targeted to the world market would be the rule rather than the exception.

This generation also marked the rise of optical discs as the storage medium of choice for the next generation, proving crucial to enabling cost effective use of increasingly sophisticated hardware and their subsequently more demanding game engines. However, CD-ROM technology was still in its primitive, formative stages, with developers struggling to find ways to fill their relatively vast capacities with worthwhile content. As with laserdisc arcade games like *Dragon's Lair,* the initial answer to filling all this space came not in the form of larger game worlds or massive amounts of content, but in digitized reels of marginally interactive video (FMV, or Full Motion Video games). It seemed that developers and publishers of the time thought the more video, the better, with little regard to niggling details like quality, resolution, set design, or acting. It seemed if it was video and there was space on the disc, in it went.

Much like the short-lived laserdisc craze that faltered at the start of this generation, these early video-centric efforts on CD-ROM would also start to peter out at the beginning of the next generation, morphing into a more balanced usage of the available storage space. Eventually, of course, even the CD-ROM wouldn't be spacious enough. The phenomenon of game developers suddenly having orders of magnitude more storage space to work with is comparable, perhaps, to the revolutions in the film and television industry when sound and later color was introduced. These punctuations in the equilibrium of technological evolution, so to speak, gave small start-up companies such as Cyan (*Myst*) and Trilobyte (*The 7th Guest*) the opportunities to compete successfully with Electronic Arts and other established houses.

The second generation of the videogame industry was a time of upheaval, with a changing of the guard and revolutionary innovations like the CD-ROM and Nintendo Game Boy. It also witnessed plenty of evolutionary dead-ends like the short-lived full-motion video craze. If the Great Videogame Crash was the asteroid that killed the Atari and Commodore dinosaurs, Nintendo and Microsoft were the new mammals on the block. The impact these juggernauts made during this era, for better or worse, is still very much with us today.

Nintendo Entertainment System (1985)

History

Nearly 30 years after its North American launch in late 1985, the Nintendo Entertainment System (NES) and its celebrated game franchises continue to thrill millions of gamers all over the world. At a time when many in the industry and the mass media assumed videogame consoles were dead, the NES leapt onto the scene like, well, a certain mustachioed plumber, thoroughly squashing the moribund competition and becoming a new global cultural icon. Indeed, according to some surveys, American children are more likely to recognize Mario than Mickey Mouse![1]

Even as late as 1988, three years after its launch, Nintendo was still apparently struggling to meet consumer demand for its best-selling console, easily outselling all the other toys during each Christmas season.[2] It may seem odd today to liken a game console to children's toys like GI Joe or Transformers action figures, but this was precisely Nintendo's strategy. At a time when most major retailers were sensibly wary of videogames and consoles like the Atari VCS and ColecoVision after the Great Videogame Crash, Nintendo worked hard to market their product as a toy rather than a game console, heavily promoting their "Robotic Operating Buddy" (ROB) and Zapper light gun in their packaging and advertisements. Indeed, the first of Nintendo's television commercials in America only showed these devices; Mario is nowhere to be seen! According to this rather misleading commercial, ROB will "help you tackle even the toughest challenge," even though in actuality he was used in only two rather underwhelming games, *Gyromite* and *Stack-Up*. Some buddy he turned out to be! As we'll see, however, perhaps the challenge the

The cover of the manual for the Control Deck, showing the Nintendo Entertainment System with its standard controllers.

---

[1] This oft-stated claim is based on data compiled by the Marketing Evaluations company, who generates "Q-ratings" of consumer appeal for personalities, characters, and brands.

[2] According to an article by Joseph Pereira in the *Wall Street Journal*, November 22, 1988, retailers demanded 1.5 million NES units in that year alone. Total console and cartridge sales for that year totaled $850 million.

Bionic Commando (1988, Capcom)

Based loosely on an arcade game by the same name, *Bionic Commando* for the NES is a platform game with a fun hook—and we mean that literally. The character, Ladd Spencer, is a commando whose shtick is a bionic arm with a grappling gun, which he can use to climb and swing. It's a good thing he has it, too, since (for whatever reason) he is unable to jump. In the original Japanese version, the plot involved Nazism and was steeped with Nazi imagery, all of which was purged for the English localization. Of course, it was the swinging mechanic that grabbed all the attention from gamers and critics, who felt it brought something fresh and original to what was quickly becoming a saturated genre of platform games.

Bionic Commando on the **FCEUX** emulator.

commercial was talking about was getting the NES into stores in the first place. Even *Electronic Games* magazine was skeptical, writing in their March 1985 issue that "considering that the videogame market in America has virtually disappeared, [launching a console now] could be a miscalculation on Nintendo's part."[3]

In retrospect, it seems incredible that Nintendo would face such resistance in marketing their console in the US, but there was plenty of pessimism. It certainly didn't help that the console was initially more expensive than a ColecoVision, with cartridges costing five times as much.[4] Nevertheless, by 1987, the upstart had systems and games in over 12,000 US retail outlets and had seized 70% of the market.[5]

Nintendo is a very old company, with roots going back to 1889. Back then, it made playing cards before diversifying into taxis and "love hotels" in the 1960s. "Love hotels," by the way, are hourly-rate hotels where we can assume the guests did not play cards. In 1966, Nintendo unveiled the Ultra Hand into the Japanese toy market. This simple toy, which was a sort of pick-up tool, was designed by Gunpei Yokoi, the company's janitor. The then president of Nintendo, Hiroshi Yamauchi, saw Yokoi playing with the contraption, which he'd whipped up in his free time. Instead of punishing or firing him for goofing off, Yamauchi promoted Yokoi on the spot and demanded he develop his toy into a product line before Christmas. Yamauchi's instincts were spot-on; the product was the first of many sweeping successes Yokoi would bring to the company. The former janitor would go on to design several key products for Nintendo, including the Game & Watch handhelds, the famous D-pad style game controller, and the Game Boy. The Ultra Hand may also have inspired ROB, which he originally designed in 1985 as the "Family Computer Robot." As we'll see, ROB will play a key role in Nintendo's takeover of the American videogames market.

Nintendo was quick to see the promise of videogames. As early as 1974, Nintendo leapt at the opportunity to distribute the Magnavox Odyssey in Japan. Nintendo soon began making their

3   Steve Bloom, "Hotline," *Electronic Games*, March 1985.

4   According to Bob Davis and Sandra Ward, "High-tech Toys are Hot Again this Year but Biggest Sellers are Repeats of 1984,"*Wall Street Journal*, December 17, 1985.

5   N. Gross and G. Lewis, "Here Come the Super Mario Bros.," *Business Week*, November 9, 1987, p. 138.

SCORE-000000 TIME 0296 STAGE 01
PLAYER ▌▌▌▌▌▌▌▌▌▌▌▌   ♥-10
ENEMY ▌▌▌▌▌▌▌▌▌▌▌▌   P-03

Castlevania on the **FCEUX** emulator.

Castlevania
(1986, Konami)

Castlevania is a side-scrolling platformer with a dark, Gothic theme. The player controls Simon Belmont, a vampire hunter with a penchant for bullwhips, which he can use to kill bats, pumas, ghosts, and other creatures, as well as burst candelabra to get the goodies underneath. He also must face off against horror-themed bosses like Frankenstein's monster and mummies. The game launched a franchise that is still ongoing.

own gaming hardware, beginning with a set of five dedicated games, the Color TV-Game series, based on *PONG*, *Breakout*, and arcade racing games. In addition to console games, Nintendo was soon producing machines for the arcade, including *EVR Race* in 1975 and, more famously, *Donkey Kong* in 1981, which changed everything.

In 1980 Nintendo rolled out Yokoi's famous Game & Watch series of handhelds, which played a single game on an LCD screen. They were another breakthrough product for Nintendo. The inspiration for the product came when Yokoi was riding the bullet train back home one evening and noticed a man playing with a pocket calculator to pass the time. If a boring old calculator could be diverting, Yokoi wondered, what about a similar device that could actually play games? Since a joystick was impractical, Yokoi designed the D-pad that has now become standard on nearly every game controller. Eventually 59 titles were released, including *Donkey Kong* and *Balloon Fight*.

Powered up by the encouraging success of Game & Watch and other videogaming ventures, Nintendo decided to up the ante with a full-on game console. The goal was to create a system that would be cheap, but with enough of a lead in technology to keep it ahead of the competition for at least a year. The result was the "Family Computer," better known as the "Famicom," which Nintendo released in Japan in 1983, launching it with the ever-popular *Donkey Kong* and *Popeye* arcade games. Unfortunately, a design fault in these systems led to a recall that cost the company millions. Even

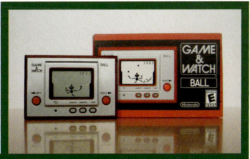

Image of the 2011 Club Nintendo exclusive recreation of the very first Game & Watch, **Ball**. Nintendo would go on to produce many electronic devices like this, including some with dual screens, tabletops, and even watches.

with this loss, the Famicom clobbered its competition, Sega's SG-1000, which had been released in Japan on the same day as the Famicom. This rivalry with Sega would continue for several generations of consoles, reaching its highest pitch with the release of the Sega Genesis (see Chapter 2.3).

Nintendo wasted little time in adapting their Famicom system for American distribution. They originally approached Atari to manufacture and distribute their system, which was to be renamed the "Nintendo Enhanced Video System." However, a complex series of events at the 1983 Consumer Electronics Show (CES) scuttled the deal. Atari had purchased from Nintendo the exclusive rights to make *Donkey Kong* ports for home computers, but Ray Kassar, the CEO of Atari at the time, saw the game running on a Coleco Adam, and felt they had been swindled. The case really gets at the ambiguity surrounding what constitutes a console versus a full computer, since the Adam is basically an add-on for the ColecoVision (see Chapter 1.8). In any case, the events apparently soured relations enough to send the deal into limbo, and it wasn't the last time the two videogame giants would be at odds.

Deciding to go it alone, Nintendo approached several major retailers, but were turned away. By this point, the Great Videogame Crash had brought the North American games industry to a grinding halt, with bargain bins all over the country filled to the brim with cut-rate cartridges and failed consoles. The company's first thought was to follow the lead of Coleco and others by turning their system into a full computer, with a datasette, keyboard, and BASIC programming cartridge. In a move prescient of their later Wii console, all of the system's components were wireless. However, when they unveiled this "Advanced Video System," or AVS, at the 1984 CES, no one was impressed with either the keyboard or the wireless capability. Once again, Nintendo had failed.

A year later, however, Nintendo returned to CES with a barebones unit they were now calling the "Nintendo Entertainment System," or NES. The keyboard, datasette, and wireless functionality were gone. In a move to distinguish it from other consoles, the cartridge slot sported a loading chamber that kept cartridges hidden from view when inserted. Instead of pushing the unit as a home computer, Nintendo sold it as a toy, and Yokoi's cutesy ROB played a key role in selling that perception. To further placate the skepticism of retailers, Nintendo offered to do their

Contra on the **FCEUX** emulator.

Contra
(1988, Konami)

The game that would come to define the "run-'n'-gun" genre began as a 1987 coin-op arcade game, before the developer decided to port it for various home computers and consoles. They produced the 1988 NES version in-house, making some subtle and not-so-subtle changes, including removing the time limit of the arcade version. Gamers loved the tight controls and fast pace, as well as the polished levels and two-player functionality. This was also the game that helped make the "Konami Code" a meme among gamers.

store setups and marketing, and even give them a three-month credit on the merchandise.[6] Any unsold units could be returned to Nintendo for a full refund. Fortunately, Nintendo was never asked to make good on that promise.

The NES was an unbelievable success in America just as the Famicom had been in Japan. At least 34 million units were sold in the US, with 61.91 million sold worldwide.[7] In five years, the NES had more active users in America than any previous console, and had replaced Toyota as Japan's most profitable corporation. By 1989, NES units were in over 20 million American homes. No one was declaring the death of the videogames industry any more. Indeed, as one reporter for *The New York Times* put it rather begrudgingly, "It takes work to avoid Nintendo. There are Nintendo television shows, a cereal and a magazine, as well as T-shirts, sweatshirts hats, pins, pajamas, beach towels and school lunch boxes."[8] Now everyone knew that videogames were here to stay.

What made Nintendo and the NES so mind-bogglingly successful? There are at least three key factors: designing great games, regulating the supply of consoles and cartridges, and patenting a "lockout" system to maximize licensing fees from third-party game developers.

First off, Nintendo had Shigeru Miyamoto at their disposal. An artist rather than a programmer by training, Miyamoto's game designs were radically fresh and different from those of his rivals, and emphasized bright and cheerful aesthetics that delighted gamers of all ages. Miyamoto established a name for himself with *Donkey Kong*, the 1981 Nintendo arcade game that also introduced us to Mario (though he was a carpenter called "Jumpman" in that game) and the classic rescue-the-damsel theme. Miyamoto built on many of the gameplay mechanics of *Donkey Kong* to make *Mario Bros.*, a 1983 arcade game that added several key innovations to the genre. The best was the ability to defeat enemies (turtles) by hitting the platforms beneath them, flipping them on their backs. At this point, Mario can jump on them from above, squash-

ing them. The game also sports the familiar pipes and coins that have become staples in the series. As impressive as *Donkey Kong* and *Mario Bros.* were, however, the brilliant Miyamoto was just getting started.

In 1985, Miyamoto and Takashi "Ten Ten" Tezuka created *Super Mario Bros.* The game was indeed a super upgrade to the original, with a partial side-scrolling feature that allowed for a much larger game world. Mario (or Luigi) can also receive a variety of fun power-ups, especially a magic mushroom that enlarges them. It is also possible to destroy blocks by hitting them from below, which allows for some fun tactics as well as locations to hide

Super Mario Bros. is the game that established Nintendo as a household name. Screenshot taken with the **FCEUX** emulator.

---

[6] Worlds of Wonder, the toy company who struck it big in the mid-1980s with Lazer Tag and Teddy Ruxpin, was Nintendo's initial partner for getting into big box stores. Within a few years, Nintendo would no longer need the company's assistance, and Worlds of Wonder, like Coleco a few years before it, would be out of business by 1990.

[7] According to Nintendo's own Consolidated Sales Transition by Region charts, available at www.webcitation.org/5nXieXX2B.

[8] A.R., "The Games Played for Nintendo's Sales," *The New York Times*, December 21, 1989.

A page from the first issue of **Nintendo Power**, July/August 1988, showing gameplay strategy for **The Legend of Zelda**'s first level. **Nintendo Power** was one of the most popular and longest running of the official console magazines, lasting until its final December 2012 issue.

bonus items. Perhaps what makes the game so compelling, however, is the fine attention to detail and precision. The game looks, sounds, and feels great, with a degree of spit and polish seldom seen from other game studios.

As if *Super Mario Bros.* wasn't enough to make Nintendo a household name, Miyamoto and Ten Ten followed up in 1986 with *The Legend of Zelda*, an "action-adventure" game that allowed even greater exploration and immersion than *Super Mario Bros.* Originally released for the Japanese-only Famicom Disk System, by the time it reached the US the following year, it had found its way onto one of the first cartridges with battery-backed memory for saved games. Eventually selling well over 50 million copies, Link is second only to Mario in terms of popularity among Nintendo's legions of fans.

Super Mario Bros. was followed by two more hit sequels in the US. Of these, *Super Mario Bros. 3*, which was released in the US in 1990, is by far the best-selling—it was even listed in the 2008 *Guinness Book of World Records* as the best-selling game of all time (that wasn't bundled with a system). Needless to say, Nintendo owes a great deal of its success to the design genius of Shigeru Miyamoto.

However, great games aren't the only part of the story. Nintendo had learned from the court battles fought by Atari and its rivals about the perils and opportunities of licensing. The second factor was American operations manager Peter Main, a former marketer for Colgate toothpaste. Despite his lack of experience with the videogame industry, Main recognized several of the NES's key advantages, including longer gameplay sessions. The older generation had specialized in what we'd call "casual" games today; games intended to be played for minutes rather than hours. After a half hour or so, you either finished the game or got bored and quit. The reason, of course, is that many of these games were based on arcade games, which were designed that way for economic reasons—you don't make money if someone can play for hours on a single quarter! Main realized, however, that games like the role-playing classic *Dragon Warrior* (1989), which can take up to 200 hours to complete, were the future.

Main also knew how to manipulate the market, limiting production runs to keep demand high without saturation. To this end, the company only partially filled retailer orders for games

Crystalis on the **FCEUX** emulator.

Crystalis (1990, SNK)

Although lesser known than *Legend of Zelda*, *Crystalis* is a solid action-RPG game that has become a cult classic among aficionados of the genre. Unlike Link, the hero of this game can move diagonally, but the plot is similar in structure—find the four elemental Swords of Water, Thunder, Fire, and Wind, and combine them to form the mighty sword Crystalis and defeat the despicable Emperor Draygon. There's also more role-playing in this game and its dialog. Allegedly influenced by the Hayao Miyazaki classic *Nausicaä of the Valley of the Wind*, *Crystalis* was called *God Slayer: Sonata of the Far-Away Sky* in Japan. The excellent music greatly enhances the mood. Unfortunately, a later version released for the Game Boy Color was inferior to its predecessor in almost every way. Stick to the original.

and systems. In 1988, Nintendo only shipped 33 of the 45 million cartridges ordered by retailers.[9] It was a strategy that infuriated these same retailers, but it only made Junior (and his frustrated parents) scream more loudly for the latest NES games at Christmas time.

Nintendo did not want to allow other companies to make games for their system without paying a hefty licensing fee. To this end, they ingeniously created and patented the 10NES lockout system. Any cartridge that did not contain a special microchip would not run on their system. Thanks to patent protection, only Nintendo could legally make these chips, and their control of a patent was much more powerful in court than a copyright would have been. This also allowed Nintendo to prevent games from being released that didn't measure up to their strict quality and moral standards. More importantly, it allowed them to make a profit from every game sold, regardless of where it originated.

In 1987, an embattled Atari had split off its console game publishing division, relabeling it "Tengen." They then tried and failed to get a better licensing deal from Nintendo. Scorned by Nintendo's prompt rejection, Tengen then asked the US Copyright office for the details on the 10NES, allegedly using this information to build their own chip called the Rabbit. As if to rub it in, Randy Broweleit, a marketing official for Atari, emphasized how the new Tengen packaging would sport a "Made in USA" logo to distinguish them from Nintendo's authorized games. To no one's surprise, Nintendo promptly sued. Although Atari/Tengen had sympathy in some political circles who agreed that Nintendo's practice felt like it was stifling competition unfairly, the point became moot when the two settled out of court.

Perhaps the most infamous court battle between Atari and Nintendo took place in 1989. By then, the *Tetris* craze was gaining rapid momentum, and everyone knew that whoever owned the rights to the NES version would make a huge fortune. Unfortunately, the copyrights were owned by the Soviet Union government, who made a real mess out of licensing. In a convoluted series of arrangements, Atari ended up with the rights to make the arcade version, whereas Nintendo was given the rights for handheld versions and non-Japanese console versions (Namco had the Japanese console rights). Atari, acting under Tengen, released an NES version anyway, an act that naturally erupted a long and costly legal response from Nintendo. Again, the issue came down to whether a game system, in this case the NES, was a console or a computer. Eventually, Tengen lost the case, and was forced to recall their version—which many fans considered superior to Nintendo's.

Although gamers loved Nintendo and their games and consoles, the company was becoming just as well known for its heavy-handedness with retailers. In 1991, they lost a price-fixing case. To keep retailers from discounting sales of their system, Nintendo had threatened to cut off their supply. The Federal Trade Commission called it a "pernicious practice" and wanted to make an example of the company, who had to cover the court costs as well as send $5 coupons to anyone who had purchased their system between 1988 and 1990.

Despite these and other setbacks, however, the NES remained the dominant console of its generation, lasting well into the 1990s. At the time of its American release in late 1985, the NES didn't have much serious competition from other consoles. By 1988, however, parents shopping in the Sears Wish Book could choose among an $89 Atari 7800, a $109 Sega Master System ($149.99 for the version with "SegaScope 3D" glasses),[10] or a $99 Nintendo Action Set (which included everything but ROB). It's telling, of course, that the catalog dedicates a full three pages to Nintendo and its games, whereas Atari and Sega get only a page each. While fans of these platforms still debate their relative strengths and weaknesses, there's no doubt that Nintendo had the decisive lead.

Nintendo made its last NES in August of 1995. By that point, their Super NES had been available for four years and had long since replaced its older brother as the king of Nintendo consoles.

Today it may be hard for some to picture a videogames industry without the heavy influence of Nintendo, Sega, and other Japanese companies. Jack Tramiel of Commodore (and later Atari) had always feared a Japanese takeover of the home computer market with the MSX standard, but that never occurred. The real invasion took place in the console market, where Nintendo, Sega, and eventually Sony replaced Atari, Mattel, and Coleco as the key players in the console market. The result of this heavy penetration of Japanese technology and games has left an indelible

Duck Tales on the **FCEUX** emulator.

DuckTales
(1989, Capcom)

What kid growing up in the 1980s didn't love Disney's *DuckTales* cartoon? We bet you can sing the catchy theme music even today. Capcom did a great job adapting the property into a fun and satisfying platform game, with an irresistibly cutesy aesthetic—this is definitely no duck-blur. Considered the gold-standard of NES cartoon-based games, *DuckTales* is a solid platform game for fans of the television series or just platform games in general. *DuckTales Remastered*, which remade the game in high definition, was released in 2013 for the Xbox 360, PlayStation 3, and Wii U. Ooh ooh!

---

10   Much like how Nintendo initially relied on Worlds of Wonder, Sega initially relied on Tonka for help breaking into the American retail market.

impression on multiple generations of American gamers, many of whom grew up playing Japanese, rather than American-made, games. With the sole exception of *Tetris*, the top ten best-selling games for the system were all made in Japan. Although American gamers continue to clamor for the latest Japanese games, the feeling is far from mutual. Even major Western franchises like *Halo* and *Call of Duty* are played by only a small fraction of Japanese gamers.[11]

All in all, the NES is without question among the most important and influential game consoles of all time. While a lot of this impact comes from the stellar quality and variety of its game library, Nintendo's shrewd business strategies paid off royally, allowing them to placate skeptical retailers in America. They had learned from Atari and Coleco and were able to capitalize on their successes while avoiding their mistakes. Perhaps more importantly from a cultural perspective, the NES helped make Japan the undisputed leader of the worldwide console market, a position the nation still enjoys today. And it owes it all to an artist, a janitor, and a toothpaste salesman.

Notable Accessories

The NES enjoyed some of the most memorable third-party accessories and peripherals of any other platform. Probably the most famous (or infamous!) of these is the Power Glove, which was featured in *The Wizard*, a 1989 movie/Nintendo promotional vehicle starring Fred Savage. Manufactured by Mattel, the Power Glove may have looked cool, but fell far short of its overblown marketing claims of "revolutionizing the video game interface." In reality, the Power Glove was a clunky and imprecise way to control most games, and certainly in no way superior to the default game pads shipped with the system. Today it ranks on several lists of the worst game controllers ever.

The Power Glove, seen here about to grab ROB, was mostly ineffective as a game controller, but it looks so bad. Not pictured is the sensor array that needed to be placed around the television for proper tracking of the glove. The dust on the glove and discoloration of the robot's plastic are two of the pitfalls of modern-day collecting.

Another seemingly innovative controller called the U-Force was introduced by Broderbund in 1989. This time, there was no glove; only infrared beams that tried to interpret hand movements. Unfortunately, much like the Power Glove, the concept was much cooler than the execution could hope to be for the technology of the time.

A slightly more successful accessory was the Power Pad, which resembles a Twister mat but with panels reminiscent of a *Dance Dance Revolution* game. Made by Bandai, it was marketed primarily as a way to curb the growing obesity epidemic. Most of the handful of games made for the Power Pad were related to athletics or exercise, such as *Athletic World* and *Dance Aerobics*.

---

[11]   There are many proposed explanations for this imbalance. According to Ryan Winterhalter of 1up.com, there is a widespread bias among Japanese gamers against Western games. According to Winterhalter, when a "high profile JRPG maker" played *Bioshock*, he threw down the controller after less than a minute, claiming the game "felt cheap."

Nintendo was impressed enough with the product's potential to take over its distribution and bundle it as part of their Power Set.

The NES Advantage was an arcade-style joystick designed to lie on a flat surface. Considered among the best accessories for the system, the NES Advantage is great for playing arcade ports and controlling the Statue of Liberty.[12]

Software Toolworks also released a musical keyboard for the NES called the Miracle Piano Teaching System. Intended to help kids learn to play the piano, the system was too expensive ($500) to generate enough sales to keep it viable. Still, what could be more fun than playing the correct note to shoot down a duck?

There were plenty of other accessories available, including a wide variety of controllers, light guns, and a cavalcade of non-game merchandise ranging from bed sheets to cereal.

This modern-day game box mock-up shows the three games—**Super Mario Bros.**, **Duck Hunt**, and **World Class Track Meet**—that were featured in the Nintendo Entertainment System Power Set, which included two gamepads, the Zapper, and the double-sided Power Pad. Nintendo would make the NES the centerpiece of a variety of bundles over the years.

Mega Man on the **FCEUX** emulator.

Mega Man
(1987, Capcom)

The NES was a haven for great platform games, and *Mega Man* is widely ranked among the best despite its difficulty. Its six-man development team had worked insatiably to produce one of the most polished and artistic games of its type. Unfortunately, some hideously bad cover art on the North American box may have played a role in its disappointing sales—several prominent publications have ranked it the worst game cover of all time! Still, the game was successful enough to warrant a sequel, and eventually it became one of Capcom's most successful franchises.

---

12   As seen in the 1989 movie, *Ghostbusters II*.

Technical Specifications

The NES featured a Ricoh RP2A03 8-bit 6502 microprocessor that ran up to 1.7 MHz, with 2K of memory. The display was capable of 256 × 240 resolution with 54 simultaneous colors, although most games were in 256 × 224 to compensate for older televisions. The system supported up to 64 sprites. The NES's audio capabilities featured four channels of mono sound: two for square waves, one for a triangle wave, and a noise generator. There were two ports for controllers. The standard controllers had an eight-way thumb pad, two action buttons, and a start and select button. Many gamers, particularly adults, found the small, boxy controllers awkward or even painful to use for extended periods. Nevertheless, due to its ubiquity on Japanese systems, it did not take long for gamepads to replace joysticks as the industry standard for console controllers.

One of the design goals of the NES was that it should be at least a year ahead of the competition in terms of technology, a goal it mostly met. One of its major advantages was hardware scrolling with support for tile-mapping, which was used to superb effect in games such as *Metroid*. Although the 2K of memory might seem like a severe limitation, Nintendo wisely designed the system so that cartridges could have their own RAM, expanding the available memory of the system. The Sega Master System, released in American in 1986, was largely technically superior. By that time, however, Nintendo had achieved enough momentum and brand recognition to prevent both the Sega Master System and Atari's 7800 from seriously threatening its dominance. Then, as now, most gamers will choose the system with the best and most abundant game library, not the one with the most impressive technical specs.

The NES did have a technological ace-in-the-hole, however, and that was the ability for the console to leverage special chips placed inside cartridges to extend the platform's capabilities. The most famous of these was Nintendo's MMC-series of chips, with for instance the MMC1,

Metroid on the **FCEUX** emulator.

Metroid (1986, Nintendo)

Metroid is one of the best games for the NES and remains one of the most engaging side-scrolling platform games of all time. Players take control of a dude in a suit named Samus (hey, no spoilers here!), a bounty hunter who must make his way through a vast fortress planet of Zebes while battling a wide assortment of enemies. What makes the gameplay stand out, however, are the many power-ups you can find for your suit, such as high jump boots and ice beams. Far more than just weapon upgrades, these items allow Samus to explore new parts of the map that were inaccessible before. Another good reason to check out this game is the amazing musical score by Hirokazu Tanaka, which really sets a profoundly somber mood.

used in games like *The Legend of Zelda* and *Metroid*, allowing for saved games, better multidirectional scrolling, and improved memory switching.

No discussion of the NES's hardware would be complete without mention of the infamous issue with its cartridge slot. These were caused by the 10NES lockout chip discussed above, which required a constant connection. Over time, the connectors would loosen or wear out, impeding or blocking the all-important connection. To temporarily "fix" the problem, gamers would blow into the cartridge connectors, slap it around, or even lick it! Needless to say, sometimes these "solutions" only led to more problems. Owners could take their system to a "Nintendo Authorized Repair Center," which were basically just shops who had agreed to pay the company a large fee to qualify for replacement parts.

In 1993, Nintendo released the NES-101, called the "Nintendo Entertainment System Control Deck." This was a much smaller version of the system usually referred to as "the top-loader," since the new design eliminated the cartridge garage in favor of a slot on top of the unit. It's also quite a bit smaller, though it did lose its composite audio-video out in favor of only RF output. The system included one "Dogbone" controller, so named because of its shape, with rounded edges rather than the harsh corners of the original. Retailing for $49.99 in the US, the NES-101 was only in production for five months. By this point, anyone who was serious about gaming had moved on to a Sega Genesis or Super NES. However, the limited production run, as well as some key advantages—such as its redesigned cartridge slot and lack of a lockout chip—make it a great collector's item today, even with the less desirable restriction on its audio-video output.

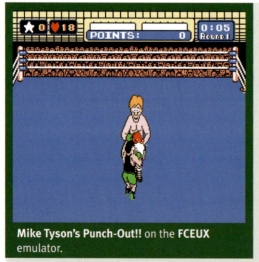

Mike Tyson's Punch-Out!! on the **FCEUX** emulator.

Mike Tyson's Punch Out!! (1987, Nintendo)

It's been over 25 years since Little Mac, the 17-year-old boxer from the Bronx, threw his first uppercut at a 21-year-old Mike Tyson in this loose interpretation of the arcade games. Still, who has forgotten about Glass Joe and Doc Louis? This seminal boxing game is ranked by many among the best games on the platform, and even if you have zero interest in boxing, you don't want to miss this one. For one thing, the designers preferred arcade fun over realism, and the goofy, cartoony graphics are much more humorous than gory. Nintendo lucked out by licensing Mike Tyson's likeness for a mere $50,000 for three years. It's a good thing they signed the contract just before he became the World Boxing Council heavyweight champion in a famous fight against Trever Berbick. After the three-year contract expired, Nintendo rebranded the game as *Punch-Out!!*, renaming the controversial Tyson's in-game character to Mr. Dream. With stellar sales and critical reviews, *Punch-Out!!* was a discombobulatingly devastating part of the NES's game lineup.

The Nintendo Entertainment System Community Then and Now

In its heyday in the mid- to late 1980s, the NES enjoyed a user base of over 30 million in the US alone. The appeal was so great that one reporter wrote that "for boys in this country between the ages of 8 and 15, not having a Nintendo is like not having a baseball bat."[13] Shortly after, an 11-year-old girl wrote back in response to the article, objecting to the term "boys" in that statement. According to her, "Just as many female adolescents like Nintendo as males do."[14] She could have added that the appeal was just as strong for adults as well, many of whom enjoyed playing games like *Duck Hunt* as much as their children. The systems were also popular at colleges, where students could pool their money to buy and share new games and compete for high scores. Much like the Wii 20 years later, the NES enjoyed nearly universal appeal, with a huge variety of games suitable for all ages.

By far the most popular magazine for the NES was *Nintendo Power*, which began publication in 1988. The magazine, an official Nintendo publication, was focused mostly on game tips and reviews, including colorful maps for popular games like *The Legend of Zelda*. Before *Nintendo Power*, Nintendo had offered a free printed publication as part of its "Nintendo Fun Club." This is the club referenced in *Mike Tyson's Punch-Out!!*, when Little Mac's trainer advises him to join the Nintendo Fun Club to learn how to win more matches.

Naturally, not everyone was pleased with Nintendo's success. Besides the understandable protests from retailers and rivals concerning the company's monopolistic tendencies, there were plenty of silly claims about the systems causing obesity, addiction, or even physical harm. The latter were usually cases of so-called "Nintendo thumb," or blisters or other ailments brought on by excessive use of a D-pad. There were also the usual litany of complaints about videogame addiction and possible links to violence, though Nintendo's strict censorship policies kept these complaints to a minimum.

Today, NES enthusiasts congregate in large numbers online. Probably the best place to get started is YouTube, where fans exchange gameplay videos, reviews, and discussions of their favorite games and accessories. Speed runs, in which players try to complete a game in the shortest possible time, have become a staple, with some truly remarkable performances by highly skilled players. Freddy Anderson's speed run of *Super Mario Bros. 3* is particularly impressive, clocking in at only ten minutes, 48 seconds.

The NES's distinctive sound hardware inspired countless memorable soundtracks. Many of these have been remixed by some truly talented artists, such as the bands Armcannon and Metroid Metal. Indeed, a whole

Blade Buster is a homebrew project with great graphics and animation. Screenshot taken with the **FCEUX** emulator.

---

13   D.C., "Nintendo Scores Big," *The New York Times*, December 4, 1988.

14   D.S. Margolin, "Nintendo Fans," *The New York Times*, January 1, 1989.

genre called "Nintendocore" has grown up around the idea of fusing modern genres with music and sounds from the NES and Game Boy. The Advantage, Power Glove, Daniel Tidwell, and The Minibosses are great examples.

One of the best sites for modern NES homebrew enthusiasts is www.nesworld.com. The site has loads of information for collectors, gamers, and history buffs alike. Some of the best NES homebrew includes Kent Hansen and Andreas Pedersen's *D-Pad Hero,* which is a fun take on *Guitar Hero* for the NES, and High Level Challenge's *Blade Buster,* a shoot-'em-up that really demonstrates the latent audiovisual potential of the platform. There is also a lively discussion forum on the site with hundreds of active members. Other popular forums for NES fans are at http://gonintendo.com, http://nintendoage.com, and http://nesforums.com.

Collecting for the Nintendo Entertainment System

Because there were so many units sold and distributed widely, it's easy and relatively inexpensive to find working NES units in good condition on online auction sites or retrogaming shops. Unless you're concerned about historical accuracy, it's probably a good idea to get a unit with a refurbished pin connector and disabled lockout chip. Although generally pricier, the NES-101 is a good system for collecting as well, especially since it's more reliable and has no lockout system to worry about, but you may wish to consider an upgrade to its RF output.

If you don't care about owning actual Nintendo hardware, you might spring instead for a clone gaming system, such as those from Retro-Bit or Hyperkin. The accuracy and reliability of these knock-offs vary widely, so you should take time to study the reviews carefully before making a purchase. One major advantage of these systems is the ability to run games from multiple systems on one unit, an important consideration for those with limited space.

The cost of acquiring game cartridges varies, of course, depending on the relative obscurity and desirability of each title. Many NES owners discarded the boxes and manuals that came with their games, so copies with intact packaging usually cost quite a bit more than loose cartridges.

There are several extremely rare and sought-after NES cartridges that any hardcore collector would love to own. *Stadium Events*, a game for the Power Pad that Nintendo quickly bought out from Bandai and rereleased as *World Class Track Meet,* is said to have only 200 copies still around. An eBay auction in 2010 for a sealed copy broke records by reaching $41,300! Another high-ticket item is *Nintendo World Championships*

Since Nintendo's patents have expired on its NES technology, many quality clones, both handheld and console, are now available for purchase. Shown here is the prototype version of perhaps one of the most interesting of such clone systems, Hyperkin's RetroN 5, which not only plays Famicom and NES cartridges, but also those for the Super Nintendo, Sega Genesis, and Game Boy Advance, among others.

Ninja Gaiden on the **FCEUX** emulator.

Ninja Gaiden
(1988, Tecmo)

Nostalgic gamers like to bemoan the state of modern gaming, in which no real skill or patience is required to beat a game. Clearly, they wouldn't last ten seconds with a *real* challenge like *Ninja Gaiden*. Celebrated for its intense difficulty, *Ninja Gaiden* is another side-scrolling platformer, but this time with a ninja named Ryu battling his way through cities, jungles, castles, and snow. It also featured some awesome cut-scenes inspired by anime. Not that you got to see very many—did we mention this game required *actual* ninja skills to win?

Gold, a promotional item for the 1990 "Nintendo World Championship." These can command tens of thousands of dollars. An alternative to these high priced originals are reproductions from companies like Retrozone, who also stock one of the several types of flash cartridges available that allow transferring ROM images for play on a real system, as well as homebrew game development.

For the most dedicated of collectors, there is the whole world of Japanese Famicom hardware, accessories, and software to explore. While emulation is the safest, most inexpensive route to investigating some of these Japanese releases, there's nothing quite like using the actual items little seen or known outside of their home country. There are even a few dozen or so releases exclusive to the European PAL television format that generally work on NES-compatible systems that don't have a lockout chip. Differences in CPU speed and display formats may cause a few peculiarities in play, however, so if you favor accuracy with these releases, either get a PAL-based system or stick to emulation.

Nintendo's earlier release of the Famicom and interesting sublicensing, add-ons, and software variations that were never released outside of Japan make it an interesting, if challenging, platform for the would-be collector. Generally speaking, with a simple pin adapter, most Famicom and NES cartridges are cross-compatible, even if many of the other items aren't.

Emulating the Nintendo Entertainment System

Emulation for the NES is generally considered 100 percent accurate, and ROM images for just about every game are freely available online. The two most popular choices for emulators are *FCEUX* and *Nestopia*. Ports of these excellent and straightforward emulators are available for

Windows, Macintosh, and Linux. Sites like virtualnes.com will even let you play many NES games right in your web browser.

Naturally, playing these games will be more authentic with the proper controller. Amazon and ThinkGeek offer USB controllers that closely resemble the original NES controllers. Ranging from $7–30, they are a cheap and easy way to duplicate the feel of an NES game without the actual hardware. Other options include USB adapters for the original controllers themselves. Using one of these definitely beats trying to play *Contra* with a keyboard!

FCEUX is a modern NES emulator for the PC and other platforms. The emulator is shown here playing **Double Dragon**.

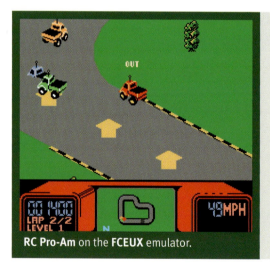

RC Pro-Am on the **FCEUX** emulator.

RC Pro-Am (1988, Rare)

Well before *Super Mario Kart* on the Super NES popularized the kart-racing genre, there was this little gem from Rare, an English company that was one of the few non-Japanese developers to realize great success on the platform. The novelty of this game was racing in remote-controlled cars, but the fun came in the form of power-ups like missiles and bombs, along with a fair share of hazards. Its modified isometric view was a refreshing change from the first-person view that was the standard of the day. Although it lacks the multiplayer mode found in its 1992 sequel, *RC Pro-Am II*, the original remains one of the most fun racing games for the system.

Of course, Nintendo and other companies have digitally rereleased large portions of their NES library for their later systems, like the 3DS and Wii U. Many unofficial emulators are also available on mobile platforms, like Android, allowing play on various smartphone, tablet, and console form factors.

Commodore Amiga (1985)

History

In his famous book *Primitive Culture*, anthropologist Sir Edward Burnett Tylor spends a great deal of time talking about fetishes. To classify something as a fetish, Tylor says we need an "explicit statement that a *spirit* is considered as embodied in it, or acting through it, or communicating by it, or at least that the people it belongs to habitually think it does." Furthermore, "The object is treated as having personal consciousness and power, is talked with, worshipped, prayed to, sacrificed to, petted, or ill-treated with reference to its past or future behavior to its votaries." Undoubtedly, there are many former Amiga owners reading this chapter who, with the possible exception of praying, can attest to engaging in all of these behaviors at some time or another with their beloved home computer!

Indeed, at the time of its release in 1985 and for many years afterward, the Amiga seemed almost mystical—an impression reinforced by the eccentric design decisions of its hardware and software teams, who left us with the famous "Guru Meditation Errors" and microchips named after their girlfriends (the word "amiga" itself, of course, is Spanish for "girlfriend"). Perhaps it is fitting that

The original Amiga, the 1000.

Andy Warhol, the avant-garde artist best known for such controversial pop art masterpieces as *Campbell's Soup Cans* and *Eight Elvises*, was a well-known fan of the system. Sadly, despite all its promise, the Amiga received little more than its 15 minutes of fame before fading from the mainstream. Today it is a rare treat even to see it mentioned in all but the best computer history books.

As told by Jeremy Reimer in a series of in-depth articles on the history of Amiga for the website *Ars Technica*, the tale of the Amiga begins essentially with one man: Jay Miner (1932–1994), an Atari engineer who had already distinguished himself by designing chips for the Atari VCS (see Chapter 1.3). Miner was not content, however, building "mere" game consoles. Instead, he wanted to make his mark on the nascent home computer industry, which at that time was dominated by the trinity of the Apple II, Commodore PET, and TRS-80. In 1979, he designed the Atari 400 (see Chapter 1.4), the first home computer to offer sprites and custom coprocessors for handling video, collision, sound, and so on. Unfortunately for Miner, Atari was afraid that its home computer line would cut into its lucrative profits on its consoles, so they advertised their utility as "serious" machines instead of showing off awesome Atari computer games like *Star Raiders.* It was, frankly, a stupid decision that hurt Atari computer sales and left the company vulnerable to competition from their vicious rival Commodore, whose ads for the VIC-20 and Commodore 64 were much more gamer-friendly. Miner was also fed up with the management style of Ray Kassar, the uptight businessman who took over Atari after the unhappy departure of founder Nolan Bushnell.

Deluxe Galaga AGA running on WinUAE.

Deluxe Galaga
(1994, Edgar M. Vigdal)

This shareware game is an enhanced (and unauthorized) remake of the popular Namco/Midway arcade game. In addition to updating the audiovisuals, Vigdal added power-ups and new types of aliens, mini-games, and even a shop for buying upgrades. The AGA version offers superior graphics, but all versions are superbly done and represent some of the best classic shoot-'em-up gameplay on the Amiga.

Miner was ready to jump ship, and when his friend Larry Kaplan called to invite him to join a startup called Hi-Toro, he didn't need much convincing. Kaplan, an Activision employee, had been selected by a group of investors (dentists and an oil baron) to start up a games company. Miner agreed to assume the role of chief engineer, but only if they'd let him work with the brand new 68000 CPU from Motorola. Miner recognized the 68000's potential, but its high price seemed hard to justify considering the success of the much cheaper 6502, whose variations had proven itself in everything from the Atari 2600 to the Commodore 64. The investors wanted Miner to design a game console, which he claimed to be doing, all the while secretly ensuring that his unit could easily be expanded into a full computer.

Fortunately for Miner (and unfortunately for his former company), the "Crash Christmas" of 1983 and ensuing collapse of the console market caused the investors to reverse their position. Now they wanted a computer instead of a console, and Miner was ready and happy to oblige.

In a twist of events, Hi-Toro was bought out by Commodore in 1984. Commodore's president, the brash but often brilliant Jack Tramiel, had recently left the company he founded and picked up the reins at his former rival, Atari. Tramiel hadn't left Commodore happily, and a morass of litigation over intellectual property stymied both companies. In the end, Commodore ended up with exclusive rights to Miner's chipset, but the slowdown gave Tramiel and Atari enough time to rush their Atari 520ST into production in June of 1985. The Amiga appeared only a month later, but its higher price ($1295 without a monitor compared to the ST's $1000 with color monitor) didn't do it any favors. Commodore also suffered production problems, giving Atari even more of a lead in the race. Naturally, the rivalry between the two companies extended into the fan communities, who are still exchanging vitriol on online forums nearly three decades later.

The Amiga platform would never seriously compete with the IBM PC platform, especially in business, education, and industrial markets. Amiga owners tended to be gamers or desktop video enthusiasts. The Atari ST and later Atari computers were also of most interest to gamers, though some musicians, including the noted synthesizer group Tangerine Dream, preferred the ST for its integrated MIDI capabilities.[1] Lack of built-in MIDI notwithstanding, the Amiga did offer great sound technology for the time. At a time when many computers were limited to a crummy internal speaker, Amiga users enjoyed four channels of 8-bit stereo goodness.

On a more positive note, the Amiga's game library is immense, covering every conceivable genre. Furthermore, several games originating on the Amiga were groundbreaking, highly innovative titles that continue to delight gamers. Several of the earliest games

One of Atari's more aggressive ads for its 520ST computer, one of the Amiga platform's bitter rivals. From the November 1985 issue of **Compute!**.

developed for the system, including Bill Williams' *Mind Walker*, Cinemaware's *Defender of the Crown*, and Damon Slye's *Arctic Fox* (all 1986), were all instant classics.

Mind Walker, a one-man production by Bill Williams, was actually a series of mini-games set in a patient's brain. The game's Freudian overtones, bizarre gameplay, and haunting music created a surreal, unsettling, and unique gaming experience.

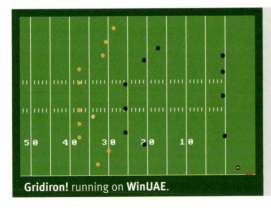

Gridiron! running on **WinUAE**.

Gridiron! (1986, Bethesda)

Well before anyone had heard of *The Elder Scrolls*, Bethesda made this football game. Gamers loved the tight controls and attention to realistic physics. As a result, the game was a triumph on the Amiga despite graphics that would have looked crude on a ColecoVision. The company's advertisements stressed that this was a game "by football addicts for football addicts," who apparently were much less concerned with atmosphere than convincing simulation of their favorite sport.

---

[1] However, the Atari ST's sound chip, the Yamaha YM2149 offered only a three voice squarewave plus one voice white noise generator, whereas the Amiga's Paula, a custom chip, offered four voices split between two stereo channels. The YM2149 was also used in the Intellivision, Vectrex, and ZX Spectrum 128, among others.

Defender of the Crown, designed by Kellyn Beck and illustrated by Jim Sachs, was an action/strategy hybrid whose graphics of medieval castles and beautiful maidens awed gamers, setting a new standard for graphical realism. Cinemaware went on to create several more classics for the system, always striving to incorporate movie-like elements into the action. For instance, *King of Chicago* (1987), which allowed gamers to become Pinky, an up-and-coming gangster striving to make his mark, took its cue from popular film noir. *Wings* (1990), as another example, was a variation on the flight simulator with a story and atmosphere lifted from World War I movies.

International Karate+ CD32 AGA version running on **WinUAE**.

International Karate+
(1988, System 3 Software)

Often abbreviated *IK+*, this beat-'em-up game offers highly polished martial arts action. Instead of the usual one-on-one fighting common in the genre, *IK+* pits three fighters on-screen at once, with intermittent mini-games designed to test a player's reaction time. Designed by Archer MacLean with music composed by Rob Hubbard and arranged by Dave Lowe, the game was better known in Europe than the United States. A version was also released for the Amiga CD32 in the UK.

Finally, *Arctic Fox*, developed by Dynamix, was a 3D tank simulation in the tradition of Atari's *Battlezone* (1980), although with greatly enhanced graphics and more complex gameplay. Like many modern first-person shooters, the player could see the avatar's hands, though this time controlling the tank rather than holding a gun. There were also several superb arcade conversions available by 1987, including Electronic Arts's *Marble Madness* and Taito's *Arkanoid*.

One of the best known of the Amiga game developers was DMA Design, a British company known for its highly polished graphics and music. One of their most popular games was *Lemmings*, a combination strategy and action game released in 1991 to instant critical acclaim. *Lemmings* players must lead tribes of the oblivious creatures to their destination using only the

mouse to rapidly issue commands to individuals. The game's cartoon-inspired graphics and humor was later ported to a variety of platforms. According to Mike Dailly, one of the game's programmers, *Lemmings* started off as a simple humorous animation of little walking men walking into a chomping mouth. Russell Kay saw the animation and thought it could be made into a game, and started using the term "lemmings" to refer to the little guys

Arkanoid, shown here running on the **WinUAE** emulator, was one of the best mouse-driven action games for the Amiga. It was inspired by the earlier arcade hit **Breakout**.

in the animation. Published by Psygnosis, *Lemmings* would soon become one of the must-have games for the system.[2]

Psygnosis also released one of the most revered of all the Amiga's many platform games: *Shadow of the Beast* (1989). *Shadow of the Beast* made exquisite use of the Amiga's ability to handle complex parallax scrolling, which simulates depth by having different background layers move at speeds relative to the player's character. Psygnosis released two sequels to *Beast*, the second of which ended as a pack-in with some Amiga 600 bundles. Other notable Psygnosis titles are the challenging scrolling shooter games *Blood Money* (1989) and *Agony* (1992), and *Hired Guns* (1993), a type of science-fiction role-playing game. *Hired Guns*, a variation on the formula established by FTL Games' *Dungeon Master* (1987), allowed players to control four autonomous adventurers, each with his or her own window and first-person perspective. Up to four players could play the game simultaneously.

Four of the last "classic" (non-AGA) games originating on the Amiga platform were *Cannon Fodder*, *The Settlers*, *Worms*, and *Pinball Dreams*. *Cannon Fodder*, released in 1993 by Sensi-

ble Software, was a strategy/action hybrid with loads of dark humor and vague political overtones. Featuring a scathing Rasta-themed soundtrack and a great deal of cartoonish violence, the game managed to arouse quite a bit of indignation in various parts of the world. Germany even banned sales of the game to minors. *The Settlers*, released in 1993 by a German developer named Blue Byte, was an early real-time strategy game. *The Settlers'*

Psygnosis games were known for their elaborate, highly stylized artwork, both in-game and on the packaging. Like Cinemaware, the Amiga was Psygnosis' premiere development platform for their state-of-the-art creations for quite some time.

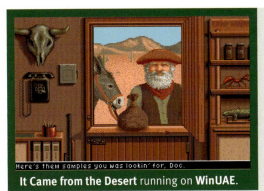

Here's them samples you was lookin' for, Doc.

It Came from the Desert running on **WinUAE**.

It Came from the Desert (1989, Cinemaware)

As their name implies, Cinemaware was a company inspired by classic cinema. As a result, their games tended to be more focused on story and style than gameplay. *It Came from the Desert* is one of their best titles, with a deep grounding in 1950s "giant insect" B-movies. The bulk of the game consists of trying to convince the incredulous townspeople of Lizard Breath that giant ants are real and about to take over their town. A strict 15-day time limit adds quite a bit of tension, as does the effective sound effects and musical score. In 1991, an updated version was released for the NEC TurboGrafx CD, which used full motion video of live actors, but proved less successful than the original.

---

2   See Mike Dailly, "The Complete History of Lemmings," www.javalemmings.com/DMA/Lem_1.htm.

catchy music, vividly detailed animations, and addictive gameplay helped make it one of the most popular games for the system. *Worms*, developed by Team 17 in 1994, remains one of the most popular of the "artillery" style games in which players take turns aiming and firing projectiles at each other. Team 17's key innovation was to introduce a wonderfully zany, cartoon-like theme to the characters and their weapons. Stuffed with allusions to *Monty Python's Flying Circus*, *Worms* infused the artillery genre with wit and charm. *Pinball Dreams*, released in 1992 by Digital Illusions CE, expanded on the computer pinball concept by offering tables that were larger than the screen, which scrolled rapidly up and down with the ball. These games were celebrated for their lush graphics and catchy melodies and spawned several sequels into the Amiga's next-generation, AGA era.

Of course, there was no shortage of ports and conversions for the Amiga. Sierra On-Line, ICOM Simulations, LucasArts, and Magnetic Scrolls offered high-quality graphical adventure games. Bullfrog Productions offered the "god game," *Populous* (1989), and the real-time strategy actionfest, *Syndicate* (1993). SSI offered versions of many of its classic strategy and role-playing games. Rainbow Arts' *Turrican* series (begun in 1990) provided one of the most compelling and recognizable of the Amiga's platform shooting games. Sports games were provided by the likes of Sensible Software (*Sensible Soccer*, 1992), Accolade (*Hardball!*, 1987), and Cinemaware (*TV Sports: Football*, 1988).

In short, the Amiga has an outstanding library of games, many of which are still avidly played, in one form or another, to this day. Furthermore, it was the proving ground of many new and highly innovative games. Indeed, perhaps the only computer platform that can truly be said to have eclipsed it in terms of depth and technical prowess is the modern PC.

Technical Specifications

The machine that would eventually become the Amiga 1000 was in many ways far ahead of its time—a fact that ended up having more negative consequences than positive. Perhaps its greatest and most innovative feature was multitasking, which even allowed multiple windows at different resolutions to display simultaneously. It was a feat of engineering genius that was sadly lost on most consumers. Another neat trick was the HAM (hold-and-modify) mode, which allowed all 4096 of the Amiga's colors to display at once through a bit of clever hacking. The rarely-used mode was probably used more for showing photo-realistic porn images than anything else, but it was a genuine marvel compared to the bulk of its competition, which had to make do with 16 or fewer colors. The sound capabilities of the Paula chip let the Amiga play four channels of sound, two on the left and two on the right. Musicians leapt at the chance to make excellent music to leverage the technology, mostly in a tidy format called MODs. Finally, after the introduction of *Deluxe Paint* by Electronic Arts in 1985, would-be artists could join Andy Warhol in creating fantastic graphics for the Amiga and other game systems, sharing them across platforms with the IFF format (which would be the industry standard for several years and is *still* included in many popular graphical editing programs).

Probably the greatest and most fantastic feature that someone would have noticed back then, however, was the graphical user interface, called Workbench. While windows, icons, and mice had been a usable concept since the 1970s, it had taken the industry a long time to rid themselves of boring and intimidating command-line interfaces like those found in CP/M and MS-DOS. Although Atari and Apple offered their own takes on the GUI, the Amiga's multitasking capability was a trump card.

The operating system was not quite ready when the Amiga 1000 was released, so Commodore included a "writable control store" of memory. When booting the machine, users

The **Deluxe Paint** series, shown here running on the **WinUAE** emulator, was a highly successful graphics editing tool used by amateurs as well as professional graphics artists.

Out of this World running on **WinUAE**.

Out of This World (1991, Delphine)

Known as *Another World* in Europe, *Out of this World* is a platform action-adventure game with a cinematic style. With its slick vector graphics based on motion-capture, *Another World* wowed gamers with some truly beautiful animation and an immersive sci-fi plot. Its richly detailed cutscenes created ripples throughout the industry. Eric Chahi, the game's designer, took advantage of the Amiga's genlock to rotoscope footage of himself performing the character's movements, lending the game its unique aesthetic and realistic character animation. It was a remarkable achievement for both Chahi and the Amiga platform.

inserted a disk called Kickstart, which contained the data read into this store and then locked down. This solution, while perhaps a bit cumbersome, allowed the company to painlessly release updates early on. The 1000 shipped with 256KB of RAM, but Miner's design included a convenient slot for a 256KB memory expansion cartridge. Since there was no hard drive, software was loaded from the internal 880KB 3.5-inch floppy drive, with the option for a second external drive. All Amiga computers came standard with two Atari-style joystick ports, which doubled as mouse ports. Conveniently, the keyboard could be stored in the "garage" under the system.

Later Models

The 1000 was the first Amiga, but it was quickly surpassed by later machines. The bestselling Amiga was the "low end" Amiga 500, released in 1987. The 500 retailed for only $600 without a monitor, a price that gave it a decisive edge over the 1000 and allowed a much larger user base to form around the platform (Commodore sold a minimum of 1 million units worldwide in 1991 alone, the best year for the 500). Despite its cheaper price, the 500 wasn't a step down in terms of

power. It was based on the same processor as the 1000, shared all of its graphics and sound capabilities, and came with 512KB of RAM, which was easily (and typically) expanded to 1MB (with battery backup clock) via a trap-door underneath the unit. By the time the 500 was released, the core operating system was much more stable and was included on a built-in ROM rather than a Kickstart disk. The

The Amiga 500 was the most successful Amiga, offering just the right combination of power and affordability.

500 included a built-in 3.5-inch floppy drive as well as a keyboard, making it more compact than the 1000. A plethora of expansions were soon available for the 500, which helped keep the system viable well into the 1990s.

Commodore also released the Amiga 2000 in 1987, a high-end computer that retailed for $1500. The 2000 was expandable to 8MB of RAM and had an optional hard drive. In general, the 2000 was larger and had far better internal expansion options. While its gaming capabilities were remarkable, the 2000 is best known for video editing, particularly when equipped with NewTek's Video Toaster, which was first released in 1990. The Video Toaster essentially turned an Amiga 2000 into a professional-quality video editing solution, complete with a 3D modeling, rendering, and animation program called *Lightwave*. For a total of $5000, a Toaster-equipped 2000 could do the work of a $100,000 professional setup, including green screening, titling, and even 3D rendering.

Speedball 2: Brutal Deluxe running on WinUAE.

Speedball 2: Brutal Deluxe
(1992, Bitmap Brothers)

This futuristic "cyberpunk" sports game offers plenty of violence and a significant step up from its predecessor. A hybrid of handball and ice hockey, *Speedball 2* was a smash hit for Bitmap Brothers and ranks highly on many "best of" lists of Amiga games on the net. Remakes of the game continue to be released to this day.

In 1990, Commodore released the 3000, another high-end machine. Like Atari's TT030 (1990) and Falcon (1992), it was based on Motorola's 32-bit 68030 processor, which was more than twice as powerful as the 68000. It came standard with 2MB of RAM (expandable to 18) and a built-in hard drive, and featured a graphic chipset called ECS, for Enhanced ChipSet. The ECS allowed for more chip RAM and three new four-color modes at 640 × 480, 1280 × 200, and 1280 × 256 resolution. It also included a built-in "flicker fixer" that stabilized these high resolution modes on compatible monitors.

Unfortunately for Amiga fans, Commodore was slow to respond to the challenge and opportunity represented by CD-ROM technology. Instead of releasing a new Amiga computer with an internal CD-ROM drive, they unsuccessfully experimented with set-top boxes. In March 1991, Commodore released a $1000 set-top box called the Commodore Dynamic Total Vision, or, simply, CDTV. The CDTV contained most of the Amiga 500's internals but was based around a CD-ROM drive and billed as a "media appliance" rather than a computer. Designed to blend with media components, it was all black, with buttons to control the unit on the front. The only other control device was a remote control that doubled as a gamepad. However, users could purchase a separate keyboard, mouse, and floppy drive and turn it into a full-blown Amiga 500-compatible unit. Unfortunately, the system failed to catch on. In fact, many Amiga 500 users were willing to wait instead for the external CD-ROM drive that would let them play games intended for the CDTV. All told, there were a little over 100 titles released worldwide for the system, all between 1990 and 1996.

In March 1992, Commodore inexplicably released the diminutive Amiga 600, another budget machine similar to the Amiga 500, although without the numeric keypad. It also featured the ECS graphics modes of the 3000 and came standard with 1MB of RAM. A hard-drive was optional. Manufactured in the United Kingdom, the 600 never achieved much success in the United States, where it was overshadowed by the next-generation AGA-based Amiga 1200 and Amiga 4000, released in October of the same year. It seems that Commodore was attempting the same low end/high end approach that had enjoyed so much success with the 500 and 2000. Unfortunately, by this time the IBM PC's graphics capabilities had long since caught up with and surpassed those of the Amiga, and the boost provided by AGA technology, which increased the color palette from 4096 colors to 16.8 million, with up to 256 on-screen at once (262,144 colors

for the new HAM mode), was simply too little and too late to save the dying platform, particularly since few other enhancements were implemented. In 1993, Commodore tried its luck with an ill-fated game console called the Amiga CD32, which was based off of technology in the 1200 and able to run most of the CDTV's library. The CD32 proved a dismal failure, and never saw wide release in the United States due to a patent dispute.

The CD32, shown here on top of a CDTV, was a bold move for Commodore, but the console failed to win over many new or existing fans thanks in part to its limited distribution.

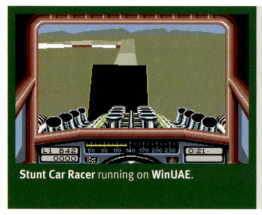

Stunt Car Racer running on **WinUAE**.

Stunt Car Racer (1989, Microstyle)

As the title implies, this racing game takes place on a stunt track, a roller coaster-like affair with lots of ramps, loops, and intense curves to deal with. Two players can race each other, provided they have two Amigas and a null modem cable. The game's designer and programmer, Geoff Crammond, formerly was a systems engineer for the defense industry, and his keen knowledge of physics is evident in the realistic feel of the gameplay. Even if you're not a fan of racing games in general, *Stunt Car Racer* is definitely worth checking out.

The End of the Amiga Line

In May of 1994, Commodore filed for bankruptcy after posting a $357 million loss in 1993. A common sentiment among Amiga fans (then and now) is that the platform was bungled or even "betrayed" by Commodore's executives. A particular source of ire is the lack of effective advertising campaigns for the system. While an outsider might think that blaming a product's failure in the marketplace on faulty advertising is a bit naïve, consider that one of the Amiga's greatest assets—the option to add full IBM PC compatibility—was seldom even mentioned in advertisements. At a time when even a crude IBM compatible would have cost twice if not three times as much as an Amiga, the marketing team apparently didn't find this optional feature, along with other add-ons that could emulate a Commodore 64 or Apple Macintosh, worth bringing up.

The Amiga, particularly the 500, enjoyed a healthy advantage over competitors; it offered superior technology over the Atari ST and was a fraction of the cost of the Macintosh or high-end IBM compatible. Most importantly (for gamers, at least), the Amiga had the best games of any other computer of the era until VGA and sound cards became a standard in the PC compatible world.

If Commodore had simply been able to market the systems better and standardized on hard drives, CD-ROMs, and enhanced visuals in a more consistent and timely manner, the company could have possibly remained a competitive option, much like the niche Apple was able to survive in with the Macintosh. As it was, even Commodore's more robust success in Europe couldn't keep

The inside of a highly expandable Amiga 2000HD, complete with an A2088 XT Brigeboard for IBM PC compatibility. With the right add-ons, the Amiga could also run Commodore 64 and Apple Macintosh software.

the company financially viable in the face of overwhelming support for and standardization on PC compatibles. Both the Commodore and Amiga brands live on independently today as the intellectual properties of other companies, leveraged for a variety of product types, some related to the original technologies, some not. In short, the Amiga's death was inglorious and disappointing for everyone involved.

The Amiga Community Then and Now

During its heyday in the mid- to late 1980s, the Amiga fan could enjoy a rich community of likeminded fans, many of whom congregated on dial-up Bulletin Board Systems and local computer clubs. Magazines such as *Amazing Computing* and *Amiga World* provided in-depth articles on hardware, gaming, productivity, development, and do-it-yourself projects. The *Portal Online System*, one of the oldest internet service providers (shut down in 1996), hosted the "AmigaZone" hub for all manner of Amiga users. Much like the "Mac addicts" of today, Amiga enthusiasts tended to have an almost evangelical spirit for their chosen platform, even though it would never seriously threaten the dominant computer or gaming platforms of the era.

Super Stardust AGA running on **WinUAE**.

Super Stardust
(1994, Bloodhouse)

This *Asteroids*-inspired shoot-'em-up game features ray-traced graphics and a mix of 2D and 3D sections. Rest assured that a lot has been added to the classic *Asteroids* gameplay—there are now end-bosses, weapons, power-ups, and many different kinds of enemies to deal with. Team 17 later released versions for AGA Amigas and the CD32. In its day, the game was widely praised by Amiga magazines and continues to receive sequels for modern platforms.

Although a great many public domain and shareware products were available for the Amiga, there was also a huge distribution network for pirated "wares." Although all computer platforms have suffered from piracy, the Amiga had it especially bad, since there were relatively few retail outlets where users could legitimately purchase software. The Amiga's relatively low adoption rate made the rampant piracy all the more damaging to software developers. An informal poll of 166 Amiga fans on the site *Amiga.org* revealed that 68.07 percent had more than 15 pirated games. While there were certainly other factors at play in the demise of the Amiga, it's difficult to deny that piracy played a role.

One sector where the Amiga flourished was desktop video editing. NewTek's Video Toaster coupled with an Amiga 2000 was a terrifically powerful package, able to deliver

commercial-quality video effects for a fraction of the cost of conventional equipment. One particular point of pride for Amiga users is the *Babylon 5* television series and the movie *Jurassic Park*, which used the technology for spectacular special effects. Even late into the 1990s, there were still plenty of professionals still using their Video Toasters to produce cost-effective television commercials.

Shown here is a scene from a 1988 episode of the legendary **Computer Chronicles** TV series, which featured, among other Amiga-related coverage, the introduction of the Amiga 3000 and this impressive real-time demonstration of NewTek's Video Toaster. In the episode, host Stewart Chiefet comments on the Amiga's undeserved lack of wider recognition.

Modern Amiga fans are still quite active online, and can now enjoy easy access to their fellow enthusiasts in Europe and beyond. Indeed, the Amiga remained viable in the United Kingdom and Germany long after support dried up in the United States. Some of the most popular sites are the *English Amiga Board* (http://eab.abime.net), *Amiga.org*, and *Lemon Amiga* (http://lemonamiga.com). In addition to bustling discussion forums, these sites also contain links to software downloads, guides, and marketplaces selling vintage or modern hardware.

One of the most vibrant Amiga communities around today is focused on demos, or short audiovisual pieces designed to showcase the artists' technical prowess and the latent capabilities of a platform. This "demoscene" regularly has competitions around the world, though mostly in Europe. The RSI Megademo and "Hardwired" by Crionics & The Silents are considered exemplars of the broader demoscene movement.[3]

Turrican II: The Final Fight running on **WinUAE**.

Turrican II: The Final Fight (1991, Rainbow Arts)

All of Manfred Trenz' *Turrican* games are excellent, but perhaps the second game offers the best graphics and gameplay. The game puts players in the shoes of one Bren McGuire, the lone survivor of an attack on his ship by an evil cyborg called The Machine. Donning a Turrican fighting suit, it's now up to McGuire to defeat The Machine and avenge his comrades. This platform game offers a wide variety of level designs and weaponry, including a cool arm beam and the ability to morph into a ball in the style of Nintendo's *Metroid*. The excellent soundtrack by Chris Hülsbeck will keep your adrenaline pumping as you explore the generously sized levels and take down wave after wave of The Machine's robotic minions.

---

3   Recordings of these demos are available on *YouTube*, though part of the fun is running them on a real Amiga computer.

Collecting Amiga Systems

There are still plenty of viable Amiga systems, software, and peripherals available on online auction sites and specialty stores. Getting a vintage Amiga system up and running might be intimidating for novices, however. There are many different versions of the operating system, for instance, and games that work fine with one might not load at all in another. Furthermore, some games require a specific chipset (OCS, ECS, or AGA), PAL or NTSC video, a certain RAM configuration, or in rare cases even a hardware "dongle" for copy protection purposes.

For broadest coverage, an Amiga 500 with 1 MB of RAM and version 1.3 of the operating system will run the lion's share of the Amiga game library and is still a cost-effective solution. A 2000 is also a good choice and is easier to expand. An Amiga 600 is another option, though the 2.x versions of the operating system are incompatible with certain games. For these systems, a Commodore 1084S stereo monitor is a great choice for display. For later, AGA games, you'll probably want an Amiga 1200, which is still much cheaper than the Amiga 4000. If money is no object, the Amiga 4000T, offering a tower case and up to a 68060 processor, certainly has appeal. Perhaps the most obscure Amigas are the CDTV and CD32, both based on CD-ROM technology. The first Amiga, the 1000, is an attractive collector's item despite its limited compatibility with later software. Opening and flipping the 1000's case reveals signatures of the design team (and even the paw print of Miner's dog, Mitchy)!

Wizkid: The Story of Wizball II
(1992, Sensible Software)

This arcade puzzle game is a humorous, zany, and downright surreal game that defies easy description. Its gameplay is a blend of other genres, including *Breakout*-inspired games like *Arkanoid*, but with many mini-games, a musical theme, and wild gameplay mechanics. Of particular note are the many varied backdrops, which range from a digitized photo of a woman with puckered lips to a platform balanced on the back of a giant tortoise. Perhaps the most apt word to describe this title is "unique."

Wizkid: The Story of Wizball II running on WinUAE.

One bit of software that makes running a wider range of software on Amiga 600s and 1200s (as well as 4000) is *WHDLoad*, which improves compatibility and allows games to run from a modern compact flash device instead of a hard drive. It's this combination, along with a large amount of expansion memory, that can allow the Amiga 1200 to run nearly all software for the platform, including all of the titles for the CDTV and CD32, making it the ideal, if somewhat pricey option for someone who doesn't want to bother with emulation.

Emulating the Amiga

The go-to solution for Amiga emulation is Cloanto's *Amiga Forever* package, available in various editions: Value, Plus, and Premium. Cloanto's package sports an attractive and easy-to-use interface for loading and configuring games, greatly simplifying the process even for experienced Amiga users. The product is regularly updated and comes pre-installed with up to 100 games and demos.

A free option, suggested only for experienced Amiga users, is *WinUAE* for Windows and *MaxUAE* for Mac OS X. *UAE* is a powerful emulation program with support for just about any Amiga configuration you can think of, including CDTV and CD32.

Amiga games downloaded from the internet are typically in ADF format, short for "Amiga disk format." The site *Back to the Roots* (www.back2roots.org) is the most extensive and active repository of Amiga software.

Cloanto's **Amiga Forever** is the go-to package for Amiga emulation. The company is also an enthusiastic supporter of the Amiga community.

Sega Genesis (1989)

History

In 1989, Nintendo was at the height of its fortune and fame, enjoying a near monopolistic hold of the videogame console industry. As we saw in Chapter 2.1, the Nintendo Entertainment System had overcome the skepticism of American retailers still reeling from the Great Videogame Crash. With a combination of hit games, cheap technology, and effective (if controversial) licensing policies, Nintendo had not only resurrected the moribund industry, but greatly expanded it, defining an entirely new generation of gamers. Competing with this behemoth would take great technology, slick marketing, and a lot of patience.

Sega had two of these qualities.

With Nintendo's dominance firmly established, Sega ramped up the hyperbole in ads for the Genesis, emphasizing its graphics and edgier games. To brand the platform, Sega used its now-familiar "Sega!" shout along with the 16-bit era's most memorable marketing tagline: "Genesis does what Nintendon't," shown here in a multipage ad from the June/July 1990 premiere issue of **Sega Visions**.

While it doesn't reach quite as far back as Nintendo's humble nineteenth-century beginnings, Sega's history is no less storied. Although best known for their Japanese operations, the company that would later become Sega was born among the beautiful palm trees and beaches of Honolulu, Hawaii. In 1940, just a year before the Japanese attacked Pearl Harbor, American businessmen Martin Bromley (originally Martin Jerome Bromberg), his father Irving Bromberg, and James Humpert started Standard Games to provide jukeboxes, slot machines, mechanical peep shows, and other coin-operated amusements specifically to the United States military. Irving Bromberg had been in the "penny arcade" business since the early 1930s, peddling his wares along the West Coast. Bromley and Humpert had found employment with the US Navy shipyard at Honolulu, providing both with invaluable contacts and marketing opportunities, particularly for their slot machines.

A federal "moral" ban on interstate shipment of slot machines in 1950, however, caused a sharp drop in the number of such devices operating within the United States and its territories.[1] As a result, in 1952 the company began importing machines into the fledgling post-war Japanese market under a new company name, Nihon Goraku Bussan, which marketed its products under the Service Games banner.

---

[1] "US Ban Cuts Operation of Slot Machines," *Sarasota Herald-Tribune*, November 3, 1952.

Disney's Aladdin running on the **Fusion** emulator.

Disney's Aladdin (1993, Sega)

It's not easy to make a compelling platform game based on a movie license. In many cases, they amount to little more than re-skinned versions of games that were mediocre to begin with. Virgin Games USA, however, raised the bar, not once, but three times, with McDonald's *Mick & Mack as the Global Gladiators* (1992), and 7UP soda's *Cool Spot* (1993). Not only did David Perry and his team of developers rise to the challenge with these games, they created two of the best platformers of their generation. However, Virgin Games USA would outdo itself with the third game when it teamed up with Disney's actual animators for *Disney's Aladdin*. The well-tested game engine, experienced development team, and Disney's genuine interest in actively participating in the game's creation all came together to create a true-to-the-movie 16-bit platforming experience quite unlike any other. The musical compositions of composer Donald S. Griffin even helped push the Genesis' sound hardware to new heights! If you like this game, check out some of the Genesis' other classics from its long list of licensed platform games, including *World of Illusion Starring Mickey Mouse and Donald Duck* (1992), with compelling cooperative gameplay between the title characters, and *Taz Mania* (1992), whose unforgiving difficulty is tempered by its enchanting cartoon-quality graphics and sound.

New York native, David Rosen, stationed in Japan during the Korean War, found similar opportunities there. After finishing his United States Air Force service term in 1952, Rosen remained in Japan, where, in 1954, he started Rosen Enterprise, Inc., to sell Japanese art to the American market, as well as create hundreds of Photorama photo studios for Japanese identification cards. In 1957, as the Japanese leisure market grew, Rosen changed strategy and began importing American coin-operated electro-mechanical amusement machines, placing them at his Photorama and additional retail locations.

In 1964, Rosen and Nihon Goraku Bussan began serious discussions about a merger, with the former bringing distribution and the latter bringing manufacturing expertise to the table. In 1965, the two companies merged under Sega Enterprises Ltd., an amalgam of the best known brand name between them, Service Games. Rosen became CEO of the new company.

As described in Chapter 1.1, Sega's history of arcade innovation began shortly after the merger with the Rosen-designed electro-mechanical breakthrough *Periscope* in 1966, followed by several other innovative arcade games. In 1969, Rosen sold the company to Gulf+Western, remaining as CEO of the Sega division. In 1972, Sega Enterprises became a subsidiary of Gulf+Western and went public. In 1982, Gulf+Western sold the US assets of Sega Enterprises to Bally Manufacturing Corporation. Hayao Nakayama—who headed Sega's Japanese operations after they acquired his former company, Esco Boueki—became the new CEO. Rosen led the US subsidiary.

By the early 1980s, after successfully licensing and developing their arcade games for various home systems, Sega tried their hand at a console of their own: the SG-1000. Similar to the

ColecoVision, the SG-1000 was released in Japan on July 15, 1983, the same day as Nintendo's Famicom. The SG-1000, the restyled SG-1000 II, and its computer variant, the SC-3000, sold reasonably well in its target Asian, Australian, and European markets. However, the platform never threatened the staggering sales figures of Nintendo's legendary console. Only in the arcades did Sega truly shine.

In March 1984, Japanese conglomerate CSK Holdings Corporation, led by Rosen and Hayao Nakayama, bought Sega's Japanese assets. The company was renamed Sega Enterprises Ltd., and was publicly traded on the Tokyo Stock Exchange. Rosen's friend and CSK chairman, Isao Okawa, became chairman of Sega. Rosen chose to remain in the United States and would later set up Sega's US operations.

Shown are several variations of Sega's SG-3000 computers from different regions. The SG-3000 computers and SC-1000 consoles gave Sega valuable experience that they further honed with the Master System before putting it all together with the Genesis.

On October 20, 1985, Sega released the SG-1000's backwards-compatible successor, the Mark III, which featured improved graphics hardware and more RAM. A redesigned version of the Mark III, with a revamped cartridge port and additional sound chip, the Yamaha YM2413, was released in North America in June 1986 as the Master System. This enhanced version of the system was released back to Japan with mostly cosmetic differences in October 1987.

Even though Sega of America, led by Rosen,[2] was established in 1986 in Los Angeles as a wholly owned subsidiary of Sega Corporation of Japan, it didn't make breaking into the US videogame market any easier. Following Nintendo's example of partnering with a toy company to help them break into the American market, Sega made its bed with Tonka, best known for their toy trucks.

Unfortunately, the Tonka partnership was not particularly successful. Like Nintendo, Sega decided in 1989 they'd be better off alone.

While the Master System was technologically more sophisticated than the Nintendo Entertainment System, Nintendo hoarded the best third-party software with its questionable exclusivity agreements. Sega had to be content with battling Atari for whatever scraps were left.[3] Sega's relative failure with

The Sega Master System was packed with features and expansion options, but failed to make much of a dent against the Nintendo Entertainment System in worldwide sales.

---

[2]   Rosen would retire at age 66 from his storied career at Sega in 1996, with his final position as a director for both Sega's Japanese and US operations.

[3]   Although a comparatively small market at the time, Sega achieved its greatest success with the Master System in Europe, where it was the top selling console for a number of years. One reason for Sega's success was that Nintendo's exclusivity agreements did not extend to that territory, creating a more level playing field.

the Master System did, however, allow them to beat Nintendo to the next generation with a 16-bit successor, a luxury Nintendo couldn't afford. For Nintendo, it just didn't make sense to cannibalize a platform with over 90 percent market share in the US, not to mention an incoming portable requiring considerable corporate attention (see Chapter 2.4).[4]

Greatest Heavyweights running on the **Fusion** emulator.

Greatest Heavyweights (1994, Sega)

Starting with their earliest arcade videogames in the 1970s, right through to the numerous creations into the 1990s for their home consoles, Sega has had a long love affair with the sport of boxing. Despite this storied history, it was only after refining the foundation of their 1992 hit, *Evander Holyfield's "Real Deal" Boxing*, itself a port of an earlier computer game,[5] that Sega properly returned the affection and captured the true essence of the sweet science. *Greatest Heavyweights* challenges players to create a boxer that can go toe-to-toe with 30 original boxers, as well as eight legends who act exactly as you'd expect them to in the ring. Michael Buffer announcing ("Let's get ready to rumble!"), instant replays, and detailed punch stats all add to the incredible audiovisual presentation that's almost as much fun for spectators as it is for players.

Released in Japan on October 29, 1988, where it was known as the Mega Drive, the Genesis wouldn't see release in the US until August 14, 1989, with initial roll-outs restricted to the New York City and Los Angeles areas at a retail price of $189.99. NEC's TurboGrafx-16 Entertainment SuperSystem, which had a similar initial roll-out period starting on August 19, 1989, retailed for $199.99. The Genesis would see wide release in North America one month later, on September 15, 1989. The 16-bit console generation was officially underway.

Although the TurboGrafx-16 could display more colors than the Sega Genesis thanks to its dual 16-bit graphics chipset, its overall design, complete with 8-bit microprocessor and two-button controller, was meant to soundly beat the Nintendo Entertainment System, not go toe-to-toe with the Genesis, or, eventually, the Super NES. As a result, Sega pulled no punches when highlighting the TurboGrafx-16's perceived deficiencies in its early advertising. NEC didn't help the situation with its reluctance to export its best Japanese titles or its occasionally heavy-handed localization censorship when it did. As if all of these disadvantages weren't enough, a series of controversial commercials—one with boiling goldfish, another with cats bouncing off the wall—aroused public indignation. As a result of all of this and lacking both Sega's arcade catalog and still having to deal with Nintendo's third-party exclusivity deals, it was difficult for NEC to compete effectively in the US with its paltry library. This despite incredible popularity in NEC's home country, a territory where, along with Nintendo after the release of its Super Famicom (Super NES in North America) on November 21, 1990, it helped relegate the Genesis to a distant third place finish.

4   www.stanford.edu/group/htgg/cgi-bin/drupal/sites/default/files2/ewu_2002_1.pdf.

5   The more sophisticated 1991 hit for the PC DOS and Commodore Amiga platforms, *ABC Wide World of Sports Boxing* (aka *TV Sports Boxing*). In 1993, Philips released its own game based off the same core engine for their CD-i platform, *Caesars World of Boxing*. While each title has its advantages, *Greatest Heavyweights* arguably features the best action.

While the Genesis faced stiff competition in Japan from NEC, in North America and Europe it was top dog for several years before Nintendo's Super NES finally began closing the gap a few years after its North American release on August 23, 1991. However, Nintendo's plodding tortoise never did manage to overtake Sega's hedgehog outside of Japan.

By 1993, even with the dominance of Nintendo's Game Boy, Sega still commanded almost 40 percent of the US game industry, to Nintendo's 51 percent.[6] Worldwide, with dominance in other territories, like Europe and South America, those figures tilted even more in Sega's favor, at close to 50 percent market share.[7] In fact, despite the release of several newer and more powerful competing consoles along the way, Sega continued to sell its aging Genesis technology for several more years, despite muted responses to the Sega CD and 32X add-ons meant to extend the core console's commercial relevance. It took several years past the late 1994 Japanese releases of Sega's own Saturn and, critically, Sony's PlayStation (see Chapter 3.2), before the market truly embraced a new generation of systems.

Technical Specifications and Models

Sega had enjoyed terrific success in the arcade, so that was an obvious source to go to for inspiration when developing the Genesis. While the Genesis was built on the foundations of its home predecessors, making sure the new console could match their Sega System 16 arcade technology positioned it well for the long haul. Worldwide arcade hits powered by the technology, like *Action Fighter* (1986), *Alex Kidd: The Lost Stars* (1986), *Fantasy Zone* (1986), *Alien Syndrome* (1987), *Shinobi* (1987), *Altered Beast* (1988), *Wonder Boy III: Monster Lair* (1988), *E-Swat* (1989), and *Golden Axe* (1989) meant there would be no shortage of games to bring over or draw inspiration from as the Genesis grew its own library of originals.

The Genesis is powered by a Motorola 68000 16-bit microprocessor running at 7.67 MHz, but also features an 8-bit Zilog Z80 as a secondary microprocessor running at 3.58 MHz. This secondary microprocessor also gives it backwards compatibility with the Master System through the use of a simple cartridge slot adapter.

The 68000 can access its own 64K of RAM, 64K of dedicated video memory, and 8K of work RAM from the Z80. The video is powered by a Yamaha YM7101 Video Display Processor (VDP), a descendent of the VDP found in the Master System, and, in its most common display modes, allows for 64 onscreen colors from a palette of 512 colors at typical resolutions of 320 × 224 or 256 × 224.

Sound on the Genesis is powered by one of two sound chips, controllable from either of its microprocessors. The first, a Yamaha YM2612 FM synthesizer chip, uses six FM channels with four operators each and runs at the same clock speed as the Motorola 68000. The second, the Texas Instruments SN76489 PSG chip, contains three square wave tone generators and one white noise generator, each of which can produce sounds at various frequencies and 16 different volume levels. Stereo sound is output through the headphone jack on model one Genesis systems, while model two Genesis systems eliminated the headphone jack and sent its stereo output through the AV out.

The front of the console features two nine-pin controller connectors, which are the same standard found on a wide variety of previous systems, including the Master System, Commodore

---

6   http://vidgame.info/sega.

7   Sega's Dream Machine," *Business Week*, September 12, 1999.

Amiga, ColecoVision, and Atari 2600. The original Genesis controller features rounded corners, a digital directional pad, a start button (often used for pausing the action), and three action buttons: A, B, and C. To support newer games like Capcom's *Street Fighter II: Special Champion Edition*, Sega released a slightly smaller six button controller in late 1993, which could be made to act like a three-button controller for better compatibility with some finicky older games.

Gunstar Heroes running on the **Fusion** emulator.

Gunstar Heroes (1993, Sega)

If there was any one game other than *Sonic the Hedgehog* that helped define the Genesis' reputation as the system with "speed and attitude," it was *Gunstar Heroes*. The perfect embodiment of the "run 'n' gun" platforming genre, *Gunstar Heroes* let one or two players use 14 different weapon combinations to blast non-stop through its many action-packed, side-scrolling levels, which culminated in epic boss battles. Developer Treasure's masterful programming allowed them to produce a large number of fast moving on-screen objects, creating an audiovisual experience unique to the platform. For more "run 'n' gun" fun, be sure to check out *Contra: Hard Corps* (1994, Konami).

Besides the aforementioned headphone jack and accompanying dedicated volume slider, the top of the original console features an on/off switch and reset button. To the rear of the console is an expansion port (EXT) that was only used for the Japanese-exclusive Meganet modem add-on, as well as a channel select switch, RF out, DIN connector for composite and RGB video and audio, and the power connector. To the side was an expansion input port, somewhat similar to that found on the ColecoVision, and was what the CD add-on would later plug into. A later version of this console model added a regional lockout chip and an accompanying license screen that would appear for a few seconds before a game started. A still later version made cosmetic changes to the console's exterior, removing the HIGH-DEFINITION GRAPHICS text, and eliminating the disused EXT port.

The first major revision to the Genesis came in 1994. Casually known as the "model two," both the internal and exterior design were streamlined, requiring a new power supply and audio-video connectors. Gone were the headphone jack, channel select switch, and dedicated RF out.

The second and final revision came in 1998, with the Genesis 3, whose production was outsourced to Majesco. The internal and exterior design were once again streamlined, making the console even smaller, but also eliminating the expansion input port, which meant no support for the CD add-on. As with its lack of support for the 32X add-on, this was considered an acceptable loss as the only new product Majesco was producing for their budget system anyway was Genesis cartridges.[8]

Similarities to the Commodore Amiga's architecture encouraged numerous ports between the two platforms, with popular computer games from top developers and publishers like

---

[8]   Majesco also rereleased the Game Gear and some new games for a short time starting in 2000. This revision of the Game Gear was incompatible with the TV tuner add-on and some Master System cartridge adapters.

Psygnosis, Accolade, and Electronic Arts helping fill out the early Genesis game library. Unfortunately, Sega's later addition of its TradeMark Security System (TMSS) regional lockout chip on its consoles rendered several of the early such games unplayable without workarounds. Accolade decided to reverse engineer Sega's copyrighted game code, a risky move that soon landed them in court with the console-maker. As Accolade's Alan Miller put it in Steven Kent's 2001 book *The Legal Game*, "One pays them between $10 and $15 per cartridge on top of the real hardware manufacturing costs, so it about doubles the cost of goods to the independent publisher." These fees were in addition to Sega's much-loathed exclusivity deal, which they'd formed along the same lines as Nintendo. The Ninth Circuit ruled that Accolade's use of reverse engineering to publish Genesis titles was protected under fair use, and that its alleged violation of Sega trademarks was the fault of Sega. The case is still frequently cited in matters involving reverse engineering and fair use under copyright law. Nevertheless, after many years of litigation, both companies settled on April 30, 1993, with Accolade finally becoming an official licensee.

Even without the onus of legal action, eventually most Sega developers became official licensees and released their games without compatibility concerns. Electronic Arts, for instance, wanted a reduction in Sega's fees, so they used their early unlicensed titles as leverage in negotiations, no doubt making use of the potential added threat of being able to share their reverse engineering technology with other companies. Whatever the details, it's safe to say that when Electronic Arts became an official licensee, the success of both companies in the 16-bit era was assured.

Electronic Arts was able to bring its expertise from its prolific, but not so profitable, 16-bit computer releases to full fruition on the Genesis. Of its many classics, like *Abrams Battle Tank* (1988), *Battle Squadron* (1989), *James Pond: Underwater Agent* (1990), *Road Rash* (1991), *Crüe Ball* (1992), *Haunting Starring Polterguy* (1993), and *General Chaos* (1994), Electronic Arts proved most clever when plugging into the American love of sports. Only hinted at with popular NES games like *Tecmo Bowl* (1989, Tecmo) and *Baseball Simulator 1.000* (1989, Culture Brain), Electronic Arts tapped into the collective competitive spirit of armchair sports fans like no other company before it. Not only did games like *Lakers vs. Celtics and the NBA Playoffs* (1989), *John Madden Football* (1990), *PGA Tour Golf* (1990), *NHL Hockey* (1991), and *FIFA International Soccer* (1993) kick off popular franchises that continue to this day, but Electronic Arts made gamers come to expect nothing less than real teams and players, forever changing the way such games were made. It didn't hurt, of course, that this expectation also meant that each of these games could be released annually with only minor improvements and updated rosters to consistently blockbuster sales.

Even though the Genesis' graphics and sound specifications were superior to most computers of the day, Sega's system would have more competition in those areas on the console side. The TurboGrafx-16 featured superior color processing, with up to 481 on-screen colors from a pallet of 512, and Nintendo's NES successor would feature both superior colors and sound (see Chapter 2.5). While its competitor's advantages were not always clear, particularly in regards to the Super NES's comparative sound clarity, it could be an obvious differentiator on multiplatform titles.

While the Genesis could demonstrate few clear technical advantages over its console rivals, it did boast a faster processor, which was put to good use in the blockbuster *Sonic the Hedgehog*

Lunar: Eternal Blue running on the **Fusion** emulator.

Lunar: Eternal Blue (1995, Working Designs)

Lunar: Eternal Blue, the sequel to the superb Lunar: The Silver Star (1993), was one of the most ambitious of the RPGs available on a platform known for its strong selection of such games. As was their standard, Working Designs translated and improved upon the Japanese original for its North American release. While the gameplay, which involved stopping a great evil that threatens all of creation, falls into the usual Japanese RPG conventions of pre-set characters, linear gameplay, and random battles, the advantages in scope afforded by the Sega CD hardware are extraordinary. With more than 50 minutes of movie content and over an hour of spoken dialog from its 15 voice actors, Lunar: Eternal Blue is as technologically epic as its ultimate mission. A clever save system, which requires magic experience points equal to a multiple of the main character's level, adds to the challenge. For a more atypical RPG experience, be sure to check out Core Design's Heimdall (1994, JVC), which is steeped in Norse mythology and offers an unusual interface and isometric perspective.

(1991) and its numerous sequels. Even though "blast processing" was as much marketing hyperbole as the words "HIGH DEFINITION GRAPHICS" plastered above the original console's cartridge port, *Sonic the Hedgehog* did indeed represent a shot of adrenaline to an incredibly crowded, increasingly stale genre.[9] While most platform games encouraged careful exploration and pixel-perfect timing, *Sonic the Hedgehog* reveled in its speed and spin dashes. While a skilled player might still want to explore every stage's nooks and crannies, Sonic's ability to rush full bore through levels laden with springs, slopes, high drops, tunnels, and loop-the-loops was irresistible. Ultimately, while the Super NES may have had better graphics and sound, the Genesis' swifter processor still had it well positioned for success well into the "Go-Go 90s."

Besides its sports games and the in-your-face attitude of its mascot cementing the Genesis' status as the "cool" system to own, Sega's more lenient censorship policy was also key to the console's popularity. Nintendo had long lauded its "family friendly" nature, scrubbing out even the subtlest references to sex and gore in their American games. While such policies may have been a hit with concerned parents, older kids (and, increasingly, adult console gamers) were ready for something more mature—and Sega was ready to deliver. Perhaps no two games made that statement more clearly than *Night Trap* and *Mortal Kombat*.

Night Trap was a 1992 release for the Sega CD from Digital Pictures, published by Sega. A type of survival horror adventure game, full motion video clips are used to tell the story of a group of young women having a sleepover at a seemingly normal house for the night. The player takes control of security cameras in cooperation with an embedded undercover agent as a plot involving vampire-like creatures unfolds. Although not a particularly great game, its voyeuristic nature and scantily clad house guests caused a furor in the mass media. Ill-informed hosts (who'd likely never played or even seen the game) launched into tirade after tirade, all in a tireless effort to whip up moral indignation at an "out of control" videogame industry.

---

9   Perhaps most importantly, unlike every other Nintendo competitor who attempted to come up with a charismatic mascot of their own to go head-to-head with Mario, Sega's Sonic had genuine staying power and is still one of the world's most recognizable characters.

Mutant League Football running on the **Fusion** emulator.

Mutant League Football (1993, Electronic Arts)

Once the *Madden* series started tackling the sales charts, most other sports games responded in kind, licensing both league and player names in an attempt to create the best digital representation of reality. Nevertheless, even in the face of this overwhelming competitive peer pressure, a few games here and there were still able to challenge convention by putting fun before fidelity. Ironically, one of the best such titles, *Mutant League Football*, came from the very same company responsible for the creatively limiting expectation of reality in the first place. *Mutant League Football* (1993), based on the solid *John Madden Football '93* (1992) game engine, features teams of aliens, monsters, and other creatures playing on fields filled with landmines, pits, and other hazards. Crazy power-ups and tricks like jet packs, exploding balls, and bribable referees who need to be killed to stop their onslaught of dirty calls, all add up to one comically mean game of football. For more monster-mashing fun, check out *Mutant League Hockey* (1994), although unfortunately the game puts a few too many demands on the otherwise superlative *NHL '94* (1993) game engine, resulting in choppier gameplay.[10] Sadly, development on a third game in the series, *Mutant League Basketball*—likely based on the *NBA Live 95* (1994) game engine—was never completed, as publishing efforts shifted away from the Genesis to the next generation of platforms.[11]

Mortal Kombat was a 1992 arcade fighting game from Midway infamous for its blood and gore. Of particular note were its "fatalities," grotesque finishing moves such as Sub-Zero's "Spine Rip," with which skilled players could graphically execute their opponents. Naturally, the game was a huge hit with teens and pre-teens, who quickly learned and memorized all of these moves. For "Mortal Monday," on September 13, 1993, Acclaim Entertainment released home ports for the Sega Genesis and Game Gear, as well as the Super NES and Game Boy. While the versions for Nintendo's systems were severely censored, replacing blood with sweat, and simply removing many of the gorier fatalities, the versions for Sega's systems were left mostly intact—particularly after a simple "cheat code" was entered. Although arguably better-looking and more faithful gameplay-wise, the Super NES version sold far fewer copies, causing Nintendo to lighten up a bit on its censorship policy for future releases.

What really earned *Night Trap* and *Mortal Kombat* their place in the history books were the infamous 1993 US Senate hearings on videogame violence, which caused the former game to be pulled from the market for a time (helping its initial run to sell out in the process), and the latter game's fatalities making regular appearances on the nightly news. In response, Sega formed the Videogame Rating Council (VRC) to voluntarily rate its own games. In September 1994, Sega's efforts and those of other companies were combined into an industry standard ratings system under the Entertainment Software Rating Board (ESRB), still in use today.

10　Many fans consider *NHL '94*, which was also ported to the Sega CD and Super NES, the pinnacle of the series. Electronic Arts even included a version of the game in *NHL 06* (2005) for the Sony PlayStation 2, though it was stripped of its official player rosters, as well as a special "NHL '94 anniversary mode" in *NHL 14* (2013) for Sony's PlayStation 3 and Microsoft's Xbox 360, which included updated graphics and rosters.

11　Despite rumors of aborted attempts at next generation revivals, and a cult following that remains to this day, Electronic Arts seems content to have let the *Mutant League* series die in deference to its popular lineup of licensed sports titles. Reality may have won out, but at what cost to gamers?

Besides Sega's more progressive stance on censorship, the Genesis differed in other ways from Nintendo's approach with the Super NES. Going back to the NES days, Nintendo would make sure they put out a competent core console, but leave it open to enhancements on a game-by-game basis with the inclusion of special in-cartridge chips. Sega, on the other hand, focused primarily on add-ons with new capabilities, but they did try a short-lived experiment with the Sega Virtua

Virtua Racing, shown here on the **Fusion** emulator, was an impressive first use of Sega's Virtua Processor, but the add-in's high cost meant the chip had no future.

Processor. While the chip was more capable than Nintendo's vaunted Super FX, it was simply not cost effective. It did, however, do an impressive job bringing Sega's own *Virtua Racing* arcade game home in 1997—maintaining much of its 3D glory. With *Virtua Racing*'s original retail price set at $100, it proved the first and last usage of the chip, with future 3D-centric games set for the 32X add-on.

The Add-Ons and Accessories

Continuing the tradition of predecessors from the likes of Nintendo, Coleco, Mattel, and Atari, the Genesis features an impressive range of add-ons and accessories. One such early Genesis add-on was the Power Base Converter, which allowed it to run nearly all of the Master System's 300+ game cartridges and game cards. Master System controllers and even the platform's famous SegaScope 3D glasses worked just like they should with the converter.

The Menacer, released in 1992, was Sega's take on the light gun, similar to Nintendo's Super Scope for the Super NES. The Menacer's three sections can be dissembled for use in various

configurations, including as its original bazooka-like design and a pistol. While only a little more than a half dozen games were released for The Menacer, it worked particularly well with popular full motion video shooting games for the Sega CD from American Laser Games like *Mad Dog McCree* (1993) and *Who Shot Johnny Rock?* (1994). Other games, like *Lethal Enforcers* (1993, Konami) came with their own, incompatible light guns.

An original Sega Genesis sporting the Power Base Converter.

While the Genesis only sported two controller ports, Sega, with their Team Player, and Electronic Arts, with their 4 Way Play, let up to four players play together in supported games. Codemasters went one step further and created games with their J-Cart system, which put two extra joystick ports right on the cartridge.

Besides the usual cheat cartridges like the *Game Genie* and *Pro Action Replay*, which had pass-through ports to allow other cartridges to connect to them, Sega developed a similar concept of its own, known as Lock-On Technology. Used in *Sonic & Knuckles* (1994), any of the three prior *Sonic the Hedgehog* games can be inserted to change the way each of the various titles play.

Phantasy Star IV running on the **Fusion** emulator.

Phantasy Star IV (1995, Sega)

As the *Phantasy Star IV* cartridge proved, epic RPGs were not the sole domain of the Sega CD. Continuing the fine tradition started way back on the Sega Master System with one of the largest console games of its time, *Phantasy Star* (1988), the final game in the original series, staked a similar claim on the Genesis, complete with matching price tag. While *Phantasy Star IV* concluded the ongoing storyline from the previous two games (*Phantasy Star III: Generations of Doom* featured a separate continuity) and played in a similar manner (just with more of everything), the series finale was also far less linear than its predecessors, with numerous side quests, and definitive moments of genuine pathos. Cover art by famed fantasy artist Boris Vallejo was the proverbial cherry on top for one of the finest 16-bit RPGs ever crafted. For a similarly themed, but more action-oriented science fiction fantasy role playing title, be sure to also check out BlueSky Software's *Shadowrun* (1994, Sega), based on the famous pen-and-paper game from FASA.

One of the more unusual Genesis add-ons was the Sega Activator, which was an octagonal controller placed on the floor. After a player stepped in the ring and a body part, like an arm or leg, was detected by one the Activator's infrared beams, it would translate to an in-game movement. Unfortunately, despite Sega promoting fighting games like its own *Eternal Champions* (1993) as an ideal companion for the contraption, no games were ever exclusively designed for the device.

Although NEC got to market first with their CD add-on (April 1988 in Japan, August 1990 in the US), it was Sega who would once again

Sega's black Mega Mouse sits in front of Sega's oversized, but modular Menacer light gun, as Konami's light blue The Justifier light gun rests on the box for Sega's Activator.

garner the most interest. The Sega CD, known as the Mega CD for its December 1991 release in Japan, wouldn't be released in North America until October 1992. The first model, designed to match the styling of the original Genesis, sat under the console and featured a front loading, motorized disc tray. The second model, designed to match the styling of the model two Genesis, sat to the side and featured a manual top-loading disc tray.

While the Sega CD featured the addition of a faster processor, more colors, and more RAM than the Genesis, the most typical use for the add-on was simply running larger games with full motion video. 64K memory was allocated for backup and save game data, but an optional CD Back Up RAM Cart could increase available storage to 1MB.

Several top computer adventure games from Sierra and LucasArts were successfully ported, and the occasional stand-out title, like *Sonic CD* (1993) and most of the role-playing games that were released, made the add-on tempting, but only approximately 6 million CD add-ons were sold worldwide. This low number was thanks in part to a large portion of the CD game library not offering much value over their cartridge-based counterparts, like the Sega CD version of the underwater action adventure classic *Ecco the Dolphin* (1993). This "new" version of the game merely featured a few additional levels and an enhanced soundtrack, hardly justifying the extra cost.

Pioneer released the LaserActive laserdisc player in the US in September 1993, at a retail price of close to $1000. Besides playing laserdisc videos, it could accept modules that added various new features, including the Sega PAC, which let it play existing Sega Genesis and CD games, as well as special laserdisc games that overlaid Genesis graphics on top of laserdisc video. Unfortunately, like the NEC PAC, which did the same for TurboGrafx-16 software, the price of the add-on was an additional $600 on top of the already sky high price of entry.

In 1994, JVC released the X'Eye in North America, which was a full-sized all-in-one officially licensed combination of the Genesis and Sega CD with improved audio and built-in karaoke capabilities. Unfortunately, it was priced higher than buying a Sega Genesis and Sega CD individually and offered few tangible gaming benefits.

Shining Force II running on the **Fusion** emulator.

Shining Force II (1994, Sega)

With the rising popularity of RPGs on consoles—and the associated glut of releases—it was no surprise that developers started to experiment with interesting variations on the genre. One of the best such hybrids was *Shining Force II*, which combined traditional RPG exploration with strategic, cinematic battle sequences. The player assumes the role of Shining Force leader, Bowie, as he leads a 12-member strike force from a selection of over 20 characters in an attempt to stop a great evil. While the bright graphics and cartoon styling may be a turn-off for some, the incredibly polished tactical gameplay is well worth overlooking any issues with *Shining Force II*'s aesthetics. Unfortunately, the next game in the series, *Shining Force III* for the ill-fated Sega Saturn, wouldn't appear until 1998 in North America, with only the first of the three self-contained scenarios releasing outside of Japan.

Sega itself attempted to make its CD add-on more appealing for consumers in 1994 by releasing the CDX, a small combination Genesis and Sega CD that also doubled as a portable CD player. It was impressive technology, but consumers balked at the $399.99 retail price.

Also in 1994, Sega released the Mega Mouse, which was meant to make controlling supported adventure and role-playing games

A Sega Genesis with its CD attachment and 32X was the proverbial elephant in the room. Shown here are the second models of the Genesis and Sega CD connected together. The extender to the left of the console is removable and allows the original, longer model of the Sega Genesis to rest comfortably next to the Sega CD.

easier, as well make creativity programs practical. Little more than a dozen cartridge and CD programs were compatible with the mouse controller.

Not content with the already dizzying array of options for the Genesis, Sega chose to develop and release the 32X, which was designed to add sophisticated 3D capabilities to the console and provide consumers a low-cost bridge to the forthcoming Saturn. Not only did the 32X contain a VDP capable of pushing 50,000 polygons per second and producing 32,768 onscreen colors, but it also contained two 32-bit RISC processors that could work up to 40 times faster than the Genesis alone, as well as additional memory and pulse-width modulation sound source.

The 32X looked great on paper, but, as with the Sega CD—which it also supported—only a handful of software took advantage of its greater capabilities. With the short window between the release of the 32X and the next generation of consoles, it's not particularly surprising the add-on failed to gain traction. The planned release for a combination Sega Genesis and 32X called the Neptune was canceled.

Virtua Fighter on the 32X, shown here running on the **Fusion** emulator, was one of just a handful of games to take good advantage of the 32X's enhancements.

On October 13, 1995, Sega took one last leap of faith with its Genesis technology and released the handheld Nomad system. Since it was region-free, the Nomad could play most both Genesis and Mega Drive cartridges on its 3.25-inch color LCD screen. Featuring six full action buttons

Streets of Rage 2 running on the **Fusion** emulator.

Streets of Rage 2 (1992, Sega)

At the time, side-scrolling beat-'em-ups were second only to side-scrolling platforming games in their ubiquity on the era's consoles, which made standing out a difficult proposition. Sega's *Streets of Rage 2* was one of the few such games that did exactly that, however, improving on its already excellent predecessor with more of everything that made the original so great. More moves, more weapons to pick up, more appropriate special attacks, more enemies, and more levels made the sequel a definitive release on the Genesis. Even the soundtrack was a stand-out, with memorable club-style music from the legendary Yuzo Koshiro, with additional contributions from Motohiro Kawashima. Though its relatively late release dulled some of its impact, the final game in the series,[12] *Streets of Rage 3* (1994), also proved a superior beat-'em-up.

and a port for a second controller, the Nomad's video could also be output to a television, making it a proper portable console. Unfortunately, the unit's bulky size, approximately two-hour battery life, and relatively high $180 retail price doomed it to failure, eventually selling just 1 million units worldwide.

Despite executing so well with the Sega Genesis, and in contrast to the relatively conservative Nintendo, it was clear Sega's missteps with its various add-ons proved costly. After fumbling both the launch and early support for the Sega Saturn, Sega would only start to get back its mojo with the release of the Dreamcast. As detailed in Chapter 3.4, even the mighty Dreamcast proved too little to erase enough of Sega's past ambitious missteps to save the company's financial fortunes.

The Sega Genesis Community Then and Now

Thanks to its strong arcade roots, the Sega brand was always defined by great games. Of its home platforms, the most successful was easily the Sega Genesis, despite the lack of similar success with its Sega CD and 32X add-ons. That combination of great Sega games married to a great Sega platform was a difficult combination for the company to replicate, even though the Saturn and Dreamcast (Chapter 3.4) have more than their fair share of fans. As a result, it's easy to find great places online to meet Sega Genesis and Mega Drive enthusiasts, and there's no shortage of old and new product available to get your 16-bit fix. Some of the better Sega-specific websites include www.sega-16.com and Sega's own forums at www.sega.com.

While new licensed games continued to be released into the 2000s in Brazil, for the most part, by the late 1990s, the best chance at getting new Sega Genesis games came from the homebrew community. The most popular such creations have been English translations

---

[12]   Sega commissioned Core Design to develop *Streets of Rage 4* as a 3D beat-'em-up for the Sega Saturn. Unfortunately, a disagreement over developing ports for rival platforms meant that version was never published. Core Design did eventually release the game as *Fighting Force* on the Sony PlayStation and PC Windows platforms in 1997, as well as *Fighting Force 64* on the Nintendo 64 in 1999. The games received mixed reviews.

from Super Fighter Team of various role-playing games released exclusively in Asian territories in the mid- to late-1990s, including *Beggar Prince* (2006), *Legend of Wukong* (2008), and *Star Odyssey* (2011). WaterMelon Co. went one step further with an original role-playing game creation in 2010, *Pier Solar and the Great Architects*.[13] All of these releases quickly sold out of multiple runs, numbering between 300

Left: The original incredible **Pier Solar and the Great Architects** homebrew package from Watermelo Co., whose included Sega CD works in conjunction with the cartridge to provide extra audio content. Right: Super Fighter Team's western release of **Star Odyssey**, also shown running below on a Sega Nomad with replacement LCD screen.

and 1500 copies, which speaks to the continued popularity of the platform, since the usual maximum for homebrew creations on most other systems is generally between 50 and 250 copies.

Collecting Sega Genesis Systems

Because of the number of Sega Genesis consoles and compatibles sold, finding an original system is relatively easy and inexpensive. The more fragile nature of the CD add-ons makes them

The Amazing Spider-Man vs. the Kingpin running on the **Fusion** emulator.

The Amazing Spider-Man vs. the Kingpin
(1993, Sega)

This enhanced Sega CD version of the 1991 Genesis original is considered one of the best Spider-Man games of all time, and with good reason. As the titular hero, the player is tasked with battling classic villains like Sandman and Hobgoblin in an attempt to obtain the keys needed to disarm a nuclear bomb Kingpin has framed Spider-Man for stealing, and will detonate within 24 hours. The perfectly tuned side-scrolling platforming action of the original blockbuster is enhanced by the Sega CD version's additions, which included animated cutscenes, extra levels and moves, an original musical score, and less linear gameplay. For even more web-slinging fun, check out *The Amazing Spider-Man: Web of Fire* (1996) on the 32X. While not a particularly distinguished game for Sega's underutilized add-on, its rarity makes it a great collectible.

---

[13] In late 2012, WaterMelon Co. ran a successful Kickstarter campaign for *Pier Solar HD*, for the Sega Dreamcast, Microsoft Xbox 360, Android/Ouya, and Nintendo Wii U, as well as for computers running Windows, Macintosh, or Linux operating systems. The fourth print run for the Sega Genesis version was also announced!

harder to find in good working condition. The all-in-one Sega CDX and particularly the JVC X'Eye, are easily the most sought after systems for collectors.

For portable fun, many Sega Genesis cartridge enthusiasts enjoy the Sega Nomad. A popular upgrade for the Nomad is replacing its LCD screen with a modern panel, which eliminates most of the motion blur found on the original.

A range of flash cartridges are available, including two popular options from Krikzz, the Everdrive MD v3 and Mega Everdrive. With these cartridges, it's simply a matter of placing game images on an SD card and then inserting it into a Genesis or clone, giving you the ability to play most of the games in the Genesis/Mega Drive, 32X, and Master System library.

ToeJam & Earl running on the **Fusion** emulator.

ToeJam & Earl (1991, Sega)

It's not surprising that a game as original as *ToeJam & Earl* had an earlier inspiration. What is surprising is the game that did the inspiring for developer Johnson Voorsanger Productions was *Rogue*. The legendary 1980 dungeon crawling computer role playing game with text-based graphics is probably the last title you'd think of when first playing *ToeJam & Earl*, but the inspiration is clear once you consider both games' random levels and item drops. Whatever its derivation, there's no denying that *ToeJam & Earl* is unique, tasking players with getting the titular funky aliens off Earth by collecting the pieces of their crashed spacecraft against a backdrop of comedic pop culture references and urban culture parodies. While a single player can take control of either alien, *ToeJam & Earl* excels in its two-player cooperative mode, which features additional character interactions and a dynamic split screen when players get too far apart. Like the first sequels to Nintendo's *Super Mario Bros.* (in the US) and *The Legend of Zelda*, the sequel to *ToeJam & Earl—ToeJam & Earl in Panic on Funkotron* (1993)—radically deviated from the original's formula at the behest of publisher Sega, resulting in a decent, but ultimately uninspiring side-scrolling platform game. A final sequel, *ToeJam & Earl III: Mission to Earth*, was originally intended for the Sega Dreamcast, but was later released only for the Microsoft Xbox in 2002. Despite switching to a third-person, 3D perspective and adding a third playable character, it was truer to the original, but still failed to capture the same magic.

Emulating the Sega Genesis

Thanks to its popularity and well understood architecture, there are a wide variety of emulators available for the Sega Genesis platform on nearly every capable system. Perhaps the most popular and versatile is *Fusion* for Windows-, Macintosh-, and Linux-based computers, which places emphasis on the accuracy of its emulation. In addition to emulating the Sega Genesis/Mega Drive, *Fusion* also emulates the Sega CD/Mega CD, 32X, Game Gear, Master System, and SG-1000/SC-3000.

Sonic the Hedgehog running on the **Fusion** emulator.

Today, Sega's Genesis library has among the best officially licensed distribution among classic console games. You can find official Genesis game collections from Sega on everything from PC and console optical media and download services to Android and iOS smartphones and tablets. This distribution extends to dedicated systems, as well, such as AtGames' Sega Arcade Classic console, which, in addition to its built-in games, accepts real cartridges, and their Sega Arcade Ultimate Portable handheld, which, in addition to its own set of built-in games, accepts an SD card that a user can load with their own game ROMs. In short, the Sega Genesis is by far the most accessible of the classic consoles to legally experience today.

Nintendo Game Boy (1989)

History

The Nintendo Game Boy, which made its North American debut in late July of 1989, was a watershed moment in the history of videogames. It was not, however, the first handheld with interchangeable cartridges. In fact, it was "obsolete" shortly after it was released. Compared to an Atari Lynx or Sega Game Gear, released two and nine months later, respectively, it was a dinosaur: a tyrannosaurus, to be precise.

Despite its cheap, underpowered hardware, the Game Boy did enjoy several key advantages over the Lynx and its predecessors. The first and most obvious was the significant brand recognition Nintendo had achieved in the wake of its Nintendo Entertainment System (see Chapter 2.1). By 1989, there wasn't a nine-year old in America who hadn't heard about Mario. Nintendo had also had great success with their Game & Watch handheld systems, which *still* remain popular among collectors. Perhaps most importantly to parents as well as gamers, however, the Game Boy enjoyed exceptional battery life. Just four AA batteries would last well over ten hours, much longer than the roughly three hours you could expect from the competition—and they required two additional batteries! Later Game Boy systems lasted even longer.

Most decisively, though, the Game Boy series had not one but two killer apps of mobile gaming: *Tetris* (1989) and *Pokémon* (1996 in Japan). Eventually, more than 600 games were released for the platform before giving way to the DS series, and today, Nintendo still has the handheld gaming market in its pocket. They owe much of that success to a Russian computer scientist, a Dutch entrepreneur, and an eccentric genius called "Dr. Bug." But let's not get ahead of ourselves!

Advance Wars on the **VisualBoyAdvance** emulator.

Advance Wars
(2001, Intelligent Systems, GBA)

Advance Wars let up to four players battle it out in a turn-based strategy game involving ground, air, and naval forces. Players could connect via a Game Link cable or on a single unit, simply passing it to the next player. It offered 114 pre-made maps, but also a map editor. The game received near-perfect scores from the critics, who praised its "easy to learn, hard to master" gameplay and the sheer joy of the multiplayer mode.

By 1989, handheld gaming had a long history. Most of these earlier units, such as the afore-mentioned Game & Watch systems or Coleco's mini tabletop arcade games (see Chapter 1.8), could only play the games built-in to their hardware. The first company to introduce a proper mobile gaming platform was Milton Bradley, who released Jay Smith's Microvision in 1979. It offered a monochrome 16 × 16 LCD display, and, like the Game Boy, was difficult to see in the absence of bright light because of the lack of backlighting. Motion blur was also a problem, even on the included *Block Buster* (1979), a clone of the arcade hit *Breakout.* Cartridges for the system contained more than just games; they had their own microprocessor, screen cover, and control panel. Thus, each game could fully customize the look, feel, and even capability of the unit—certainly a novel feature with exciting potential for game developers. However, much like Smith's other game system, the Vectrex, creativity and innovation weren't enough to make the platform a hit. With little external support and only 13 games in its lineup, the Microvision faded from the scene within a few years. Other systems with interchangeable cartridges, such as the Adventure Vision from Entex Industries, failed to make even the impression of the Microvision on the market.[1] There just didn't seem to be much future in the handheld videogaming market beyond what the cheaper, fixed-game units could provide. Once again, entering this market proved that Nintendo was willing to take big risks, convinced it could succeed where others had failed.

Naturally, the design of the Game Boy fell to Gunpei Yokoi, the janitor-turned game developer introduced in Chapter 2.1. Yokoi was a logical choice for the job, given his reputation for ingenuity and his proven success with the Game & Watch. Unlike many engineers in the gaming industry then or now, Yokoi was interested in what could be done with cheap, readily-available parts rather than cutting-edge components that would only

The original Nintendo Game Boy and some of its games. Marketing photos tended to show a misleadingly clear image versus the reality of the Game Boy's low contrast, low resolution screen.

ratchet up costs. He called this philosophy "lateral thinking with withered [sometimes translated as 'seasoned'] technology." It was a philosophy that clashed strongly with the dominant ideology of the industry, which still continues to privilege the latest, greatest tech above all else. Yokoi realized, however, that technophiles were only a small fraction of the potential market. Then as now, most people simply don't care about what's inside a system, assuming it's cheap enough to fit within their budgets and "good enough" to let them play their favorite games.

Yokoi was content to design his unit with a 2.5-inch monochrome LCD screen, even though rivals were already promising full-color graphics. Yokoi guessed correctly that a cheaper price, better battery life, and Nintendo's reputation would more than compensate for whatever gee-whiz audiovisuals the competition would offer.

Let's be clear. Nintendo's Game Boy was crude, cheap, and obsolete even before it was released. But it had three points in its favor: *Tetris,* and *Tetris.* Oh, and *Tetris.*

---

1   It should be noted that the Entex Adventure Vision (and the similar Colorvision), which resembled an arcade machine, was intended to be placed and played on a tabletop rather than held in the hands. It was also too fragile and bulky to be carried in your pocket or backpack. In short, it's not the in the same category as the Microvision or Game Boy.

Golden Sun: The Lost Age on the **VisualBoy Advance** emulator.

Golden Sun: The Lost Age
(2003, Camelot Software Planning, GBA)

This sequel to 2001's *Golden Sun* is widely regarded as one of the best role-playing games for the platform. It's certainly one of the most ambitious, with more than 40 hours of gameplay and brilliant graphics. Although the second game is better than its predecessor, you should probably play them in order to get the most out of the story—and when you're done, you can transfer your party to this one.

Yokoi contented himself with the look and feel of the system, and turned to his partner Satoru Okada to do the internal work. Okada, an electronics engineer by training, had distinguished himself by directing the hit NES games *Metroid* and *Kid Icarus.* Okada didn't quite share Yokoi's commitment to "weathered" technology. He worried that the design—particularly the "four shades of gray" 160 x 144 pixel display—just wasn't good enough, and that upgrades were required. He pleaded with Yokoi, who stubbornly held his ground.

It wasn't just the monochrome scheme that Okada feared would turn off gamers. At the time, most videogames offered a two-player mode, but how would this work on a handheld? While various wireless technologies had been around for many years, none were as cheap and effective as today's Bluetooth or Wi-Fi. Yokoi's rather awkward solution was to connect systems using a wire called the "Link Cable," which would allow gamers to connect two Game Boys together—assuming they both had copies of the cartridge. It was a kludge, but it would later prove its value to a degree unimagined by its designers.

The Game Boy was an instant hit in Japan, where it landed in shops in late April of 1989. In just two weeks, it had sold 300,000 units—its entire stock.[2] Surprisingly, the Japanese launch titles did not include *Tetris*—for reasons we'll get into in a moment. Instead, the big game was *Super Mario Land,* which Yokoi had produced and Okada had directed.

A well-built platform game featuring the famous Mario characters, *Super Mario Land* was indeed a great hit, earning stellar reviews and spurring sales of the handheld. Nintendo felt it would be the perfect title to bundle with

An excerpt of a page from the 2001 premiere issue of **Nintendo Power Advance** magazine, showing a Game Link Cable scenario between two Game Boy Advances. With the right combination of cables and games, Game Boys from different eras could link together for connected multiplayer gaming.

2   Travis Fahs, "IGN Presents the History of Game Boy," *IGN*, July 27, 2009, www.ign.com/articles/2009/07/27/ign-presents-the-history-of-game-boy.

the unit for its North American debut. The man who changed their minds—and the future of handheld gaming—was a tenacious Dutch entrepreneur named Henk Rogers.

Rogers had moved from the Netherlands to Japan in 1976, starting his own publishing company called Bullet-Proof Software. The company's claim to fame was *The Black Onyx*, originally for the NEC PC-8801 computer, but later ported to several other systems, including the Game Boy. Released in 1984, it was one of the first Japanese role-playing games, and sold over 150,000 copies, paving the way for *Dragon Quest* and other popular Japanese role-playing games.[3] This feat is all the more surprising considering that Rogers couldn't speak or read Japanese!

Four years later, Rogers was at the 1988 Consumer Electronics Show (CES) in Las Vegas, where he played a fun little computer game called *Tetris* at the Spectrum Holobyte booth. Rogers had heard about Nintendo's plans to build a handheld, and he immediately recognized the revolutionary potential that *Tetris* held for such a system.

Rogers approached Minoru Arakawa, head of Nintendo of America, and convinced him that *Tetris* would be a much better game for selling Game Boys than *Super Mario Land*. His argument was simple: *Super Mario Land* would appeal to young boys; *Tetris* would appeal to everyone. Arakawa was finally convinced and sent Rogers to secure the licensing rights for the Game Boy.

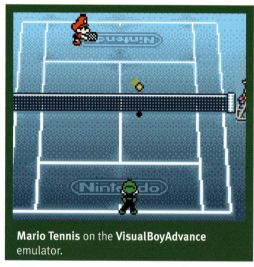

Mario Tennis on the **VisualBoyAdvance** emulator.

Mario Tennis
(2001, Camelot Software Planning, GBC)

This GBC title is much more than a simple tennis game. Instead, you get an RPG-style world in which Mario and his friends earn experience points to level up their tennis skills. There are also mini-games and you can use your Link Cable to play against friends. With a Nintendo 64 Transfer Pak, you can connect to the earlier *Mario Tennis* (2000) on the Nintendo 64 and unlock secrets and "supercharge" your champion. This fun and innovative game earned top scores from nearly every publication that reviewed it.

Like everyone else at the time, however, Rogers had a hard time figuring out just who owned and was legally entitled to license the rights to *Tetris*.[4]

Rogers' first strategy had been to sign deals with Spectrum Holobyte and Tengen, the Atari-spinoff, who both claimed they had the rights to sublicense *Tetris*.[5] To cover all his bases, Rogers even secured them from Mirrorsoft, a software publisher in the United Kingdom, yet another company who made a similar claim. Mirrorsoft had bought their license from Robert Stein, president of Andromeda.

Stein, however, had no authority from either Pajitnov or the Soviets—he had lied instead, telling everyone that the game had been created by some Hungarian programmers. The fiasco came to the

3   Edge Staff, "The Making of Black Oynx," *Edge*, January 20, 2013. www.edge-online.com/features/the-making-of-the-black-onyx.

4   See "Tetris (1985): Casual Gaming Falls into Place," Chapter 20 in Bill Loguidice and Matt Barton, *Vintage Games: An Insider Look at the History of Grand Theft Auto, Super Mario, and the Most Influential Games of All Time* (Focal Press, 2009), for more on the game.

5   See Chapter 2.1 for a discussion of Tengen's *Tetris* and the fight over the NES versions of the game.

attention of *CBS Evening News,* who ended up exposing Stein's duplicity and revealing Pajitnov as the actual creator. When the Soviet authorities finally got involved, they began by informing everyone that they hadn't licensed the game to anyone—and all the existing copies of the game were illegal. Stein did eventually sign a deal with them, but not for console or handheld versions. In the meantime, both Spectrum Holobyte and Mirrorsoft had been sublicensing *Tetris,* further adding to the chaos.[6]

Rogers decided to fly to Moscow and deal with the authorities in person. Luckily for Rogers, he got there first, and impressed the Russians with his honest assessment of the licensing situation. His only faux pas was showing them a Japanese version of *Tetris* his company did for the Famicom back in 1988. The Soviets were outraged, but Rogers was able to soothe their anger with a check for $41,000 and a promise of more to come.[7] Soon Rogers was signing an exclusive deal for the American handheld version of the game. It took another two months to settle all the legal disputes, but the ink was dry just in time for the Game Boy's North American release.

It's hard to exaggerate the significance that *Tetris* held for the Game Boy and handheld gaming in general. Rogers' prediction that its appeal would extend far beyond traditional gamers was spot-on. In *Augmented Learning,* Eric Klopfer writes that he gave a Game Boy with *Tetris* to his father, who played it regularly despite having no interest in any other videogames. The situation is comparable to games like *Farmville, Bejeweled, Angry Birds,* and hidden-object games, today. Many "real" gamers and game journalists tend to ignore or disparage these sorts of games, even though they are actively played by vast numbers of people who couldn't care less about the latest *Call of Duty.*

Metroid Fusion on the **VisualBoyAdvance** emulator.

Metroid Fusion
(2002, Nintendo R&D1, GBA)

Metroid Fusion is the sequel to *Super Metroid* for the Super NES. This time, Samus Aran is infected by the "X" parasite, only to be saved by a vaccine made from a Metroid. The X parasite can mimic whatever abilities are used against it. It's up to Samus to find and eliminate all traces of the parasite on a research station. If you enjoyed the first two *Metroid* games, you'll definitely enjoy this incarnation, which offers much of their style with some welcome enhancements and expansions.

Klopfer adds that the "small screen and flexibility of playing place made it feel less socially isolating and awkward."[8] Even though people could see you playing with your Game Boy, they wouldn't be able to see how well you were playing—an important consideration for sensitive gamers. We could also add the obvious point that you didn't need your own television or monitor—there was no need to battle mom or dad for the remote. In short, the Game Boy made gaming a lot more accommodating and convenient for everyone.

---

6 For a detailed account of the *Tetris* licensing fiasco, see "The Tetris Saga," *Atari HQ,* www.atarihq.com/tsr/special/tetrishist.html

7 A great deal of ink has been spilt telling this story. See Harold Goldberg, *All Your Base Are Belong to Us: How Fifty Years of Videogames Conquered Pop Culture* (Three Rivers Press, 2011) and David Sheff, *Game Over: How Nintendo Conquered the World* (Vintage Press, 1994). Both give dramatic accounts of the *Tetris* debacle. Steve Rabin also covers the story in his *Introduction to Game Development: Second Edition* (Cengage, 2010). Hopefully, there will be a movie soon.

8 See Eric Klopfer, *Augmented Learning: Research and Design of Mobile Educational Games,* Cambridge: MIT Press, 2008, p. 38.

While no one knows how many people bought a Game Boy just to play *Tetris,* it sold 35 million copies and caused at least some to wonder if the game's hopelessly addictive gameplay is a type of electronic drug—a "pharmatronic," as Jeffrey Goldsmith of *Wired* would have it.[9] It's often been called the perfect videogame; the ultimate example of the "easy to learn, hard to master" dynamic. It also relies almost entirely on its gameplay for its appeal; you certainly don't need advanced graphics or sound to enjoy *Tetris.* That said, the version that Nintendo whipped up for the Game Boy really did it justice, even featuring catchy music by Hirokazu Tanaka of *Metroid* fame. It also features an intense two-player competitive mode that connects two Game Boys via the Game Link Cable. Many gamers and critics consider it among the best games ever made, including Steve Wozniak, the celebrated designer of the Apple II discussed earlier in this book. The Game Boy version is his favorite videogame of all time.[10]

Nintendo's Game Boy didn't enjoy a monopoly for long. Just two months later, Atari unleashed the Lynx, which was technologically superior to the Game Boy in almost every conceivable way. Most obvious, of course, was the 3.5-inch color LCD display with a backlit display. Instead of four shades of gray/green, Lynx games could offer 16 on-screen colors from a palette of 4096, the same number of colors the mighty Commodore Amiga could draw from. It also boasted better sound and could be flipped around to accommodate lefties. Instead of just a two-system connection, the Lynx accepted up to an 18-unit network! Unfortunately, the Lynx's battery life was far less impressive, sucking down six-AA batteries in just a few hours. This fact, coupled with a $179.99 introductory price (the Game Boy was $90 cheaper) limited its appeal.

The Lynx had originally been developed by the game publisher Epyx, who had called it the Handy. Two members of its design team, R.J. Mical and Dave Needle, had helped develop the Commodore Amiga (see Chapter 2.2). Unfortunately, Epyx was not doing well, and managed to sell the ambitious project to Atari just before filing for bankruptcy. Sadly, much like the Amiga, the Lynx was never able

On the far left is the original Game Boy shown next to an original Atari Lynx (top) and Sega Game Gear (bottom) for scale. To the right of the Atari Lynx is NEC's TurboExpress and one version of the Watara Supervision, which was a poorly distributed budget competitor to the Game Boy first released in 1992.

to rise above the competition despite its obvious technological advantages, and sold fewer than 3 million units. Fortunately for fans of this system, it now enjoys a vibrant homebrew community.

Sega's Game Gear, despite being based on the powerful Master System console technology—and able to use its cartridges with a simple adapter—didn't fare much better. It boasted a 3.2-inch screen capable of displaying 32 colors at 160 × 144 resolution, and Sega had its popular *Sonic the Hedgehog* and arcade properties it could leverage. Sega also had a viable response to *Tetris* in its launch lineup, *Columns,* which offered similar casual gameplay. Unfortunately, like the Lynx, the Game Gear was a battery hog, and its introductory price of $149.99, while cheaper than the

9   Jeffrey Goldsmith, "This is Your Brain on *Tetris,*" *Wired,* Issue 2.05, www.wired.com/wired/archive/2.05/tetris_pr.html.

10   Daniel Terdiman, "Woz and I Agree: 'Tetris' for the Gameboy is the Best Game Ever," *CNet,* December 11, 2007, http://news.cnet.com/8301-13772_3-9832348-52.html.

Lynx, was still much more than a Game Boy. Though far more successful, it also failed to pose a serious threat to Nintendo, only selling 11 million units.

A third contender at the time, NEC's Turbo-Express, was the least successful of all the handhelds of the era, selling only 1.5 million units, despite being arguably the most powerful. A portable version of the TurboGrafx-16 (PC Engine in Japan) and compatible with all of its cartridges, its impressive 400 × 270 resolution couldn't make up for its high price ($249.99) and lack of big-name games designed for a smaller screen.

The original Game Boy line, through the Game Boy Color, eventually sold over 118.69 million units (with the Game Boy Advance chipping in another 82 million), which is almost double the worldwide sales of the Nintendo Entertainment System. This disparity

Many third-party manufacturers came up with various add-ons to try and make the Game Boy more usable, including an assortment of lights and magnifiers. Some such manufacturers, however, like this advertisement for STD's Handy Boy demonstrates, clearly didn't know when to stop.

Pokémon Crystal on the **VisualBoyAdvance** emulator.

Pokémon Gold/Silver/Crystal
(2000, Game Freak, GBC)

This GBC title is the follow-up to the original *Pokémon* for the Game Boy. It leaves much of the gameplay intact, but with a new world, creatures, and a greatly improved interface. The game made great use of the new handheld's color, adding even more personality to the already charming series. The *Crystal* version, released in 2001, adds the option to play as a male or female, new locations, moves, and much more—it's probably the one to get, especially if you are new to the series.

between Nintendo's handhelds and consoles has continued to the present day. Consider the data in the table below, in which we've juxtaposed the consoles chronologically with the handhelds of their era:

CONSOLES	HANDHELDS
Nintendo Entertainment System: 61.91	
Super Nintendo Entertainment System: 49.10	**Game Boy** through **Game Boy Color**: 118.69
Nintendo 64: 32.93	
GameCube: 21.74	**Game Boy Advance**: 81.51

Data from Wikipedia in millions of units sold.

While even today most of the hardcore or "serious" gaming community seems focused on consoles or computers, it's clear that many other gamers (and many who would probably object to that title) prefer these handheld devices. Gaming had moved from the arcade, to the living room, and now to pretty much anywhere without direct sunlight. In short, the Game Boy was what Clayton Christensen calls a "disruptive" technology:

> Disruptive technologies bring to a market a very different value proposition than had been available previously. Generally, disruptive technologies underperform established products in mainstream markets. But they have other features that a few fringe (and generally new) customers value. Products based on disruptive technologies are typically cheaper, simpler, smaller, and, frequently, more convenient to use.[11]

Christensen also found that it was these disruptive technologies coming from outside that posed the gravest threat to the leading firms he studied. As we'll see later, it was another disruptive technology—the CD-ROM—that led to Nintendo's own defeat in the console market by Sony in the 1990s (see Chapters 3.2 and 3.3). It's curious to think what would have happened had Yokoi not had his way, and the Game Boy ended up being as expensive as the Lynx or the Game Gear—or, more sensationally, if Atari had won the battle over *Tetris* and offered it as an exclusive game for the Lynx.

The last major event in the original Game Boy's career occurred in 1996, when Satoshi Tajiri released his first *Pokémon* game. As a youngster growing up in the Tokyo suburbs, Tajiri loved nothing more than exploring the outdoors in search of insects, a passion that led to his nickname "Dr. Bug." His father intended for him to become an electrician, but his love of playing and writing about videogames led him to a career as a designer. His debut was *Mendel Palace* (1989, Hudson Soft), an arcade/puzzle game for the NES. He was also one of the programmers on Shigeru Miyamoto's *The Legend of Zelda*.

However, Tajiri's real breakthrough came in 1990, when he observed children playing a game together on their Game Boys via the Link Cable. He began to conceive a game that would also use this cable, but not just so players could compete head-to-head. Instead, his mind turned back to his childhood love of insects, and he imagined bugs growing in Game Boys and traveling through the cables to visit other Game Boys. When he approached Nintendo with the idea,

---

[11]   Clayton M. Christensen, *The Innovator's Dilemma: When New Technologies Cause Great Firms to Fail*, Harvard Business Press, 1997, p. xv.

they swatted him away. Later attempts were also repulsed. Fortunately, at least one person at Nintendo was sympathetic: Miyamoto, Nintendo's star game designer. Miyamoto adopted his friend's cause, and this time the company listened.

Miyamoto himself was assigned to help Tajiri develop the idea into the now-familiar game of catching, training, and trading a huge variety of creatures. It took six years, but finally the game was ready. Of course, by this time, the Game Boy was nearing obsolescence, but they were still avidly enjoyed by younger children and anyone who couldn't afford a newer console. Sales were modest at first, but momentum built steadily as the social networking kicked in over "Mew," a secret creature. Although the game officially had 150 creatures, this hidden one could only be "caught" by trading with your friends. As unlikely as this ploy might seem, it worked, creating an insatiable buzz for more *Pokémon* players. The franchise soon expanded into a popular trading card game, manga, anime, toys, and pretty much anything else you can think of.

It seems laughable today, but when the developers were localizing the game for North America, some thought that gamers here would be turned off by the "cuteness" of the creatures and wanted them redesigned with a more threatening look. Fortunately, the team was able to convince them otherwise.[12]

A scan of the fold-out **Pokémon** poster from the August 1998 issue of **Nintendo Power** released in anticipation of the upcoming "Red" and "Blue" games. The "Gotta catch 'em all!" slogan could not only be applied to the in-game activities, but also come to represent all the merchandise that popped up in support of the franchise that fans eagerly snatched up.

Pokémon arrived in America in two versions: Red and Blue. Each version came with different creatures, and, much to the dismay of parents, you needed both to "catch 'em all" and become a "Pokémon master." The major game publications gave it their highest possible ratings, and sales climbed to 9.85 million, making it both the best-selling role-playing game (although some disagree with the classification), and not just on the Game Boy, but of all time. Everyone agreed that it was

---

[12] Developers Fred Ford and Paul Reiche III designed a computer game in 1985 called *Mail Order Monsters*, whose gameplay bears a striking resemblance to *Pokémon*. These two would go on to develop *Skylanders: Spyro's Adventure* in 2011, which expanded the concept to include physical toys and a "Portal of Power" interface that transfers data between game or PC systems and the toys.

Pokémon Pinball
(1999, Jupiter Corp., GBC)

As the title suggests, this game takes the best-selling franchise into a new domain: pinball! It's also one of the first-ever GBC games to leverage the Rumble Cartridge. While some critics criticized its physics engine, most agree that it was more than just a cash-in on the popularity of the franchise. In any case, if you love pinball and *Pokémon*, it's hard to see how you could go wrong with this game.

Pokémon Pinball on the **VisualBoyAdvance** emulator.

one of the best games ever released for the Game Boy, where much like *Tetris,* the appeal extended far beyond the normal "gamer" stereotype. The franchise has continued to expand into the modern era, but many serious fans still clamor for the original Game Boy versions—especially the "Yellow" version, called *Pokémon Special Pikachu Edition*, distinguished primarily by a Pikachu who surfs and clearly says "Pika Pika." This game's artwork also more closely matches that of the anime, which by the time of its release had become a staple of children's television programming.

Like the platform it originated on, *Pokémon* is clearly a disruptive technology, something that seems cheap, strange, and let's face it—downright silly—to the established market, but has an overwhelming and transformative appeal for large groups outside of that sector.

Writing for *The New York Times,* Edward Rothstein tried to explain why the Game Boy was still selling in large numbers as late at 1997. After pointing out the unit's obsolescence—even when it was released—Rothstein gets at what might very well be the reason for the system's appeal:

> [The] Game Boy is almost bracing. It has so few details that each one becomes essential... In the best games, which range from puzzle games like *Tetris,* to the newest so-called narrative game, *Donkey Kong Land III*—leanness provides focus...It begins to seem like an upgrade to solitary pre-tech activities like crossword puzzles.[13]

While Nintendo's later handhelds greatly enhanced the audiovisual capability, Rothstein's analysis is still insightful. After all, plenty of other handhelds were vastly superior technologically speaking, but the charming simplicity of the Game Boy line still managed to draw more sales.

Nintendo finally discontinued the original Game Boy in 2003 after a full 14 years on the market, though the Game Boy Advance was backward compatible and available as late as 2008. Furthermore, many classic Game Boy games can be played on modern Nintendo handhelds via their Virtual Console service on their newest systems. Although the Nintendo DS has the distinction of being the best-selling console of all time, it owes a large part of its success to its humble, "withered" predecessor, the Game Boy.

---

13   E. Rothstein, (1997, Dec 08). Technology. *New York Times* (1923-Current File). Retrieved from http://search.proquest.com/docview/109731363?accountid=14048.

Later Models and Accessories

Nintendo's cartridge-based handhelds have a long, storied history. Here are a few of the highlights:

- **1995:** A commercial failure, The Virtual Boy offered 3D graphics and promised a new era of virtual reality games. Designed to be played on a table, the system required users to peer into an eyepiece, like binoculars. The monochrome graphics were an unsettling red, and some users complained about eye fatigue or headaches. It was rumored that the disappointing sales led to Nintendo's asking for the resignation of its late designer Gunpei Yokoi, but he claimed otherwise.

The Virtual Boy, shown next to the original Game Boy for scale, was a miserable failure for Nintendo. The company wouldn't take another stab at a dedicated 3D system until the 3DS.

- **1996:** The Game Boy Pocket was sleeker and smaller than the original Game Boy, plus had a better screen with less blur during action sequences. Unfortunately, its serial port was resized, requiring owners to buy special adapters if they wanted to connect their unit to a classic system.

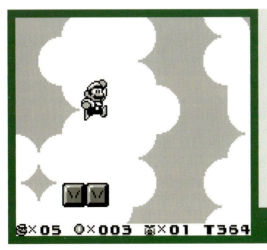

Super Mario Land 2: 6 Golden Coins on the VisualBoyAdvance emulator.

Super Mario Land 2: 6 Golden Coins
(1992, Nintendo R&D1, GB)

This title for the original Game Boy improves upon its predecessor with better graphics, tighter controls, new moves, and a storyline that introduced the world to Wario, a villain who quickly became a favorite with fans of the franchise. The battery pack saves your in-game progress, which is a good thing considering the size of this adventure.

- **1997:** The Game Boy Printer was an intriguing add-on that was intended mostly as a way for players to print out their high scores and photos taken with the Game Boy Camera attachment. Unfortunately, it wasn't a big success, and requires special paper that is hard to find nowadays.

- **1998:** The Game Boy Camera was, for a time, recognized as the world's smallest digital camera. It uses the four "shades of gray" palette of the Game Boy to take pictures at 256 × 224 resolution, which can then be printed out on the Game Boy Printer or shared via a Game Link cable. Perhaps its most famous application was the cover of Neil Young's *Silver & Gold* album. At any rate, you'd surely be a hit with the Game Boy Printer and Camera at any Nintendo convention.

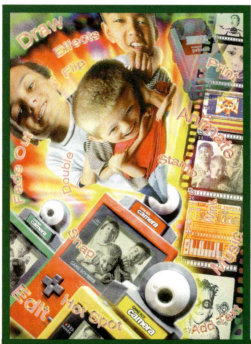

- **1998:** Color finally arrived to the platform with the Game Boy Color. Fully backward compatible with the original, this Game Boy could display up to 56 colors from a palette of 32,768. It also offered an infrared port, so *Pokémon* fans could at last connect to each other without wires or cables. While some games for the Game Boy Color also play fine in the older units, there are also plenty of games exclusive to this system. The memory was increased to 32K, and the processor had a "double mode" that ran at 8.4 MHz, which was used for the GBC-exclusive games.

- **2001:** The Game Boy Advance was a significant step forward for the platform, with a new form factor (wide instead of tall) and shoulder buttons. It also upped the resolution to 240 × 160, increased the screen size to 2.9 inches, and added two sound channels. Its

A colorful ad for the Game Boy Camera and Printer from the August 1998 issue of **Nintendo Power**. The camera and its software allowed for a primitive version of the type of interactive virtual reality play experiences common on later consoles, beginning with Sony's PlayStation 2.

CPU runs at 16.8 MHz—twice as fast as the GBC. It's backward-compatible, but doesn't have the infrared port—the Game Link Cable had returned. An interesting add-on for the Game Boy Advance was the e-Reader, which had an LED scanner that read e-Reader cards with specially encoded data. Some of the cards included classic NES games to scan in and play, while others unlocked content in games like *Animal Crossing* (2002) on the Nintendo GameCube (Chapter 3.7) when used with the link cable.

- **2003:** The Game Boy Advance SP was another significant revision. Nintendo finally added front lighting, so players could at last play in the dark. It also had a redesigned case that clamped shut like a wallet. These units have rechargeable lithium ion batteries. A later version allows you to adjust the brightness instead of just toggling the light on and off.

Systems shown, left to right: Game Boy, Game Boy Pocket, Game Boy Color, Game Boy Advance, Game Boy Advance SP, Nintendo DS, and Nintendo 3DS.

- **2004:** The Nintendo DS is widely regarded as one of the best-ever handhelds. The biggest change was the introduction of a second screen, which accepts touch or stylus input. It has a 256 × 192 resolution, 260,000 on-screen colors, and 16-bit stereo sound. It is oriented horizontally, but can clamp shut like the SP, protecting the screen when not in use. It is backward-compatible with the Game Boy Advance, but not the earlier systems. It, and future versions of the DS, remain Nintendo's best-selling system of all time.

- **2005:** The Game Boy Micro, the last of the original Game Boy series systems, is a much smaller, thinner version of the Game Boy Advance, but isn't compatible with Game Boy or Game Boy Color games. The company made a big deal out of the interchangeable faceplates, but the tiny system was overshadowed by the popularity of the DS.

- **2006:** The DS Lite slimmed down the original DS and improved the display, while retaining backwards compatibility with Game Boy Advance games.

- **2008:** The DSi enlarged the screens of the DS and added cameras. It also has rewriteable internal and external storage via SD cards. The only real downside to this model is the lack of a port for Game Boy Advance games. In 2009, Nintendo introduced the XL version, which, as the name suggests, is larger, with screens that have a wider viewing angle.

- **2010:** Nintendo's 3DS introduced stereoscopic 3D—that is, 3D without the need for any special glasses. They also added an accelerometer and a gyroscope, which open up some intriguing options for controlling games. While the unit has fared much better than Nintendo's earlier attempt at 3D, the Virtual Boy, the 3DS has failed to achieve the same popularity of its predecessor in light of increased competition for eyeballs from smartphones and tablets. An XL version, released in 2012, offers much larger screens, better battery life, and a higher capacity SD card than the original. The 2DS, introduced in late 2013, plays all of the same 3DS games, just in 2D and with a non-folding, slate form factor, making it a budget friendly alternative to the original 3DS and those adverse to the idea of 3D gaming.

The Legend of Zelda: The Minish Cap
(2004, Flagship Co., GBA)

Link is second only to Mario in terms of popularity with Nintendo fans, and this game does the venerable franchise justice. The Minish are tiny people, so Link must use the power of the titular hat to shrink himself down small enough to explore their world. This shrinking dynamic is used to great effect in the game's puzzles. It's also one of the best-looking games on the platform.

The Legend of Zelda: The Minish Cap on the **VisualBoyAdvance** emulator.

The Nintendo Game Boy Community Then and Now

Nintendo's Game Boy enjoyed a tremendously broad appeal that extended far beyond the traditional gamer demographics. After all, how else were you going to play *Tetris* on the go? Although the bulk of Nintendo fans were 8–12-year-old boys, there were quite a few women and girls playing as well. Some of Nintendo's television commercials showed 30-something-year-old business professionals playing Game Boys as the narrator said, "You don't stop playing because you get old. But you could get old if you stop playing." The relatively cheap price of the Game Boy and its long battery life made it ideal for travelers, students, or anyone without easy access to a television.

The *Pokémon* craze that swept across America in the late 1990s had less appeal for adults. Children were playing so much of the videogame (and the related card game) that some schools

banned them. As discussed above, the need to play the game with other people to acquire all the monsters spiked a social gaming movement. It's hard to exaggerate the impact that the franchise has had on a generation of children, many of whom still play the original game or its many sequels.

One intriguing part of today's Game Boy culture is in music, where artists use Game Boys to make "chiptunes." While other systems are also widely used to make chiptunes, the portability and familiarity of the Game Boy make it a fun instrument for performers.

Shown here via the **VisualBoyAdvance** emulator is **Fatass**, a music tracker for the Game Boy Color. Many chiptune artists use programs like this to create fantastic, retro-sounding digital tunes.

The Legend of Zelda: Oracle of Ages on the **VisualBoyAdvance** emulator.

The Legend of Zelda: Oracle of Seasons/Ages (2001, Flagship Co., GBC)

While both great games in their own right, what makes these games unique is the way they interact with each other—either via passwords or Game Link cable. As the titles imply, one game focuses on weather-based puzzles and abilities, whereas the other is concerned with time travel. *Seasons* is more action-based, with *Ages* being more puzzle-oriented. If you complete one, you're given a password that will create a "linked game" with the other one, changing its story line and ending. Can you say replay value?

Today, there are countless websites that cater to the needs of all types of Game Boy fans, although these skew mostly toward the Game Boy Advance and DS systems. YouTube is full of videos featuring fans playing games, repairing or modifying their systems, or just reminiscing about the good old days. Online forums are plentiful, although few seem to be focused exclusively on the original Game Boy.

There's also an impressively active homebrew and modding community. The Game Boy Development forums at http://gbdev.gg8.se/forums are a great place to learn about all manner of exciting projects. A recent example is *Super Connard*, a French cartridge with three different casual mini-games. Most homebrew for the Game Boy line, however, is made for the Game Boy Advance or DS systems. A program called *Dragon BASIC*, written by Jeff Massung, makes it easy for even novice programmers to create new games for the Game Boy Advance.

Dragon BASIC is an easy-to-use interpreter for programming games on a computer for the Game Boy Advance. Shown on the left is the IDE with the source code for the game on the right. The game was programmed by Jason Bullough and is entitled **Chegg**.

Collecting Nintendo Game Boy Systems

Acquiring an original Game Boy is neither expensive nor difficult. For units with the inevitable scratched screen, buying and installing a replacement screen can be easily done with an inexpensive kit. It's also trivial to find and replace the battery cover, which are often missing on systems formerly owned by small children, or very forgetful adults.

However, it probably makes sense for most people to go with one of the later units. The Game Boy Advance SP is a great choice for many people, since it is backward-compatible with the original Game Boy and Game Boy Color, and of course has a nicer form factor and lighting.

Emulating the Nintendo Game Boy

There are many ways to emulate the Game Boy. One of the most popular and versatile is *Visual-BoyAdvance*. It emulates the classic Game Boy, Game Boy Color, and Game Boy Advance lines, and is available for Windows, Macintosh, and Linux computers. Another option is *BGB*, which has TCP/IP support for emulating the game link. *BGB* is also known for its accurate sound emulation, an important factor for chiptune composers. Similar emulators are available for a variety of smartphones and tablets.

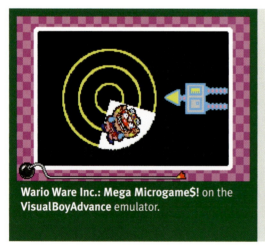

Wario Ware Inc.: Mega Microgame$! on the **VisualBoyAdvance** emulator.

Wario Ware Inc.: Mega MicrogameS!
(2003, Nintendo R&D1, GBA

This GBA title features the villainous Wario, who debuted in *Super Mario Land 2*. Otherwise, the two games couldn't be more different. This one is a huge assortment of brief mini-games that span the history of Nintendo—there are games based on everything from the old Game & Watch systems to later NES hits like *Duck Hunt* and *Metroid*. Several of the mini-games border on the surreal, with one, for instance, having you rapidly clicking the buttons to suck the snot back into a woman's nose! The casual, "pick up and play" nature of this game hearkens back to the days of *Tetris*.

If you own a Super NES, a fun option is the Super Game Boy. This special cartridge has a slot for Game Boy cartridges, and some later Game Boy games actually have special enhancements that take advantage of this setup. While this is mostly limited to enhanced audiovisuals, some games, such as *Wario Blast*, actually let you use the Super NES's second controller for two-player gameplay. The Game Boy Player is a similar device for the GameCube, but also accepts Game Boy Color and Game Boy Advance cartridges. Unfortunately, it doesn't support the Super Game Boy's enhancements.

Of course, an obvious problem with PC or console-based emulation is that you lose out on the mobility! Thankfully, it's also possible to emulate the Game Boy on modern gaming hand-helds. The *Lameboy* emulator offers support for playing older Game Boy games on a DS. There's also *GameYob*, which has a number of cool features such as save states and support for a Rumble Pak. It uses the DS's wireless capability to emulate the game link. Note that both options will require the purchase of a micro SD card and reader, as well as a Flash cartridge.

Of course, you should always check Nintendo's own Virtual Console store on their latest systems to see if the game is already available as part of that service. Many of the classic Game Boy titles, such as *Tetris* and *Super Mario Land,* are sold on the Nintendo eShop for reasonable prices.

Nintendo Super NES (1991)

History

As the 1980s drew to a close, Nintendo was at the top of its game, easily dominating both the console and the new handheld market thanks to its Game Boy. While the Game Boy easily fended off all comers, the NES was feeling its age. Nintendo was losing ground in both Japan and America to NEC's PC Engine series and Sega's Genesis, respectively. The company was naturally reluctant to threaten its well-established NES with a new, non-compatible console. However, when Nintendo finally struck with the Super Famicom on November 21, 1990, it never looked back: 8-bit was dead.

The Super Famicom was designed by master Famicom creator Masayuki Uemura, who was brought back from retirement to direct its creation. It was an instant success, selling out of its initial shipment of 300,000 units in just a few hours. The company had released it on a Wednesday evening, and tried other secretive measures to avoid unwanted attention from the Yakuza (a transnational organized crime syndicate).[1] However, the public disturbance was so great that the Japanese government formally requested that all future videogame console releases take place on a weekend.[2]

The Super Famicom, or Super Nintendo Entertainment System (Super NES or SNES), as it would be known after its release in North America (August 23, 1991, retailing for $199.99) and Europe (April 11, 1992), gave Nintendo its first crack at updating its popular franchises, enhancing favorites such as Mario and Zelda for the "next generation." In this regard, the Super NES delivered. These new games were more than just audiovisual facelifts of stale classics, however. They were indeed "Super," as their titles suggested, taking full advantage of the new hardware to offer gamers a richer, more in-depth experience than ever before. More importantly, they allowed Nintendo to shift console sales momentum back in their favor.

A still from one of the earliest Super Nintendo commercials in 1991, showing a simple addition to the NES's famous slogan, "Now you're playing with power."
www.youtube.com/watch?v=BrI-A94aLfo

---

[1] David David, *Game Over: How Nintendo Zapped an American Industry, Captured Your Dollars, and Enslaved Your Children*, New York: Random House, 1993.

[2] Steven L. Kent, *The Ultimate History of Video Games: The Story Behind the Craze that Touched our Lives and Changed the World*, Prima Publishing, 2001.

Super Mario World, which was the pack-in game for North American consoles, was a brilliant addition to the Mario platforming dynasty (and first introduction to new series favorite, Yoshi), and showed that producer Shigeru Miyamoto was just as good with 16-bits as he was with 8-bits. *F-Zero* was a genre-defining futuristic racing game that showed off the new system's inherent scaling and rotation effects, much like casual flight simulator *Pilotwings*.

The software at the Japanese launch was anemic at best. Only **Super Mario World** and **F-Zero** were available to showcase the new hardware. Nintendo waited nearly a year to launch the system in North America, which allowed developers to add **Pilotwings**, **SimCity**, and **Gradius III** to the lineup.

Chrono Trigger on the **ZSNES** emulator.

Chrono Trigger (1995, Squaresoft)

Even against the NES and Sega Genesis before it, and the Sony PlayStation after it, it's been argued that the Super NES featured the greatest selection of original role-playing games ever produced for a console. With releases like *Chrono Trigger*, it's easy to see why. While *Chrono Trigger* tasks the player with controlling the usual group of adventurers through the standard types of forests, towns, and dungeons in an attempt to prevent an obviously world-shattering catastrophe, the game presents several interesting twists to the usual genre conventions. These twists include seamless enemy encounters that are visible on and take place on the same map used for exploration; time travel, where actions that occur in the past have an impact on future events; and not just one, but 13 unique endings. The game also further refines the "Active Time Battle" system first implemented in the 1991 classic *Final Fantasy II* (known as *Final Fantasy IV* in Japan), where the player has to input character orders in real-time during battles. Detailed, colorful graphics, and a masterful soundtrack round out *Chrono Trigger*'s appealing total package.

SimCity had been an absolute mega-hit on the PC, but it was unclear if the city-building game's complex interface and gameplay mechanics would translate well to consoles. The resulting game could either make or break the platform's reputation. Therefore, Nintendo took on the responsibility of porting the game itself. Although their port suffered from noticeable slow-down with large cities, it demonstrated that complex computer simulations were not major hurdles for the new console. The developers even added their own flourishes, including replacing the *Godzilla*-like monster from the original game with Bowser, Mario's nemesis.

The only third-party title at the launch, *Gradius III*, was a competent, if somewhat mundane port of Konami's own side-scrolling arcade space shooter. The lack of third-party support didn't bode well for the system, particularly now that the company was facing stronger competition. It had also allowed many of its infamous exclusivity agreements with major publishers to expire. Nevertheless, third-party software support for the Super Nintendo quickly gained momentum. Some third parties continued to deal exclusively with Nintendo, obtaining both licenses and cartridges, but most others would simply purchase the required security chips and manufacture their own cartridges. This option left them free to support the Genesis and other systems. Of course, to get the required license and accompanying security chip, third parties still had to agree to produce at least three Super NES titles a year.[3] It wasn't a popular clause with publishers, but old habits die hard.

Technical Specifications

The Super NES featured a boxy grey exterior accented with purple and grey features. On the top of the console was a cartridge port with a noticeably different shape than its Japanese counterpart. This shape, combined with an internal lockout chip, means the North American Super Nintendo could only play cartridges made for its region without the use of special adapters. Below the cartridge port, from left to right, were a purple power button, grey eject button for removing cartridges after power off, and a reset switch.

Donkey Kong Country 2: Diddy's Kong Quest on the **ZSNES** emulator.

Donkey Kong Country 2: Diddy's Kong Quest (1995, Nintendo)

As sequels go, *Donkey Kong Country 2: Diddy's Kong Quest* had one of the tougher acts to follow. No longer afforded the luxury of surprising gamers with the original game's audiovisual "wow factor," developer Rare succeeded by simply focusing on improving nearly every aspect of *Donkey Kong Country*'s already winning formula, from even better graphics fidelity to larger, more varied stages. One or two simultaneous players take on the role of Diddy, or his girlfriend Dixie, as they try to rescue Donkey Kong from Kaptain K. Kool through Crocodile Isle's eight unique environments. Hidden bonus stages with collectible tokens add to the returning ability to "ride" various animal buddies with unique abilities, including Squitter the Spider, Glimmer the Anglerfish, and Squawks the Parrot. David Wise's compositions, which were also released separately on CD, provide a fitting soundtrack to Diddy Kong's continued adventures. The last sequel to appear on the Super NES was *Donkey Kong Country 3: Dixie Kong's Double Trouble!* (1996), which, while combining some of the best elements from the first two games, had the unfortunate distinction of releasing shortly after the launch of the Nintendo 64, lessening some of its potential impact.

---

[3] David Sheff, *Game Over: How Nintendo Zapped an American Industry, Captured Your Dollars, and Enslaved Your Children*, Random House, 1993.

To the front of the console were two controller ports. Included with each Super Nintendo console were two eight button controllers with a color scheme that matched the console. Unlike the rectangular NES controllers, the Super NES controllers were rounded and slightly larger, which made them far more comfortable for extended use. From left to right on the front of each controller were a digital direction pad, select button, start button, and Y, X, B, and A action buttons. Left and right digital triggers were at the top of the controller.

Although not in a traditional arcade layout, the fact that the Super Nintendo's controllers supported six action buttons by default (counting the two shoulder triggers) made the system a natural for fighting game conversions. Combined with its impressive audiovisual capabilities, games like *Street Fighter II* (1992, Capcom), *Super Street Fighter II: The New Challengers* (1994, Capcom), *Killer Instinct* (1995, Rare), and *Ultimate Mortal Kombat 3* (Midway, 1996), shined whether using the stock controller or dedicated arcade stick.

Street Fighter II running on the **ZSNES** emulator. Although the controller didn't have a traditional layout, its six action buttons in combination with the console's quality graphics and sound made the Super NES one of the era's best platforms for fighting games.

On the right rear of the console were, from left to right, a multi out, RF out and CH 3–CH 4 switch, and AC adapter input (DC 10V). The versatile multi out audiovideo output connector, which would also later be found on the Nintendo 64 (Chapter 3.3) and GameCube (Chapter 3.7), allowed for composite, S-Video, and RGB signals, as well as RF with an external RF modulator.

On the bottom of the console was an EXT expansion port, covered by a removable slot cover. Only two Japanese exclusives made use of this port: the Satellaview modem and an exercise bike. If the planned CD add-on ever saw release, it too would have made use of this port. Since it saw so little use, the expansion port, dedicated RF output, and related channel select switch weren't included in the later Super Nintendo model, the SNS-101, released in 1997 at a budget-friendly $99.99 retail price.

The Super NES contains a custom Ricoh 5A22 CPU, which was based on the Western Design Center (WDC) 65816, which itself was the 16-bit successor to the 8-bit WDC 65C02 class of CPUs found in systems like the NEC TurboGrafx-16, Atari Lynx, and Apple IIe Enhanced/IIC+ (Chapter 1.2). The Rico 5A22 CPU ran at 3.58 MHz, faster than the 2.8 MHz from the similar CPU found in the Apple IIGS, which was often used as an early development system for the Super NES. While Nintendo's choice of CPU and related clock speed was somewhat underwhelming in terms of raw performance, critics were impressed with the system's ability to pass processing demands onto other parts of its architecture, like its video and audio subsystems.

The Picture Processing Unit (PPU) was made up of two IC packages that act as a single unit. The versatile PPU contained 64K of SRAM for storing video data, 544 bytes of Object Attribute

Memory (OAM) for storing sprite data, and a 256 × 15-bit Color Generator RAM (CGRAM) for storing palette data. This translated to a common output resolution of 256 × 224 pixels, with up to 256 colors on-screen at one time from a palette of 32,768.

The system's background layers were made up of 32 × 32 to 128 × 128 tiles on one of two foreground or background planes, with eight different color palettes. Each of these layers could be scrolled horizontally and vertically, allowing for some impressive effects. The Super NES featured eight such graphics modes, numbered 0–7, but the most famous was Mode 7. In this mode, one layer of 128 × 128 tiles from a set of 256 could be rotated and scaled using matrix transformations, with HDMA used to generate perspective effects. Put simply, background images could be rotated and scaled freely to simulate 3D environments without any performance hits to other processing activities. While the Atari Lynx and Sega CD had similar capabilities in hardware, it was the Super NES that made the most consistent and innovative use of the feature, defining the unique aesthetics of *Super Mario World*, *Pilotwings*, *F-Zero*, *Super Mario Kart*, and *Kirby Super Star*. The remarkable scaling and rotation effects in games like these made "Mode 7" one of the unlikeliest household phrases ever.

EarthBound on the **ZSNES** emulator.

EarthBound (1995, Nintendo)

Known in Japan as *Mother 2* (1994), *EarthBound* was the first game released in the series in the US after Nintendo chose not to release the Famicom original *Mother* (1989), as *Earth Bound* in 1991 for the NES, despite being fully translated and ready to go. Luckily, bad timing didn't affect the sequel's release, and North American gamers were able to experience this unique, bizarre take on console role-playing. Ostensibly a parody of overused fantasy role-playing tropes, *EarthBound* also ruthlessly skewered American culture. The player is tasked with controlling 13-year-old Ness, who is gifted with psychic abilities, and other strange characters in the town of Onett, where one night a meteor landed, unleashing an evil alien named Giygas, who, of course, wants to take over the world. All activities take place from a single seamless 2D gameworld, including the turn-based battles. While poor sales meant no other sequels would be released outside of Japan, *EarthBound* is deserving of its cult classic status, well worth downloading on the Wii U's eShop if a boxed original copy of this highly collectible game (complete with included player's guide!) is out of your price range.

While the Super NES's graphics capabilities deservedly received a lot of attention, the audio subsystem is arguably even more impressive sounding than its colorful PPU looked. An 8-bit Sony SPC700 and a 16-bit DSP shared 64KB of SRAM and a clock speed of 24.576 MHz. In combination, these two processors generated a 16-bit waveform at 32 kHz by mixing input from eight independent voices and an eight-tap FIR filter. Each of the eight voices could play its sound sample at a variable rate, with Gaussian interpolation, stereo panning, and ADSR, linear, non-linear, or direct volume envelope adjustment. All of these features combined to create some of the cleanest and richest sound output of its era, which could be further augmented by passing stereo audio data from a cartridge, expansion port, or both, before sending the combined output to a television or audio receiver.

Besides the memory found in its video and audio subsystems, the console itself used a separate 128KB of DRAM. As with all of its other features, the base memory of the system could be expanded with chips in game cartridges, an innovation Nintendo had leveraged in the NES. While the NES was known for its in-cartridge game enhancer chips, the Super NES took the concept to the next level.

Two of the most popular such cartridge add-ins were the DSP- and Super FX-series chips, although they certainly weren't the only ones. The DSP chips were a series of fixed-point digital signal processor chips that allowed for fast vector-based calculations, bitmap conversion, 2D and 3D coordinate transformation, and other enhancements. These were often used as in-cartridge math co-processors to provide faster floating point and trigonometric calculations needed by 3D math algorithms in games like *Pilotwings* or *Super Mario Kart.*

The Super FX chips were a series of RISC CPUs primarily used for creating the type of 3D game worlds consisting of the types of polygons, texture mapping, and light source shading that the Super NES by itself could never hope to reproduce. In some cases, these chips also enhanced the elements of regular 2D games.

The first game to make use of the Super FX chip was the third-person space shooter *Star Fox. Star Fox* used scaling bitmaps for lasers, asteroids, and other obstacles, but the ships and other objects were rendered with hun-

Star Fox, shown here running on the **ZSNES** emulator, was the first game to use the Super FX chip to render 3D polygonal graphics on the Super NES.

dreds of polygons, creating the game's unique look. Other games that made use of the Super FX chip included racing games *Stunt Race FX* (1994, Nintendo) and *Dirt Trax FX* (1995, Acclaim), and 3D shooter, *Vortex* (1994, Electro Brain), which featured a transforming robot.

The Super FX 2, which was an enhancement of the original chip designed for larger games, was featured in three releases: *Doom* (1996, Williams), *Super Mario World 2: Yoshi's Island* (1995, Nintendo), and *Winter Gold* (1996, Nintendo), the latter of which was a European exclusive. The chips helped make these games critically and commercially successful, but their high cost and late availability limited their impact.[4]

Doom, shown here running on the **ZSNES** emulator, was one of a handful of games to use the Super FX 2 chip. Although the game ran in a window and with a relatively low frame rate, its faithfulness to the PC original is still an impressive demonstration of the versatility of the Super NES's architecture.

Final Fantasy III on the **ZSNES** emulator.

Final Fantasy III (1994, Squaresoft)

Released as *Final Fantasy VI* in Japan, it was the third game in the series released in the US, thus the confusing disparity in numbering that would take until 1997—and a completely different platform—to eventually sync up across all regions. Whatever it's referred to as, the fact remains that this cartridge is considered not just among the greatest ever console role-playing games, but among the greatest ever console games period. While it put the usual industrial spin on classic fantasy elements that the series was already known for, *Final Fantasy III* featured a large cast of characters who have to deal with serious dramatic issues (e.g., teen pregnancy and suicide) as they develop over the course of the game. *Final Fantasy III* would be a triumph based on its scope alone—which even included a tragic opera—but it was also successfully married to extremely polished gameplay. The game's greatness was such that it received several later ports that became classics in their own rights, including to the Game Boy Advance and Sony PlayStation, although, fittingly, little needed to be changed from the original.

---

4   One casualty was *Star Fox 2*, which, while completed and intended for a 1995 release, was shelved in favor of focusing on the Nintendo 64's launch. Ironically, the Nintendo 64's intended release date was missed by over a year, which would have provided an ample window for *Star Fox 2* to succeed at retail.

The Accessories and Add-ons

The Super NES had nowhere near the volume of add-ons enjoyed by the Sega Genesis or the NES, but there were still fun accessories available. While the Super NES came with great controllers, there were a wide variety of third-party replacements, as well as Nintendo's own Super Advantage arcade-style joystick with adjustable turbo settings.

The Super Nintendo also received an official bazooka-shaped light gun, the Super Scope. Only a dozen games were released with support for the light gun, including *Super Scope 6*, a bundled collection of mini-games, and *T2: The Arcade Game* (1995, LJN), a quality port of the popular arcade game.

Like the Genesis and NES before it, the Super NES also featured a variety of multitaps, including Hudson Soft's Super Multitap, which featured four controller ports and came bundled with the hectic multiplayer classic *Super Bomberman* as the *Super Bomberman Party Pak* (1993). While up to two multitaps could be connected to the console, giving a theoretical limit of eight players, the maximum that was ever supported in an original retail game was five.

In 1992, Nintendo released the Super NES Mouse in a bundle with a plastic mouse pad and *Mario Paint*, a clever drawing, animation, and music composition cartridge. While support wasn't exactly universal, the Super NES Mouse faired far better than its Genesis counterpart, since it was usable with several dozen games, including obvious targets like strategy games *Utopia: The Creation of a Nation* (1993, Jaleco) and *Sid Meier's Civilization*

To the left is the Super Scope surrounded by a few of its games. The Super NES mouse sits next to the Super Game Boy cartridge. At the top right of the photo is the Victormaxx Stuntmaster virtual reality helmet, which was really nothing more than a low resolution LCD screen in a bulky headset.

(1994, Koei), as well as role-playing games such as *Might and Magic III: Isles of Terra* (1995, FCI) and casino games such as *Super Caesars Palace* (1993, Virgin Games).

As mentioned in Chapter 2.4, while Nintendo never released a compatibility option for NES games for the Super Nintendo, they did release one for the original Game Boy. The Super Game Boy cartridge let all original Game Boy games (as well as black Game Boy Color cartridges and the Game Boy Camera in monochrome compatibility modes) run on a TV, mapping the four shades of green to various other colors. It also could display special graphical borders and other enhancements in games that provided special support for those features. Two games that showcased these extra features were *Donkey Kong* (1994, Nintendo), a wonderful fusion of the original arcade game and puzzle elements with more than 100 stages that added custom music and voice samples in addition to a colorful arcade machine border, and *Kirby's Dream Land 2* (1995, Nintendo), a platform game that came with a custom color scheme, special game border, and additional sound effects.

Secret of Mana on the **ZSNES** emulator.

Secret of Mana (1993, Squaresoft)

Thanks to the Super NES's multitap accessory, up to three players can control the three protagonists, a warrior boy, a magic user girl, and an amnesiatic con artist orphan sprite in this innovative action role-playing game.[5] While employing the traditional top-down perspective of other console role-playing games, *Secret of Mana* utilizes a real-time battle system and "Ring Command" menu system, which pauses the game and allows for a wide range of actions to be quickly performed without switching out from the main screen. The second or third players could drop out from the game at any time, where they would be immediately replaced by a customizable artificial intelligence, keeping the cooperative gameplay elements intact. The usual colorful Super NES graphics and excellent musical score from composer Hiroki Kikuta round out *Secret of Mana*'s compelling package.

Cartridges like the Pro Action Replay and Game Genie not only allowed in-game cheats, but could also be used for other useful functions like playing games intended for other regions. As is typical for add-ons like these, any Super Nintendo cartridges with special chips tend not to work.

Of course, arguably the most famous add-on for the Super NES was something that was never even released. Sony Engineer Ken Kutaragi had developed the SPC700 chip that helped power the Famicom's audio subsystem, which led to Nintendo signing a deal in 1988 with Sony for development of a CD-ROM add-on and Sony-branded combination Super Famicom and CD-ROM console.

At the June 1991 Consumer Electronics Show, Sony unveiled the Play Station, which played both Super NES cartridges and new SNES-CD titles. Despite demonstrating a viable prototype, Nintendo corporate became uncomfortable with the idea of a Sony developed and controlled CD format, and instead announced an alliance with Philips to produce their own CD add-on the very next day. Despite a new deal being reached in 1992 where Sony could once again produce Super NES-compatible hardware, the damage from the surprise announcement was already done and the company instead focused its corporate might on a new console of its own, the PlayStation, described in Chapter 3.2.

The infamous Philips CD-i games and muted reception to its properties that appeared on PC and Macintosh computers probably contributed to Nintendo's decision to end future sublicensing experiments.

---

5   Interestingly, Free Fall Associates' 1989 release for the Commodore Amiga, *Swords of Twilight*, had a somewhat similar gameplay structure and simultaneous three-player mode. Only some rough edges and being limited to a platform where console-like role-playing games were not looked upon favorably kept this title from having wider influence. Why publisher Electronic Arts never bothered to port or rework the title for later use on console platforms like the Sega Genesis remains a mystery considering how well-regarded *Secret of Mana* later became.

Unfortunately for Nintendo, their partnership with Philips didn't turn out any better. Philips released a handful of mostly mediocre (*Hotel Mario*) and infamous (*Link: The Faces of Evil*) games for their ill-fated CD-i multimedia platform,[6] but never a CD add-on for the Super NES. Partnerships with computer software publishers, Interplay and Software Toolworks, to release DOS, Windows, and Macintosh Nintendo-themed edutainment and casual entertainment titles like *Mario Teaches Typing* (1992) and *Mario's Game Gallery* (1995) produced similarly uninspired results.

With no CD-ROM add-on forthcoming, Nintendo instead doubled down on maximizing their console's potential. Games like Rare's *Donkey Kong Country* (1994), which made revolutionary use of pre-rendered 3D graphics from Silicon Graphics workstations, breathed new life into the Super Nintendo, helping the system remain competitive against a growing lineup of next generation consoles. Those same Silicon Graphics workstations would provide similar inspiration for and help bridge the gap to the release of Nintendo's next console in 1996, the Nintendo 64, described in Chapter 3.3.

Ultimately, the Super NES sold close to 50 million units worldwide, almost 10 million more than the rival Genesis.[7] The last Super Nintendo system rolled off the production line in 1999, while the last Super Famicom was September 2003, almost a full 13 years after its original Japanese launch.

Super Mario All-Stars on the **ZSNES** emulator.

Super Mario All-Stars (1993, Nintendo)

Once the decision was made during the Super NES's development to give up on the idea of backwards-compatibility with its predecessor, it seemed that platforming fans without an NES would have to miss out on some truly legendary *Super Mario Bros.*-series games. Original Super NES pack-in *Super Mario World* was of course a brilliant new take on the legendary series, as was the later, *Super Mario World 2: Yoshi's Island*, which, among its other distinctions were its unusual graphics that looked hand-drawn, but neither game really offered quite the same experience as the originals. That all changed in 1993 when Nintendo released *Super Mario All-Stars*, which contained audiovisually enhanced versions of *Super Mario Bros.*, *Super Mario Bros.: The Lost Levels* (the Japanese *Super Mario Bros. 2*), *Super Mario Bros. 2*, and *Super Mario Bros. 3*. The games were lovingly presented behind an animated startup screen and menu system that gave the titles their proper historical due, which was further enhanced with the welcome addition of a modern save game feature. In 1994, the game package was made even better with a version of the cartridge that also contained *Super Mario World* and included as a pack-in game with new Super NES systems. No wonder the Super NES started catching up in sales to Sega's Genesis! Fans with a Wii or Wii U would do well to check out *Super Mario All-Stars: Limited Edition* (2010), which was released to celebrate the 25th anniversary of *Super Mario Bros.* and is an authentic recreation of the Super NES original. While it's missing *Super Mario World*, the package does include the addition of a nice soundtrack CD and history booklet.

---

6   One CD-i game from the partnership, *Super Mario's Wacky Worlds*, developed in 1993, never saw release. While never quite finished, the game was shaping up to be a promising sequel to *Super Mario World*.

The Nintendo Super NES Community Then and Now

Nintendo fans have never suffered a shortage of support. Nintendo's own *Nintendo Power* magazine was just one among many publications that supplied fans with news about their favorite 16-bit system. Almost every site dedicated to classic gaming today has continued this support with discussion forums dedicated to the Super Nintendo, including Nintendo's own website (http://nintendo.com).

While there have been only a handful of homebrew games released for the Super Nintendo to date, the list is growing all the time. One of the most high profile homebrew releases to date has been the Kickstarter-driven *Super 4 in 1 Multicart*, which was funded on May 5, 2013, and features puzzler *Mazezam*, platformer *UWOL—Quest for Money*, cooperative multiplayer platformer *Skipp and Friends: Unexpected Journey*, and the up-to-eight-player fighting game *N-WARP Daisakusen*, as well as fifth bonus action game, *Balloon Attack*. Another popular homebrew title that has gained some attention is *Nightmare Busters* (2013) from Super Fighter Team, an enhanced version of a previously unreleased game from Nichibutzu.

Super Mario Kart on the **ZSNES** emulator.

Super Mario Kart (1992, Nintendo)

Super Mario Kart's release marked one of gaming's rare defining moments. Not only was it the first time Nintendo truly leveraged the combined power of its roster of characters, becoming a staple feature in future Nintendo game franchises, it also single handedly established the subgenre of kart racing. Like many Nintendo originals, *Super Mario Kart* was released fully formed, incredibly polished and highly playable. From the balanced roster to the imaginative tracks and now iconic power-ups, right through to the competitive battle modes, there was little to criticize about the game. Bright cartoon-style visuals, split screen multiplayer, and well implemented Mode 7 graphics rounded out its complete package.

Besides *Super Mario Kart*'s many excellent sequels on later Nintendo platforms, for more racing thrills, check out the earlier *F-Zero* (1990), a faster, futuristic racing game that also put Mode 7 to the test. For more kart racing action, be sure to check out *Street Racer* (1994, Ubisoft), which lacks *Super Mario Kart*'s personality, but makes up for it with fun competitive game modes, like Rumble, where you try to force your opponents from the arena, and Soccer, where you try to knock the ball into your opponent's goal. Although ported to a number of other platforms over the years, the Super NES original is by far the best, even supporting four-player simultaneous split screen with a multitap!

7 www.webcitation.org/5nXieXX2B.

Collecting Nintendo Super NES Systems

Super Nintendo systems and games are easy to find and inexpensive on online auction sites, although, as is usually the case, complete, boxed items hold considerably more value. Of Nintendo's Super NES consoles, the SNS-101 version has somewhat limited appeal to collectors since its audio-video output is restricted to composite. However, once modified to restore the missing multi out functionality, the system's appeal jumps considerably. The fact remains, however, that there are enough original Super Nintendo models available to make the purchase of an SNS-101 generally more trouble than it's worth. Fortunately, the SNS-101's companion controller only differs from the original cosmetically, with slightly darker buttons and different logo placement. Finally, like many older systems with light colored casings, it's not uncommon for the grey plastic on Super NES items to become discolored over time with an unattractive yellow tint.

A large aftermarket of Super NES clone consoles and handhelds has sprung up, though these vary wildly in terms of quality and compatibility. Hyperkin's SupaBoy is one of the more popular such options, letting you plug in both Super Nintendo and Super Famicom cartridges into the handheld's top slot and play them on its built-in 3.5-inch color screen. In addition to working like a portable

Hyperkin's SupaBoy is a versatile clone system that can work both as a handheld and console.

Super Nintendo, the SupaBoy's two front facing controller ports let you plug in original controllers and play your games on the TV like a regular console.

Several flash cartridges are available for the Super Nintendo and Super Famicom that let you play many of the platform's games region-free on any compatible console. Two of the most popular such options are the SNES PowerPak from Retrozone, which works with compact flash cards, and Krikzz's Super Everdrive, which works with SD cards.

A deluxe version of the Krikzz Super Everdrive from reseller Stone Age Gamer. Most NTSC and PAL games are directly supported, save for those requiring special chips.

Super Mario RPG: Legend of the Seven Stars
on the **ZSNES** emulator.

Super Mario RPG: Legend of the Seven Stars
(1996, Nintendo)

On a platform overflowing with legendary role-playing games, it's only fitting that Mario and company would join in on the fun. A collaborative production between Square and Nintendo—led by Shigeru Miyamoto himself—this action role-playing game combines the story and game mechanics from the *Super Mario Bros.* games with conventions found in the likes of the *Final Fantasy* series. Players control Mario and a small group of teammates as they take on Smithy, who has stolen the seven star pieces of Star Road. Combat is turn-based, but has the innovation of correctly timed button presses that amplify an attack, special move, defense, or item usage. Filled with humor and lovingly rendered in an isometric perspective, *Super Mario RPG* was a fitting final appearance for Mario and Square on the Super NES. Because Square would not return to Nintendo platforms again until the 2002 Japanese release of puzzler, *Chocobo Land: A Game of Dice,* for the Game Boy Advance, Nintendo's next Mario-themed RPG was more of a spiritual successor than a direct sequel—*Paper Mario*—which came out in 2001 in the US for the Nintendo 64.

The Legend of Zelda: A Link to the Past on the
ZSNES emulator.

The Legend of Zelda: A Link to the Past
(1992, Nintendo)

The third game in the series and a return to the original game's top-down perspective, *The Legend of Zelda: A Link to the Past* proved once and for all that Nintendo would have no trouble bringing improved versions of non-Mario NES classics to its future generations of consoles. Players take the role of Link who must rescue Princess Zelda from an evil wizard who wants to unleash main series antagonist, the sorcerer Ganon. Under the direction of mentor Sahasrahla, players must guide Link between parallel Light (normal) and Dark (evil) versions of the land of Hyrule. With increased mobility, power-ups, new items to discover, and special attacks to unleash, *A Link to the Past* took all that was great about the first game and made it even more epic, setting the standard for the series to achieve ever greater heights going forward. This game was rereleased in 2002 for the Game Boy Advance as *The Legend of Zelda: A Link to the Past & Four Swords*, which added additional sound effects and a new multiplayer adventure that can interact with the main game.

Emulating the Nintendo Super NES

The Super Nintendo is one of the most popular platforms to emulate, with emulators available for nearly every type of capable computer, console, and handheld imaginable. Two of the most popular are *Snes9x*, which runs on an impressive range of platforms, and *ZSNES*, which runs on Linux, PC DOS and Windows, and Macintosh computers, and even has an unofficial port for modded Xboxes. Simple USB adapters can even let you use original controllers with these emulators.

Of course, the best official way to play great Super Nintendo classics is via Nintendo's own Virtual Console service for the Wii, 3DS, and Wii U. A growing collection of games—some never released outside their home territories—make the Virtual Console the perfect destination for those wanting to check out Nintendo's classics, Super Nintendo or otherwise.

Configuring options in the **ZSNES** emulator to run the original pack-in game, **Super Mario World.**

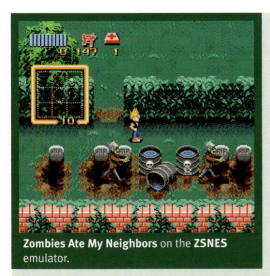

Zombies Ate My Neighbors on the **ZSNES** emulator.

Zombies Ate My Neighbors
(1993, Konami)

Developed by Konami and LucasArts (back when its games didn't always feature a *Star Wars* tie-in), *Zombies Ate My Neighbors* is a one- or two-player cooperative "run-'n'-gun" shooting game that can be seen as a precursor to modern-day classics like *Dead Rising* (2006, Capcom) for the Xbox 360. Unlike *Dead Rising*, however, *Zombies Ate My Neighbors* is overflowing with humor and horror movie satire, and is far less burdened with advancing the in-game plot. Players take the role of either Zeke or Julie, as the teenagers try to rescue their titular neighbors from all kinds of monsters through 55 levels of mayhem. Imaginative weapons like squirt guns and weed whackers join power-ups like secret potions and clown decoys to add to the gory fun. While there have been several sequels and offshoots of the core gameplay found in *Zombies Ate My Neighbors*, including its direct follow-up *Ghoul Patrol* (1994), none have managed to recapture the fun of the fondly remembered original.

Part 3
Generation Three
(1995–2001)

The mid-point of the 1990s brings us to the third and final generation covered in this book: Generation Three, the 3D generation. This generation saw the rise of several technologies that have been with us ever since: advanced 3D graphics, optical discs, and a Microsoft Windows suited to more than just spreadsheets. It saw the collapse of the "sick man of the videogame industry," Sega, and the final console to bear their name. It also saw the introduction of two new console contenders who rapidly rose to prominence: Sony and Microsoft. Finally, and perhaps most importantly, this generation experienced the first major wave of internet adoption across America, a decisive cultural and sociological phenomenon that radically altered the videogame industry and its culture in ways we are still feeling today.

Both the beginning and end of this generation are dramatic. In 1995, Nintendo and Sega were firmly entrenched, seemingly impervious to upstart contenders. They had easily kept their competitors at bay, including the wave of CD-ROM consoles introduced in the early 1990s, which included Philips' CD-i (1991), Commodore's CDTV (1991), and Panasonic's 3DO Interactive Multiplayer (1993). The systems they introduced this generation, the Nintendo 64 and Sega Dreamcast, were both quite capable machines with exciting possibilities for both gamers and developers.

The real threat to the status quo came from two sources: Sony and Microsoft. Although the console market had long been dominated by 2D games—especially platform games like *Super Mario Bros.,* overhead-perspective action adventures like *The Legend of Zelda,* and beat-'em-up games like *Street Fighter II,* Sony gambled that the future was in fully 3D games similar to Frederick Raynal's *Alone in the Dark* (1992) and id Software's *Doom* (1993). Compared to their 2D contemporaries, these games may have looked crude and blocky, but they were also much more immersive. These weren't games you so much looked *at* as *through*, perceiving the action in a way that *felt* more realistic than even the best 2D artists could match.

Since the introduction of the Atari 2600 in 1977 (see Chapter 1.3), one of the major factors distinguishing gaming *consoles* from *computers* was cartridge-based storage. These plastic devices were usually read-only, meaning that users couldn't easily modify or copy their contents. The advantages were clear: less piracy and greater control, especially once Nintendo developed and patented its lockout technology, which prevented rival manufacturers from flooding the market with their own games (although they certainly tried). They were also substantially faster— there was no waiting around for a game to load. What nine-year-old kid would be content sitting around for five minutes watching a loading screen? Even though cartridges were much more expensive to produce than floppy disks or cassette tapes, these advantages were too strong to ignore.

CD-ROM technology, however, was something different. At the time, most floppy disks could store up to 1.44 MB. Games were shipped on as many as a dozen different disks, which users would either install to a hard drive (a process that could take hours), or, worse, swap out the disks during gameplay—an aggravation, to be sure. By contrast, a CD-ROM could hold hundreds of megabytes without issue—and were *cheaper* to boot! While loading times were still an issue, these optical discs were much more difficult for consumers to copy illegally than floppies had been, at least for a time. Still, Sony shrewdly developed its own copy protection measures for its console, a step that Sega did not take with most of its CD-based systems.

Sony's gamble on 3D graphics and optical storage paid off. The PlayStation's 3D graphics made Sega's Saturn system look primitive by comparison, since it required far more effort and resources to do what the PlayStation did by default. By the time Sega was able to launch the more 3D-capable Dreamcast, they had lost too much momentum to catch up, caught between the high profile releases of Sony's first two consoles. Nintendo was quicker to adopt powerful 3D graphics, but stubbornly stuck to cartridges with its Nintendo 64. Thus, neither company realized the advantage of embracing both 3D and optical storage the way Sony did—a failure that the upstart company leveraged to the fullest possible advantage, ensuring that their PlayStation and PlayStation 2 consoles would dominate the competition.

In the computer world, the DOS era was coming to an end. The previous generation had witnessed the rise of the GUI, or graphical-user interface—the mouse, windows, and icon-driven interface we are so familiar with today. Much of this technology had been developed by Douglas Engelbart of Stanford Research Institute and Alan Kay of Xerox PARC, but it was commercialized by Apple, whose introduction of the Macintosh in 1985 was a huge leap forward for home computing. Later machines from Commodore and Atari further popularized the GUI by offering lower-cost computers, but, despite all of their advances, could not seriously compete against the ubiquity of machines running Microsoft's DOS.

When Microsoft *finally* began getting serious about GUIs in the early 1990s, it was hardly revolutionary. The early versions of Windows were basically just extensions to DOS rather than a full operating system. It wasn't until the development of Windows 95 that PC owners could at last make the transition to a fully integrated product. Windows 95 was finally able to replace DOS as the dominant operating system, introducing countless millions of computer users to the user friendliness of GUI-based computing. Microsoft also developed the first version of DirectX around the same time, a set of application programming interfaces (APIs) that made life much easier for game developers targeting the platform. While the bulk of today's high-profile gaming attention is still focused on the console market (and increasingly smartphones and tablets), the Windows platform continues to enjoy broad and diverse support as competing systems continue to come and go.

In 2001, the Xbox became the first major American console since Atari's ill-fated Jaguar in 1993 to seriously challenge the Japanese dominance of the market. Spearheaded by a superb new franchise, *Halo*, Microsoft's Xbox brought back much-needed diversity to the industry—and also provided an attractive option for many Windows game developers. As its title suggests, the Xbox was based on DirectX, making it easier than ever for developers to make the transition from computer to console development.

PC Windows Computers (1995)

History

Today, Microsoft's Windows operating system is virtually synonymous with personal computing. According to NetMarketShare, a company that collects statistics on internet technologies, as of August 2013, 91.56 percent of desktops ran some version of Windows. The second largest system, Macintosh, occupied only 7.19 percent, which may seem trivial, but that was actually up a few percentage points from previous years.[1] Linux, the "revolutionary" free operating system that some thought would finally give Microsoft a run for its money, had only a tiny 1.18% piece of the pie. Like it or not, Microsoft Windows has become the industry standard operating system for home and office computers; the question when buying a new PC isn't whether to buy Windows, but rather which version of Windows you want installed.

However, back in 1983, when Microsoft first announced it was working on a GUI, or Graphical User Interface, for its fledgling MS-DOS operating system, the landscape of home computing was much, much different. As you've seen in previous chapters, the field of personal computing was fiercely competitive, with companies such as Apple, Commodore, Tandy, Atari, and Texas Instruments

Bill Gates showing off Windows 3.0, the first commercially successful version of the software. http://microsoft.com.

(just to name a few) fighting tooth and nail for control of the desktop. If you think buying a personal computer is intimidating today, imagine what it was like back before MS-DOS, when making a bad choice could leave you with an obsolete machine with little-to-no software to run on it.

When the IBM PC showed up in the early 1980s, it made a huge impression, but it wasn't so much the technology itself than the clever licensing arrangement between Microsoft and IBM that made the real difference (see Chapter 1.6). This arrangement made possible the huge array of "IBM PC compatibles," which, although owing little to IBM, were able to sell cheaper (and even superior) machines that, thanks to MS-DOS, were just as good as the "real thing." The strategy worked well for Microsoft, who was soon the undisputed king of the desktop.

---

[1] See http://netmarketshare.com for these and other stats.

Baldur's Gate II: Shadows of Amn
(2000, BioWare)

The *Advanced Dungeons & Dragons* license had fallen into disrepair, at least as far as videogames were concerned, when BioWare released the first game in this series in 1998. While that game is inarguably a classic that every fan of role-playing should experience, BioWare was able to greatly refine the formula in this epic masterpiece. Who could forget Minsc's obsession with his hamster, Boo, or the eerie chambers of the Illithids? Many fans of the genre, including the authors, consider this game to be the best of its kind, with a richness

Baldur's Gate II: Shadows of Amn.

and depth that are simply timeless. Check out *Planescape: Torment* (1999) for a brilliant single-player variation on this game engine.

However, by the mid-1980s, the old command-line interface of MS-DOS was showing its age. Compared to the sleek new interfaces of an Apple Macintosh, Atari ST, or Commodore Amiga, it looked painfully antiquated. It was the opposite of user-friendly. In 1986, even the humble Commodore 64 had a GUI! Even though today it's easy enough to find diehards who still prefer the old command-line interfaces, most of us couldn't imagine computing without icons, mice, and, of course, windows. So far, these competing systems hadn't managed to make much of a dent in Microsoft's enormous user base, but the future was apparent. Text-based interfaces were about to go the way of text adventures.

In the early 1980s, Microsoft began working on a product called Interface Manager, but this boring name was soon replaced by "Windows." In 1983, Microsoft announced the product, but it was a full two years before they were able to ship the first version. In the meantime, several GUI-based packages had been developed, including VisiCorp's Visi On (1983), Quarterdeck Office Systems' DESQview (1984), and IBM's TopView (1985). While ambitious, all of these systems were expensive, slow, and poorly supported by external developers. Reviews were harsh—stick with DOS if you want anything resembling performance. Indeed, there was significant skepticism that even Microsoft would be able to deliver on its promises.

When Windows 1.0 finally shipped, it wasn't a stand-alone product. Like the older GUIs, it ran from MS-DOS. If you had a powerful computer with enough memory,

IBM's TopView was an early competitor of Windows, but was a commercial flop.
Source: Wikipedia.

it could run more than one program simultaneously, but reviewers weren't impressed with the speed. Erik Sandberg-Diment of *The New York Times* put it this way: "Running Windows on a PC with 512K of memory is akin to pouring molasses in the Arctic. And the more windows you activate, the more sluggishly it performs."[2] Getting most software to run in Windows was a complex, painful process. Finally, few PC users at the time owned mice, which were bundled with the Macintosh. Try to imagine moving your mouse pointer with a keyboard—it's no wonder so many people preferred to stick to DOS. Windows 1.0 is notable, however, for including the first-ever Windows game: *Reversi*.

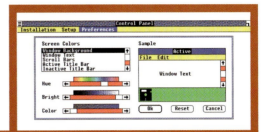

Windows 1.0 was slow and compatible with very little software. Shown here is the Control Panel screen demonstrating the customization options for window preferences.
Image courtesy of Marcin Wichary at www.guidebookgallery.org.

Windows 2.0 debuted in 1987, and offered some nice features that had been sorely lacking in the first iteration, including overlapping windows, desktop icons, and keyboard shortcuts. Advances in PC technology, particularly Intel's beefier processors, helped make the Windows experience much smoother than before. Microsoft later released special versions of Windows 2.x called Windows/286 and Windows/386, which could take better advantage of Intel's respective processors. Still, even when all tallied together, by 1990 Microsoft had still managed to sell fewer than 2 million copies of its Windows operating systems.[3]

During this time, Microsoft had been working with IBM on OS/2, a new operating system for IBM's upcoming PS/2 line of personal computers. The idea was to learn from the "mistakes" of the previous generation, when hundreds (if not thousands) of "IBM PC compatible"

Diabolo II.

Diablo II (2000, Blizzard Entertainment)

Before *World of Warcraft*, there was *Diablo*. It introduced gamers to the concept of an "action role-playing game," that is, a game with the addictive leveling, gearing up, and stats of a traditional RPG, but with real-time combat sequences. They also featured procedurally generated maps, greatly upping the replay value. For the sequel, Blizzard pulled out all the stops, with a huge world, intricate leveling system, and awesome online multiplayer options. The long-anticipated third game in the series was finally released in 2012, earning perfect or near-perfect scores from almost every major critic despite some infamously oppressive DRM.

---

2   E. Sandberg-Diment, "Personal Computers; Windows are Open at Last," *The New York Times*, February 25, 1986.

3   These and the other Windows-sales statistics in this chapter are from Harry McCracken's "A Brief History of Windows Sales Figures, 1985–Present," from *TIME Tech*. 7 May 2013, http://techland.time.com/2013/05/07/a-brief-history-of-windows-sales-figures-1985-present.

manufacturers had ripped into IBM's profits. Gates and business manager Steve Ballmer were adamant about Microsoft's support for the new system. Gates declared it the "environment for office computing in the 1990s," and Ballmer promised that "Microsoft would cease development of its Windows software after the release of Windows 3.0... IBM's OS/2 would become the main PC operating system of the 1990s."[4] They cut the Windows team down to a skeleton crew, shifting the bulk of their resources to the OS/2 camp.

IBM's OS/2 represented the company's concerted effort to introduce a new, more tightly controlled PC architecture (PS/2) and operating system. Shown here is a portion of a multi-page Microsoft ad from the December 1988 issue of **Byte** magazine, describing Microsoft's key role in supporting Windows-, Macintosh-, and OS/2-based computers, like the one shown here. Of particular interest is Microsoft's obvious need to still talk up the value of a mouse.

Fortunately for Microsoft, David Weise and Murray Sargent were still part of the crew—and they had a radical new idea. One night at a party, Murray told his friend Weise that Windows 2.x was a joke. "What one really should do," said Murray, "was get Windows into protected mode and blow away the 640 KB RAM barrier altogether." The original IBM PC reserved the memory addresses above 640 KB for I/O and ROM—the rest, called "low memory," was what operating systems like Windows had left to work with. When Intel developed its 80286 processor, it introduced "protected mode," which allowed access to more memory, but it wasn't widely used. The problem was that the processor had to be reset whenever a program switched back to "real mode," which gave it direct access to hardware, but without the safeguards necessary to keep it from crashing when accessing the greater memory.

Not realizing that Murray was joking, Weise said, "Sure!" When? "Right now!" So the two left the party and immediately went to work on the project. Over the next two weeks, the pair made enormous progress, but kept their mission secret—"OS/2" was the buzzword at the office, after all. But the team was successful—the 640 KB RAM barrier that had reduced earlier versions of Windows to "pouring molasses in the Arctic" was shattered. Still, the team was worried that Gates and Ballmer would reject their new approach.[5] Although firmly in the OS/2 camp at the time, the heads at Microsoft were excited about their team's breakthrough, and gave it their full support.[6]

It's a good thing they did. The new version of Windows sold over 10 million copies in just two years. Gates had never made a better decision. The new Windows was everything the old version had wished it could be. It was also the first to come pre-installed on PC compatibles, a strategy that has served Microsoft well ever since.

---

[4]   Paul Ormerod, *Why Most Things Fail*, Faber & Faber, 2010.

[5]   Paul Ormerod, *Why Most Things Fail*, Faber & Faber, 2010.

[6]   See Murray Sargent's account of these events in "Saving Windows from the OS/2 Bulldozer," *MSDN Blogs*, December 7, 2006, http://blogs.msdn.com/b/murrays/archive/2006/12/07/saving-windows-from-the-os-2-bulldozer.aspx.

Meanwhile, IBM's new PS/2 line of computers were creating a different kind of buzz. Still smarting from the "IBM Compatible" phenomenon that had stolen sales, IBM built a proprietary bus architecture called Micro Channel Architecture (MCA), and insisted on draconian licensing terms for anyone else hoping to build compatible hardware for its PS/2 line. The companies that had made so much money with the older "open" architecture balked. The PS/2 had plenty of great innovations, some of which would become standard in DOS and later Windows machines, such as VGA graphics, the 1.44 MB floppy disk format, plug-and-play BIOS management, and new keyboard and mouse ports. IBM lavished funding on the platform's marketing, but it was to no avail. PS/2s were selling, but few were buying.

The problem for IBM was that its name no longer carried the clout it once did in the PC market. Consumers were quite happy to buy a less expensive "IBM PC compatible" from the likes of Gateway, Dell, or Compaq, and no one was eager to leave the older ISA (Industry Standard Architecture) bus that had served the industry so well. Another problem was that the first PS/2 computers were high-priced "premium" models for business. IBM had planned to release cheaper consumer-oriented versions, but problems at the chip factory delayed them. "IBM has clearly lost momentum in the personal computer business," declared Richard Zwetchkenbaum from the International Data Corporation. Compaq's president Eckhard Pfeiffer described IBM as "having some troubles... especially [with] its PS/2 position,"

The Windows 3.x series of operating systems was Microsoft's first commercially successful GUI and marked the turning point for the chances of competing computer systems to remain commercially relevant. Screenshot from Windows 3.0 courtesy of Marcin Wichary at www.guidebookgallery.org.

Grim Fandango.

Grim Fandango
(1998, LucasArts Entertainment)

Tim Schafer's *Grim Fandango* is one of the last and greatest achievements of LucasArts' famous graphical adventure game division. The main character, "Manny" Calavera, lives in the Land of the Dead, a strange (and rather comical) version of the afterlife based on Mexican mythology blended with "hardboiled" detective novels and modern art. Players loved the unforgettable characters and clever puzzles, and Peter McConnell's jazz and bebop musical score complements the themes perfectly.

lines which he surely delivered with a smile.[7] Soon newspapers were reporting the resignation of IBM's president of its personal computing unit, Robert J. Corrigan. Never again would IBM play a significant role in the personal computer market.

By this point, most computer users had upgraded to at least a 286 or 386-based machine with a CGA or EGA color video card. The better graphics technology allowed Microsoft to build a much nicer-looking interface into Windows 3.x, with sharper icons and better performance. It was at this point that the famous Windows game folder showed up, with the ever-popular *Solitaire*, *Hearts*, and *Reversi*. Version 3.1 hit in March 1992, and introduced TrueType fonts, better stability, and multimedia support to an already popular system. It also replaced *Reversi* with *Minesweeper*, a game that is still included for free with most Windows releases. In short, although Microsoft itself had lost faith in Windows along the way, it was now apparent to all that they had finally gotten the product right.

However, despite the breakthrough that was Windows 3.x, it was Windows 95 that really won over the masses. Released in August of 1995, it sold 7 million copies in just five weeks. For the first time, Microsoft had integrated their Windows interface and MS-DOS (you no longer needed to buy Windows and DOS separately), and advanced the underlying architecture from 16-bit to 32-bit. They also added the famous start button, taskbar, and "plug and play" capabilities that made life infinitely easier for folks installing

Windows 3.x. Games shown, clockwise starting from top left corner: **Minesweeper, Solitaire,** and **Hearts**.

software or connecting peripherals to their computer. They'd also gone to fantastic lengths to hype the new software, including licensing "Start Me Up" by the Rolling Stones. They bought out an entire print run of *The Times of London* so they could run their ads on its front page and give it away for free. They also tried to light up the Empire State Building in New York with the distinctive colors of the Windows 95 logo: red, yellow, green, and blue. To everyone's frustration, though, they couldn't get the blue light to work, but fans need not have worried. They would have plenty of opportunities to view the bold color on their own machines soon enough.

Of course, the mid-1990s is when America (and the world) saw the first big bursts of the internet revolution. Although Gates had been slow to move to the GUI revolution, he immediately grasped the importance of the internet. In a memo he sent on Mar 26, 1995, he declared the internet "the most important single development to come along since the IBM PC was introduced in 1981."[8] To secure a foothold in this wild and rapidly expanding frontier, Microsoft quickly released its first version of Internet Explorer—for free. This move resulted in immediate action from Spyglass, from whom Microsoft had licensed the technology, promising royalties for each copy sold. Later, when they began bundling the browser with Windows,

7   S.L., "IBM's Head of PC Unit Resigns Post," May 3, 1994, *The New York Times*.

8   www.lettersofnote.com/2011/07/internet-tidal-wave.html.

they brought on more litigation from Netscape and Opera Software, who accused them of violating antitrust law.

Since Windows 95, Microsoft has steadily released new versions of its operating system. Some of these releases, such as Windows 98 in 1998 and Windows XP in 2001, were warmly received, whereas others, especially Windows ME (2000) and Vista (2006), were derided by both critics and users alike.

Game developers were slow to support Windows before Windows 95. Most games for Windows 3.x were low-budget shareware or freeware games.[9] Microsoft released its own Entertainment Pack for the system, which included versions of *Tetris* and a few puzzle games. Perhaps the most important game released for 3.x is *SimCity for Windows* (1992), which was quite well-suited to the Windows environment. Other notable releases for Windows 3.x were *Myst* (1993) and *Sid Meier's CivNet* (1995).

Most PC gamers, however, preferred MS-DOS, which was viewed as a much better system for gaming. Unlike Windows, MS-DOS had the advantage (for gaming, at least) of monopolizing the hardware, taking direct control of the graphics and sound cards, and doesn't have to worry about "sharing" its resources among simultaneously running programs. The situation was comparable to games for the Commodore Amiga (see Chapter 2.2), which usually required booting from disk rather than running as a multitasked application in Workbench.

Minecraft is as much a set of virtual building blocks as it is a game. Shown here is one of the many fantastic creations possible, this one from Armchair Arcade's Mark Vergeer.

Minecraft (2010, Mojang AB)

There have been many great indie games in recent years, including Introversion's *Darwinia* (2005), Jonathan Blow's *Braid* (2010), and Edmund McMillen and Florian Himsl's *The Binding of Isaac* (2011). None of these excellent games, however, have enjoyed the widespread popularity of Markus "Notch" Persson's *Minecraft*. Players mine and build during the day, then defend against monsters at night. While there's no set goal to the game, players still enjoy building fantastic levels with their friends online, or posting videos featuring narrated tours of their recreation of the *Millennium Falcon* or ancient Egypt. While *Minecraft* has been ported to everything from Android to Xbox One, the original PC version is still where the game feels most at home.

Windows 95 marked a turning point largely because of the release of DirectX, a set of Application Programming Interfaces (APIs) that made it much easier for third-party developers (especially game developers) to make software for the platform. As its name implies, DirectX allows programs to talk directly to hardware, without any of the speed-cutting workarounds necessary for most Windows applications. Another major advantage is that DirectX would take care of the problems associated with accommodating so many different possible PC configurations (i.e., whether a gamer had an AdLib or Sound Blaster sound card). The development of DirectX is worthy of a feature film, with essentially three brilliant men—Craig Eisler, Alex St. John, and Eric

---

[9]   The .x convention is a way of grouping together the various updated releases of a product. "Windows 3.x," for instance, include 3.0, 3.1, etc.

Engstrom, working non-stop to hammer out the first version before the Computer Game Developers Conference of April 1995. The CDs they needed for the presentation arrived just hours before they were on stage touting the software.

Unfortunately for the DirectX team, 3D hardware acceleration was just around the corner, and they weren't ready for it. DirectDraw, the part of the DirectX suite that handled graphics, was only good for 2D. Meanwhile, OpenGL, a rival API that had originally been developed by Silicon Graphics Inc. (SGI), had been supporting 3D graphics for some time, mostly for serious or high-end applications like computer-aided design, virtual reality, and flight simulation. Instead of including OpenGL with Windows 95, Microsoft opted to develop its own "lightweight" 3D API called Direct3D. To expedite the process, they bought Servan Keondjian's company RenderMorphics, who had developed a 3D CAD and medical imaging API called Reality Lab.[10] Keondjian worked frantically with the DirectX team to rapidly develop the product in time to ship with the second version of DirectX.

Microsoft's **Hover!** (1995) was a game intended to show off Windows 95's 3D and multimedia capabilities. It still runs great on modern Windows systems.

Reactions to Direct3D were mixed. Famously, John Carmack, the celebrated coder behind *Doom* and *Quake,* refused to use it, supporting OpenGL instead. Whereas OpenGL was time-tested and easy to use, Direct3D was overly complicated and downright confusing. Coming from Carmack, this criticism carried a lot of weight, and ignited an OpenGL vs. Direct3D debate that is still a hot topic in some programming circles. Fortunately, Microsoft was able to resolve many of these issues in version 8.1 of Direct3D in 2001, a point at which many programmers feel the product had at last surpassed OpenGL. While OpenGL is still a popular choice for mobile gaming applications, even Carmack now acknowledges its rival's superiority—although he has no plans of switching anytime soon.[11]

With DirectX and either OpenGL and/or Direct3D in place, Windows 95 was finally able to hold its own against DOS—although many developers continued supporting the older system for several more years. However, eventually Microsoft was able to leverage its relationship with hardware makers—especially graphic card makers like NVIDIA and ATI—to ensure that DirectX would work seamlessly with their new 3D accelerated products. Without comparable support for DOS-based machines, gamers wanting the latest and greatest games had no choice but to make the move.

We saw in Chapter 1.6 how PC graphics technology had evolved from CGA to VGA and beyond, each time adding tremendous increases in resolution, color palette, and on-screen colors. These advances were great in terms of color and resolution, but 3D graphics were still a tremendous challenge. Early 3D games did this work entirely in software, meaning that the

---

[10]   Previously, Keondjian had worked for Magnetic Scrolls, a company specializing in illustrated text adventure games.

[11]   Kevin Parrish, "Carmack: Direct3D Now Better Than OpenGL," March 11, 2011, *Tom's Hardware*, www.tomshardware.com/news/john-Carmack-DirectX-OpenGL-API-Doom,12372.html.

Starcraft.

Starcraft (1998, Blizzard Entertainment)

Although Blizzard's *Warcraft: Orcs & Humans* (1994) was the company's first foray into real-time strategy games, it was this science fiction follow-up that turned it into what can only be described as a sport. Offering near-perfectly balanced gameplay and just the right amount of complexity and intensity, *Starcraft* became a cultural phenomenon—especially in South Korea, where the 2005 *Starcraft* championship drew a larger crowd than the Super Bowl did in America that year. Indeed, a new unit called "actions per minute" was invented as a metric to test a player's skill. It also introduced the meme and Google doodle "zerg rush," named for one of the alien races in the game known for its rapid spawning. Other great real-time strategy games for Windows are *Command & Conquer: Red Alert* (1996, Westwood), *Total Annihilation* (1997, Cavedog), and *Age of Empires III* (2005, Ensemble).

computer's CPU was taxed to generate the 3D animation in addition to executing all the rest of the game's code. While some critics felt that CPUs would continue to improve to meet the demands of 3D programming, others felt that specialized devices were needed to help out the CPU.

Enter the GPU, or Graphics Processing Unit, which, thanks to OpenGL or DirectX, could take over the burden of transforming, clipping, and lighting 3D scenes. Then as now, hardcore PC gamers doled out for the latest and most expensive GPUs to power their systems, but it didn't always result in noticeable differences unless DirectX or OpenGL *and* the game in question specifically supported its new features. Fortunately for PC gamers (and GPU companies), high-profile games such as id's *Quake II* (1997) and enhanced versions of Activision's *Mech-Warrior 2: 31st Century Combat* (1995) soon showed off the advantages of the new technologies. Indeed, many new GPUs shipped with special versions of a popular game specifically built to showcase its abilities, a practice still common today. It's also still an important consideration when buying a GPU to check its compatibility with the latest DirectX version.

Shown here are two Voodoo2 3dfx graphics cards from 1998 intended for a Scan-Line Interleave (SLI) configuration. In SLI mode, two Voodoo2 boards were installed in a PC and ran in parallel, with each unit drawing half the lines of the display, supporting a then-impressive resolution of 1024 × 768. A third, 2D video card, was still required for this setup for all non-3D activities, creating quite the web of cable interconnections between the three cards and target monitor.

Incidentally, Microsoft quickly learned it could use its latest DirectX as a way to goad laggards into upgrading to an unpopular version of Windows. For example, DirectX 10 was exclusive to Vista, and Direct X 11.1 is limited to Windows 8.x. The need for such a strategy reveals one of the unique problems faced by operating system developers: do your job too well, and your users may not care to "upgrade" to your next system. Indeed, as of September 2013, there were still over 500 million users of the 12-year-old Windows XP, which still enjoys a reputation as one of the most stable and reliable incarnations of the software.

Windows 95 coincided nicely with the rise of 3D gaming and the first-person shooter boom. As these games became increasingly complex, they required faster processors and better GPUs—most of which were only supported on Windows. Later Windows versions would continue this trend. Even though today there is more support than ever for gaming on Macintosh- and Linux-based systems, Windows is still the best choice for gamers who want to play the latest and greatest games at the highest possible performance specifications.

Technical Specifications

Since Windows is software rather than hardware, it makes more sense here to talk about the computers it runs best on. Microsoft recommended a 386-based machine for Windows 3.x, with 640 K of conventional memory, 2048 K of extended memory, 30 MB hard drive, and a VGA or higher graphics card. A mouse was, of course, recommended. You also needed to have MS-DOS 3.1 or later.

For Windows 95, Microsoft recommended a 486 (these ran up to 133 MHz), with 8 MB of RAM, 256-color SVGA card, a modem, an audio card, and speaker. Obviously, later versions would increase these specifications as the operating system grew larger, more sophisticated, and more demanding on the hardware. For comparison, Windows 8.1, the latest version as of this writing, requires a 1 GHz or faster processor, 1 GB of RAM (2 recommended), and a DirectX 9-compatible graphics device. As always, upgrading to the latest Windows usually necessitates a subsequent upgrade in hardware, a policy that has worked out well for Microsoft, but also for the supporting hardware industry.

Windows Versions

What follows are some of the major Windows release highlights (and lowlights):

- **1985**: The first incarnation of Windows, version 1.x, attracted little fanfare. Its sluggish performance was hardly a match for MS-DOS despite its more attractive interface.

- **1987**: Windows 2.x offered some nice innovations, such as overlapping windows, desktop icons, and the Control Panel. Designed for higher performing 286-based machines, it was slightly faster than the previous version, but reviewers and software developers were still quite happy with DOS.

- **1990**: With Windows 3.x, Microsoft had finally stumbled upon the right mix of speed and efficiency. The new version offered better graphics, support for 386-based machines, and much greater performance.

- **1995**: Windows 95 marks the tipping point for Windows and the end of the DOS era. The new version was perfectly poised to take advantage of the multimedia craze as well as the internet, which was just beginning to take off. The taskbar and start menu make their debut.

  To assist novice computer users, Microsoft introduced *Microsoft Bob*, a suite of applications that included a word processor and email client. It had an interface built on a house metaphor, complete with living room, furniture, and cartoony characters like Scuzz the Rat and Clippy the Paper Clip who helped you with your computing chores. The cutesy product turned out to be a fiasco for the company, harshly criticized (and then lampooned) by the press. Although Ballmer later admitted it was a mistake, Gates remains adamant that "we were just ahead of our time, like most of our mistakes," and promises that Bob will return.[12] You've been warned!

- **1998**: Windows 98 was marketed as the system that "works better, plays better," which was a fitting description. It was more stable than the previous release, and had a cool "Quick Launch" bar. It was also the last Windows based on MS-DOS.

The Last Express.

The Last Express (1997, Broderbund)

Jordan Mechner's *The Last Express* is widely considered one of the best graphical adventure games designed, with an engaging story set aboard the Orient Express in 1914, just before the outbreak of the first World War. The game is set in real-time, and was celebrated for its non-linear approach to the genre. The distinctive art style is "art nouveau," which was period appropriate for the time in which the game was set. To create the look, real actors were filmed in front of a bluescreen. The resulting footage was converted to black and white and then colorized by hand. It's truly a remarkable achievement that demonstrates the artistic and narrative possibilities of the medium.

- **2000**: Windows ME was a stumble for the company. This "Millennium Edition" was roundly criticized for being slow, buggy, and downright unstable. It was billed as the "home edition" of Windows; serious users were urged to buy Windows 2000 Professional instead. It was marketed as the most secure Windows ever, but was subsequently the target of a series of infamous virus attacks. *PC World*, who ranked it #4 on their list of the

---

12   Dan Farber, "Bill Gates Says Microsoft Bob Will Make a Comeback," **CNet**, July 15, 2013, http://news.cnet.com/8301-10805_3-57593736-75/bill-gates-says-microsoft-bob-will-make-a-comeback.

worst tech products ever, quipped that "users reported problems installing it, getting it to run, getting it to work with other hardware and software, and getting it to stop running. Aside from that, ME worked great."[13]

- **2001**: Windows XP showed up the following year, no doubt rushed to quell the bad press generated by Windows ME. Still preferred by many Windows users even today, XP was fast, solid, and reliable. It was easier than ever to get online, and Microsoft used this feature to roll out regular "security updates" to fight the increasing number of viruses targeting the system. It was so successful that Microsoft took five years before releasing another version.

- **2006**: Windows Vista was billed as having the "strongest security" ever, and the interface got a stylistic overhaul with "Aero." Gates announced the "Trustworthy Computer Initiative" as a way to hype the system's laser focus on security. Reactions to all this were mixed, at best. The new bells and whistles made Vista slower than XP, and no one seemed to like all the emphasis on DRM (Digital Rights Management). Many programs (especially games) that worked fine on XP would not run on Vista, at least without patches or workarounds. Users also disliked being inundated with prompts asking them if they were sure—absolutely sure?—they wanted to install the software they had just commanded the computer to install. In short, many gamers stuck with or went back to XP.

- **2009**: Windows 7 is to Vista what Windows XP was to 95/98: A faster, sleeker, and more reliable Windows. According to Microsoft, 8 million beta testers helped them root out bugs and glitches before release, which seems plausible enough given its stability. Most of the gamers who had stuck with XP were now happy to upgrade to the new system.

Half-Life 2 from **The Orange Box**.

The Orange Box (2007, Valve Corporation)

This is a collection of five games built with Valve's "Source" 3D engine: *Half-Life 2*, its two follow-up "episodes," *Team Fortress 2*, and *Portal*. *Half-Life 2*, originally released in 2004, is widely regarded as the best first-person shooter ever designed, mostly due to its well-developed characters, unforgettable settings, and thought-provoking story arcs. *Team Fortress 2* is a "class-based" multiplayer team shooter with a comical look. Each of the nine available classes has a special skill that, if used correctly, can help the team win the match. *Portal* is a brilliant puzzle game that introduced us to GLaDOS and the "cake is a lie" meme. You really can't go wrong with any of these games; get the box and we'll see you next year.

---

13   Dan Tynan, "The 25 Worst Tech Products of All Time," *PC World*, March 26, 2006, /www.pcworld.com/article/125772/worst_products_ever.html?page=2.

- **2012**: The radical new interface of Windows 8, designed to work smoothly with touch controls as well as the standard mouse and keyboard, had a tortured release, thanks in part to being designed to work with devices outside of traditional desktops and laptops. The addition of the Windows Store, which might have been a boon for game developers, was instead criticized for its strict policies. Features in previous versions that users found convenient, such as the Start button, were missing altogether, causing frustration and making Windows experts suddenly feel like novices again. While competing products from Google and Apple were a hot commodity, tablet and touchscreens powered by Microsoft technology failed to catch on the way the company hoped. In particular, their first generation of high profile Microsoft Surface tablets floundered. Par for the course for Microsoft, the first Windows 8 update, Windows 8.1, released October 2013, addressed many of the complaints about the first version—including the return of the start button, and the second generation of Surface tablets was much better received. As history has shown for Microsoft, dogged persistence, even in the face of obvious failure, pays off, you just have to keep at it.

The PC Windows Gaming Community Then and Now

Considering the massive size of the Windows installed user base, it makes little sense to talk of a community of all Windows users. Even if we focus just on gamers, we find ourselves confronted with an extremely unwieldy mass of disparate elements. No doubt, most Windows users are those who, if they game at all, restrict themselves to the included *Solitaire*, *Hearts*, and *Minesweeper*, or migrate to browser-based offerings, casual hidden-object type games, or the social games genre available on social networks like Facebook.

If we narrow our focus just to those described as "hardcore gamers," however, a more coherent community emerges. This community began forming after Windows 95, as it became clear that DOS could no longer support the cutting-edge graphics demanded by the latest batch of first-person shooter games. This community had initially formed around LAN parties, where dozens (or hundreds, or thousands!) of gamers would lug their heavy PCs and CRT-monitors to a central location, network them together via cable, and play "death match" games until they collapsed from exhaustion. These events were comparable to sports; it was all about skill, teamwork, and endurance. After the internet rose to prominence, these groups could simply meet to frag each other online, an activity that has continued ever since.

They don't get much attention from the regular gaming press, but here are three of the most popular games ever made for Windows: **Solitaire, Hearts,** and **Minesweeper.** Shown here are the Windows 7 versions.

Although first-person shooters get the most attention from the popular press, there are plenty of other types of Windows games that have attracted huge communities of dedicated players. Prominent examples include Blizzard's *Diablo* (action role-playing) and especially *Starcraft* (real-time strategy) games. Of course, it's impossible to imagine today's Windows gaming landscape without MMOs (Massively Multiplayer Online games) like *World of Warcraft*, which command tens of millions of paying subscribers. While most fans of these games are happy just to play casually, others take the competition quite seriously, spending hundreds if not thousands of hours playing, researching, and devising strategies to hone their skills.

The Sims.

The Sims (2000, Maxis)

The Sims is a real-time simulation of social and family life; a microscopic view of the "Sims," the tiny citizens in the earlier hit, *SimCity*. While the characters go to work or school, work out, and have babies, the player can remodel their home. A classic "sandbox" or "dollhouse" game, there's no stated way to win *The Sims*. Instead, the thrill comes from meticulously managing so many different aspects of your Sims, while reveling in all the fun shopping options. The game was a huge hit, especially with previously underserved female gamers.

Compared to their console-gaming cousins, Windows gamers tend to be more obsessed with hardware, often going so far as to upgrade or even build their own gaming rigs to take advantage of the latest components. If asked, they can likely give you a plethora of details about their system, such as the make and model of their processor, and easily slip into impassioned discussions of the ins and outs of SLI-based configurations, liquid CPU coolers, or overclocking. Of course, few, if any, games are available that truly take advantage of such expensive configurations, but that's not the point. In many ways, the hardcore Windows gaming community is comparable to the "hot rod" culture of the 1950s, when a "souped up" car was a point of pride for many people—regardless of whether they actually participated in any street races.

Microsoft's Xbox 360 and Sony's PlayStation 3, as well as their respective successors, Xbox One and PlayStation 4, have helped further narrow the gap between console and computer games. Except for a handful of high-profile exclusives, most popular games were available on all three current platforms, and it's often difficult to tell the versions apart. That said, most modern Windows games still offer superior graphics over their console versions, assuming the user has the hardware to take advantage of it—a process called "running at ultra spec." Windows gamers also enjoy greater access to "indie" games, that is, games made by small developers and sold exclusively online—though again this gap has steadily closed as more of these titles are available via Microsoft's and Sony's digital game stores for their respective consoles. Of course, many Windows gamers would still insist that no console could ever match the power of their beloved gaming rig.

Thief II: The Metal Age.

Thief II: The Metal Age
(2000, Looking Glass Studios)

Mention "stealth game" to anyone of a certain age, and they'll undoubtedly refer you to the *Thief* series. The first game, *Thief: The Dark Project*, debuted in 1998, enriching the adrenaline-soaked first-person shooter scene with a spine-tingling new subgenre. Instead of "running 'n' gunning" your way through a monster-packed level, you snuck around, sticking to the shadows and trying to avoid detection. The second game ups the ante with better graphics, higher resolution, and some fun new abilities like listening at a door for enemy movement.

Collecting PC Windows Systems

To most Windows gamers, the idea of a "vintage Windows system" is ludicrous. Why would anyone want an obsolete machine? Indeed, there are really no Windows-based systems that are "collector's items" in any general sense.

There are, however, occasions when a particular game works best on the hardware it was designed for. For this reason, some gamers keep around an older machine running Windows 98 or XP. Occasionally, this blossoms into a desire to create the ultimate "vintage" Windows rig. Perhaps you could not afford the best possible machine back in 2001, but now that those same components are available for little more than the cost of shipping on eBay, it could be time to return to your dream of building that perfect rig. The best part is, if you screw up and damage something, who cares?

Before heading to eBay, though, check your local craigslist, classified ads, and thrift stores to see if anyone local is selling or giving away their old PC. You might get lucky and score a machine for little more than the gas it takes to drive out and pick it up.

The screen that greets the user when Windows 95 is first run. Image courtesy of Marcin Wichary at www.guidebookgallery.org.

Emulating PC Windows

Almost every Windows gamer has, at some point or another, discovered that a favorite game will not run on the current version of the operating system. In many cases, this problem can be solved within Windows using the compatibility troubleshooter, which can rollback many features that might conflict with an older program. There are also authored and fan-made patches that can update or modify an older game to play friendly with a newer machine. It's always worth doing a thorough internet search to see if anyone else has had similar problems and found a workable solution.

Sometimes, however, no matter what you do, an old Windows game just won't run on your version of Windows. If all else fails, the best advice is to acquire an old Windows PC (see above). Older PCs running Windows 98 or XP are plentiful and cheap. There are, however, other solutions.

World of Warcraft.

World of Warcraft
(2004, Blizzard Entertainment)

The MMORPG to rule them all went online in November 2004, handily crushing the previous champ, Sony's *EverQuest* series. While the concept of a Massively Multiplayer Online Role-Playing Game had been well-established since the success of Richard Garriott's *Ultima Online* in 1997, Blizzard was able to broaden their appeal to a staggering 10+ million base of subscribers. Beyond just offering better graphics than the competition, Blizzard offered better gameplay, with more intuitive controls and a near-immaculate progression system. They also ensured that you could have (nearly) as much fun playing the game by yourself as with other people. Over the years, newer MMORPGs have been hailed as a "WOW Killer," but none have come close to even causing a minor wound. Although Blizzard had only released four expansions from 2004 to 2014, the team steadily issued updates and patches to refresh the content and rebalance the stats.

If you're on Windows 7, you can try downloading and installing the "Windows XP Mode" tool by Microsoft. This program essentially fools your program into thinking you're running Windows XP, but there's an important caveat—it's intended for legacy business applications, not 3D games. If you need something older than XP, you can try VirtualBox. It's a free third-party "virtualization" tool, but this one also supports Windows 2000—provided you have the installation discs.

A more drastic option is to create a dual boot partition on your PC. A chapter of its own would have to be devoted to describe the process here, but it boils down to creating a special partition of your hard drive. If you're on Windows 7, this can be done with the "Disk Management" tool available through the control panel. Once you've successfully created and formatted your partition, you can install your old Windows version onto it. After this, you'll need a program such as EasyBCD (free; available at http://neosmart.net) to give you the option of which system to load up when you turn on or reset your machine. This technique, by the way, can be used to install a Linux partition as well. You may run into compatibility issues with your newer hardware, though, especially if you're installing something older than XP.

If Windows 3.1 is your thing, you're in luck. Michael Vincent of CrunchGear has put together a great XHTML website that replicates the experience—all in your browser. Just visit www.michaelv.org and click the "games" folder for some classic *Minesweeper.* It's also possible to emulate Windows 3.x using DOSBox, though it's a fairly involved process. If you're feeling ambitious, check out the illustrated guides at sierrahelp.com.

Sony PlayStation (1995)

History

From the 1970s into the 1990s, the home videogame industry had been dominated by three companies: Atari, Nintendo, and Sega. Nintendo had managed to buck Atari from the top spot, a feat made easier thanks to the Great Videogame Crash. Atari's failed Jaguar (launched on November 15, 1993) was the last time the former giant's brand would grace a console. With Atari out of the picture, Nintendo and Sega settled in for what would hopefully be a long and relatively unchallenged rivalry for control of the console market.

When Sony announced its new PlayStation console, the executives at both companies had little reason to panic. The PlayStation seemed like only the latest in a line of failed CD-based systems. Why should they take Sony seriously when Commodore, Philips, and Panasonic had all tried a similar tactic and failed miserably? Even if no one else believed they had a shot, Sony was ready to go big or go home—a fact attested by the minimum $500 million they invested in the new device.[1] Ready or not, Mario and Sonic were about to meet their match.

Crash Bandicoot on the **ePSXe** emulator.

Crash Bandicoot
(1996, Universal Interactive Studios)

Prior to *Crash Bandicoot*, Naughty Dog (nee Jam Software) was perhaps best known for their mediocre photo-realistic fighting game for the 3DO, *Way of the Warrior* (1995),[2] one of many such titles that failed to match *Mortal Kombat*. It's surprising, then, that Naughty Dog was the first to create a 3D platform game with the approachability and accessibility of the best traditional 2D side-scrollers. Even when the perspective changed between stages to mix up the challenge, there was no camera control to fight with, as the linear setup allowed Naughty Dog to always provide a clear view through the lushly illustrated levels. The game's vibrant aesthetics and charming personality helped propel its titular character to mascot status. The success of *Crash Bandicoot 2: Cortex Strikes Back* (1997) and *Crash Bandicoot: Warped* (1998) proved the first hit was no fluke. *Crash Team Racing* (1999) was yet another hit, and one of the few successful attempts at mimicking *Super Mario Kart* from Nintendo's Super NES. If you're looking for a less linear 3D platformer, try *Spyro: Year of the Dragon* (1998, Universal Interactive Studios), from Insomniac Games, which kicked off another franchise.

---

[1]   "PlayStation," *NEXT Generation*, Issue 1, January 1995, p. 42.

[2]   To be fair, they were also responsible for solid Apple IIGS adventure games *Dream Zone* (1988) and *Keef the Thief* (1989), but overall, their track record was mixed and certainly didn't suggest their future greatness.

On the back of a successful Japanese launch in December 1994, Sony unleashed its PlayStation on the US market on September 9, 1995. The timing couldn't have been better. The Atari Jaguar and 3DO Interactive Multiplayer (launched on October 4, 1993) had joined the Sega Genesis and Nintendo Super NES on their respective deathwatches, hoping to eke out a few last orders before the inevitable next generation consoles rendered them all obsolete. Gamers were ready for something new, and not many were willing to wait patiently for Nintendo or Sega to rise to the occasion.

Sega was the first to respond to Sony's threat, hurriedly releasing their own next generation console called the Saturn on May 11, 1995. They'd rushed it to production well ahead of schedule, and succeeded in beating everyone else to the punch. Unfortunately, the truncated production cycle had left them with a poor selection of buggy launch titles. It was difficult even for some Sega diehards to get excited about the system. Adding further insult to injury, the Saturn's retail price was $399, while Sony promised their PlayStation's would only cost $299—a promise they were willing and able to keep. Sega clearly had good reason to worry about what Sony was up to. However, their decision to prematurely launch the Saturn was a poor one with disastrous consequences for the company's future (see Chapter 3.4).

Still, what did Sony really know about videogames? While the company was well regarded for the high quality of their electronics—especially the Sony Walkman—they were neophytes in the world of videogames. Their previous videogame experience consisted mostly of mediocre titles for the Genesis, Sega CD, and Super NES. Meanwhile, the PlayStation's bizarre-looking controller suggested that the company just didn't grasp gaming.

With so much skepticism growing among consumers, Sony clearly needed a tight and effective marketing campaign. Unfortunately, their early efforts were clumsy and potentially ruinous. Intended as a sarcastic, literally edgy, mascot, "Polygon Man" appeared in pre-launch ads featuring upcoming PlayStation games. While striking in appearance, the disembodied head had all the charm and cha-

An early two-page ad in the August 1995 **NEXT Generation** magazine for the Sony PlayStation featuring the short-lived "Polygon Man" mascot. The game featured in the ad, **Battle Arena Toshinden,** was a mediocre fighting game, but its 3D graphics dazzled and helped make it a hit when the PlayStation was officially released.

risma of... a disembodied head. Among the unimpressed was Ken Kutaragi (see Chapter 2.5), the global head of the PlayStation brand. As recounted by Phil Harrison, former head of Sony's European publishing business, Kutaragi was furious about wasting their limited resources developing an alternative brand. What really incensed him, however, was that the design of the character was flat shaded, not Gourad shaded.[3] This was a significant misstep because the advanced PlayStation technology featured the noticeably smoother and better lit polygons that Gourad shading offered; flat-shading was obsolete. By the US launch, Polygon Man was phased out in favor of actual in-game characters, although the basic style of the ads remained the same.

---

3   www.edge-online.com/features/making-playstation/5.

Fear Effect 2: Retro Helix on **ePSXe**.

Fear Effect 2: Retro Helix (2001, Eidos)

Fear Effect 2: Retro Helix may be best known for its puerile advertising campaign, which featured protagonists Hana Tsu-Vachel and Rain Qin romping around together in a sexually suggestive manner. However, the actual game featured an unusually mature and sophisticated storyline for its era. The relationship between the two of the four main characters was indeed romantic and at times gratuitous (in one scene, Hana and Rain make out in an elevator to distract some male guards), but with just a few such exceptions, this action-adventure broke new ground with its rich character development. This puzzle-driven game was also notable for its striking visuals, which used cel-shaded 3D character models on top of 3D backgrounds that were themselves overlaid with looping full-motion video clips. The player alternated between four different characters as the story progressed, providing a dynamic, multilayered narrative. The vibrant visuals and complex story, spanning four discs, made this game a unique entry in the survival horror genre. Unfortunately, a planned PlayStation 2 sequel was canned when publisher Eidos ran into serious financial problems, which also doomed plans for a movie.

Despite the rocky lead-up to launch, the console's debut went smoothly. While the launch fanfare paled in comparison to Windows 95 (see Chapter 3.1), gamers lined up in front of retailers like Electronic Boutique, eager to get their hands on Sony's product. Sony owed this momentum to a solid launch lineup that was both diverse and effective at showing off the PlayStation's impressive 3D capabilities. These titles included *Air Combat* (Namco), *Aquanaut's Holiday* (Sony), *Battle Arena Toshinden* (Sony), *ESPN Extreme Games* (Sony), *Jumping Flash!* (Sony), *Kileak—The DNA Imperative* (Sony), *NBA Jam TE* (Acclaim), *Power Serve 3D Tennis* (Ocean), *Rayman* (Ubisoft), *Ridge Racer* (Namco), *Street Fighter: The Movie* (Acclaim), *The Raiden Project* (Sony), *Total Eclipse Turbo* (Crystal Dynamics), and *Zero Divide* (Time Warner Interactive). There was something for nearly every taste, thanks in part to Harrison's uncanny ability to attract talented developers and publishers like Namco and Ubisoft.

Sony also rejected convention by omitting a pack-in game. Instead, they bundled a pack-in sampler disc, *PlayStation Picks*. No doubt, some gamers were appalled by what looked like a miserly move on Sony's part. However, the sampler disc contained lots of fun, playable game demos. Some retailers even tossed in the *PlayStation Developer's Demo*, which was

The "Dino" tech demo from the **PlayStation Developer's Demo** disc. While the dinosaur looked great and was fully interactive, 3D models in actual games were necessarily lower in quality because of the extra demands on the console.

a pre-release audio CD with a special track, only playable on a PlayStation, which featured amazing tech demos. If Sony had faltered before, they were making up for it now, and soon gamers all over the world were buzzing about the PlayStation.

Sega's Saturn was a competent system, but the PlayStation's inherent 3D capabilities put it in another class. The competition stiffened

A scene from the "Movie" tech demo from the **PlayStation Developer's Demo** disc, an excellent example of the improved colors and motion video quality possible on the PlayStation. While nowhere near the near DVD-level video quality of the next generation of systems, it was a marked improvement over what the previous generation of CD-based systems was capable of.

after Nintendo finally released the Nintendo 64 in the US on September 29, 1996—over a year later. Nintendo hadn't squandered the time, though. *Super Mario 64* was a masterpiece of 3D game design, perfectly matched to an innovative new controller. Sony may have clobbered Sega, but Nintendo seemed more than capable of dealing with the upstart Sony head-on. In fact, if not for Nintendo's decision to stick with cartridges instead of moving on to optical discs, they might well have succeeded. Instead, Sony's decision to embrace optical discs made them extremely popular with developers, many of whom switched sides to support the newcomer.

Among these renegades was Squaresoft, who delighted Sony (and mortified Nintendo) by making their masterpiece, *Final Fantasy VII*, exclusive to the PlayStation. For legions of role-playing gamers, this title alone was worth the price of admission. Supported by an ambitious marketing campaign and the technical wizardry to back it up, *Final Fantasy VII* (published by Sony in 1997) made Nintendo's decision to cling to cartridges look foolish, and set the tone for the remainder of the gen-

The infamous **Final Fantasy VII** ad that drove a dagger through the hearts of Nintendo's fans and helped establish PlayStation's dominance once and for all.

eration. There had been plenty of epic Japanese role-playing games before it, but *Final Fantasy VII*'s three CDs worth of content took the genre to the next level. It sold close to 10 million copies worldwide, placing it third in total platform sales—just behind Sony's remarkably detailed (and obsessive) racing simulations *Gran Turismo* (1998) and *Gran Turismo 2* (1999).[4]

By March 31, 2005, Sony had shipped a total of 102.49 million PlayStation consoles,[5] becoming the first videogame console to move so many systems. Sony would repeat this stunning feat

4   http://en.wikipedia.org/wiki/List_of_best-selling_PlayStation_video_games.

5   http://web.archive.org/web/20120609161621/http://scei.co.jp/corporate/data/bizdataps_e.html.

Final Fantasy Tactics on the **ePSXe** emulator.

Final Fantasy Tactics (1998, Squaresoft)

Despite leveraging themes from previous games in the *Final Fantasy* series, *Final Fantasy Tactics* was still a risky new venture for Squaresoft that, ultimately, paid off handsomely. Not only were they trying a new concept with the idea of a tactical role-playing game, they also introduced a new game world and engine, which used a fully 3D, isometric, rotatable playing field, complemented by detailed character sprites. Set in a fantasy kingdom called Ivalice, the game's story followed Ramza Beoulve, a highborn cadet who finds himself thrust into the middle of the Lion War, where two opposing noble factions are fighting over their respective claims to the kingdom's throne. Players recruited generic player characters and customized them using the Job system made famous in the original *Final Fantasy* role-playing series (whose characters made appropriate cameos). Composers Hitoshi Sakimoto and Masaharu Iwata teamed up to create more than 70 stirring orchestral scores. While the localization of this Japanese original was not without issues, enough of its brilliance shown through to establish it as the first entry in a popular new franchise.

with the PlayStation 2 (Chapter 3.5). "Playing Atari" and "playing Nintendo" were once common parlance for playing videogames. Now gamers were "playing PlayStation."

Technical Specifications

A look inside the PlayStation reveals the progressive attitude of its designers. Unlike Nintendo, who favored value over performance, Sony was all about the cutting edge. The PlayStation contained an LSI LR333x0-based Core, which consisted of a 32-bit MIPS Computer Systems R3000A-compatible RISC chip running at 33.8688 MHz and 2MB of RAM. Inside the main CPU chip was a geometry transformation engine, which provided additional vector math instruction processing that enabled 66 MIPS of operating performance. That translates to 360,000 polygons per second, or 180,000 that are texture mapped and light-sourced. An MDEC was responsible for decompressing images and full-motion video.

The PlayStation's GPU processed 2D graphics separately from the main 3D engine. This allowed for resolutions from 256 × 224 to 640 × 480 (320 × 240 being the most common), with a maximum of 16.7 million colors. There was 1 MB of Video RAM (VRAM). The Sound Processing Unit (SPU) supported ADPCM sources with up to 24 channels, as well as a sampling rate of up to 44.1 kHz. There was 512 kB of memory dedicated to sound processing.

The internal CD-ROM drive ran at 2x speed, with a maximum data throughput of 300 kB/s. Besides PlayStation CDs, the CD-ROM drive could also play audio CDs with a built-in player program.

The original PlayStation console model, the SCPH-1001, had three buttons on top. To the right of the CD lid was the button that flipped it open. To the left of the CD lid was a power button placed just above an LED indicator. Above the power button was a small reset button.

Two controller ports, each with a memory card slot above them, were on the front of the console. The optional memory cards, which had an initial capacity of 128 kB, were used to store saves and other game data. Using the built-in utility, owners could manage the data on the memory cards, including copying the information to other cards.

Klonoa on the **ePSXe** emulator.

Klonoa: Door to Phantomile (1998, Namco)

In this uniquely styled platforming adventure, players took control of the titular anthropomorphic cat creature and a "spirit" encapsulated in his ring, Huepow. A crashed airship, foretold in one of Klonoa's dreams, set the two friends off on an epic, branching adventure. While the game was rendered in three dimensions, all action took place on a 2D plane, which allowed for the type of precise maneuvering and enemy-bashing jumps reserved for the best games in the genre. For more platforming fun, check out *Tomba!*

2: The Evil Swine Return (1999, Sony), which, while played from a more traditional side-scrolling perspective, featured an even wackier theme.

To the rear of the console, from left to right, was a parallel I/O, serial I/O, audio out (stereo R and L connectors), RFU DC out (for an RF modulator), video out (composite), AV multi out (up to S VIDEO), and AC in (for the power plug). The parallel I/O was primarily used for unofficial cheat/region free cartridges, while the serial I/O enabled two PlayStation consoles to be connected via the PlayStation Link Cable. A few dozen or so games supported this feature, which required two PlayStation consoles, two TVs, and usually two copies of the game. While seldom supported and hardly a major selling point, the feature marked a significant improvement over split screen multiplayer.

Three cosmetically similar major revisions were introduced after the SCPH-1001. The first revision was the SCPH-5001, which dropped the dedicated audio out, RFU DC out, and video out ports. The second revision was the SCPH-7001, which came standard with the DualShock controller and introduced SoundScope, which was a graphical light show representation of the music that was playing when an audio CD was inserted. The buttons on the controller could change between 24 patterns and other effects, which could be saved to a memory card. The third revision was the SCPH-9001, which also dropped the parallel I/O.

While several model variations were introduced before and after the three major revisions, in 2000, Sony released a completely new design to go along with the PlayStation 2's launch. The PSone as it was called, which for a time outsold the PlayStation 2, was considerably smaller than any of the previous PlayStation consoles. Besides the obvious cosmetic differences, the PSone also dropped the SERIAL I/O port and utilized an external power supply. This would be the last PlayStation model produced, with production officially ending in March 2006, over 11 years after its original Japanese launch in December 1994.[6] Freeing up production (and focus) helped Sony launch the PlayStation 3 in November 2006.

Sony had made the right move by focusing on 3D gaming. Whereas most of the previous competition had lesser capabilities (3DO) or tacked on support (Sega Saturn), the PlayStation was designed with 3D games firmly in mind. Still, one area where they stumbled was in the design of their original controller, which mimicked designs from 2D consoles.

On the front of the controller, from left to right, was a digital directional pad, select button, start button, and circular action buttons that featured a green triangle (top), a red

The original PlayStation shown with its first (left) and revised DualShock controller (right).

Metal Gear Solid on the **ePSXe** emulator.

Metal Gear Solid (1998, Konami)

While the concept of a stealth-driven action-adventure was nothing new, console gamers had yet to experience the anxiety-provoking gameplay of masterpieces like *Castle Wolfenstein* (1981) or *Thief: The Dark Project* (1998). That changed with the release of Hideo Kojima's *Metal Gear Solid* for the PlayStation. While previous games in the *Metal Gear* series were brought to the NES, they were pale, heavily modified imitations of the classic MSX computer original. With *Metal Gear Solid*, console gamers finally had a definitive, no compromise stealth game of their own. The sequel to Kojima's previous masterpiece, *Metal Gear 2: Solid Snake* (1990), for MSX2 computers, *Metal Gear Solid* took the series into a bold new third-person 3D direction. Featuring cinematic cutscenes rendered with the powerful in-game graphics engine and full voice acting, Kojima and his team leveraged the full power of the PlayStation's hardware. Players took the role of soldier Solid Snake, who must infiltrate a nuclear weapons facility to both liberate hostages and neutralize a terrorist threat from renegade special forces unit, FOXHOUND. While there's plenty of action, players must often resort to using Solid Snake's stealthier capabilities to remain undetected, including crawling under objects, ducking behind walls, and making noises to distract an enemy's attention. With such masterful execution, it's no wonder that all future titles in the series would expand upon its foundation. If you like this game, be sure to also check out Activision's *Tenchu 2: Birth of the Stealth Assassins* (2000), which featured similarly stealthy gameplay, but also let players design their own missions, including level layouts, usable characters, and mission objectives.

---

6   www.gamespot.com/news/sony-stops-making-original-ps-6146549.

circle (right), a blue X (bottom), and a pink square (left). These geometric shapes would soon become iconic and be incorporated in PlayStation branding. On the top of the controller were two pairs of shoulder buttons. Since the middle fingers were used to press the bottom shoulder buttons, there were elongated grip handles for better balance. Crucially, the controller was missing an analog joystick.

Early PlayStation games, such as the innovative first person platformer, *Jumping Flash!* (1995, Sony), and the legendary third-person action adventure, *Tomb Raider* (1996, Eidos), were easy enough to control. However, *Super Mario 64* (1996) on the Nintendo 64 (Chapter 3.3), which took full advantage of that console's analog controls, revealed the inherent flaws in the PlayStation controller's design.

Fortunately, Sony developed a superb series of retrofits in 1997, starting with the Dual Analog Controller, which had dual analog sticks. The design culminated in the classic DualShock, which further refined the Dual Analog Controller's design and added rumble effects. An additional analog button turned the feature on or off for greater compatibility with past titles. The addition of dual analog sticks finally made a PlayStation controller ideal for nuanced movement and camera control in the newest generation of 3D games, like *Tomb Raider III—Adventures of Lara Croft* (1998, Eidos) and third-person platformer, *Ape Escape* (1999, Sony). In short, the DualShock was just the controller the PlayStation needed to secure its place in videogame history.

The Accessories

Besides the various Sony gamepad controllers, a variety of other add-ons and accessories were made for the PlayStation. Naturally, the most common accessories were various third-party controllers, including arcade sticks. Sony released two additional first party controllers that are worth mentioning: the Analog Joystick and PlayStation Mouse.

The Analog Joystick featured two large button-laden flight sticks mounted on a base along with all eight of the standard action buttons, as well as select and start. A mode switch made the

Analog Joystick function like a regular digital gamepad, with both sticks functioning as the directional pad. A thumb-operated hat switch on the right joystick functioned as a standard directional pad when in analog mode. About a dozen games, listed as "Analog Joystick Compatible," were released, including appropriate titles like flight simulator, *Ace Combat 2* (1997, Namco), and mech simulator, *MechWarrior 2: 31st Century Combat—Arcade Combat Edition* (1997, Activision).

At the top of the photo is the Hori Fighting Stick PS; a Game-Enhancer from modchips.com, which plugs into the console's PARALLEL I/O port, rests on top. Nyko's Classic Trackball and Sony's PlayStation Mouse and mouse pad are at the bottom of the photo.

Abe's Exodus on the **ePSXe** emulator.

Oddworld: Abe's Exoddus (1998, GT Interactive)

Developed by Oddworld Inhabitants, *Oddworld: Abe's Exoddus* was platform gaming as twisted as its spelling. Hearkening back to a time when platformers didn't scroll, *Abe's Exoddus* is broken up into discrete screens, which include challenging puzzles that must be solved using the titular character's unique abilities to directly and indirectly control various objects. Abe discovers that the Glukkons are enslaving his fellow Mudokons to produce Soulstorm Brew, a drink that uses their bones and tears as ingredients. Naturally, you must put a stop to this. As well received as its equally atmospheric and eccentric predecessor, *Oddworld: Abe's Oddysee* (1997), *Abe's Exoddus* added the crucial ability to save your progress at any point, resulting in far less frustration. Future installments in the *Oddworld* series entered the third dimension and were released on a wider variety of platforms, but many fans feel that these games were at the height of their charm on the PlayStation.

The PlayStation Mouse was a two-button ambidextrous mouse that came with a PlayStation-themed mouse mat. A few dozen or so titles supported the mouse, including adventure games, *Broken Sword: The Shadow of the Templars* (1998, THQ) and *Discworld* (1995, Psygnosis), and strategy games *Dune 2000* (1999, Westwood Studios) and *X-COM: UFO Defense* (1995, MicroProse).

Light guns were also plentiful on the PlayStation. Besides Konami's The Justifier, which only worked with a few games, there was Namco's Guncon, which other companies shamelessly cloned. Guncon compatible games include Namco's popular arcade conversions of *Time Crisis* (1997) and *Point Blank* (1998), as well as Working Design's *Elemental Gearbolt* (1998) and Fox's *Die Hard Trilogy 2: Viva Las Vegas* (2000), which featured third-person shooting, action driving, and light gun game modes.

Namco also released two specialty steering wheel controllers: neGcon and Jogcon. These were soon joined by an avalanche of other, more traditional steering wheel controllers that purported compatibility. The neGcon was a standard gamepad design with its right and left halves connected by a swivel joint, which registered analog movements. The Jogcon, which was initially bundled with *R4: Ridge Racer Type 4* (1999), took a slightly more traditional approach and placed a force feedback dial at the bottom of the front of a standard gamepad design.

The PlayStation Multitap and its clones let up to four controllers and four memory cards connect to a single controller port on the console. While supported only by a few dozen games or so, most of the titles that would have benefited from its use supported it, including arcade sports classic *NBA Jam TE* (1995, Acclaim), competitive racer *Rally Cross* (1997, Sony), and combat racer *Twisted Metal III* (1998, 989 Studios).

Konami's popular arcade dancing game *Dance Dance Revolution* was brought home to North American gamers in 2001, along with the Dance Dance Revolution controller, a plastic dance mat. Additional rhythm games from Konami and others followed, as did other types of dance mats, including more rigid designs that better mimicked the arcade experience.

The small size of the PSone encouraged its own line of add-ons, including carrying cases and power adapters for use in a car. The most popular add-ons were LCD screens, with Sony themselves coming out with the best, a seamless 5-inch diagonal attachment that was also offered in a bundle with the console itself.

The compact PSone with its optional 5-inch diagonal LCD screen attachment. The actual console is approximately the same width as the standard controller. Courtesy of Evan-Amos, Vanamo Media.

The Sony PlayStation Community Then and Now

Because it came from Sony and had an earlier Japanese launch to help provide context, the PlayStation received a good deal of attention from the gaming press in North America well before its release. *NEXT Generation* magazine in particular provided substantial coverage, which began in their first issue dated January 1995. Other popular magazines, such as *Electronic Gaming Monthly* and *GameFan*, also contributed to the buzz.

PaRappa the Rapper on the **ePSXe** emulator.

PaRappa the Rapper (1997, Sony)

Even though rhythm gaming has become a staple of casual gamers, the pioneering *PaRappa the Rapper* still stands out with its unique visuals, catchy soundtrack, and quirky plot. Players controlled the titular character—whose motto is, "I gotta believe!"—as he tries to win the heart of flower-girl Sunny Funny through six crazy stages. While really nothing more than a challenging game of "Simon Says," PaRappa the Rapper's seemingly endless charm will keep you coming back for more. Also be sure to check out the PlayStation Portable port released in 2007, the 2002 sequel for the PlayStation 2, as well as the PlayStation's own follow-up, *UmJammer Lammy* (1999), which plays similarly, but instead features the sweet story of a shy lamb rock guitarist.

As the PlayStation's popularity grew, it became feasible for publishers to launch dedicated magazines for fans to rally around. Magazines like *Dimension PS-X*, whose first issue appeared in November 1995, and *PSM*, which followed in September 1997, provided extensive PlayStation coverage for the steadily growing fan community, which was starting to rival that of Nintendo's and exceeding that of a downward-trending Sega's.

Of course, the magazine with the greatest impact was *Official US PlayStation Magazine*, whose first issue was dated October 1997. What set this magazine apart from its rivals was its bundled discs full of playable demos. Month-after-month, eager PlayStation gamers could sample exciting new games and see preview videos for future releases, building anticipation and free word-of-mouth advertising. The success of this model was clear to Sega and Microsoft, who bundled discs with their official magazines for Dreamcast and Xbox, respectively. Only Nintendo refused to jump on the demo disc bandwagon.

Sony was also a pioneer in promoting indie game development. Sony released the Net Yaroze development kit for the PlayStation in Japanese, North American, and European/Australian variations in 1997. For less than $800, users could get a package containing a special black-colored PlayStation debugging console

Official US PlayStation Magazine served the community for almost ten years, from its first issue dated October 1997, cover shown here, to its final issue dated January 2007. Every issue of the magazine came with a disc full of playable demos. PlayStation-specific demos lasted until issue 54, after which all further demo discs were targeted exclusively to the PlayStation 2.

with two controllers, documentation, software, and no region lockout. Using a PC Windows- or Macintosh-based computer (as well as NEC PC-9801 in Japan), users could write code, compile it, and send the program to the debugging console for testing. Although purposely limited in comparison to the official PlayStation Software Developers Kit used by Sony's commercial licensees, with the right skillset, commercial quality games could still be developed. In fact, one such game, puzzler *Devil Dice* (1998, Shift), was one of a handful of retail releases that started life as a Net Yaroze title.

While there has not been a lot of activity in PlayStation homebrew software outside of Net Yaroze projects, there is one homebrew hardware item of particular note. The PSIO, although still undergoing a great deal of additional development and revision, allows ISO images of PlayStation CDs to run from an SD card. Not only does this allow commercial software to run from an SD card, but should also help spur further homebrew software development.

Resident Evil: Director's Cut on the **ePSXe** emulator.

Resident Evil: Director's Cut (1997, Capcom)

Resident Evil: Director's Cut was the special edition of the original, genre-defining survival horror classic from 1996 that spawned a multimedia empire. This version changes item and enemy placements and tweaks certain gameplay elements. As a bonus, the original version of the game was also included, along with an easier beginner's mode, which less dexterous players will appreciate. Although it still has the original's infamously campy voice acting and somewhat crude visuals, this game still has an amazing ability to scare, and is a fun glimpse into the genesis of the historically important game series. Also be sure to look out for the updated release of this game, labeled as the "Dual Shock Ver.," featuring support for the DualShock controller's analog joysticks and vibration, as well as a new symphonic soundtrack by Mamoru Samuragoch, replacing the original soundtrack by Makoto Tomozawa, Akari Kaida, and Masami Ueda.

Silent Hill on the **ePSXe** emulator.

Silent Hill (1999, Konami)

It's hardly surprising that eventually a new series would give *Resident Evil* a run for survival horror fans' money. More shocking was the fact that it only took about three years to release a solid alternative—not a mere clone, but a unique and equally compelling take on the genre. *Silent Hill* relied on the third-person perspective of *Resident Evil*, but added real-time 3D environments with liberal use of eerie fog and shadow. These techniques made the game much more frightening, but also much less demanding on the PlayStation hardware. Instead of playing a tough combat expert, players assumed the role of an everyman, Harry Mason, as he searches for his missing adopted daughter in the fictional American town of Silent Hill. Eventually, players stumble upon a cult conducting a ritual to revive a deity it worships, and in the process discover the true origins of Mason's daughter. Depending upon the player's in-game actions, there were five possible endings, including one intended as a joke.

Collecting and Emulating Sony PlayStation Systems

The earliest PlayStation games came in over-sized cardboard or plastic game cases, the latter being the same type that Sega used for its Saturn games. After a few years, all PlayStation software came on standard CD jewel cases, including rereleases of some of the earlier titles. This makes the original long boxes more collectible, although not necessarily rare.

Early PlayStation games came in long cardboard or plastic cases, before eventually moving to standard CD jewel cases.

The earliest PlayStation model (with the audio out ports) has been compared to high-end CD players. As Jeff Day breathlessly described in an April 2007 review on www.sixmoons.com,

> The Sony Playstation 1 SCPH-1001 is another giant killer that's a darling of the audio underground. If you're looking for audio sonic fireworks, the PS1 might not be your cup of tea but if you're looking for an outstandingly musical digital front end that can play music better than just about every multi-kilobuck digital source, look no further—way recommended.[7]

While there's considerable debate over the true fidelity of its sound output, the hype does tend to make the SCPH-1001 more collectible than the later models.

If you're looking for maximum portability, however, the PSone's combination of compatibility and low cost on the various auction sites makes it ones of the easier systems to acquire, though its value is much higher when bundled in its original combo package with the LCD

Syphon Filter on the **ePSXe** emulator.

Syphon Filter (1999, 989 Studios)

A third-person shooter, *Syphon Filter* did away with most of *Metal Gear Solid*'s stealth trappings to deliver an action game filled with a variety of hazards and puzzles spread over 13 missions. Players took on the role of Gabriel Logan and three other operatives, neutralizing terrorists and destroying a biological weapon before it threatens Washington, DC. Each operative contributed a different set of skills that must be properly leveraged to complete the high concept mission. The game's concluding scene foreshadowed future games in the series, which, like many great PlayStation originals, continues to this day.

---

7   www.6moons.com/audioreviews/zigmahornet/zigmahornet.html.

screen. Third-party LCD screens are generally lower quality and as a result hold less value than Sony's official offering. Net Yaroze systems are available for only slightly less than their original retail prices, and not always complete.

Of course, as described in Chapter 3.5, most of the early models of PlayStation 2 did a great job of playing PlayStation games, so that opens up even more possibilities. Perhaps the ultimate such console, though, are the original CECHBxx (20 GB) and CECHBAxx (60 GB) models of the PlayStation 3, which not only play PlayStation 3 discs, but also PlayStation 2 and PlayStation discs, all in hardware. Many PlayStation games are also available via software emulation on Sony's PlayStation Portable, PlayStation 3, PlayStation Vita, and PlayStation 4 platforms via purchase from their respective digital stores. PlayStation Certified Android tablets and smartphones

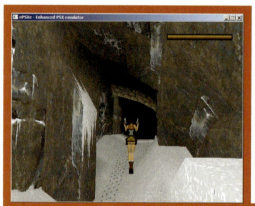

offer similar options. All of Sony's offerings in this area also provide various configuration settings that allow the low resolution PlayStation games to look better on the higher resolution devices they're being played on.

Besides Sony's official offerings, two of the more popular unofficial emulators are *pSX* and *ePSXe*, both of which work with Windows- and Linux-based computers. A variety of other unofficial emulators are available for those and other platforms, including Android, with overall compatibility improving all the time.

The **ePSXe** emulator showing the original **Tomb Raider**.

Nintendo 64 (1996)

History

Nintendo's original Nintendo Entertainment System had enjoyed a virtual monopoly on the console industry (see Chapter 2.1). Its Super NES, however, had faced considerable competition from Sega, who had successfully wrestled third-party developers away from the stranglehold of Nintendo's licensing terms, which forbid them from porting their games to other systems. Other companies had also entered the fray. Despite these threats, Nintendo's leaders had absolute confidence—or perhaps arrogance—that no matter what the competition brought to the table, the Nintendo brand would always reign triumphant. Alas, the next few years would challenge this hubris as never before.

The story of the Nintendo 64 begins with a company named Silicon Graphics (SGI), an American company famous for its high-end graphics workstations. In 1992, SGI spent $406.1 million acquiring MIPS technologies, a semiconductor company who specialized in high performance RISC chips. MIPS, who designed the CPUs for SGI's workstations, had fallen prey to vicious office politics, which had key employees—including their president—walking out the door. Jim Clark, SGI's founder, saw a golden opportunity to not only salvage his company's favorite chip-maker, but to leverage their expertise in building the next generation of game consoles. Less than a year after the acquisition, Clark, prototypes in hand, was ready to talk business.

Blast Corps on the **Project 64** emulator.

Blast Corps (1997, Rare)

A clever mix of action and puzzle game, as its title implies, *Blast Corps'* primary focus was making things go boom. Using one of a variety of heavy vehicles, including trucks and robotic power suits, players needed to destroy any obstacles that stand in the path of an out-of-control nuclear missile carrier, which would explode the second it touched something. Adding to the challenge was the fact that some obstacles couldn't be destroyed at all, but still needed to be bridged or moved. Once cleared, levels could be returned to at a later time for additional play types or simply to find all the hidden objects. *Blast Corps* was released too early to take advantage of the Rumble Pak, but it was still a blast.

First, Clark approached Tom Kalinske, Sega of America's CEO. Kalinske liked the design, but was unable to persuade his company's Japanese headquarters to take it seriously. They believed that their own research and development team could design something better, and, unwilling to reject the offer outright, instead demanded exclusive rights to the chips.[1] Naturally, Clark was unwilling to agree to such demands, since they would severely limit his company's future profits. Fortunately, Clark made a much better impression on Nintendo CEO, Hiroshi Yamauchi. Yamauchi immediately recognized the prototype's potential and was willing to license it on a non-exclusive basis.[2] Clark was happy, and unlike Kalinske at Sega, nobody said "no" to Mr. Yamauchi.

In the spring of 1993, Nintendo took the first step towards its next generation initiative with a formal partnership with Silicon Graphics to design a new console. Nintendo hoped that the project, code-named "Project Reality," and later "Ultra 64," was the secret weapon that would finally send the competition scurrying back to the fringes of the industry. With its 64-bit microprocessor based on MIPS Technologies' proven R4300i design, Nintendo's new console would have more than enough power to achieve this goal.

Silicon Graphics' technology first proved its value in Rare's *Donkey Kong Country* (1994) for the Super NES. As described in Chapter 2.5, it was one of the first mainstream games to use pre-rendered 3D graphics, which were created on Silicon Graphics' workstations. *Donkey Kong Country* and other games using similar technology kept the 16-bit Super NES relevant long after 32-bit systems hit the market.

Similar technology would also find its way to the arcade, with favorites like Rare's fighting game, *Killer Instinct* (1994, published by Midway and Nintendo), and Midway's racer, *Cruis'n USA* (1994). While their hardware wasn't identical to the Ultra 64's, they still provided a tantalizing glimpse at its possibilities.

To help bridge the gap between the release of the Super NES and Ultra 64, Nintendo released the Virtual Boy (Chapter 2.4), first in Japan on July 21, 1995, and then in North America on August 14, 1995. The concept behind the device seemed infallible at the time—a 32-bit tabletop 3D console that, as the name suggested, would bring virtual reality to the masses. Unfortunately, it was a virtual disaster, and it was discontinued months later. Ultimately, the Virtual Boy was only a stumble for Nintendo, but it painfully revealed that the company was anything but infallible.

Meanwhile, all was not going smoothly with the Ultra 64, either. The console's design was first revealed to the public in the spring of 1994, but its first public unveiling was on

A few pages of an article from the August 1995 issue of **NEXT Generation** magazine. The article—entitled "Why the hell has Nintendo delayed the Ultra 64?"—echoed the growing exasperation over the final release date of Nintendo's next console. Note how closely the design of the pictured Ultra 64 console and its cartridge matches that of the Nintendo 64, which would finally launch in North America over one year after the article's publication.

---

[1]   http://wayback.archive.org/web/20090207173139/http://www.sega-16.com/feature_page.php?id=214&title=Interview:%20Tom%20Kalinske.

[2]   Richard L. Brandt, "Nintendo Battles for its Life," *Upside*, 7.10, 1995, p. 50.

Conker's Bad Fur Day on the **Project 64** emulator.

Conker's Bad Fur Day (2001, Rare)

Conker's Bad Fur Day should have never existed on the Nintendo 64. Besides being one of the few cartridge games that could rival the scope of the best CD-based games of the day, it was also unapologetically crude and vulgar. It sold poorly thanks to its offensive nature and high retail price,[3] but it did enjoy nearly universal critical acclaim. The remarkable game engine for this 3D platformer featured dynamic shadowing, colored lighting, long draw distances, detailed facial animation with lip syncing, elaborate textures, and even individually rendered fingers for some of the characters. Perhaps the game engine's greatest accomplishment, however, was the amount of audio, with properly synchronized speech and even fully vocalized songs. The game was far from perfect—its camera was noticeably lower to the ground than other games of its type, and the main character's curse-laden tirades are sometimes a bit over-the-top. Still, the fun factor found in the overall package was a testament to Rare's capabilities. After Rare was purchased by Microsoft in 2002, they did a remake called *Conker: Live & Reloaded* for the Xbox in 2004. While more polished, particularly with its online multiplayer mode, the remake didn't fare any better than its predecessor.

November 24, 1995. There, at the 7th Annual Shoshinkai Software Exhibition in Japan, it was finally introduced as the Nintendo 64. Nintendo promised its first shipments in time for Christmas, but was forced to push that date forward by four months. Unfortunately, this embarrassing and costly delay would not be the last.

It was unclear who or what was responsible for these disastrous setbacks. Some claim it was a calculated move on Nintendo's part to give software developers more time to make games for the launch lineup. Others believe SGI engineer Andrian Sfarti's claim that underperforming chips needed to be redesigned. In any case, the Japanese didn't get their systems until June 23, 1996,[4] nearly eight months later than expected. The North American release (at $199.99) was pushed to September 29, 1996. European and Australian gamers had the longest wait, not getting their systems until March 1, 1997.

Perhaps these delays would have been acceptable if Nintendo only had Sega to deal with. True, Sega had gotten their 32-bit Saturn console to market nearly a year and a half earlier, but it hadn't managed to get much traction even with its considerable head start. Unfortunately, Nintendo also had Sony to deal with, who the company previously scorned and was doing remarkably well with its upstart PlayStation console, which was released just over a year earlier in North America.

Nintendo's tortoise-speed development of the Super NES had allowed Sega's Genesis to undermine their control of the industry, which they never fully recovered. Likewise, Nintendo's heel dragging gave Sony a full year to exploit their new PlayStation brand. Sega had ultimately

---

[3]   Because of all the extra technology packed into the cartridge, it's actually noticeably heavier than other games for the system.

[4]   Richard L. Brandt, "Nintendo Battles for its Life," *Upside*, 7.10, 1995, p. 50.

failed to give Nintendo more than a flesh wound, but the PlayStation was no Genesis. It enjoyed terrific success in every territory, including Nintendo's home market of Japan.

Despite all this, Nintendo's leaders scoffed at the foolish antics of this brash young upstart. Just wait until the Nintendo 64 hit the market; the PlayStation would be history. And they were right. Sony's PlayStation would indeed make history, but not in the way they thought.

Diddy Kong Racing on the **Project 64** emulator.

Diddy Kong Racing (1997, Rare)

Since the first *Mario Kart* title on the Super NES, it was a forgone conclusion that the best kart racing game on any Nintendo platform would be from this series. *Diddy Kong Racing*, however, was an exception. While Nintendo 64 fans got an excellent new *Mario Kart 64* shortly before *Diddy Kong Racing*, it suffered from a fatal flaw despite the watchful eyes of Shigeru Miyamoto. While *Mario Kart 64* had stellar multiplayer, the single player mode suffered from irritating "catch up" artificial intelligence, which meant that no matter how far ahead a player got in a race, the computer opponents would "cheat," automatically getting whatever boost they needed to catch up. In contrast, *Diddy Kong Racing* suffered no such balance issues. It also had better audiovisuals and more varied levels, with planes and hovercrafts added to the standard karts, as well as an adventure mode. Rare followed up with perhaps the third-best kart racer on the platform, *Mickey's Speedway USA*, in 2000, although outside of its Disney characters and themes, the game didn't make any notable advances.

Somehow, even after all of the blown deadlines at the factory, only three games were ready in time for the system's Japanese release: *Super Mario 64*, *Pilotwings 64*, and *Saikyō Habu Shōgi*, a gamed based on shogi, a traditional Japanese chess-like game that was, by all accounts, better

made from wood. In any case, North America didn't even get that, having to be content with only the first two titles. Despite a further delay, Europe and Australia only got two additional titles over North America: *Star Wars: Shadow of the Empire* and *Turok: Dinosaur Hunter*. It seems likely that Nintendo bungled the launch so badly on purpose, perhaps in response to a schoolyard dare. To think otherwise seems too unkind.

The Nintendo 64 console, with Expansion Pak inserted, and its famous controller. Unlike previous Nintendo consoles, no game was included in the original box, although later system bundles would address that deficiency.

The Nintendo 64's game library eventually numbered some 387 games, a poor figure indeed when compared to the PlayStation's 1100+. While the Nintendo brand still carried considerable prestige, many developers were fed up dealing with cartridges, which were a losing proposition: they were more expensive to make, yet less capacious, than discs. Fortunately, the Nintendo 64 still received its fair share of classics, and they still held three trump cards in their hand: Mario, Zelda, and their creator, Shigeru Miyamoto. If Miyamoto couldn't singlehandedly save his company, it was game over for Nintendo. Fortunately, Miyamoto was the best game designer in the business.

The game that saved the Nintendo 64 was *Super Mario 64*, which sold over 11 million copies and sold more systems than all of Nintendo's marketing forces combined.[5] Indeed, so fundamental was this game's success that Nintendo had designed the system's default controller around it. It was a bold move, but, as a result, the game and controller felt like natural extensions of one another. Both game and controller were extraordinary. The controller, with its analog stick, was an ideal way to freely move around the 3D worlds of *Super Mario 64* and the many games that followed its example. While most previous 3D worlds often felt cramped or even claustrophobic, *Super Mario 64*'s, with its dynamic camera system and 15 unique environments (courses), made gamers feel they'd just stepped outside. For the first time, a 3D game was just as natural and easy to control as the 2D games of the 1980s. It was a revelation that few gamers (and developers) ever forgot. *Super Mario 64* wasn't just a breakthrough for the Nintendo 64; it advanced the state of the industry.

On the back of *Super Mario 64*, the Nintendo 64 sold over 500,000 units in its first four months on sale in North America.[6] Ultimately, the Nintendo 64 sold just over 32 million units worldwide, with over 20 million of those sales coming from North America. While this total was small in comparison to the Sony's PlayStation's 100 million units sold worldwide, it was far more than Sega's Saturn or Dreamcast, which sold just over 9 and 10 million units each, respectively, across all territories.

A two-page Nintendo ad from the October 1996 issue of **NEXT Generation** magazine, indicating the Nintendo 64's September 29 launch date and the first game you'd want to own.

Thanks to its relative success in North America, Nintendo was able to keep the system in production until November 30, 2003, a little over two years after the launch of its successor, the GameCube (Chapter 3.7). Although many at the time thought Nintendo had erred in going with cartridges rather than discs, now nostalgia has painted things with a softer brush. The Nintendo 64 was the last major console that used cartridges, a format that will forever remain an icon of gamer culture. Their durability ensures that, long after the discs of other systems have succumbed to the rays of sun and claws of cat, a gamer somewhere will still be firing up *Super Mario 64*. Nintendo might have made many foolish decisions with the Nintendo 64, but they are mistakes that all true gamers cherish.

---

5   http://web.archive.org/web/20060221044930/http://www.ownt.com/qtakes/2003/gamestats/gamestats.shtm.

6   "Sega Dreamcast Sales Outstrip Expectations in N. America," *Comline Computers*, 1999.

ExciteBike 64 on the **Project 64** emulator.

ExciteBike 64 (2000, Nintendo)

A sequel to the classic NES launch title *ExciteBike* (1985), *ExciteBike 64* took the series in a bold new direction. Clearly inspired by the earlier *Wave Race 64*, *ExciteBike 64* shifted the perspective from its predecessor's 2D side-scrolling to 3D third-person, and integrated finely crafted physics into its robust game engine. Besides standard race modes, several fun mini-games are available for unlocking, including the original *ExciteBike* and a 3D reimagining called *Excite 3D*. Of course, the original's popular track editor also received an update for this spectacular sequel. A spiritual successor, *Excite Truck*, debuted on the Wii in 2006. While a solid game, it failed to generate the same excitement as its predecessors, though it did spawn sequels of its own.

Technical Specifications

The Nintendo 64 may not have been the competition-crushing technological powerhouse that Yamauchi envisioned, but it was definitely not a wimp. Its heart was the NEC VR4300 RISC-based CPU, an inexpensive derivative of the 64-bit MIP Technologies R4300i. While the VR4300 used a 32-bit system bus, it retained most of the other 64-bit computational properties of its forbearer and had an impressive clock speed of 93.75 MHz. In deference to execution speed and the limited cartridge storage space, most Nintendo 64 software relied on 32-bit, rather than 64-bit, data operations.

The Nintendo 64's audiovisuals, particularly 3D graphics, were awe-inspiring. Had the console not been hamstrung with cartridges, it might well have trounced the PlayStation. They were powered by a 64-bit SGI chipset, dubbed the Reality Co-Processor (RCP). The RCP is a 64.5 MHz chip with two major components capable of high bandwidth cross-communications: the Reality Drawing Processor (RDP) and the Reality Signal Processor (RSP).

The RDP performs graphics rendering operations and supports resolutions of 256 × 224, 320 × 240 (most common), and 640 × 480 (uncommon) with 16.8 million unique color variations. The RSP typically performs audio processing, which is also possible from the CPU, with a maximum sampling rate of 48 kHz with 16-bit audio. Its maximum sampling rate and theoretical limit of 100 channels of PCM audio are impressive, but limited system resources and the albatross of cartridge space resulted in only modest real world performance.

The Nintendo 64 uses a unified memory system, meaning any subsystem or process could access the 4 MB of RDRAM. Made by Rambus, the RDRAM offered large amounts of high speed bandwidth, which was expandable to 8 MB with the addition of the Expansion Pak.

The console itself featured a streamlined (some would say toy-like) design. On top is the cartridge slot. Just below the cartridge slot was the memory expansion door, where the Expansion Pak went. To the left of the memory expansion door is the on/off power switch; to the right is the

GoldenEye 007 on the Project 64 emulator.

GoldenEye 007 (1997, Rare)

GoldenEye 007 was the first console-based first-person shooter to make PC gamers take notice. At the time, it was "common sense" that you needed a keyboard and mouse to play a shooter, but Rare taught gamers otherwise, paving the way for later console shooters like *Halo: Combat Evolved* in the process. Not only did Rare craft a breakthrough first-person shooter, they accomplished the equally difficult task of doing justice to the *James Bond* movie license, something few other developers have achieved before or since. Based on key events from the *GoldenEye* (1995) film, in which Bond must deal with a satellite weapon that can fire an electromagnetic pulse, the videogame featured innovative mission objectives, a zooming sniper rifle, stealth elements, context-sensitive hit locations (like shooting a hat off a head!), and a local multiplayer deathmatch mode featuring unlockable likenesses of famous *Bond* characters. A spiritual successor, *Perfect Dark*, debuted in 2000, with a number of enhancements, including full voice-acting—players could even eavesdrop on guards having conversations about the events going on around them. While a classic in its own right, *Perfect Dark* pushed the Nintendo 64 past its limits, resulting in occasionally choppy framerates. The Expansion Pak enabled higher resolution graphics, Dolby Surround Sound, and access to more of the game's campaign and multiplayer features.

reset button. On the front of the console are four controller ports. To the rear of the console is the AC adapter bay, which accepts the removable power supply. To the left of the AC adapter bay is the multi out port, which supports the same RF, composite, and S-Video cables as the Super NES and GameCube.

The Nintendo 64 was capable of trilinear filter, allowing for much smoother textures. This was in contrast to the Sega Saturn and Sony PlayStation, both of which used nearest-neighbor interpolation, producing more pixelated-looking textures. However, again because of the limited cartridge space, Nintendo 64 games had fewer textures available, and were stretched and rendered in lower resolution. These workarounds often resulted in an unacceptably blurry or "Vaseline-smeared" appearance. However, the graphics were often much sharper if gamers used the S-Video connection instead of RF or composite.

A scene from one of the more subversive Nintendo 64 commercials from 1996, ending with "Change the system." Based on the promise of its technical prowess alone, many gamers surely heeded Nintendo's advice. www.youtube.com/watch?v=4uQj3hL9SPI.

Mario Party on the **Project 64** emulator.

***Mario Party* (**1999, Nintendo)

Developer Hudson Soft's innovative party game kicked off yet another enduring franchise for publisher Nintendo's platforms. As many as four players could compete in up to 56 different mini-games to get the most stars by the end of a play session. Players chose to play as Mario, Luigi, Princess Peach, Wario, Yoshi, or Donkey Kong in a suitably Nintendo-themed world that took the form of a traditional board game. There was even a dice block, numbered one through ten, which indicated the number of spaces a player moves. Be warned, however— some of the mini-games hearkened back to classic sports videogames, requiring players to rotate the Nintendo 64 gamepad's analog stick as quickly as possible. The result? A sore hand, or worse, a broken controller! With sequels now numbering in the double digits, however, the potential pain and expense deterred few gamers.

Underneath the console is the EXT. door, which covers the Extension Port. The only add-on to make use of the Extension Port was the 64DD, which allowed the Nintendo 64 to use proprietary 64 MB magneto-optical disks for inexpensive data storage. After the 64DD's release was delayed in Japan until December 1, 1999, where it was then met with a muted consumer response and limited software support, the add-on's planned release elsewhere was scrapped.

The Nintendo 64's cartridges were more durable than optical discs, and eliminated the load times associated with the Sega Saturn and Sony PlayStation. However, the downsides of the cartridge format were obvious and painful. Because cartridges were more time-consuming and expensive to produce than a CD, production runs had to be carefully managed. In addition, the cost of a cartridge escalated with the amount of data it was required to store. This led to prices as high as $79.99 at retail, or $116 in today's dollars. Then as now, these prices are simply non-competitive. Many developers, particularly makers of epic-scale role-playing games, like Squaresoft (*Final Fantasy*) and Enix (*Dragon Warrior*), required the enormous storage capacity of optical discs to realize their expansive new game designs. As they switched sides, they brought their hordes of fans with them.

One thing Nintendo got right was its decision to bring back analog controls. In fact, the entire design of its controller was innovative and inspired, thanks in part to having to meet the unusual requirements of the console's Shigeru Miyamoto-produced showpiece, *Super Mario 64.*

The front (left) and back (right) of the Nintendo 64's famous controller. Images courtesy of Evan-Amos, Vanamo Media.

The controller, which features three grips (shaped a bit like an "M") to allow for the different hand positioning required to get access to all of its controls, was quite unlike anything before it. On the face of the controller, from left to right, was a digital directional pad (D-pad), a red start button, an analog control stick, a green B action button, a blue A action button, and four small yellow C buttons, with up, down, left, and right arrows, respectively, often used for camera control or secondary game functions. On the top of the controller were Left and Right triggers, and below the middle grip, a Z button. Just above the middle grip was a single expansion port, which was initially for the Controller Pak (memory card), and later, the Rumble Pak, which provided haptic feedback during gameplay in games that supported it.

Super Smash Bros. on the **Project 64** emulator.

Super Smash Bros. (1999, Nintendo)

Leave it to Nintendo to revitalize yet another genre: fighting games. Players tried to knock Nintendo characters, including Mario, Samus Aran, Donkey Kong, Fox McCloud, and Link, outside the arena's boundaries with all manner of attacks. The arenas were large and required players to be adept at moving around, both in the air and on various platforms. Perhaps the game's best feature was that each character controlled exactly the same, but with different abilities—master control of one character and you know how to control all of them. A four-player multiplayer mode makes this a great party game. With such beloved characters combined with timeless gameplay, it's no surprise that a new *Smash Bros.* game is always the most requested addition to each new Nintendo system's game library.

The controller came in a wide range of colors, including grey, black, red, green, yellow, blue, gold, atomic purple, extreme green, banana bunch yellow, and more, some of which were designed to match the special edition console they were bundled with. The colors were also useful for identifying which of the four controller ports a controller was plugged into during hectic multiplayer matches.

The Add-Ons

Two of the most popular add-ons were the aforementioned Controller Pak and Rumble Pak, each of which plugged into the controller's single expansion port. The Rumble Pak initially came bundled with *Star Fox 64* (1997, Nintendo), the first game to support it, and the required two AAA batteries. There was also a variety of third-party options, including combination Controller and Rumble Paks, where each respective function was accessible via a switch. In-game prompts would indicate when to insert and remove (or switch on) a Controller Pak for games that supported it. While some third-party Controller Paks could store more data than the 123 pages of information on Nintendo's memory card, they still had to be contained in separate blocks of 123 pages each, with a particular block selectable with a switch.

Another popular add-on was the Expansion Pak, also mentioned earlier in this chapter, which doubled the Nintendo 64's memory and allowed for higher quality graphics and other advanced features in some games. Two games, *Donkey Kong 64* (1999, Rare), which originally came bundled with it, and *The Legend of Zelda: Majora's Mask*, required the Expansion Pak. Other games were enhanced with the Expansion Pak, like *Resident Evil 2* (1999, Capcom),

Two third-party controllers and three third-party memory cards and rumble packs are surrounded by some of the Nintendo 64's classic games.

which increased its graphics fidelity; *Gauntlet Legends* (1999, Midway), which enabled a four play simultaneous mode; and *Indiana Jones and the Infernal Machine* (2000, LucasArts), which added a high resolution (640 × 480) display mode. The only downside of the Expansion Pak was that it got hot when the console was running. Some third-party alternatives to the Expansion Pak ran even hotter.

The usual third-party selection of alternative controllers, including steering wheels, was also available. Interact's GameShark series of cheat cartridges also made an appearance, as did their unusual SharkWire Online, a GameShark with modem and PC-style serial port for keyboards. While allowing for emailing and updates, the SharkWire Online depended upon the short-lived sharkwire.com dial-up service for connectivity. Good luck getting it to work now.

The Legend of Zelda: Ocarina of Time on the **Project 64** emulator.

The Legend of Zelda: Ocarina of Time
(1998, Nintendo)

The fifth Nintendo Zelda game, but the first such title in 3D, *Ocarina of Time* was a paradigm shift for the franchise. A high concept action-adventure game with role-playing and puzzle elements, players controlled series hero, Link, as he explored an open world, protected by his trusty sword and shield, plus projectiles and magic spells. Link's quest was to stop the evil Ganondorf, King of the Gerudo tribe, from obtaining the Triforce, a sacred relic that grants the wishes of whoever possesses it. As part of a player's progression, they must learn to play and perform several songs on an ocarina, a formerly obscure musical instrument the game made famous. Despite the high concept, the game was a breeze to control thanks to the innovative context-sensitive actions that were highlighted on-screen, and Z-targeting, which let Link keep his focus on an enemy or other object as he moved about. Its sequel, *The Legend of Zelda: Majora's Mask*, was released in 2000 and had better visuals and a more complex story enabled by the required Expansion Pak. Versions of both classic games are available on Nintendo's later systems.

The Nintendo 64 Community Then and Now

As usual for most Nintendo systems, the Nintendo 64 had strong interest from fans even before its release. The magazines of the day helped fuel the fires of anticipation, which only grew along with the delays. *Nintendo Power*, as expected, was still the go-to magazine resource for dedicated Nintendo 64 fans.

Today, as the last of the major cartridge-based consoles, and the last of the Nintendo consoles to attempt to exceed the best technology that its generation offered, the Nintendo 64 holds a special place in the hearts of many gamers. Despite this, homebrew activities have been relatively limited, though devices like the development and backup unit, Doctor V64, or the development and flash-drive cartridge from Retroactive, 64drive, theoretically make running code on a real console easier.

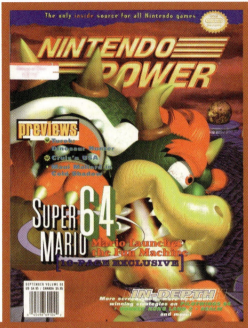

As the official magazine, **Nintendo Power** helped fuel anticipation for Nintendo's next great console. Shown here is issue 88, which discussed the console's pending launch and its killer app, **Super Mario 64**. www.retromags.com/magazines/category/usa/nintendo-power/nintendo-power-issue-88#.Ui3ascakp5B.

The newest and perhaps most versatile such device is Krikzz's Everdrive 64, which claims to run 99 percent of all known Nintendo 64 games, supports both SD and SDHC flash cards, and even includes a built in NES emulator. As a bonus, not only does the Everdrive 64 play games from any region, it can also be used on a Nintendo 64 from any region.

The front side of Krikzz's Everdrive 64, which not only lets you play region free Nintendo 64 games, but also has a built-in NES emulator.

Turok: Dinosaur Hunter on the **Project 64** emulator.

Turok: Dinosaur Hunter (1997, Acclaim)

The Native American warrior Turok dates back to a 1954 Western Publishing and Dell Comics comic book, *Four Color Comics #596*, which was set in a "lost land" featuring demons, aliens, and dinosaurs. Not long after, the popular character graduated to his own series, eventually ending up in Valiant Comics. Videogame publisher Acclaim, betting its future on internally developed games and licensed merchandise, bought out Valiant Comics and developer Iguana Entertainment in 1994, then set to work on *Turok: Dinosaur Hunter* for the Nintendo 64. Acclaim's finances were deteriorating rapidly, and Iguana Entertainment came through just in time. The game hit retail outlets late February 1997, stunning gamers with its intricate graphics—among the first to show what the Nintendo 64 was really capable of—and intriguing gameplay, with traditional first person shooter gameplay mixed with adventure game elements. The character controls were surprisingly versatile, and included jumping, swimming, climbing, crawling, and running. While the game spawned multiple sequels on a variety of platforms (delaying Acclaim's inevitable demise until 2004), none, not even the excellent follow-up, *Turok 2: Seeds of Evil* (1998), could match the impact of the original.

Collecting and Emulating Nintendo 64 Systems

Finding a Nintendo 64, various accessories, and loose games is easy and fairly inexpensive online or off. Boxed systems and, particularly boxed games, hold considerably more value and are more challenging to collect.

Nintendo 64 systems are made more collectible by their variety of colors (with matching controllers), as well as a series of special editions. The latter includes packages like the Star Wars

Episode I Racer Limited Edition Set and the Pikachu Nintendo 64 Set, each themed on its included game. While the latter set was recommended for kids aged 12 and under, it was a particularly impressive bundle, with not only a copy of the *Hey You, Pikachu!* game cartridge, but also a special interactive console, Voice Recognition Unit and Microphone (only used with the one game), and an

One of several later variations of the Nintendo 64 console, this one a limited edition yellow-and-blue console featuring a raised-relief Pikachu on top. The power is turned on by using the Poke Ball on/off switch, and Pikachu's cheeks light up. Pressing Pickachu's foot resets the console.

Wave Race 64 on the **Project 64** emulator.

Wave Race 64 (1996, Nintendo)

Wave Race 64 eschewed the top-down perspective of its primitive 1992 predecessor on the Game Boy, *Wave Race*, for a thrilling new third-person perspective. Boasting accurate wave physics, *Wave Race 64* had some of the most realistic water effects of its era, adding to the excitement of its various race modes. Excellent controls made racing the jet skis or performing crazy stunts a pleasure rather than a pain. *Wave Race 64*'s sequel, *Wave Race: Blue Storm*, appeared on the GameCube in 2001. Blue Storm had even better water effects, but few other improvements over its predecessor. In fact, in some ways the series took a serious step back when many players found the game's overly sensitive controls difficult to wrangle, particularly in comparison to its finely-tuned predecessor.

animated/talking Pokémon watch. It's well worth picking up if you happen upon one at a yard sale or flea market.

For those not into the intricacies and expense of physical items, there's always emulation. While the earliest emulators, like *UltraHLE*, released in 1999, showed how much a higher resolution favored the Nintendo 64's games, compatibility wasn't always the greatest. Luckily, that began to change to the point where the emulators that are available today not only offer improved resolutions and smoother gameplay, but are also highly compatible.

Two of the best modern emulators are *1964 UltraFast* and *Project64*, each of which runs on Windows PCs. Of course, many other emulators are available that also support other platforms, including Macintosh, Linux, and Android.

Perhaps the easiest way to get your Nintendo 64 fix today, however, is through Nintendo's official Virtual Console digital store for the Wii and Wii U. While the selection is not particularly robust, new games are added on a regular basis and are relatively inexpensive, although you will need a Wii Classic Controller (Original or Pro) to join in on the fun.

The **Project64** emulator running **Super Mario 64**.

Sega Dreamcast (1999)

History

Sega was the competition that Nintendo needed and deserved. The brand had risen to prominence with the Genesis, whose powerful technology and provocative advertisements allowed Sonic the Hedgehog to stand proudly next to his friendly rival, Mario. Although fans of both platforms like to emphasize their differences, in reality, Sega and Nintendo had much in common. Sure, Sonic was less polite than his plumbing counterpart, but he wasn't about to start shooting cops and smacking bitches, either. The two companies played nice with the public, the media, and, for the most part, each other, keeping each other on their toes and moving the industry along at a pace they were both comfortable with.

Historically, Nintendo had relied on the popularity of its key franchises, Mario and Zelda, to move its systems. These games were popular for a reason: they were designed by Shigeru Miyamoto, a perfectionist with an uncanny skill for matching ambitious new game designs with marvelously intuitive controls. Sega, on the other hand, had based most of its appeal on its high-tech image, tirelessly pointing out the alleged technical superiority of its systems and gadgets. After the Genesis, rather than waiting to release a completely new system, Sega had hedged its bets (and baffled consumers) with a bevy of add-ons, including the Sega CD and the Sega 32X. This experimentation might have been harmless enough; Nintendo was legendary for its lengthy hardware development cycles. However, when Sega learned that Sony was set to release their PlayStation, they panicked. Convinced that their new 2D-optimized console would compare unfavorably to the 3D-optimized PlayStation, they hastily rushed the Saturn into production before anyone—including their own engineers and developers—were ready for it. All that mattered was getting something, anything, onto the shelf before the PlayStation hit. The result, predictably, was a catastrophic failure, selling only 2 million units in North America before Sega threw in the towel just three years later.[1] The PlayStation had won this round.

Sega regrouped, knowing they only had one last, desperate shot to stay in the console manufacturing game. The past series of failures had hurt them financially, but there was still hope they could make things right with a new console. Unfortunately, even with help from Microsoft, the Dreamcast would not be Sega's salvation, but rather their tombstone.

The story of the Dreamcast begins in 1996, a year after the Saturn's North American launch, when Bernie Stolar took over as CEO of Sega of America. Stolar had been the president of Atari's home division, and he'd also oversaw the PlayStation's development as executive vice-president of Sony Computer Entertainment America. He immediately saw that the originally 2D-oriented Saturn, despite its dual CPUs and 3D-capable graphics processors, could not compete with the

---

[1] Sega continued selling the system until 2000 in Japan.

ChuChu Rocket!

ChuChu Rocket! (2000, Sega)

Despite its modest audiovisuals, Yuji Naka's quirky puzzle game was still a technical achievement—it was the first online-enabled Dreamcast title. The object of the game is to guide one or more ChuChus (mice) on a level into one or more goals, while avoiding the roaming KapuKapus (cats). The ChuChus and KapuKapus move in predictable patterns and can be redirected with strategically placed arrows. Various play modes were available for up to four simultaneous gamers, which is where the fun factor really kicks in. As a nice value-add, a level editor allowed players to create their own puzzle levels to share with others online. Sega released ports of the game for the Game Boy Advance in 2001, iOS devices in 2010, and Android devices in 2011. As with any good puzzle game, several unofficial ports have also been released for a variety of additional platforms, though the Dreamcast original is arguably still the best. Forget about that bowling game; next time you have your non-gaming friends over, fire up *ChuChu Rocket!*

PlayStation or Nintendo 64, which were both optimized for 3D gaming. The Saturn was capable of impressive results, but the system was just too complex for most developers to handle. For Stolar, Sega only had one option: kill the Saturn.

Aborting the Saturn stopped the financial hemorrhaging, but it also left Sega without an actively supported console on the market for over a year. It was a painful period, but Stolar knew that there was no other way to ensure there would be sufficient resources left for their last stand. The Saturn had been a costly mistake, but if the Dreamcast were to have any chance of success, Sega must keep looking forward, not back.

Earlier, Stolar had set the plan in conjunction with Sega of Japan CEO Hayao Nakayama. In contrast to earlier regimes, where American opinion on key company decisions held little value (see Chapter 3.3), Nakayama agreed to let Stolar shape the direction of the new platform and help restructure Sega.

Sega established two different teams to develop the Saturn's successor. The American project, called Katana, was led by IBM's Tatsuo Yamamoto. It was centered on the 3Dfx Voodoo graphics chipset, which had been a hit with PC gamers. The Japanese project, Dural, was led by Genesis designer Hideki Sato, and based on Hitachi and NEC technology. While NEC's PowerVR graphics chipset didn't have the same cachet as 3Dfx, its potential was just as strong. The competition was on, and the stakes had never been higher. Yamamoto and Sato knew that, whatever the outcome, the fate of the company was in their hands.

The best available technology won out. NEC's PowerVR would not only lay the foundation for Sega's next console, but also their next arcade board, NAOMI. In earlier days, Sega's arcade technology had inspired related developments on the Genesis. Now it would be NAOMI's turn to influence games on the Dreamcast. In fact, the arcade and home technology were closer than

Grandia II.

Grandia II (2000, Ubisoft)

While not as deep as the role-playing game library found on its 16-bit predecessor, Sega's Dreamcast still featured several genre-defining stand-outs. Arguably the best of the bunch was Game Arts' *Grandia II*. The sequel to the Japanese-only Sega Saturn original, *Grandia* (1997, 1999 for PlayStation), *Grandia II* was a more mature and technically advanced entry in the series. The plot follows a young mercenary, Ryudo, and his talking bird, Skye, as they protect a church songstress, Elena, and uncover the true history of their world, which was nearly destroyed a thousand years before by the gods. Featuring fully 3D graphics, the game sports a unique hybrid turn-based battle system that allowed for real-time actions, including moving into a better position to strike opponents or blocking at just the right time to mitigate damage. Later ports to the PlayStation 2 and Windows were technically inferior and bug-ridden, so the Dreamcast original remains the best. If you like this game, be sure to also check out *Skies of Arcadia* (2000, Sega), which, despite an excess of random battles, is another brilliant Dreamcast RPG classic that also makes a compelling case for best-in-class.

ever, especially with the NAOMI's interchangeable games and economical, powerful hardware. It translated almost perfectly to the Dreamcast's design.

Stolar had a few more tricks up his sleeve. First, he convinced his Japanese colleagues that the new console should be bundled with a modem. This idea was clearly ahead of its time; online gaming had only just starting catching on with PC gamers. Next, he turned his focus to shifting developer resources to Dreamcast projects, including giving Sonic back to Yuji Naka's Sonic Team. This time, the blue blur would get the chance to shine in a way denied him on the Saturn.

Unfortunately, all of this planning and effort didn't help the Japanese launch on November 27, 1998. There were only four games available—the cutesy racer *Pen Pen Trilcelon*, city destroyer *Godzilla Generations*, adventure game *July*, and a poorly done arcade port *Virtua Fighter 3tb*—and none were any good. The Dreamcast had made its first impression, and it was a bad one. The publication of *Sonic Adventure* shortly thereafter better demonstrated the system's capabilities, but it still left many Japanese gamers uncertain why Sega had abandoned the Saturn so quickly. Unlike their American counterparts, Japanese gamers had been much more forgiving of the Saturn's flaws, and the Saturn fans there felt neglected, or even betrayed. So far, they'd seen little on the Dreamcast that justified abandoning the platform.

In the end, however, great games trump everything else, and Japanese fans finally had a Dreamcast game they could rally around: *Seaman*. Released on July 29, 1999, the bizarre virtual pet game was bundled with the official Dreamcast microphone for voice commands. It was the fledgling console's first hit and was, if nothing else, unique. The gameplay had players helping to evolve a fish with a human face (that of its designer, Yoot Saito) from "Mushroomer"

to "Frogman," mostly by talking to it. Best described as a Monty Python-esque virtual pet "conversation" game, *Seaman* had players listening to trivia, trading insults, and witnessing some downright creepy facial expressions. It's not clear (to us, anyway) why the game was so popular in Japan, but, like so many things, it did not translate well to other countries. Even after recruiting the great Leonard Nimoy of *Star Trek* fame to narrate it, *Seaman*'s North American release on August 9, 2000 had more gamers asking "What the hell?" than "How much?"

In the meantime, Sega was preparing for the Dreamcast's North American debut. A soft launch in July 1999 at Hollywood Video retail chains gave gamers a chance to rent the console, but the full launch was targeted to September. The delay gave Sega a chance to get both its marketing and launch lineups in order.

Sega's Dreamcast received lots of pre-release hype, including from its **Official Dreamcast Magazine**, which came with a PC CD-ROM preview disc to help potential owners know what they'd be getting at launch. Shown here is a promotional cardboard insert.

The Genesis' strong sales in the United States were due in no small part to its excellent sports titles. By contrast, the Saturn's sports selection was miserable in comparison to the PlayStation's. Stolar was determined to recapture the sports crowd with a mix of superior first and third-party games. He first purchased Visual Concepts, who had earlier attempted to develop a debut *Madden* title for Electronic Arts on Sony's PlayStation. Although the game was never released, Stolar, who had architected the publishing deal, had liked what he saw. Visual Concepts was immediately put to work on a next generation football title. Stolar now turned his attention to the undisputed champion of sports gaming: Electronic Arts (EA).

When Stolar first knocked on their doors, he was told that EA wanted exclusive rights to develop sports games on the Dreamcast. Obviously, this request came at a bad time. The ink was still wet on the Visual Concepts deal, and there had long been plans to bring Sega's arcade sports games to the Dreamcast. Therefore, Stolar had little choice but to refuse EA's terms. Stung by the rejection, EA's vice-president, Bing Gordon, angrily told Stolar, "You can't succeed without us." When Stolar still refused to sign, EA retaliated by refusing to release a single game on the Dreamcast. Stolar probably knew deep down that Gordon was right—without EA's support, the Dreamcast was more than likely doomed. But he still refused to sign.

Dreamcast fans have little love for EA.

Jet Grind Radio.

Jet Grind Radio (2000, Sega)

Called *Jet Set Radio* everywhere except North America, *Jet Grind Radio* featured one of the early uses of cel-shading, which outlined polygon graphics in such a way to make them look like cartoons. These innovative graphics were combined with an inspired street style that perfectly matched the funky soundtrack. Players take the role of a member of The GGs, a gang "fighting" to gain control of Tokyo-to while "battling" rival gangs and the police. Instead of using weapons, the player's avatar rides on inline skates to jump, slide on rails, and skitch on the back of cars, while performing tasks like spraying graffiti over rival gangs' work. A similar playing sequel, *Jet Set Radio Future*, appeared in 2002 for Microsoft's Xbox, while an isometric reimagining of the Dreamcast original appeared on the Game Boy Advance in 2003, courtesy of THQ. A high definition update of the original also appeared on the respective digital stores for PlayStation 3, Windows, and Xbox 360 in September 2012. If you like the cel-shaded art style of *Jet Grind Radio*, be sure to also check out *Wacky Races* (2000, Infogrames), which takes the somewhat obscure Hanna-Barbera cartoon license and places it into a polished kart racer for the Dreamcast, brought down only by an unforgiving difficultly level later on in the game.

Legacy of Kain: Soul Reaver.

Legacy of Kain: Soul Reaver (2000, Eidos)

While released earlier for the Sony PlayStation and Windows computers, action adventure *Legacy of Kain: Soul Reaver* looked best on the Dreamcast, which is high praise for what was already a stellar looking game. While its predecessor, *Blood Omen: Legacy of Kain*, never appeared on the Dreamcast, *Soul Reaver* takes place 1500 years after the first game's events, so no prior experience is necessary. Players take the role of vampire-turned-wraith Raziel, lieutenant to vampire lord Kain. Raziel is murdered by Kain, but is revived by the Elder God to become the titular Soul Reaver, which is also the name for the sword he acquires during the game and uses to help exact his revenge. The third-person gameplay consists of a combination of hack and slash fighting, switching between the material and spectral planes at will, and puzzle solving. While sometimes criticized for leaving its player wondering where to go next, the fact remains that *Soul Reaver* is one of the best third-person action adventures of its generation. For a more action-oriented third person game, be sure to check out BioWare's *MDK2* (2000), which features three very different playable characters.

When Stolar returned with the bitter news about EA, the team at Visual Concepts stepped up to the challenge. The burden was on them to prove that the Dreamcast didn't need EA to bring the sports—and they delivered. Sega Sports' launch title, *NFL 2K*, outclassed anything Electronic Arts would come out with for several years. In fact, after the Dreamcast launched in North America, *NFL 2K* was joined by a full and diverse lineup of titles that included *AeroWings*, *AirForce Delta*, *Blue Stinger*, *Expendable*, *Flag to Flag*, *Hydro Thunder*, *Monaco Grand Prix*, *Mortal Kombat Gold*, *NFL Blitz 2000*, *Pen Pen Trilcelon*, *Power Stone*, *Ready 2 Rumble Boxing*, *Sonic Adventure*, *Soulcalibur*, *The House of the Dead 2*, *TNN Motorsports Hardcore Heat*, *Tokyo Xtreme Racer*, and *TrickStyle*. Clearly, Sega had learned from their mistakes with the Japanese launch, this time offering a truly representative selection of games that demonstrated the Dreamcast's technical superiority over the PlayStation and Nintendo 64.

Luckily for Sega, US gamers responded well to the launch. The 300,000 pre-orders set a new record, and 500,000 of the $199.99 consoles went home in just two weeks. Amazingly, 225,132 Dreamcasts were sold in the first 24 hours alone.[2] Needless to say, the champagne was flowing at Sega headquarters. The long nightmare was over; Sega was saved.

Tragically, the momentum was short-lived. Despite strong North American and European sales (where it launched on October 14, 1999), sales remained tepid in Japan, contributing to large consecutive annual losses for the company. As described in Chapter 3.5, after the PlayStation 2's launch in Japan on March 4, 2000, interest in the Dreamcast waned even further. Six of the PlayStation 2's launch titles were EA's, including sports juggernauts *Madden NFL 2001* and *NHL 2001*. Back at his Sega headquarters, Stolar watched miserably as the sales reports grew bleaker. The Dreamcast was a great system, but it was just too little, too late. Perhaps things would have gone differently if he'd signed with EA, perhaps if he'd killed the Saturn sooner or perhaps let it live a bit longer, or perhaps if people weren't still laughing about the fish game—maybe then the Dreamcast would have made it. But now the dream was over, and perhaps wasn't going to help move the furniture out of the building.

Sega officially discontinued Dreamcast production on March 30, 2001. The last North American release was, fittingly, *NHL 2K2* in February 2002, which again proved itself one of the best sports games on the market. Interestingly, Sega supported the Dreamcast longest in Japan, where it had been the least successful. Sega of Japan continued selling refurbished systems and releasing new software until 2007, when the company finally stopped producing the Dreamcast's GD-ROM optical discs. Many of the final titles were ports from Sega NAOMI arcade hardware, which was still a thriving business in the region.

Free roaming adventure game **Shenmue** (1999 in Japan, 2000 in North America), was one of the most ambitious and costly titles ever produced, with a budget of $47 million. Combined with its sequel, development cost Sega an estimated $70 million. Disappointing relative sales for the titles did Sega's financial situation no favors.

---

2   www.g4tv.com/gamemakers/episodes/1259/Sega_Dreamcast.html.

Power Stone 2.

Power Stone 2 (2000, Capcom)

Released in 1999, *Power Stone* was a remarkably innovative Naomi-based arcade and Dreamcast fighting game. The sequel, released for the same two platforms in 2000, took the best features from its predecessor and added more options. Up to four players can duke it out in different arenas using in-level melee and projectile items, like tables, chairs, rocks, guns, flamethrowers, hammers, bear traps, and more. There's also an interesting adventure mode, which plays similarly to the main battle modes, but with an ongoing item and money inventory that can be traded for and mixed in an item shop, extending the game's longevity far beyond that of typical brawlers. As a bonus, there's a VMU application called the Mini-Book, which lets players inspect their inventory and trade items with other players. Whether played alone or with three other friends, *Power Stone 2* won't disappoint. In 2006, Capcom ported the two games to Sony's PlayStation Portable as the *Power Stone Collection*.

While hardly a smashing success in its short life, the Dreamcast still sold over 10 million consoles worldwide, with over 2 million in Japan, 4 million in North America, just under 2 million in Europe and Australia, and just over 2 million everywhere else.[3] Afterward, Sega abandoned console manufacturing and became a third-party software developer.

Despite its tragic flaws, the Dreamcast, thanks to its unusual hardware and strong games library, is worthy of an honored place in the annals of gaming history. And if reading this chapter has made you sad, we know a fish you can talk to.

Technical Specifications

The Dreamcast had a powerful and versatile internal architecture. The CPU was a 32-bit SH-4 running at 200 MHz, but enhanced by an on-die 128-bit vector graphics engine. Its graphics hardware was the PowerVR2 CLX2 chipset, capable of a peak performance of 7 million polygons per second with trilinear filtering—and a variety of built-in hardware effects to boot. Resolution was 640x480 interlaced or progressive scan, with up to 16.78 million colors. Sound hardware was equally impressive. The Yamaha AICA Sound Processor had a 32-bit ARM7 RISC CPU operating at 45 MHz, and a 64 channel PCM/ADPCM sampler with 4:1 compression, XG MIDI support, and a 128 step DSP. Suffice it to say, this box could bring the bump.

The Dreamcast had 16 MB of main RAM, 8 MB of dedicated video RAM, 2 MBs for system ROM, 128KB of flash memory, and 2 MB just for sound. The proprietary optical GD-ROM drive (Gigabyte Disc Read-Only Memory) was capable of reading discs up to 1.2 GB in capacity. The GD-ROM drive was also compatible with standard CD-ROMs, including music CDs, which the Dreamcast can also play. It could not, however, play DVD movies like the PS2 or Xbox.

---

3 Blake Snow, "The 10 Worst-Selling Consoles of All Time," *GamePro*, May 4, 2005.

On the top of the console was a power button and an open button, which opened the GD-ROM door. To the rear of the console, from left to right, was the line in for the detachable 56 kbit/s dial-up modem, AV out, serial port, and AC in, for the power cable.

Like the Nintendo 64 before it, the Dreamcast not only had four controller ports, found on the front of the console, but also further

The Dreamcast's controller had two expansion slots, or dock connectors, often used for the VMU and Jump Pack.

expanded upon the idea of expandable controllers with not one, but two expansion slots, or dock connectors. The controller features an analog stick, digital direction pad, triangular start button, two analog triggers, and four action buttons, which include a yellow X button on the left, a red A button on the bottom, a blue B button on the right, and a green Y button on top. To the frustration of some gamers, instead of the controller's connection cord coming from the top of the controller, it comes out the bottom.

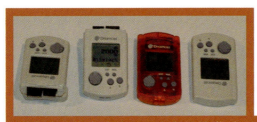

Typically, the controller's two dock connectors were filled with some combination of memory card or Jump Pack (haptic feedback rumble pack), first- or third-party, and a Visual Memory Unit (VMU). The VMU could be snapped into the controller's first dock connector so that its screen showed through

While the VMU had a low resolution LCD display, the screen's contrast was still sharp.

the opening. This allowed the VMU's low resolution LCD screen to be used as an auxiliary display—a cool innovation with a lot of potential, only some of which was realized in the Dreamcast's brief lifespan.

Of course, the VMU was more than just a secondary display. Without batteries, the VMU still functioned as a memory card and auxiliary display, but when powered by two CR-2032 lithium batteries, it can also work independently from the Dreamcast. In this mode, it could play simple downloadable games and facilitate transfers (or even multiplayer gaming) when plugged into another VMU. Helping the VMU with this extra functionality were a front-facing digital direction pad and four buttons, including small sleep and mode buttons, and large A and B action buttons. A built-in speaker allowed sound from its simple 1-channel PWM sound source. The VMU has 128KB of flash memory for storing saved games and other data, although 28KB of space was reserved for system use.

Finally, no discussion of the Dreamcast's technical features would be complete without mentioning the operating system. There is no built-in operating system; instead, it's always loaded

Resident Evil Code: Veronica.

Resident Evil Code: Veronica (2000, Capcom)

While the first three *Resident Evil* games debuted on the Sony PlayStation, *Resident Evil Code: Veronica* was the first new entry in the survival horror series to debut on a rival platform. Sony's loss was Sega's gain, as Capcom pulled out all the stops to make this the best *Resident Evil* game yet, and arguably, the best for many sequels yet to come. *Resident Evil Code: Veronica* kept the series' tank-like character controls, but the pre-rendered backgrounds were now in true 3D, allowing for real-time lighting and limited camera movement. It also added two new weapons that could be fired from a unique first person perspective. Further improvements abound, including brilliant new cut scenes made possible by the Dreamcast's more powerful hardware, various dual-wielding pistols, which allowed targeting two enemies at the same time, and more finely tuned difficulty, allowing players to retry failed scenes and quickly pick up and use healing herbs even if the character's inventory is full. Several updates of the game were released, including *Code: Veronica X* for the Dreamcast (2001, Japan only), PlayStation 2 (2002) and Nintendo GameCube (2003), which featured new and updated cutscenes, as well as minor graphical changes to the main game. If you like this game, be sure to check out Capcom's *Dino Crisis* (2000), which was their take on "*Jurassic Park*-meets-*Resident Evil*." While a port of the PlayStation original and not as well implemented as *Resident Evil: Code Veronica*, it's a nice change of pace from traditional survival horror themes.

SoulCalibur.

SoulCalibur (1999, Namco)

Namco's *SoulCalibur*, the sequel to *Soul Edge* (1996), started life as a Namco System 12 arcade game in 1998. For its 1999 Dreamcast port, Namco greatly enhanced the audiovisual quality and added in new features, creating one of the finest fighting games ever made in the process. A one-one-one 3D weapons-based fighting game, *SoulCalibur*'s greatest innovation was its unprecedented freedom of movement. Beyond simple sidesteps or rolls, *SoulCalibur* let players maneuver in any direction, creating deeper strategic gameplay possibilities than almost any other fighter of its era. What's perhaps most amazing, however, is that this was one of the Dreamcast's launch titles, so the remarkable degree of polish and audiovisual mastery of the console's hardware by the developers is a true tour de force. Fighting game fans owe it to themselves to play this masterpiece, which many Dreamcast fans consider the best game on the console. While not quite as dazzling, Tecmo's *Dead or Alive 2* (2000) is also worth checking out for fans of the genre.

from a disc. The advantage to this was that developers could ship their games with the latest version of the operating system, complete with all the newest features and performance enhancements. There was, therefore, no anxiety about their games suddenly breaking after an official update from Sega. Microsoft wanted their Windows CE, which supported DirectX, as the primary operating system for the Dreamcast, but Sega decided to go with a two-pronged approach instead: developers could choose to use Windows CE or Sega's own custom operating system. Most games were developed using Sega's operating system, which had better performance, but the Windows CE option made it easier to bring over a fair number of ports. Unfortunately for both companies, the potential benefits of the Windows CE option was never fully realized in the Dreamcast, but it clearly whet Microsoft's appetite for greater investment into the console business (see Chapter 3.6).

The Online Connection

While there were online or connected experiments for everything from the Atari 2600 and Mattel Intellivision to the Sega Genesis, Super Nintendo, and Sega Saturn, the Dreamcast was the first console to offer a truly modern, unified experience. Even with a relatively primitive implementation, the Dreamcast's built-in online capabilities cannot be overstated, and it's what later allowed Microsoft's Xbox Live to dominate the console world. The important thing was that *every* Dreamcast had access to the online component, not just ones who sprang for an add-on. That guaranteed that developers would be much more likely to support the functionality.

Using its built-in dial-up modem, players could connect with their own ISP or sign up for Sega's Seganet service. While the configuration process was a bit of a hassle, it had the virtue of actually working as advertised. The included PlanetWeb Browser went through several revisions, each of which added functionality or improved compatibility. Later, Sega offered a broadband adapter (BBA) as a one-to-one replacement for the dial-up modem, though this saw limited release. It would take the competition years to catch up.

Space Channel 5.

Space Channel 5 (2000, Sega)

A rhythm game following the quirky exploits of charismatic space reporter Ulala, players must copy the sequence of movements performed by her onscreen opponents, synchronized to the music. As with any good rhythm game, the music and atmosphere make it or break it, and *Space Channel 5* has both in abundance. If you like your rhythm games eccentric, *Space Channel 5* delivers. For example, keep an eye out for a cameo from Michael Jackson later in the game as Space Michael. HEE HEE! If you want to spice up your rhythm gaming, be sure to grab some maraca controllers and check out a copy of *Samba de Amigo*.

Naturally, there was more to do with the Dreamcast's modem than browse the web. Several dozen games were released that either allowed for competitive online play (*Bomberman Online*), online rankings (*Crazy Taxi 2*), or provided access to extra content (*Floigan Bros.*). While all of the official servers have long gone offline, multiple unofficial servers are still active that provide support to those gamers who still want to get online with their Dreamcast. That should tell you something about the quality of the Dreamcast's online experience.

The start screen for version 2.62 of the PlanetWeb Browser.

The Accessories

The Dreamcast supported a proprietary keyboard and mouse, which was useful for the web browser, as well as select games, like first-person shooter, *Quake 3* (2000, id), or MMORPG *Phantasy Star Online* (2001, Sega). Several third-party options and adapters were also available.

Beyond the usual third-party controllers, arcade sticks, and light guns, the Dreamcast featured two rather unusual controllers in its lineup: the Fishing Controller and the Samba de Amigo Maracas Controller. The motion sensitive Fishing Controller lent a "reel-alistic" haptic dimension to games such as *Sega Bass Fishing* (1999) and *Reel Fishing Wild* (2001, Natsume). The Samba de Amigo Mara-

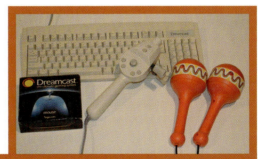

The official Dreamcast keyboard shown above the box for the official mouse. The Fishing Controller is shown next to a pair of third-party maracas.

cas Controller and its third-party alternatives consisted of a plastic mat that players stood on and two wired maracas that connected to a sensor bar. There might be someone out there who wouldn't enjoy playing the wacky and hilarious rhythm game *Samba de Amigo* with these controllers—if such a person is found, please feel free to apply the maracas in a different manner.

One of the more popular accessories is the VGA adapter (or third-party equivalents), which allowed Dreamcast games to be played on high resolution monitors or HDTVs in the console's highest resolution, 480p. While this is a significant improvement over standard RF, composite, or even S-VIDEO output, not every game supports VGA. As a result, many VGA adapters also have composite and S-VIDEO outputs for maximum compatibility. Of particular note is that VGA is what the Dreamcast outputs natively.

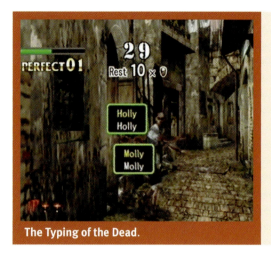

The Typing of the Dead.

The Typing of the Dead (2001, Sega)

The best use of a Dreamcast keyboard is not in fact, the web browser, but instead is this unusual shooting game. Loosely based on *The House of the Dead 2* (1998) light gun-based arcade game, *The Typing of the Dead* had you blasting zombies by typing the words that appear above their heads as quickly as possible. It's funny, strange, and a challenge for even the best typists, as well as a classic example of Sega's willingness to experiment. If you like the zombie typing fun, be sure to grab a light gun and check out the regular Dreamcast ports of the arcade *House of the Dead* games, which are a literal blast to play.

Two link cables, which connected to the SERIAL port, were released for the Dreamcast. One, the Vs Link Cable, connected two Dreamcasts together for head-to-head play and was supported by just a half dozen games, including robot battler, *Virtual On: Oratorio Tangram* (2000, Sega). The other was the Dreamcast to Neo Geo Pocket Color link cable from SNK, which connected SNK's failed Game Boy competitor, the Neo Geo Pocket Color, to the Dreamcast and allowed for data transfer between the small selection of compatible games, including fighting game, *Capcom vs. SNK: Millenium Fight 2000* (2000, Capcom).

Virtua Tennis.

Virtua Tennis (2000, Sega)

On a system filled with so many great sports games (although oddly, never a good interpretation of baseball), it's surprising that a tennis title would make the list. With no particular dependence upon having the latest and greatest rosters, and gameplay that has arguably not been improved upon since, *Virtua Tennis* was actually an easy choice to make. With a quick learning curve, wide variety of fun training mini-games, and choice of several game modes, this modern update of *Pong* will have you making a racket. Who cares if you're not into tennis? The only major downside is the lack of female athletes—you'll need to play the 2001 sequel for that.

The Sega Dreamcast Community Then and Now

Although the Dreamcast was short-lived, its fan community was not. Indeed, now is the best time ever to own a Dreamcast. The homebrew selection alone is worth buying a system for.

All of the general gaming magazines of the day provided excellent coverage of the Dreamcast. No magazine did a better job, though, than the *Official Dreamcast Magazine*, whose first issue was September/October 1999. It ran for 12 issues, with its last being the March/April 2001 edition. Almost every issue was bundled with an impressive GD-ROM disc filled with demos. The editorial style was fun, witty, and informative. Many of its best design elements were recycled for the *Official Xbox Magazine*.

Unlike the majority of disc-based consoles, copy protection is usually not an issue with the Dreamcast. Depending upon the exact model of Dreamcast, both games from other regions and burned CD-R discs can usually be played on the console with no fuss, though sometimes a special boot disc, like *Utopia*, is required. That, too, however, can easily be burned onto a regular CD-R disc.

Official Dreamcast Magazine's inspired content provided a wonderful resource for fans of Sega's underdog console to rally around. http://archive.org/details/Official_Dreamcast_Magazine_The_Issue_01_1999-09_Imagine_Publishing_US.

Because of its flexibility, not only can the Dreamcast play backups of commercial games, but also a diverse array of emulators. A Dreamcast SD card adapter even allows software to be run without any further intervention from the GD-ROM drive. Did we mention that now is the best time ever to own a Dreamcast?

Homebrew software is particularly robust, with not only the aforementioned emulators and ports from other systems, but plenty of original games as well. As a favorite of hardcore gamers, shoot-'em-ups are particularly well represented on the Dreamcast, with

A selection of boxed original Dreamcast games, as well as three modern homebrews: **Inhabitants**, **Maquipai**, and **Cool Herders**.

games like *Last Hope* (2007, RedSpotGames), *DUX* (2009, HUCAST.Net & KonTechs Ltd.), and *Sturmwind* (2013, RedSpotGames) giving many commercial releases a run for their money. Of course, if shooting stuff is not your thing, other releases, like multiplayer collect-'em-all *Cool Herders* (2002, HarmlessLion Games), rhythm game *Feet of Fury* (2003, GSP), and puzzle game *Wind and Water: Puzzle Battles* (2009, RedSpotGames), will surely fit the bill. Better yet, playing all these fun homebrew titles might well inspire you to take a stab at creating your own!

Collecting and Emulating Sega Dreamcast Systems

Finding a working Sega Dreamcast console is not a costly proposition, though you do need to pay attention to how well the GD-ROM works, which is a typical point of failure. Most software is still easy to find, although there are the usual selection of rarities for which demand exceeds supply.

The two major North American console colors were the standard light grey and black, which was originally available in the Sega Sports Pack bundle with *NBA 2K* and *NFL 2K*,

Released September 9, 2000, the Sega Sports Pack included a black console (pictured), black controller and VMU, and copies of the Sega Sports titles **NBA 2K** and **NFL 2K**. Photo courtesy of Evan-Amos, Vanamo Media.

as well as matching controller. Other, more limited special editions with minor cosmetic variations were released by select retailers or for special events. Many aftermarket colored shells were also sold, which were relatively easy to apply to the system to change its coloring.

Although the Dreamcast can be a challenge to emulate for today's systems, there are presently two worth noting that do a commendable job: *Chankast* and *nullDC*. The former supports Windows computers, while the latter supports both Windows and Linux.

The **Chankast** emulator running the popular comic sports game **Ready 2 Rumble Boxing**.

Sony PlayStation 2 (2000)

History

Sony's PlayStation 2 might well be the last single console to truly dominate the industry. More commonly known as the PS2, this console sold over 150 million units, easily making it the best-selling console of all time. More importantly, it enjoyed the lion's share of the market. Some reports show its market share reaching as high as 70 percent in 2005.[1] Shortly after its launch, it crushed its first serious competitor—the Sega Dreamcast. By the time Microsoft and Nintendo finally rolled out their Xbox and GameCube, respectively, the PS2 had built up such an enormous lead that neither console stood a chance of catching up. Indeed, the PS2 was such a successful machine that even Sony's own PS3 had a difficult time competing with it. As late as 2009, the PS2 was outselling both the PlayStation 3 and the PlayStation Portable![2]

The PS2 boasted some of the best hardware ever designed for a console, a huge games library with plenty of major hits, and a competitive price. However, it owes much of its success to impeccable timing.

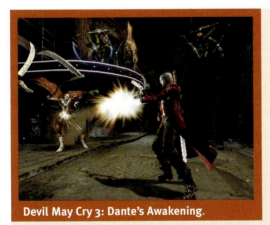

Devil May Cry 3: Dante's Awakening.

Devil May Cry 3: Dante's Awakening
(2005, Capcom)

Perhaps no word better epitomizes *Devil May Cry 3: Dante's Awakening*'s gameplay better than "challenging." The game pulled no punches, even in the opening segments. Once you'd mastered the game's sophisticated combat system, however, you'd be treated to some of the most stylish sword- and gun-fighting ever to grace a console. It also featured some of the best in-game graphics and cutscenes of any PS2 game. Like a good anime, there's a spicy quirkiness here that, while occasionally bizarre, is always intriguing and memorable. The game was set before the previous two games, with a younger (and cockier) Dante who has just opened his first demon-hunting agency. To defeat his many foes, Dante has four combat styles and dozens of creative combos to work with—and there's even some puzzles thrown in to challenge your mind as well as your reflexes. In 2012, Capcom released *Devil May Cry HD Collection* for the PlayStation 3 and Xbox 360, which re-mastered the first three games in high definition.

---

[1]   See Vladimir Cole, "PS2 51%, Xbox 34%, GameCube 15%, says Gartner," *Joystiq*, November 13, 2005. Note that Cole disagrees with Gartner's numbers.

[2]   See Michael Humphries, "PS2 is outselling PS3 and PSP," *Geek.com*, July 31, 2009.

When Sony's second generation of its PlayStation arrived in North America in October of 2000, Sega was the sick man of the videogame industry. Its failed Saturn console had damaged the company's finances, as well as its reputation. To avert total disaster, Sega hurriedly rushed its next generation console, the Dreamcast, into production (see Chapter 3.4) in November of 1998; ten months later, shipments made their way to American retailers. The Dreamcast was superior in almost every conceivable way to the Saturn, and it also had the advantage of being the first new generation console on the market by a long shot. However, poor sales led to Sega's withdrawal from the console industry in 2001, just 18 months after the Dreamcast went on the market.

Meanwhile, Microsoft's Xbox and Nintendo's GameCube were still in the planning stages, and wouldn't make their American debuts until November of 2001. This gave Sony's PS2 more than a year to build up its user base without serious competition. Even when these competing consoles finally arrived, they offered no obvious advantage to the well-established PS2, either in terms of technology or game libraries. While the Xbox was able to carve out a nice slice of the American pie, worldwide, the PS2 was barely fazed. Clearly, having such a huge head start to build up its games library and user base had made the PS2 virtually unstoppable.

A less obvious explanation for the PS2's broad appeal was that it was both a great game console and a decent DVD player—and cost just a little more than a dedicated device. At a time when DVDs were finally beginning to replace VHS tapes as the medium of choice for home movies, the PS2 was an exceptional value for gamers and movie lovers alike. The GameCube, of course, was incapable of playing DVDs or audio CDs, and the Xbox required an optional add-on to duplicate the DVD functionality. It's easy to overlook this seemingly mundane feature, but for many PS2 owners, their console played just as many movies as it did games.

Finally, we have to consider the prestige attached to the PlayStation brand. As we saw in Chapter 3.2, the first PlayStation had been a major breakthrough, introducing hordes of gamers raised on 2D platformers to the amazing world of full 3D gaming. For countless thousands of gamers all over the world, the brand represented the bleeding-edge of videogame technology. When Sony announced its plans to develop the PS2 on March 1, 1999, the gaming world took notice, generating endless speculation on online forums and even the evening news circuits. Dazzling demonstrations of planned games such as *Gran Turismo 2000* (released as *Gran Turismo 3: A-Spec* in 2001) and *Tekken Tag Tournament* at industry events fanned the flames, and Sony fueled specu-

lation about its mysterious "Emotion Engine" technology that would allegedly not only harness the number-crunching power of a supercomputer, but even simulate human emotion. By the time the device was ready, the hype had grown to such proportions that one breathless anchor on CNBC struggled to find words to express it: "The PS2 is the biggest thing to come along since... TV was invented!"

The original **"Fat"** version of the PlayStation 2. Fun fact: the raised multicolor PlayStation badge on the front of the console can be rotated to match the alignment of the console.

Dragon Quest VIII: Journey of the Cursed King.

Dragon Quest VIII: Journey of the Cursed King
(2005, Level-5)

The *Dragon Quest* series has long been a favorite among fans of Japanese role-playing games. With this title, the developers pulled out all the stops, creating one of the most massive adventures ever. Of particular note were the character and monster designs, created by the celebrated Akira Toriyama of *Chrono Trigger* fame. The 3D cel-shading technique allowed for attractive visuals, but also convincing emotional expressions and body language. In the words of reviewer Jeremy Dunham of *IGN*, it gave "the feeling that you're playing an anime." The combat was also fun and interesting, even after hundreds of hours of gameplay, thanks to a well-developed enemy AI. While not especially original from a storytelling point of view, *Dragon Quest VIII: Journey of the Cursed King* made up for it by its sheer size, anime-like graphics, and tireless attention to detail.

Sony's vice-president, Mike Morimoto, was more reserved: "The PS2 will be more important than the Betamax," he vowed to reporters from *TIME* magazine.

There's no question that the PS2 was a marvel of modern technology. Ken Kutaragi, the "Father of the PlayStation" and head of Sony's game subsidiary, had partnered with Toshiba to develop the "Emotion Engine CPU." This radical technology consisted of eight different components, each assigned to a specific role. The entire architecture was designed and optimized for 3D gaming. The original PlayStation could generate 360,000 polygons per second. The Emotion Engine could generate 66 million. Such a leap forward was necessary for Kutaragi to achieve his grand vision for the system: "Today's videogame graphics look like computer graphics. Our goal is to achieve a film-like graphics quality that won't make viewers conscious of or annoyed by the fact that they are indeed looking at computer graphics."[3] While the PS2 didn't quite reach this standard, gamers and critics alike were still amazed by the detail seen in games such as *Metal Gear Solid 2*, which featured convincing raindrops, breaking glass, and bullets whose spent casings fell to the floor.

Still, not everyone was thrilled about the PS2. As we've seen throughout this book, a key part of any console's survival hinges on support from third-party developers. Ultimately, gamers buy a console to play great new games, not marvel at its technical specifications. As we'll see in Chapter 3.6, Microsoft was able to lure many prominent PC developers to its ranks by making the transition from Windows to Xbox programming as painless as possible. The radical design of the PS2, while arguably more effective, had a much steeper learning curve. Capcom's Shinji Mikami, creator of the hit *Resident Evil* series, was so frustrated by the PS2's development tools that he considered making his franchise exclusive to the Xbox. His colleague Keiji Inafune had another complaint: the machine was so powerful that developers would go bankrupt before they could build up enough assets to take advantage of it.[4] Even Kutaragi was willing to admit that PS2 development was no easy task, estimating that it would take even experienced developers a full two years to really grasp the system.

---

3 See Douglas C. Perry, "Early PlayStation 2 Rumblings," *IGN*, October 2, 1998.

4 See Dave McCarthy, "The History of PlayStation 2," *Games Industry.biz*, November 22, 2006.

The daunting challenge faced by PS2 developers is evident in its first titles. Enough developers were onboard to provide nearly 30 games for the PS2's launch lineup. Most of the games were mediocre and forgettable at best, and critics weren't impressed. A common lament was that these games would have looked almost as good on the old PlayStation. Many games also suffered from the lack of anti-aliasing, which made the edges of graphics appear jagged, which was shocking to those expecting a console that could exceed the graphical fidelity of Sega's Dreamcast.

Fortunately, a few of the launch titles did a better job showing off the PS2's eventual potential as developers harnessed the system's capabilities. Among these solid launch titles were Electronic Arts' *Madden NFL 2001*, the latest entry in the immensely popular sports franchise, and *SSX*, a snowboarding stunts game; as well as Namco's *Tekken Tag Tournament*, an impressive-looking fighting game. Perhaps the most unusual launch title, however, was Sony's own *FantaVision*, a

SSX is widely considered the best game in the launch lineup, but the artfully executed **FantaVision**, DVD insert shown here, also impressed critics.

colorful action puzzler somewhat comparable to the old *Missile Command* arcade game, although with fireworks rather than missiles. More than any other game, *FantaVision* showed Sony was serious about advancing gaming as an art. They'd do something similar in 2009 with the publication of *Flower* for the PS3.

God of War.

God of War (2005, SCE Studios Santa Monica)

There are few games as brutal, savage, visceral, and—let's face it, *totally badass*, as *God of War*. Set in a land based on ancient Greek myths, this game puts players in the role of Kratos, a demigod whose only chance for salvation lies in murdering Ares, god of war. To achieve that, players will have to guide him through a 3D world loaded with platforming action, puzzles, and plenty of opportunities to put Kratos' blades to good use. Critics marveled at the superb special effects, lavishly detailed environments, and epic fighting combos. Indeed, many critics consider it the best game ever made for the PS2. In 2009, a re-mastered *God of War Collection*, featuring the first two games in high definition, was released for the PS3. No matter which version you play, you'll surely arouse some ancient god's wrath if you don't check it out!

The fact that the PS2 was backward-compatible with the original PlayStation was, at this stage, a vital point in its favor. Many PlayStation games were enhanced when played on a PS2, loading up to 25 percent faster and rendering smoother looking polygons.

The PS2's future brightened considerably when Rockstar, the creator of the popular *Grand Theft Auto* series of open-world action-adventure games, announced that its third entry in the series would debut exclusively on the PS2 on October 22, 2001. This revolutionary title updated the previous installments with a new 3D game engine, and players and critics alike raved about the unprecedented level of detail and freedom offered by the interface. Rockstar followed up with *Grand Theft Auto: Vice City* in 2002,

Rockstar's **Grand Theft Auto** franchise, **Grand Theft Auto III** shown here, played a pivotal role in the PS2's rise to dominance. The controversial games weren't suitable for children—a fact that didn't bother Sony one bit.

a 1980s-inspired take on the genre, and in 2004 with *Grand Theft Auto: San Andreas*, set in a semi-fictional version of 1992 California and Nevada. While all of these games were hits, *San Andreas* was a juggernaut, becoming the best-selling of all PS2 titles with well over 17 million copies sold.

Following a month behind *Grand Theft Auto III* and just in time for the vital 2001 holiday season, *Metal Gear Solid 2: Sons of Liberty* was another undisputed masterpiece. Directed and produced by Hideo Kojima, this stealth-focused action-adventure game was far more than just an audiovisual facelift of its predecessor. Now enemies had advanced artificial intelligence, able to work in squadrons to coordinate deadly flanking and blocking maneuvers. The play-

Metal Gear Solid 2: Sons of Liberty, DVD insert shown here, was a breakthrough title for the PS2 and remains a favorite among fans of stealth games.

er's character also has new abilities, most notably the ability to use cover, and non-violent players can actually complete the entire game without killing a single enemy. Furthermore, the plot and complexity of the narrative has led some critics to classify it as a postmodern work of art. In any case, this title certainly lent credence to Kutaragi's claim that the PS2 was just as capable of artistic and emotional expression as the gritty realism demanded by most action titles.

In 2002, Sony released two PS2 Network Adapters, one for dial-up and another for broadband internet connections. They also cut the price of the system by $100, making it as cheap as a GameCube and much cheaper than an Xbox. Though the PS2's network functionality would never equal the Xbox's, games such as Zipper Interactive's *SOCOM: US Navy SEALs* were quite popular. Rather than offer a unified service like Xbox Live, Sony left it up to individual publishers to run their own third-party servers. Digital Illusions' *Battlefield 2: Modern Combat* was another popular online game; as of this writing, the PS2 servers are still in operation. Guerilla Games' *Killzone* was another solid choice for online gamers, but its servers were finally shutdown along with *SOCOM*'s in 2012.

The PS2 remained in production for a full 12 years, an impressive feat for any console. By the end, its library boasted over 10,000 games. Sadly, its successor, the PS3, released in November of 2006, has not shared its spectacular success; the PS4's final story has yet to be written. In any

case, it's hard to imagine any other console enjoying a window of opportunity like the one presented to the PS2. Unlike the Game-Cube, it could easily serve as a DVD player, and, unlike the Xbox, it was custom-built for 3D gaming, with no Windows or PC vestiges to worry about. In short, the PS2 was the right machine, at the right time, for the right price. It may not have been the biggest thing since TV, but it sure beat out the Betamax.

Sony's PS2 Network Adapter, shown here attached to a third-party hard drive, was inserted into the expansion bay. Both the Network Adapter and hard drive were required to play **Final Fantasy XI**.

Technical Specifications

The PS2's most remarkable feature was its Emotion Engine CPU, co-designed with Toshiba. Optimized for 3D processing, it handled all the geometry, world and behavior simulation (including AI and physics), and housekeeping functions. It ran at 294.912 MHz, with 32 MB of main memory and 4 MB for video. Most games ran at standard 640 × 480 resolution, although some games supported 480p, 720p, and even 1080i. The original "fat" version weighed 4.9 pounds and was 11.9 inches wide, 3.1 inches tall, and 7.2 inches deep. The PS2's disc drive could support both CD-ROM and DVD-ROM discs, running up to 24x and 4x, respectively.

The console had two controller ports, two USB ports, one proprietary AV output, an SPDIF output for sound, and an expansion bay. There were also two slots for memory cards. It also included an IEEE 1394 port for connecting PS2s together for multiplayer. The USB ports could be used to attach standard PC accessories such as mice and keyboards. The expansion bay was for adding a network adapter and hard drive.

Ico.

Ico (2001, Team Ico)

Ico was one of the first critical triumphs for the PlayStation, and arguably an important step forward for videogames as an expressive medium. Everyone gushed about the artwork, effects, and convincing character animation. But what really makes the game special is the story and emotional attachment players have for its characters, Ico and Yorda. Ico is a boy with an odd birth defect—horns—and to ward off evil, his people seal him into a sarcophagus inside an old castle. Of course, Ico manages to escape, and quickly runs into a mysterious princess named Yorda. The two must work together to escape, and much of the gameplay is focused on Ico helping the less-athletic Yorda follow him up, down, and around the castle's many platforms, obstacles, and puzzles—all the while protecting the princess from the evil shadowy beings that lurk the grounds. The developers created new languages for the game, which, with the exception of Yorda's speech, are rendered in subtitles for the player's benefit. Ico's inability to talk to Yorda was a good justification for one of the game's key mechanics—holding hands, which helped players bond with the princess and heightened the desire to keep her safe from the shadows. Few who have played Ico can speak about it without a certain wistfulness—it's emotional stuff. If you're delighted by _Ico_, check out _Shadow of the Colossus_, another superb game that is far more than the sum of its parts. You can also check out both games in the high definition re-mastered package _The Ico & Shadow of the Colossus Collection_, released for the PS3 in 2011.

The "DualShock 2" controller was, at first glance, just the old DualShock with a new color scheme. However, it was a considerable improvement. Almost all of its buttons, including the directional pad, were pressure sensitive, enabling more refined control. While some reviewers chided Sony for not introducing something more radical, most commended them for making only minor adjustments to an already excellent device. It was also backward compatible with the original PlayStation. All in all, the DualShock 2 was a wonderful controller that is still widely regarded as the best of its class.

The DualShock 2 closely resembled the original, but had more refined controls. Image courtesy of Evan-Amos, Vanamo Media.

The Accessories and Later Models

Considering the vastness of the PS2's user base, it's hardly surprising that a great many accessories were built to support it. Perhaps the most significant of these is the PlayStation Network Adapter, which allowed owners to play with their friends online using a dial-up or broadband internet connection. While only supported by some games, this add-on was crucial in reducing the PS2's vulnerability to the Xbox. Another multiplayer option was the Multitap, which allowed owners to plug in up to four controllers for simultaneous use; adding a second Multitap allowed up to eight people to join in.

Another highly anticipated accessory was the Hard Disk Drive (PS2 HDD). Sony released a version in Japan in 2001, but delayed until 2004 to offer it in the United States. It had a 40 GB capacity and, if supported by the game in question, would reduce loading times, store saved games, and backup memory cards. Unauthorized products allowed users to copy entire games to their drives or other hard drives. A few games used the drive in conjunction with the network adapter to provide additional content, such as extra maps for the *SOCOM* games titles. The network adapter and HDD were required for the MMORPG, *Final Fantasy XI*. One version of the game included the HDD with the game pre-installed on disc.

The memory cards contained 8 MB of Flash Memory, and were all but a necessity, since without one you couldn't save games or transfer your data to another system. Third parties offered their own memory cards of varying capacity.

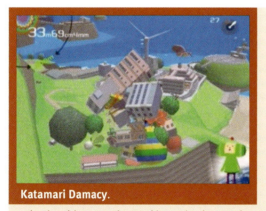

Katamari Damacy.

Katamari Damacy (2004, Namco)

The developers of this title had four driving goals: novelty, simplicity, enjoyment, and humor. After playing *Katamari Damacy* for a few minutes, you'll see they nailed each one. The core of the gameplay is guiding a magical sticky ball (the "katamari") around some truly creative levels. Any item that the ball rolls over becomes stuck to it, eventually culminating in a giant, unwieldy ball that becomes a star. The game's bizarre, surreal aesthetics are enough to make you think the game was designed on another planet. Critics rightfully praised its uniqueness and enjoyable gameplay, and it received several awards for its innovative game design.

Another key PS2 accessory was the DVD remote control. As stated above, the PS2 could play DVD movies straight out of the box, but, naturally, a wireless remote made things more convenient. The DVD remote control, available from both Sony and various third parties, requires a controller port for the infrared dongle (some featured a pass-through), and space on a memory card for software enhancements.

Perhaps the most innovative of all PS2 accessories was the EyeToy USB Camera. Its marketing promised that the device would allow players to use their body movement to control games, map their face onto game characters, and record video messages onto memory cards. Its collection of casual mini-games seemed to anticipate the flood of

The EyeToy anticipated many later devices as well as the casual/party games movement that would drive sales of Nintendo's Wii and Microsoft's Kinect for Xbox 360.

casual party games that would help make the Nintendo Wii so successful. The camera was designed by Richard Marks, who envisioned it as a way to build a more intuitive, "natural" interface with implications for mixed reality games. Like the Wii, the EyeToy had broad appeal that extended far beyond traditional gamers. The 12 cutesy games that were bundled with the device let players dance, box, spin plates, wash windows, and much more. One reviewer claimed that if "you get this for your girlfriend, she'll be hogging the PS2 forever."[5]

In 2004, Sony released the "Slim" version of the PS2. Obviously, it was smaller than its predecessor—far smaller—but it also had the added utility of a built-in Ethernet port. However, one major limitation is that it lacks the expansion bay necessary for the hard drive.

The PlayStation 2 "Slim," shown with its included DualShock 2 controller. Image courtesy of Evan-Amos, Vanamo Media.

---

[5] See Douglass C. Perry, "EyeToy: Play," *IGN*, November 4, 2003.

> You hear that? Sounded like something closed.

Kingdom Hearts.

Kingdom Hearts (2002, Square)

What videogame character is more popular than Mario? The producers of this game weren't sure there were any, including their own highly successful *Final Fantasy* cast. So, they turned outside the world of videogames to recruit Mickey Mouse and his friends from Walt Disney. The result was a role-playing game like no other, in which Donald Duck and Goofy join a young boy named Sora in his search for Mickey Mouse and his friends Riku and Kairi. Of course, the party must battle plenty of enemies—dark creatures called Heartless, to complete their epic quest. The game was an instant hit, selling millions of copies and launching a new franchise, and even a manga series. The fun gameplay would have been enough to recommend it anyway, but the novelty of seeing your favorite Disney characters alongside those of *Final Fantasy*'s is well worth the price of admission. In 2013, Square Enix released *Kingdom Heart HD 1.5 Remix* for the PS3, which includes *Kingdom Hearts Final Mix* and *Re:Chain of Memories* in high definition and with trophy support.

The Sony PlayStation 2 Community Then and Now

It's no exaggeration to say that many PS2 owners truly loved their console. This was particularly true of fans of Japanese games, an area where the PS2 was a clear winner. However, there was no shortage of first-person shooters, sports, or action-adventure titles, both of domestic and overseas origin. There truly was something for everyone. That said, while close, it didn't quite nail the casual audience as effectively as the Wii.

As the major system of its era, the PS2 also enjoyed regular, in-depth coverage in major gaming magazines, as well its own *Official US PlayStation Magazine*, which included a sampler disc with demos and videos. Given the PS2's lack of built-in networking, these sampler discs were vital in marketing new games.

In 2002, Sony released Linux for PlayStation 2 (PS2 Linux). It included the operating system, keyboard, mouse, VGA adapter, and the network adapter. With this tool, users could turn their

PS2 into a full-fledged computer. Naturally, this package was exciting for amateur game developers, hackers, and modders, who met on the official site and Internet Relay Chat (IRC) to discuss their projects. Most support and communities around this initiative, however, have since died off.

The original kit for Linux for PlayStation 2. A hacker's dream.

Maximo: Ghosts to Glory.

Maximo: Ghosts to Glory (2002, Capcom)

While 3D hack and slash action games are common on the PS2, 3D action games as easy and intuitive to control as their 2D forefathers are rare indeed. In many ways, this game is an homage to the fun yet grueling challenge of the old *Ghosts 'n Goblins* arcade game from 1985, but remade in full 3D with a third-person perspective. You control the titular character, a warrior who must whack and thwack his way through five different areas in search of a princess. Don't let the campy, cartoonish graphics fool you—this is no cakewalk, but instead a game demanding skill and precision. If you want a modern action game that captures that good old arcade feel, *Maximo: Ghosts to Glory* is hard to beat.

The PS2 homebrew scene is still quite active, supported by sites such as http://psx-scene.com. So far, the community has focused on applications, especially modding tools, hacks, graphical demos, and emulators, rather than original games. This situation might change soon, however, as the last few commercial publishers have stopped supporting the PS2, possibly leading to broader support for more independent and hobbyist development.

Ratchet & Clank: Up Your Arsenal.

Ratchet & Clank: Up Your Arsenal
(2004, Insomniac Games)

This game was the third in the franchise, and by most accounts the best—and that's saying something, considering how well the earlier games were received. While the new action-adventure game made plenty of refinements, the biggest was a new online multiplayer game option. The story has the titular characters in pursuit of Dr. Nefarious, whose mission in life is to destroy all of it. Fortunately, the good guys have an abundance of weapons, gadgets, ships, and dune buggies to aid their cause. While the audiovisuals and memorable characters are definite bullet points, it's really the insanely compelling gameplay that sells this one. Critics went beyond mere praise in their reviews, instead simply ordering readers to immediately go out and purchase the game. It sold millions of copies and is found on most of the "best of" lists of PS2 games. If you like this game, also try *Jak 3*, another slick and well-honed action adventure that was released around the same time. In 2012, Sony released *Ratchet & Clank Collection* for the PS3, which includes the first three games in the series re-mastered in high definition.

Collecting Sony PlayStation 2 Systems

Now is the ideal time to begin collecting for the PS2. Systems in excellent condition can be found for little effort or money. Furthermore, PS2 games are still readily found in bargain bins and used games section in many shops. The system hasn't aged enough to assume "collector" status, so expect to find amazing deals on complete systems accompanied by dozens of games on online auction and related sites. As always, some games are particularly rare and desirable: *Baldur's Gate: Dark Alliance II, Capcom vs. SNK 2: Mark of the Millennium 2001*, and *Marvel vs. Capcom 2: New Age of Heroes*, as just three examples, all fit into that category.

Sly Cooper and the Thievius Raccoonus.

Sly Cooper and the Thievius Raccoonus
(2002, Sucker Punch Productions)

If you're into stealth games but don't like the gritty realism of the *Metal Gear Solid* series, this game might be just the thing. Featuring a cast of anthropomorphic animals, this stealthy action game was acclaimed for its tight, precise controls and addictive gameplay. Avoiding enemies, dodging spotlights, and spotting tripwires are all fun, but the developers also threw in some delightful mini-games, including kart-racing and rhythm. The splendid cel-shaded art and superb voice work add to the charm of this cartoon come to life. In 2010, Sony released *The Sly Collection* for the PS3, which re-mastered all three of the PS2 *Sly Cooper* games in high-definition, and even added 3D support for *Sly 3: Honor Among Thieves*, for those players with 3D-capable televisions.

The biggest choice to make is whether to get one of the older "fat" models or the "slim." If space is an issue, go for the slim, but keep in mind you won't be able to use an official hard drive with it. That's not a deal breaker for most people, but if you want to benefit from its faster loading times in select games, you'll need the "fat" model instead.

Another factor to consider when purchasing a used PS2 is whether it's been "modded" or "chipped." Such a system has the questionable advantage of being able to run homebrew and pirated software without any extra hassle. Otherwise, you'll need a modded PS2 memory card, such as "Free McBoot," or a boot disc.

Sony released several different colors of its PS2 over the years, including limited editions Super Red, Metallic Silver, Light Yellow, Snow White, and Star Blue. Expect to spend at least twice as much acquiring these systems, even though the differences are purely cosmetic.

Emulating the Sony PlayStation 2

By far the easiest way to play PS2 games today is to buy a used console. For the broadest flexibility, consider picking up an early model PlayStation 3 (CECHBxx or CECHAxx), which plays original PlayStation as well as PS2 games in hardware.

SSX Tricky.

SSX Tricky (2001, Electronic Arts Canada)

The PS2's mediocre launch lineup lent some credence to developers' complaints about how difficult it was to program for. Programmers needed time to figure out its hardware and build a new bag of tricks. No title better exemplifies this than *SSX Tricky*, a follow up to the earlier, already excellent, *SSX*, and the game it really aspired to be. Whether or not you care for the actual sport, *SSX Tricky* will lure you in with its fun tracks, awesome tricks, and characters based on and voiced by celebrities like Billy Zane and Lucy Liu. The acclaimed soundtrack boasts cuts from 15 artists, including Mixmaster Mike and Run DMC. The innovative controls made it easy to perform tricks including death- (and physics-) defying maneuvers like Triple Back Flip Superman and the 1080 Morgan Grinder. The DVD also featured over an hour of special features. Receiving near-perfect scores by every major critic, *SSX Tricky* is definitely not a game your PS2 collection should be without.

Emulating a PS2 on a modern PC can be frustrating, especially if you don't have a powerful system. That said, emulation is surprisingly robust for such a recently deprecated system. The standout emulator is *PCSX2*, which runs many games at near 100 percent accuracy. This program is available for Windows, Macintosh, and Linux, and is highly customizable and configurable. Of course, not every game will work well or at all with the emulator, but most major games are covered.[6]

There are two other notable emulators available: *PS2emu* and *NeutrinoSX2*. As of this writing, there's little reason to prefer these to *PCSX2*.

In any case, you'll need a PS2 bios file to run these emulators. To get around the obvious legal issues involved with hosting these

PCSX2 is the most capable PS2 emulator.

---

6   A complete list of games playable in the PCSX2 emulator is available at http://wiki.pcsx2.net.

files themselves, most emulator sites will not include these files in their download package. You'll either need to work out the technical means necessary to extract one from an actual PS2, or simply download one elsewhere. Keep in mind, though, that BIOS files vary by region and version, so select the one that is compatible with the software you intend to run with it.

Microsoft Xbox (2001)

History

When Microsoft first announced its plans to enter the console market at the Game Developers Conference in 2000, many people thought the company had lost its way. There were three good reasons to doubt that even the richest company in the world could bully its way into the console market: Microsoft's reputation as a business-oriented company, Japan's undisputed dominance of the console industry, and a long-standing prejudice by many console fans against PCs.

First of all, while Microsoft always dabbled in games publishing, they were primarily known as a serious, business-centric corporation, making the bulk of its money from operating systems and productivity software. In 1996, their much hipper rival Apple had tried to enter the console market with their Pippin—a multimedia console that had failed miserably. Sure, Microsoft had deeper pockets than Apple, but would it really be willing to invest the billions of dollars it would take to convince their skeptics that they really understood gaming? Certainly, Microsoft's past experiments in the console space, like in 1992 with the Tandy Memorex Visual Information System (VIS) multimedia console (which used a version of Windows 3.1), and in 1998 with Sega's Dreamcast (which used Windows CE as one of its operating systems)[1], didn't exactly instill any confidence either.

Secondly, after the Great Videogame Crash, the bulk of the console industry moved to Japan, where it had dominated from ever since. For many years, Nintendo ruled, but the upstart Sony had wrestled control away from them and their rival Sega with the PlayStation. The PlayStation

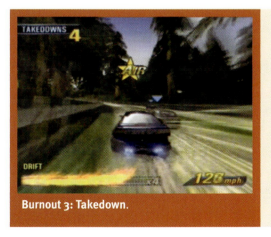

Burnout 3: Takedown.

Burnout 3: Takedown (2004, Criterion Studios)

In many car racing games, the objective is to *avoid* smashing into things. This game reverses that mechanic, rewarding players for causing as much mayhem as possible. The more damage you do, the more cars you unlock—up to 70. There are also 40 tracks to play on. You could also race with up to six others online. The game received several awards and accolades, and most critics agree that the arcade-style gameplay will appeal even to gamers who dislike traditional racing games. If you don't care for the soundtrack, which features over 40 licensed tracks, you can create your own mix.

---

[1] See Chapter 3.4.

was a juggernaut, and had already lured away several prominent Windows game developers. Sony had announced its successor, the PlayStation 2, back in March 1999, and it would hit American shores like a tsunami in October 2000, wowing everyone with its promise of amazing graphics and processing power. Even if Microsoft could somehow design a system that was technically superior to the PS2, would gamers and developers pay it any attention? After all, Japanese gamers tend to be fiercely loyal to companies from their own country.[2] Even if Microsoft could get a foothold in America, as a non-Japanese company, they would struggle with this cultural bias, hampering their ability to compete globally. While many gamers were curious about what Microsoft was up to, the smart money was on Sony and Japan.

Finally, and perhaps most importantly, few gamers were interested in what they assumed would be a boring Windows PC in console clothing. Then as now, many gamers preferred a device dedicated solely to gaming. Although several manufacturers over the years have tried to blur the boundary, the results have seldom been good.[3]

The story of the Xbox begins in 1998, when four men—Kevin Bachus, Seamus Blackley, Otto Berkes, and Ten Hase met secretly to take apart some Dell laptops. Their idea was to study the laptop's components and see if they could come up with a prototype for a Windows-based game console. When their "DirectX Box" prototype was ready, they brought it to Ed Fries, head of Microsoft's gaming division. Fries liked the idea, particu-

The original Xbox was dismissed by some gamers as a PC masquerading as a console, but, in reality, its operating system and hardware components were highly customized for gaming.

larly its reliance on Windows and DirectX, which would make it a snap for Windows game developers to make the transition to console development.

It was time to pitch the idea at a staff meeting. In proper Microsoft fashion, Hase created a PowerPoint presentation that detailed the team's vision for a gaming console based on DirectX. Much to Hase's embarrassment, the staff thought the whole thing was a joke. They felt there was simply no way the team could mass produce such a device at a price that could compete with other consoles. Consoles cost hundreds of dollars; computers cost thousands. What the team had proposed was not only infeasible—it was laughable.

Luckily, Bill Gates had been growing anxious that Sony posed a grave threat to the future of Windows as a gaming platform. At the Game Developer Conference in 1999, Ken Kutaragi, CEO of Sony Entertainment, declared the death of PC gaming in the wake of the new PlayStation 2. "Entertainment content requires an entertainment device," he said to thunderous

2   See Brian Ashcraft, "Square Enix Says Japanese Retail 'Prejudiced' Against Western Games," *Kotaku*, March 1, 2010. Yoichi Wada, a business executive at Square Enix, said that "even now, there have been people in Japan using the label *youge* (Western games) with a terribly discriminatory meaning." For these gamers, a *youge* product doesn't even count as a game, but rather something cheap, fake, or alien. Wada argued that it was retailers who were most guilty of this prejudice, refusing to stock non-Japanese titles on their shelves.

3   See Chapter 1.8 on the Coleco Adam or Chapter 1.5 on Mattel's attempts. With that in mind, Microsoft did do a fusion of sorts in 2013 when it was announced that the Xbox One would run an operating system functionally similar to Windows 8, whose core technology now powers all of their platforms.

Crimson Skies: High Road to Revenge
(2003, FASA Studio)

The first *Crimson Skies* was released in 2000 for Windows. Set in a memorable alternate reality version of 1937, it was an arcade-inspired flight simulator with a fun role-playing mechanic by FASA (a tabletop role-playing, war game, and board game maker). *High Road to Revenge* updated the formula and customized the interface for the Xbox controller. In addition to a superb single-player campaign, you could also play with four others (split screen) or up to 16 others using the system link.

Crimson Skies: High Road to Revenge.

applause.[4] Gates sensed the tide was turning against PC gaming, and that didn't bode well for the future of Windows. After all, it was gaming that had been the driving force behind the steady stream of upgraded, yet cheaper components that had made Windows viable in the first place. Without the rapid advances in technology demanded by the gaming industry, we might still be computing with monochrome monitors and internal beepers for sound.

Gates asked the DirectX team to survey the situation and report back. They concluded that the PC was likely to maintain its edge in hardware, providing better graphics and processing power than any device Sony could possibly deliver. Furthermore, the price of these advanced components had been steadily dropping due to intense competition. The team argued that they *could* build a console based on these components at a reasonable price point.

Unlike those at the staff meeting, Gates didn't laugh at the idea—instead, he asked the team to step up their efforts to build a unit that could compete head-to-head with Sony's PlayStation 2. He gave them until the end of the year to have the unit ready for retail—which gave them fewer than six months to turn their clunky prototype into something resembling a true gaming console.

The team set out to define what the "console experience" actually meant. They decided that the unit had to boot up immediately, not go through the lengthy startup sequence of a PC. Furthermore, loading a game should be as easy as inserting a disc—not wading through menus and installation procedures. They realized that Windows 2000, which they'd been building their console around, was simply too bulky for their purposes. They needed something much lighter and faster, but still close enough to Windows for PC developers to make the transition easily.

The result was a new gaming operating system based on the Windows 2000 kernel, but heavily customized for speed and efficiency.[5] Programming Xbox games would be similar to making games for Windows, with APIs (application programming interfaces) familiar to Windows developers. However, software built for the Xbox would not be directly compatible with Windows PCs.

---

4 See "The Xbox Story," *VG24/7*, August 5, 2011, www.vg247.com/2011/08/02/the-xbox-story-part-1-the-birth-of-a-console.

5 A "kernel" is a middle manager that shuffles between software applications and hardware. This frees up developers from having to worry about interacting directly with the CPU or other components, which requires a great deal of highly specialized knowledge. The Xbox team had a massive advantage over their Windows counterparts, since they knew the exact make and model of the components installed in every Xbox.

The team shopped around to get the best deals on a processor and components like the GPU and hard drive. They ended up with an Intel Pentium III CPU and a custom GPU from Nvidia. Since their Windows-based operating system couldn't run without a hard drive, they included an 8 GB hard disk for internal storage—a first for the console industry. The hard disk would add considerably to the manufacturing cost, but, as we'll see, it would play a key role in the success of the Xbox.

Gates knew his company needed a major publicity splash to build momentum for the console, so he did something he'd never done before: attend and present at the Game Developer Conference in person. It was there, in San Jose, that Gates first traded his business casuals for the famous X-emblazoned black leather jacket and announced that the era of the Xbox had arrived. Perhaps the jacket alone would have been enough to convince gamers and developers that Microsoft was now cool, but just to be safe, they churned a half billion dollars into marketing for the device.[6]

Bill Gates (left) donned an X-emblazoned black leather jacket to announce the Xbox at the Game Developer Conference. On the right is Seamus Blackley, one of the Xbox's designers. www.gdcvault.com/play/1014852/GDC-2000-Opening-Keynote-Bill.

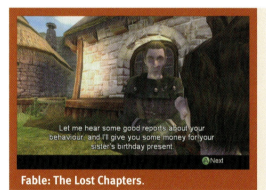

Let me hear some good reports about your behaviour, and I'll give you some money for your sister's birthday present

Next

Fable: The Lost Chapters.

Fable (2004, Lionhead Studios)

Long in development, Peter Molyneux's epic *Fable* was one of the most ambitious roleplaying games ever attempted. The idea was to control a character from cradle to grave, with the character's appearance altering based on his actions (think *The Picture of Dorian Gray*). While there was still plenty of combat, the roleplaying went much deeper. Other characters in the game will notice and begin to treat the character differently based on his behavior. While critics generally praised the game, Molyneux failed to deliver many of the more intriguing features he promised, including multiplayer options and the ability for the character to marry and have children. Perhaps the most infamous, though, is the "acorn incident," in which Molyneux boasted that if the character knocks an acorn out of a tree, it'll eventually grow into a new tree. When the feature failed to appear, he swore it would show up in the sequel—but it wasn't there, either. Fortunately, what Lionhead was able to deliver was more than enough to please most fans of the genre, and the 2005 release, *Fable: The Lost Chapters*, enhanced the game significantly. In 2014, Microsoft released Fable Anniversary for the Xbox 360, a remastered version of *Fable: The Lost Chapters*.

---

6   See Jeffrey M. O'Brien, "The Making of the Xbox," *Wired*, November 2001, www.wired.com/wired/archive/9.11/flex.html.

Gates realized, however, that no amount of advertisements could sell a machine without a great software lineup. To that end, Microsoft spent $30 million acquiring a little-known company called Bungee, whose new *Halo* game would serve as the platform's premier first-person shooter. The move proved incredibly fortuitous later on, but we should keep in mind that, at the time, first-person shooters were a rarity on consoles. Indeed, to that point, the only console first-person shooter really worth talking about was Rare's *GoldenEye 007* for the Nintendo 64 (see chapter 3.3).

All in all, Microsoft was able to sign on 150 developers, and rapidly sent out 500 development kits to spur their efforts. The only major holdout was Electronic Arts, who was dubious that Microsoft would really have their back if the Xbox flopped in the marketplace. Unlike for Sega and the Dreamcast, they'd eventually come around, but the lack of support from one of the world's biggest game companies didn't look promising for the future of the console.

When the console was at last revealed at the Consumer Electronics Show in 2001, Gates was on stage again, this time sharing it with Dwayne "The Rock" Johnson. The Rock was, as always, a crowd pleaser, and his witty banter with Gates had the place rolling. What was less impressive, though, was the Xbox itself. Journalists criticized the big, clunky unit and its even more awkward controllers that even looked large in The Rock's hands. Compared to the sleek PlayStation 2 control-

Microsoft brought on Dwayne "The Rock" Johnson to promote their new console. Their witty banter and antics delighted the crowd at the 2001 Consumer Electronics Show. www.youtube.com/watch?v=IdjAeoqWskU.

lers, these looked primitive and monstrous. These would eventually be redesigned, but the first impression was in—and it was bleak.

Fortunately, the dire predictions or blunt criticisms weren't enough to scuttle the launch on November 15, 2001. Even at the initial price of $299, the company quickly sold out. It was a much more impressive reception, in fact, than Nintendo had received following its GameCube launch, which had no must-play launch title of its own like *Halo: Combat Evolved*. In fact, it's impossible to overstate *Halo*'s value to Microsoft's early success.[7]

In a little under five months after its release, *Halo: Combat Evolved* broke sales records at the time, with a little over 1 million units sold.[8] The success of future console's launch-day game releases would continue to be compared against the Xbox's *Halo: Combat Evolved* for years to come. As IGN's Ryan McCraffrey would tweet on August 20, 2013, in regards to the Xbox One's *Titanfall* (2014), "If @Titanfallgame was a Day One launch title, it would be the killer-est killer app since Halo 1 on OG Xbox. Still a likely system-seller." While sales for the Xbox were understandably dismal in Japan, it was a hit nearly everywhere else, especially after its first major price drop in April of 2002 helped spur on sales even further.

---

[7]   The Xbox sold 1.53 million units in its first three months in North America alone, a record that wouldn't be broken until the blockbuster launches of both the PS4 and Xbox One in November 2013.

[8]   www.microsoft.com/en-us/news/press/2002/apr02/04-08halomillionpr.aspx.

Although masterpieces like *Halo: Combat Evolved*, *Fable*, and *Knights of the Old Republic* would do much to secure the console's reputation, the real "killer app" was not a game, but a service: Xbox Live. As we saw in Chapter 3.1, Microsoft had been quick to realize the revolutionary potential of the internet, supporting it in Windows 95 and even creating their own web browser, Internet Explorer. It's hardly surprising, then, that the Xbox would connect to the internet. At the time, many people still relied on dial-up for internet access, and Sega had opted for a dial-up modem in their Dreamcast (Chapter 3.4). It was a sensible move, considering that only 4.4 percent of American households had broadband in 2000.[9] Sony wouldn't add built-in support for networking until the second iteration of its PlayStation 2, the "Slim," in 2004. Until then, PlayStation 2 owners had to settle for the $40 Online Adapter and tedious, confusing, title-by-title configurations for online games. Microsoft, however, built an Ethernet port into every Xbox. The advantages were obvious, and they predicted (correctly) that significant broadband adoption was just around the corner.

Ninja Gaiden Black.

Ninja Gaiden Black (2005, Team Ninja)

In 2004, Team Ninja released *Ninja Gaiden* for the Xbox, a reimagining of the popular arcade game from 1988. The team had planned to release the game for the PS2 instead, but Tomonobu Itagaki, the game's creator, was impressed with the development kits Microsoft had put together. The decision might well have been part of their larger strategy to target gamers outside of Japan—and they succeeded; the game was a hit everywhere *but* its mother country. The game offered a third-person "over the shoulder" perspective, and combined the puzzle-solving and exploration of the *Zelda* series with a mature martial arts theme—with gore and violence aplenty. *Ninja Gaiden Black*, released a year later, added new foes, cutscenes, and integrated the two "Hurricane" bonus packs from the original game.

The big question, though, was how exactly the company would utilize this high-speed connection. One idea was to use the Xbox's hard drive to allow game developers to sell additional game content online, such as new levels and maps. This concept, later called DLC for "Downloadable Content," was soon an industry buzzword. Before, game publishers only made money at the time the game was purchased. Now, they could continue to reap profits long after the game had faded from retail—and recoup some of the losses incurred from the rapidly expanding used game market. It would also allow developers to cheaply "patch" games that had already shipped. Instead of sending out replacement discs, developers could simply upload fixed versions of the troublesome binaries. There was a negative side to this: now publishers could feel better about shipping games with bugs, knowing these could be fixed later with patches.

More famously, though, Xbox Live would become the hub for online competitive gaming, exponentially upping the replay value of games such as *Halo* and the *Call of Duty* series. From

9   See Mike Futter, "The Complete History of Xbox Live (Abridged)," *Game Informer*, May 19, 2013, www.gameinformer.com/b/features/archive/2013/05/19/the-complete-history-of-xbox-live-abridged.aspx.

now on, finishing the single-player campaign was only the start of your "training." After that, it was time to head online to fight against human opponents from all over the world. Gaming had finally returned to the glorious competitive days of the arcade (see Chapter 1.1).

Xbox Live wasn't available until November 2002, a full year after the Xbox launch. They charged $49.99 per year for the service, a figure that hasn't varied much since. Unlike their computer gaming counterparts, Xbox gamers wouldn't have ready access to a keyboard to chat with other players. To address this limitation, Microsoft insisted that Xbox Live-enabled games would offer voice chat. Inevitably, many users have abused this service, spewing foul language, including sexist and racist rants. Dealing with the problem has been a persistent problem for Microsoft, who has overreacted on a number of occasions—such as deleting user names (called "Gamertags") like "Gaywood," which turned out to be legitimate surnames. They also offered the option to mute offensive players and "voice-masking" headsets for gamers that could, in theory, at least, disguise one's gender or age. In any case, fears over voice chat abuse didn't stop over 350,000 users from signing on within the first three months. By 2005, they had 2 million.

Xbox Live also gave gamers access to lesser known, "budget-priced" games that weren't available at retail. This service, called Xbox Live Arcade, featured many titles from 1980s' arcades, such as *Ms. Pac-Man*, *Joust*, and *Gauntlet*, as well as casual games such as *Bejeweled* and *Bookworm.* Microsoft would continue to evolve its online offerings, especially after the release of the 360 in 2005.

As expected, former Windows developers would play a large role in building the Xbox's games library. To bolster its lineup, Microsoft acquired FASA Studio and made them part of Microsoft Game Studios. This company had established itself with its *Mech*-franchise, and their Xbox exclusives *MechAssault* (2002) and *Crimson Skies: High Road to Revenge* (2003) were praised by critics and sold well. Indeed, IGN singled out *MechAssault* as the best game for Xbox Live. Bethesda Game Studios was another prominent PC developer who made the move, releasing their open-world role-playing game *The Elder Scrolls III: Morrowind* for Xbox in 2002. Microsoft Game Studios would publish Lionhead Studio's *Fable* for the Xbox in 2004, another critically-acclaimed role-playing game. Microsoft acquired Lionhead Studio in 2006. Valve Corporation, which had been founded by former Microsoft employees Gabe Newell and Mike Harrington, brought its mega-hit *Counter-Strike* to Xbox in 2003, which quickly became a staple of Xbox Live. BioWare's *Star Wars: Knights of the Old Republic,* released in 2003, was another masterpiece, and arguably one of the best *Star Wars* games ever produced for any system. They'd release *Jade Empire* in 2005, another great RPG, and introduce their *Mass Effect* series for the 360. The presence of these and other notable former Windows developers helped distinguish the Xbox from the competition.

Despite all of these innovative games and features, the Xbox was only a minor irritant for Sony, even though their online gaming options were much less unified and convenient as Xbox Live. Microsoft sold over 24 million Xboxes, placing the console just above Nintendo's GameCube at just over 21 million. Both consoles are dwarfed, however, by Sony's staggering figure of 155 million units for its PlayStation 2, which remains the best-selling console of all time (see Chapter 3.5). As many expected, the Xbox flopped miserably in Japan despite a robust marketing campaign, selling only 2 million units compared to Sony's 21.[10]

---

[10] Fortunately for Microsoft, the playing field would even out dramatically in the next generation—the PS3 and 360 each sold around the same number of units worldwide.

Oddworld: Stranger's Wrath

Oddworld: Stranger's Wrath
(2005, Oddword Inhabitants, Inc.)

Lorne Lanning's *Oddworld* series traces its roots back to a seminal platforming/puzzle game from 1997 (see Chapter 3.2). *Stranger's Wrath* departs from the formula, using the third-person perspective popularized by the later *Zelda* games as well as first-person shooter mechanics for combat. You could freely switch between these modes. It was marketed as a "shooter unlike any you've seen before," and they certainly hit the mark. Unlike the cutesy lead characters from the earlier games, this time you play as "The Stranger," a tough, Clint Eastwood-inspired bounty hunter. Load up your double-barreled crossbow with live ammo, and we mean that literally—your ammo consists of living creatures such as Chippunks and Boombats.

If there was one thing that Microsoft had, it was money, and they knew they had to spend it freely if the Xbox were to survive. Beyond lavishing money on expansive marketing campaigns, they set the retail price of the Xbox so low ($299) they actually lost money on each unit sold. This move was felt necessary to keep them competitive with Sony, who was charging $299 for the PS2. In April of 2002, Microsoft dropped the price by $100, forcing Sony to follow suit two months later. According to some estimates, Microsoft lost $168 for each Xbox sold.[11] However, underpricing consoles is a common strategy for manufacturers, who recoup their losses through software and licensing. In the Xbox's case, licensing fees brought in $7–9 per game sold.[12]

Perhaps the peak of the original Xbox came in November of 2004, with the long-anticipated release of Bungee's *Halo 2.* Within 24 hours, the game had sold 2.5 million copies, making it the most successful product launch in the history of entertainment. Eventually selling over 8 million

copies, *Halo 2* received near-perfect reviews in major gaming publications and solidified Bungee's reputation as a master of the genre. While the game's epic storyline and incredible graphics were lauded by critics, it also introduced a new matchmaking system of playlists and parties with a skill-ranking system. Now, joining online sessions was much faster and friendlier for novices.

The long-anticipated release of **Halo 2** was a pivotal event for Bungee and the Xbox as a platform. While the epic single-player campaign was praised by critics, the multiplayer action on Xbox Live was the major draw.

11   See Dean Takahashi, "The Making of the Xbox: Microsoft's Journey to the Next Generation (Part 2)," *Venturebeat*, November 15, 2011, http://venturebeat.com/2011/11/15/the-making-of-the-xbox-part-2. Read more at http://venturebeat.com/2011/11/15/the-making-of-the-xbox-part-2/#Swm5uWsdgVOqw6k1.99.

12   This figure is according to CNN's analysts. See Chris Morris, "Microsoft Launches Xbox," *CNN Money*, November 15, 2001, http://money.cnn.com/2001/11/15/technology/xbox.

Electronic Arts published its first games for the Xbox in the last few months of 2001. This lineup included its bestselling sports franchises, *Madden NFL 2002, NBA Live 2002,* and *NHL 2002.* The company's strategy was to spread its wares across all major platforms, avoiding the situation they'd faced in the 1980s when Nintendo held the reigns. In any case, it must have been a relief to Microsoft to finally have these titles available, since legions of fans would pass on any system that didn't offer the latest and greatest sports titles. Indeed, EA's failure to support Sega's Dreamcast clearly contributed to it its early demise.

Sega also played an important role in establishing the Xbox in the early years. With their console manufacturing days behind them, the company turned to software development, and released several key games for the Xbox in 2002. These included a string of sports titles as well as *Jet Set Radio Future, Panzer Dragoon Orta, Crazy Taxi 3: High Roller,* and *Sega GT 2002.* These Xbox-exclusive titles may well have convinced many former Dreamcast fans to choose the Xbox over the PlayStation 2 for their next console.

The last Xbox rolled off the assembly line at the end of 2008, purportedly to clear the deck for the 360. However, Nvidia had stopped making graphic chips for them back in 2005, following a vicious falling out over pricing. For the 360, Microsoft turned to Nvidia's fierc-est rival, ATI, who supplied them with a new chip called the Xenos, a Greek word whose meaning roughly translates to "uncertain

The **Official Xbox Magazine** had two preview issues prior to its first official issue. Shown here is the second preview issue for November 2001. From issue 1 to issue 52, the magazine came with a demo disc playable on the Xbox. Starting with issue 53, all demo discs were targeted exclusively to the Xbox 360. Like all of the official console magazines, the **Official Xbox Magazine** provided a key resource in helping to grow the Xbox's community.

Outlaw Golf.

Outlaw Golf (2002, Hypnotix)

While the sport of golf has seen plenty of videogame adaptations over the years, none have been quite like this zany, *Happy Gilmore*-like take on the genre. Forget about old white men in plaid plants and polo shirts. These golfers include strippers, failed rappers, and former inmates. Steve Carell of *The Office* fame is the game's hilarious announcer. While the theme, dialog, and crazy antics are certainly part of the game's appeal, the team did a great job with the gameplay, allowing up to four players and featuring a fully adjustable camera. Be sure to check out its sequels, *Outlaw Golf: 9 Holes of X-Mas* and *Outlaw Golf 2*, as well as *Outlaw Volleyball* and *Outlaw Tennis*.

relationship." By contrast, Sony didn't halt production of the PlayStation 2 until January of 2013. Fortunately for fans of the older games, the 360 is backward-compatible with many games for the original system, assuming your 360 is equipped with an official hard drive.

The fact remains that the Xbox is an intriguing chapter in the history of the videogame industry. In the late 1990s, the industry was completely dominated by Japan, and only a company with vision, highly skilled workers, and—most importantly—bottomless cash reserves, had a chance to alter the status quo. Microsoft was able to muscle its way in by sheer force, restoring to the West at least some of the control ceded to Japan after the Great Videogame Crash. They also made it much easier for Windows game developers to transition to the more lucrative console market, becoming a prominent source for key genres like first person shooters that were previously dominant on computers.

Technical Specifications

The original Xbox had a 32-bit CPU based on Intel's Pentium III Coppermine chip. This chip was capable of speeds up to 733 MHz. It had 64MB of main memory. Most games run at 640 × 480 resolution, which was fine for standard televisions. However, after HD displays became more common, some games began supporting 720p or even 1080i resolutions with the VGA and Xbox High Definition AV Pack cable options.[13] Its Nvidia-built GPU was a powerful beast in its day, with twice the memory bandwidth of the PS2 and better anti-aliasing.[14] Sound output was stereo, with up to 256 channels. The aforementioned AV Pack enabled Dolby Surround Sound, provided you had the sound system to take advantage of it. Famously, the Xbox was the first game console to feature an internal hard drive: an 8-gigabyte drive spinning at 5400 RPM. 8 MB memory cards were used to transfer data from system to system. The Ethernet support was integrated. Unlike the later 360, the four controller ports of the original Xbox were proprietary and would not function with standard USB-compatible devices without modding.

Psychonauts.

Psychonauts (2005, Majesco)

Tim Schafer's *Psychonauts* remains one of the developer's best-known and best-loved titles. Self-described as a "psychic odyssey though the minds of misfits, monsters, and madmen," *Psychonauts* is certainly one of the most bizarre, yet endearing games you'll find on the system. This 3D-platformer features great level design, unforgettable characters, and plenty of fun sequences and puzzles. If you like the originality found in *Psychonauts*, be sure to check out *Blinx: The Time Sweeper* (2002, Microsoft).

---

[13]   A list of 157 Xbox games with HD support can be found at Wikipedia, http://en.wikipedia.org/wiki/List_of_Xbox_games_with_HD_support. *Dragon's Lair 3D: Return to the Lair* (2002, Ubisoft) was the first console game capable of 1080i resolution.

[14]   Aliasing is a fairly technical concept, but it amounts to using color blending techniques to smooth out the jagged-looking lines of pixel-based computer graphics. To picture this, draw a diagonal on graph paper by coloring in the squares with dark black pencil. Now imagine filling in the squares around this line with a lighter gray. If you step back from the paper, the line will look smoother than before. If you'd like to learn more, see Jason Cross's detailed explanation at Extremetech, www.extremetech.com/computing/78546-antialiasing-and-anisotropic-filtering-explained.

The Xbox was often criticized for its bulk and weight, but it was actually quite comparable to the original PS2. It weighed in at 8.5 pounds, which was really only a little over a pound heavier than the original PS2. The Xbox's dimensions were 12.5 × 4 × 10.5 inches; the PS2's were 12 × 7 × 3 inches. The later PS2 "Slim" was 4.3 pounds and 10 × 5 × 1 inches in size.

The Accessories

The standard Xbox Controller was nicknamed "The Duke" or, less kindly, "Fatty." Although Microsoft insisted that it was "lighter than it looks," it weighed just under a pound. Its dimensions were 6.5 × 5 × 3 inches. It was also widely regarded as one of the worst controllers ever released. IGN ranks it as the second worst controller ever. Chris Harris, who compiled the list for IGN, wrote,

> I may be able to palm a bowling ball, but even I couldn't comfortably or effectively wrap my mitts around Microsoft's original monstrosity. The gargantuan thing was clearly made for the Rock Biter from *The Neverending Story.* What a shame the Nothing took him away.[15]

The controller was award-winning, however. Unfortunately, the award in question was a Guinness World Record for biggest controller ever.

While few were especially pleased with the controller, at least it was built with 3D-gaming firmly in mind. It offered two analog sticks, a D-pad, six pressure-sensitive buttons, and start/back buttons. The two trigger buttons on the sides were great for both left- and right-handed gamers. It also had two slots for accessories, which included a memory card or headset. It also had "rumble," which meant it could vibrate to provide more visceral feedback.

In 2002, Microsoft replaced the Duke with the Controller S, nicknamed "Akebono." Originally only released in Japan, this controller was 8.3 × 6.3 × 1.7 inches, and weighed in at 8 ounces— about half the weight of the original. Although nearly the same length and width as its predecessor, it was also thinner, a profile most gamers found more accommodating. There were, of course, plenty of third-party controllers. Logitech offered the best wireless controller, although some still complained of issues with latency (especially in competitive Xbox Live matches).

On the left is the original Xbox game controller, "The Duke." On the right is the Controller S or "Akebono" replacement. Below the two controllers is the remote control contained in the optional DVD Wireless Remote Control Kit.

Perhaps the most interesting Xbox controller is the one required to play Capcom's *Steel Battalion* (2002). This mech-style affair had two joysticks, dial, thumb pad, switches, forty buttons, and three foot pedals. Bundled with the game, it cost $200, and was easily the most ambitious third-party product released for the Xbox. It's since become a collector's item, even though only

---

15   See Craig Harris, "Top 10 Tuesday: Worst Game Controllers," *IGN*, February 21, 2006, www.ign.com/articles/2006/02/22/top-10-tuesday-worst-game-controllers.

one other game supported it, the online multi-player-only sequel, *Steel Battalion: Line of Contact* (2004).

Another popular accessory for the Xbox was the $30 DVD Wireless Remote Control Kit, which was basically a controller port dongle and remote control that enabled users to play movie discs on their Xbox. While obviously useful, many users complained about having to spend the extra money just to play

Steel Battalion cost $200, but it boasted one of the most impressive-looking controller setups ever available for this or any other platform. Shown is the second release of the controller with the blue, rather than green, buttons.

DVDs. After all, the PlayStation 2 didn't need an add-on for this purpose. Apparently, Microsoft didn't want to increase the cost of the Xbox by including built-in support for DVD playback, which would have required paying substantial fees to the DVD Format/Logo Licensing Corporation, a Japanese company. Instead, only people who bought the remote would shoulder this cost.

Finally, for gamers who wanted to compete without having to go online, there was the Xbox System Link Cable. Playing with this setup required two Xboxes as well as two copies of the game in question—provided it had support for this option. Multiple Xboxes could also connect over a LAN (local area network). In this way, up to 16 players could play games like *Halo: Combat Evolved* in four-way split-screen mode, using four Xboxes. This setup was quite common in college dormitories, especially where policies prohibited online gaming.

Star Wars: Knights of the Old Republic.

Star Wars: Knights of the Old Republic
(2003, BioWare Corporation)

BioWare rose to prominence with its *Baldur's Gate* series for Windows in the 1990s, which revitalized the *Dungeons & Dragons* license for videogames. This 2003 game, however, trades long swords for light sabers and blasters. It was custom-built for the Xbox, with gameplay eminently suited for playing with a controller. The game's polished graphics, story, characters, and "real-time with pause" combat were a big hit with Xbox fans, and many still consider it the greatest *Star Wars* game ever made. The best part is, you can role-play the character as a noble Jedi—or an evil Sith. If you love the polish found in this hybrid RPG, be sure to check out the equally excellent *Jade Empire*.

The Microsoft Xbox Community Then and Now

While there are obviously many different kinds of people who enjoyed many different kinds of play on the Xbox, the most visible were the competitive Xbox Live crowd. Games such as *Halo: Combat Evolved, Call of Duty, Counter-Strike*, and *Tom Clancy's Rainbow Six 3*—to name a few—provided endless hours of multiplayer action. When these players weren't gaming, they might be visiting one of the many online forums dedicated to the platform and its games, comparing strategies, notes, or setting up their own tournaments and challenges.

As with any popular console, videogame magazines, both multiplatform and dedicated to the platform, were a great source of information for the Xbox. Perhaps the greatest of these magazines was the *Official Xbox Magazine*, which started producing monthly issues just before the console's official launch. Each issue came with a demo disc playable on the Xbox, which lasted for 53 issues until coverage shifted primarily to the Xbox 360.

After the introduction of the 360 in November 2005, official support for the original Xbox dried up quickly. That said, there's still plenty of enthusiasm for modding and hacking the original Xbox. You can even buy a book by Andrew "Bunny" Huang called *Hacking the Xbox: An Introduction to Reverse Engineering*, which promises to teach you "how to enjoy a Microsoft Xbox game console without the mindless tedium of playing video games." It's certainly a must-read for anyone interested in this often subversive community of electronics hobbyists.

Homebrew for the original Xbox is plentiful, with over 500 games listed at *The ISO Zone* (www.theisozone.com). Many of these are ports of games from other systems, such as *Beats of Rage*, but there are also plenty of originals available. Many of these projects are compiled with unauthorized copies of the Microsoft System Development Kit for Xbox, which means they're technically illegal.

The **CoinOPS** MAME arcade emulator for modded Xbox consoles.

Collecting Microsoft Xbox Systems

Acquiring an original Xbox in good condition is cheap and easy from a variety of sources, including the usual auction sites. Of course, you'll need to fire it up to make sure it still works. It's relatively easy to replace broken hard drives, disc drives, and power boards, and if you're really feeling ambitious, even motherboards. Still, unless you get a broken Xbox for free or just enjoy tinkering, you're probably better off just buying another Xbox in working condition. In fact, if you'd like to use an Xbox as a multimedia center or emulation machine, even modded Xbox consoles are not that difficult to find or particularly expensive.

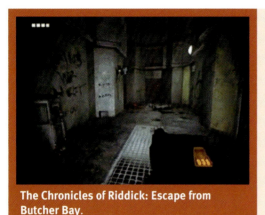

The Chronicles of Riddick: Escape from Butcher Bay.

The Chronicles of Riddick: Escape from Butcher Bay (2004, Vivendi Games)

Most games based on movie licenses are quickly made cash-ins that rely almost entirely on the appeal of the movie to sell copies. This game is a rare example of the reverse: a game that is better than the film it's based on. Voiced by Vin Diesel (who had a hand in development), this game allows you to switch between first-person and third-person mode, which allows for both stealth and intense combat sequences. Critics raved about the happy marriage of story and gameplay. When the only recurring complaint about a game is that it left gamers wanting more, you know the designers did a great job. No matter what you think of Vin Diesel, you'll find much to enjoy about this game.

Microsoft released several "special edition" Xbox consoles themed on certain games. The *Halo Special Edition Green Console* is translucent green and included a matching green controller. Then there's the lime green *Mountain Dew*-branded edition, which the soda-maker gave away in a sweepstakes. There are also many editions that weren't released in the United States, such as the *Panzer Dragoon Orta* edition only available in Japan. Surprisingly, even these rare special editions seldom sell for more than a few hundred dollars. There are also two editions, one for the launch team and another for partners, which feature a silk screened message from Bill Gates on the jewel (the circular logo on the top of the Xbox). The chances of encountering one of these in the wild are quite slim, since only 60 of each exist. If you do manage to find one, though, you're in luck—they can bring in $1500 or more at auction.

As the box copy proudly proclaimed, the **Halo Special Edition Green Console** included an "Exclusive Green Halo Console, Special Edition Green Controller, and a full version of Halo!"

Games for the original Xbox are also quite cheap and plentiful, with few rarities. Perhaps the most collectible games are *Steel Battalion*, mentioned above, and *Marvel vs. Capcom 2*, an extremely popular title that is nevertheless becoming hard to find. Expect to pay triple digits for an unopened copy. Another unexpectedly collectible game is *Barbie Horse Adventure: Wild Horse Rescue*, which has a reputation for being so unbelievably bad, you have to see it to believe it.

Tom Clancy's Splinter Cell: Chaos Theory.

Tom Clancy's Splinter Cell: Chaos Theory
(2005, Ubisoft)

Although the late Tom Clancy is best known for writing action-packed military-themed novels, among gamers his name conjures up this series of stealth games. The series launched in 2002 with *Tom Clancy's Splinter Cell*, which introduced Sam Fisher, an agent of the NSA's "Black Operation." Instead of blasting through levels with a grenade launcher, Fisher must rely more on brains than brawn, using all manner of cool gadgets—like a snaking camera to look under doors. The multiplayer mode was a huge hit on Xbox Live. *Chaos Theory* was the third Fisher game, and is less linear than the preceding titles, with more viable solutions for the problems Fisher encounters. While everyone raved about the graphics, it was really the highly flexible gameplay and ambience that sealed the deal. For another excellent Tom Clancy game series and game, be sure to check out *Rainbow Six 3*.

Emulating the Microsoft Xbox

At this point, it's much, much easier to buy either an original Xbox or hard drive-equipped Xbox 360 to play Xbox games. Although many people assume the Xbox is just a PC in disguise, it's actually only similar. The proprietary Nvidia hardware, in particular, is a problem, since the company has not released the technical specifications—information vital for anyone attempting to build an emulator. The audio system, BIOS, and video encoding systems are problematic as well. Furthermore, even if emulator developers had full access to the schematics, source code, and other secret documentation, you'd likely need an extremely powerful PC to run the games at a decent frame rate.

That said, there are two options currently available: *Xeon* and *Cxbx*. *Xeon* only runs *Halo: Combat Evolved,* but is still quite rough. *Cxbx* has a larger list of games that work with it, but its authors acknowledges that Direct3D, sound, and networking support are still lacking. *Turok Evolution* is the only fully playable retail game.

In short, emulating the Xbox is not a viable option, and probably won't become so until at least another generation or two. For now, get a used Xbox for full compatibility, or a backward-compatible Xbox 360 instead.[16]

The **Cxbx** emulator running the Xbox dashboard.

---

[16]   For the full list of Xbox games compatible with the Xbox 360, see http://support.xbox.com/en-US/games/xbox-games/play-original-games.

Nintendo GameCube (2001)

History

In the late 1990s, when Nintendo began development on the console that would become the GameCube, the once seemingly invincible company had proven vulnerable after all. As we saw in Chapter 3.3, its previous console, the Nintendo 64, was innovative in some ways and old-fashioned in others. It hadn't been a total failure, but it did allow Sony to rip into Nintendo's share of the console market and steal a great deal of its thunder. Even though Nintendo was still the undisputed king of handheld gaming (see Chapter 2.4), their mostly G-rated games library, which reassured so many parents and sold many Nintendo Entertainment Systems in the past, was a liability now that the majority of gamers were in their twenties or thirties. Nintendo needed a system that could right the perceived wrongs of the Nintendo 64, whose cartridge-based format, odd controller, and toy-like aesthetics had turned off many gamers and developers.

Nintendo needed a new console that would represent a clear alternative to what the likes of Sony and Microsoft brought to the public. They needed a console with innovative controls and games that would truly appeal to all ages. With such a platform, they could win back third-party developers and reclaim the throne, not only taking back what they'd lost, but expanding the videogames industry beyond what anyone had thought possible. Nintendo would build this system. But this chapter is not about the Wii, but its older brother: the GameCube.

The Nintendo GameCube was a great choice for gamers on a budget, with respectable technology and a selection of great original games. However, it lacked the strong appeal to casual gamers that would propel the Wii to super stardom.

The GameCube was not destined for greatness. Instead, it languished in third place, well behind Sony's PlayStation 2 (see Chapter 3.5) and Microsoft's Xbox (see Chapter 3.6). Indeed, were it not for their hugely successful line of mobile devices, Nintendo might well have joined Sega (see Chapter 3.4) in their transition away from console manufacturing to a purely software-driven business.

Animal Crossing on the **Dolphin** emulator.

Animal Crossing (2001, Nintendo)

Animal Crossing is among the most popular, endearing, and unusual games for the GameCube. Like Maxis' classic PC game *The Sims* or Zynga's *Farmville*, *Animal Crossing* has no obvious goals or objectives. Instead, players choose whether to perform various activities such as digging, chopping, writing letters, and fishing in an adorable village of anthropomorphic moles, owls, hedgehogs, and other creatures. One neat feature is that the game takes into consideration the actual time and date. Assuming you set the clock correctly, if it's dark outside, it'll also be dark in the game. Village life continues while you're away, too. Multiple players can interact with each other by leaving messages and borrowing tools, and connecting a GBA allows you to visit an island and play classic NES games. *Animal Crossing* was designed by Takashi Tezuka, a longtime friend and collaborator with Shigeru Miyamoto. It's hopelessly addictive and well worth picking up a GameCube just to play it.

When Nintendo's designers first began work on "Project Dolphin," the company was still driven by a vision of cheap, child-safe, game-playing toys than the general-purpose "media centers" of Sony and Microsoft. Genyo Takeda, director and general manager of Nintendo's research and development team, believed that making consoles was like making cars. Obviously, not all cars are built for street racing. Most people are happy with cheap, fuel-efficient vehicles that can get them from point A to point B. Much like Gunpei Yokoi's "lateral thinking with seasoned technology" approach (see Chapter 2.4), Takeda's approach prioritized serviceable rather than cutting-edge technology. Takeda also held fast to another principle: the various components of a console should work in harmony, with no single element rising above the other. This Taoist tenant put him at odds with the Silicon Valley engineers who developed the console's components. They wanted to show off, but Takeda demanded moderation. "It was most difficult to ask [them] to swallow their pride," he told reporters in 2000.[1]

Takeda might sound conservative here, but he was hardly a slouch when it came to innovation. It was Takeda who had proposed the battery backup in *The Legend of Zelda* cartridge for the original Nintendo Entertainment System, a critical breakthrough that allowed console gamers to painlessly save and restore their gaming sessions. Back in 1975, he'd designed the first Nintendo arcade game to include a video screen, *EVR Race*, a monstrous six-player gambling simulation for horse or auto racing based around an early video tape system. While certainly ambitious, the complicated and delicate machinery was easy to break and hard to maintain. No doubt this painful experience contributed to Takeda's later demand for simplicity and reliability.

As we saw in Chapter 3.3, the Nintendo 64 had been heavily criticized for its reliance on cartridges for data storage. Every other major platform had shifted to optical discs for storage, which had the combined benefits of being cheaper to make, yet holding exponentially more data. They were, however, slower and much easier to copy and distribute illegally. Nintendo had stubbornly maintained that these disadvantages outweighed the perks, but third-party developers

1   Yoshiko Hara, "Designers Bring Practical Touch to GameCube," *EE Times*, July 9, 2000, www.eetimes.com/document.asp?doc_id=1224761.

disagreed. The cartridges drove up development costs and severely limited the scope of their games.

Takeda realized that cartridges (at least on consoles) were a losing proposition, but his company wasn't quite ready to embrace a DVD format. To hedge their bets, Nintendo chose a proprietary miniDVD-based format that was incompatible with both audio CDs and movie DVDs. The proprietary format allowed them to avoid the licensing fees associated with regular DVDs, and the 8-centimeter discs were faster. They were,

however, limited to a mere 1.5 gigabytes (Xbox and PlayStation 2 discs could hold up to 8.5). Nintendo was greatly concerned (some might say paranoid) about piracy and bootlegging, and implemented a complex disc authentication and data encryption scheme that was thought unbreakable—at least until some persistent hackers found a way to exploit a security vulnerability in Sega's *Phantasy Star Online* game to bypass it in 2003.

Nintendo finally embraced optical discs for its GameCube, but hedged its bets with a proprietary miniDVD format. They were much smaller and faster than conventional DVDs, but could not hold as much data. On the right is a PlayStation 2 disc for comparison.

The GameCube's inability to play movies or audio CDs was hardly a selling point. Takeda was firm, however, insisting that he wanted "users to play games, not to watch movies or access non-game internet sites. Movies and internet are practically competitors to gaming."[2] Although Nintendo would finally add an internet browser to its Wii console in 2007, none of its consoles have supported movie or audio discs.

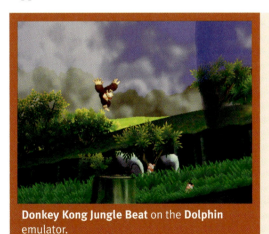

Donkey Kong Jungle Beat on the **Dolphin** emulator.

Donkey Kong Jungle Beat (2004, Nintendo)

If Maynard G. Krebs of *The Many Loves of Dobie Gillis* had ever designed his own videogame, it would surely have been something like *Donkey Kong Jungle Beat*. This quirky title lets you beat on a pair of bongos to guide the famous titular ape, making him run, jump, pound, leap, and do backflips to your beat. You can also clap your hands together to stun or knock out enemies. There's no story or other frills to worry about; this game is just pure, goofy fun. While most critics ticked off a few points for its brevity, everyone enjoyed its unique and addictive gameplay—and who could resist those cool looking bongos?

2　Yoshiko Hara, "Designers Bring Practical Touch to GameCube," *EE Times*, July 9, 2000, www.eetimes.com/document.asp?doc_id=1224761.

Another oft-made complaint about the Nintendo 64 was its lack of support for online gaming. The Xbox (see Chapter 3.6) would owe much of its success to its excellent Xbox Live service. Nintendo,

however, made baby steps. Instead of built-in support for dial-up or broadband internet, the GameCube required an optional add-on—and there was no unified marketplace or online interface, either. Instead, publishers would have to individually create their own interfaces and online experience. Connecting Game-Cube consoles together locally also required an add-on. As a result, very few GameCube games had support for either LAN or online play, particularly in comparison to the competition.

The Nintendo GameCube did not have built-in LAN or internet support. Instead, gamers had to pony up for a Modem Adapter or Broadband Adapter, shown here, which sat flush in Serial Port 1 on the underside of the console. Image courtesy of Ben Wood.

Nintendo hoped to leverage the massive support for its best-selling Game Boy Advance (GBA) handheld by allowing gamers to connect them to their GameCube. Doing so would allow the GBA to function as a second controller and display. It was put to good use in *The Legend of Zelda: Four Swords*, where it was used as a controller, and *Final Fantasy: Crystal Chronicles*, where it allowed for a unique multiplayer mode. Since so many GameCube owners also had handhelds, it was a great idea to marry the two. Nintendo would later use many of the ideas developed at this time in its Wii U console.

Takeda partnered with three different companies to manufacture the GameCube's components. The GPU, called "Flipper," was developed by ATI—and explains the codename "Dolphin" for the project. The main processor, "Gekko," was made by IBM, and could run at 485 mhz.

Matsushita Electric Industrial built the disc drives. Cleverly designed texture compression techniques allowed the GameCube to hold its own in terms of graphics power.

The Nintendo 64's unique controller was loved by some and despised by others, so Nintendo returned to the drawing board for the GameCube. Shigeru Miyamoto led the design team, and admitted later that he'd never had so much trouble designing one. It seems apparent that much of the struggle was

The GameCube's controller was more mainstream than the Nintendo 64's, but it's clear from the button and joystick arrangement that Miyamoto wasn't content to just copy Sony's DualShock. Also shown here is the GameCube sitting on top of the Game Boy Player.

over how much, or how little, the new design should borrow from existing models—particularly Sony's DualShock controller, which was widely admired by gamers and developers alike. The resulting "handlebar" design lacked the middle grip of the Nintendo 64's controller. Unlike the DualShock, whose analog sticks are placed side by side, the GameCube controller's joysticks are diagonal, with a D-pad in the lower left corner and four digital buttons on the top right. While a bit jarring when moving between systems, the GameCube's controller was often lauded for its comfort, if not its overall practicality.

Nintendo had felt the sting of rejection from third-party developers with the Nintendo 64. To better woo potential GameCube developers, Takeda and his team developed a memory technology that reduced latency, thereby eliminating the tedious, console-specific optimizing routines required to make games run at a decent frame rate. Nintendo also created a helpful software development kit, but was slow getting them out to Western companies. This, coupled with production delays of the console itself, gave Nintendo's competitors an advantage in securing and bolstering third-party developer support—a fact that Nintendo president Satoru Iwata attributes to the GameCube's ultimate demise.

The GameCube was first unveiled at Nintendo's Space World event. Several of the games shown that day were never completed, including an infamous Zelda game demo called *The Legend of Zelda 128*, which featured dark, gritty graphics. Many fans of the series saw this demo as evidence that Nintendo was at last ready to shed the franchise's childish image, but when *The Wind Waker* was at last revealed—with its cutesy, cel-shaded cartoon aesthetics—some fans felt

The Legend of Zelda 128 was one of the demos shown at Nintendo's Space World even in 2000. The realistic aesthetic thrilled gamers who were eager for a more mature take on the franchise. However, when **The Wind Waker** was actually released, its art style was even more cartoony and cutesy than its predecessors. Source: Wikipedia.

betrayed by a bait-and-switch. In any case, other games demonstrated that day were much less controversial, including the hits *Super Smash Bros. Melee*, *Metroid Prime*, and *Luigi's Mansion*.

The GameCube launched in Japan on September 14, 2001, followed by a North American launch two months later. To the shock and dismay of the Nintendo faithful, there was no Mario-title in the launch lineup, and the closest thing to it—*Luigi's Mansion*—was criticized for its short length. Early reviews of the system were lukewarm. Some of the criticism was focused on the paucity of launch titles, which consisted of only 15 games. Unlike the PlayStation 2, the GameCube was not backward-compatible with its predecessor. In short, if you didn't see anything you liked in the launch lineup, there was no reason to buy a GameCube. Precious time flew by as Nintendo struggled to get its own titles and those from third-party developers on the shelf, a situation eerily similar to what would become of the Wii's waning years and the Wii U's post launch years.

Eternal Darkness: Sanity's Requiem on the **Dolphin** emulator.

Eternal Darkness: Sanity's Requiem
(2002, Silicon Knights)

Games like *Eternal Darkness: Sanity's Requiem* show how far the company was willing to stray from the likes of Mario and Princess Peach. This mature-rated game is a masterpiece of psychological horror. Players must carefully monitor the characters' sanity as well as their mana and health. If the sanity meter drops too low, you'll be treated to in-game meddling, including a skewed camera and eerie sound effects such as whispers and distant cries. Designed by Silicon Knights (the team responsible for *Legacy of Kain*), *Eternal Darkness* boasts a massive scope, with 12 different characters and a story that spans several different time periods. The magic system is also well developed and sophisticated, even allowing you to create new spells by mixing up ingredients. Critics praised the graphics, atmosphere, story, and keen attention to detail. If you're still convinced that the GameCube is a children's toy, turn off the lights, put on headphones, and let *Eternal Darkness* set you straight.

Perhaps the greatest complaint about the system was its squeaky clean, "kiddie" image. The unit was colored purple and shaped like a giant block, an aesthetic that one acerbic reviewer likened to a Fisher-Price toy. Instead of wowing the gamers at E3 2003 with a gritty first-person shooter or sexy open-world crime game, Nintendo showed the assembled mob of 20–30+-year-olds a new take on *Pac-Man*. Needless to say, the GameCube had more gamers scratching their heads than reaching for their wallets. Many felt that Nintendo was simply oblivious, hopelessly stuck in a 1980s time warp.

Beth Llewelyn, senior director of corporate communication for Nintendo of America, squarely placed the blame for the Game-Cube's dismal sales on Nintendo's headquarters in Japan, who simply refused to listen to their urgent and persistent requests for more

Nintendo's American branch tried to extend the systems' appeal to adults with a series of unusual partnerships, including a marketing campaign with Heineken beer, shown here.

mature-themed games. "[We were] like the misfit child sent off to the strange land full of strange people," said Llewelyn. Nintendo of America tried to reach out to older gamers, including partnering with *Maxim* magazine and Heineken beer in a "Cube Club" marketing campaign, but gamers seemed more interested in the scantily clad models, free beer, and musicians on stage than the GameCube.

For their part, Nintendo's chairman, Hiroshi Yamauchi and Nintendo of Japan were nonplussed by the GameCube's poor reception. Kyle Mercury, the man in charge of much of the United States marketing for the console, claims that his increasingly desperate pleas for a rapid change in direction were ignored by his Japanese superiors:

> No one I talked to at Nintendo could understand why the company was struggling, why the whole brand was in danger of collapsing much like Sega before them. *"But we're Nintendo."* I can't even recall how many times I heard that as a catch-all excuse... No one could believe that Nintendo was capable of being unseated as Number 1.[3]

Yamauchi later acknowledged that "the culture of Japan is very different," and that it was becoming increasingly difficult to "develop software that appeals to everyone," which he felt was the "lifeline" of their business.[4]

Despite its shortcomings, the Nintendo 64 did boast two amazing games that truly spurred system sales: *Super Mario Bros. 64* and *The Legend of Zelda: Ocarina of Time*. Both were undisputed masterpieces that made significant contributions to videogames as a medium. By contrast, GameCube hits such as *Super Mario Sunshine*, *Animal Crossing*, and *Metroid Prime* just didn't

Final Fantasy: Crystal Chronicles.

Final Fantasy: Crystal Chronicles
(2003, Game Designers Studio)

Square, the developer behind the *Final Fantasy* series, stabbed Nintendo in the back during the Nintendo 64 era, snubbing the console in favor of Sony's PlayStation. *Crystal Chronicles* marked the franchise's return to the Nintendo fold after a decade-long hiatus, but it was a very different game than those that had come before. Gone were experience points and turn-based combat; *Crystal Chronicles* is an action role-playing game comparable to *Diablo*. Some versions of the game were bundled with the GBA link cable, which was used for the fun and innovative multiplayer mode. The GBA served as a controller and for personalized menu navigation. Almost every review of the game stresses the need to play this one with friends; solo play pales in comparison. While some critics considered the GBA Link feature a gimmick to sell more handhelds, there's no doubt that it does genuinely add to the gameplay and is essential to get the most out of the game. If you've ever had to kick back while a friend navigates on-screen menus, you'll see the value of each player having his own screen and interface to work with. While few fans of the series count this game as their favorite, it does show off the potential of the GBA/GameCube link and is a fun take on the genre.

3   Yoshiko Hara, "Designers Bring Practical Touch to GameCube," *EE Times*, July 9, 2000, www.eetimes.com/document.asp?doc_id=1224761.

4   Gamesindustry.biz, "Nintendo's Yamauchi Speaks," July 3, 2003, *The Register*, www.theregister.co.uk/2003/07/03/nintendos_yamauchi_speaks.

seem worth the admission price to many gamers outside the ranks of the faithful. By December of 2003, *Time* magazine had declared the GameCube an "unmitigated disaster," remarking that far from reclaiming its dominant position at the top of the industry, Nintendo was "struggling just to stay in the game."[5]

In September of 2003, Nintendo dropped the price of the GameCube by $99, but sales still lagged behind Sony and Microsoft. However, calling it an "unmitigated disaster" is a wild exaggeration. It ended up selling some 22 million units, which places it just shy of the Xbox's 24 million (although well behind the PlayStation 2's 155 million). The GameCube was certainly no NES or Super NES, but it still sold in respectable numbers and represented a viable alternative to Xbox and PlayStation 2. Fortunately, Nintendo's handhelds would continue to keep the company well in the black, and the Wii's release in 2006 would shatter records and rocket Nintendo back to the top of the videogames industry for another generation.

In the end, the GameCube proved a brief but interesting chapter in the history of one of the industry's largest and most influential companies. While Nintendo's approach with the Game-Cube may have been flawed, the runaway success of the Wii shows that they were smart to focus on games for the whole family rather than just the *Grand Theft Auto* and *Call of Duty* crowd. With the GameCube, Nintendo tried to play it safe, correcting many of the perceived flaws of the Nintendo 64 with a console more in line with the status quo. Ultimately, however, Nintendo would return to glory not by imitating its competition—but by daring to be different.

Technical Specifications

The GameCube was designed to do more with less, representing a cheaper alternative to the Xbox and PlayStation. Nevertheless, its hardware is actually quite capable and arguably superior to the PlayStation 2 in some regards.

According to Nintendo's webpage for the console, the case was intended to be "small, cute, and desirable." Apparently, someone at Nintendo was enamored with purple blocks. At 11.4 ×

Metroid Prime.

Metroid Prime (2002, Retro Studios)

Metroid is one of Nintendo's best-loved properties, so it was a shock to some that the company turned to a game developer out of Austin, Texas, to revamp the franchise for GameCube. When fans heard that it was going to be a first-person shooter, eyes were rolling faster than Samus' morph ball. However, the resulting game was a masterpiece, successfully updating the classic *Metroid* exploration and puzzle-solving formula with a great first-person shooter engine. It quickly became one of the GameCube's most popular and endearing titles, and led to a sequel in 2004. The third game, *Corruption*, was released on the Wii in 2007, followed by a collector's edition with all three games in 2009. For many fans, though, the first *Metroid Prime* is still the best.

---

5   Jim Frederick, "The Console Wars: Game On," *Time*, December 15, 2003.

15 × 16 centimeters, it wasn't a precise cube, but it was unquestionably more compact than the hulking Xbox. Its design was minimalist, with a top-loading disc drive and a front panel with four controller inputs and two slots for memory cards. There were three ports underneath the console, labeled Serial Port 1, Serial Port 2, and High Speed Port. Serial Port 1 supported the Modem Adapter or Broadband Adapter, and the High Speed Port supported the Game Boy Player, which allowed Game Boy, Game Boy Color, and Game Boy Advance cartridges to be played on a TV via the console. Serial Port 2 was never utilized.

Internally, the GameCube featured a miniDVD drive built by Matshushita. The discs were 8 centimeters in diameter and could hold up to 1.5 gigabytes. The drive transferred data between 16 and 25 megabits per second. Combined with the excellent texture compression routines, the GameCube was soon noted for significantly shorter loading times than the Xbox and PS2. Still, compared to the full-sized discs of the competition, the GameCube certainly put developers at a disadvantage when it came to storage space for cutscenes.

Pikmin.

Pikmin (2001, Nintendo)

Shigeru Miyamoto was the producer of this off-the-wall title, a hybrid with elements of adventure, puzzle, and real-time strategy games. The player controls Olimar, an alien who has crashed on a strange planet and must rely on the helpful "Pikmin" natives to help him recover the pieces to his spaceship. Much of the gameplay is focused on controlling these Pikmin and coordinating their abilities and attributes to solve puzzles. If you mess up, you can always breed more Pikmin, but it will take time—and the game enforces a strict 30-day time limit (each day in the game is around 15–20 minutes in real time). The game was lauded for its originality, memorable characters, gorgeous environments, and unique challenges. Perhaps more than any other GameCube title, it shows that the company took the "Nintendo Difference" seriously, offering an experience quite unlike any other found on a PlayStation 2 or Xbox. *Pikmin 2* was released for the GameCube in 2004, and *Pikmin 3* was released for the Wii U in 2013. Both sequels received similar critical acclaim.

The GameCube's "Flipper" GPU, designed by ATI Technologies, may not have been faster than lightning, but it did hold its own against its rivals. At a standard resolution of 480p (640 × 480 progressive scan) for many games, the GameCube's graphics are as good if not better than the Xbox and PS2, though the latter consoles can go up to 1080i (1920 × 1080 interlaced), despite few games supporting it. The Flipper ran at 162 MHz compared to the PS2's 147. IBM's "Gekko" PowerPC processor ran at 485 MHz, which was slower than the Xbox but a good deal faster than the PS2 (733 and 294.9 MHz respectively). Likewise, the GameCube had 40 megabytes of memory, again placing it between the Xbox at 64 and the PS2 at 32.[6]

---

[6]   For a handy matrix showing these figures and more for easy comparison, see http://wars.locopuyo.com/cwsystemspecsold.php.

The Accessories

The GameCube's default controller featured a handlebar design, with staggered analog sticks,

d-pad, built-in rumble motor, six digital buttons, and two pressure-sensitive triggers on the left and right (pressing these all the way down resulting in an audible click and a digital signal). The A, or main button, was oversized and placed in the middle of the other buttons. Later, Nintendo released the rumble-less Wavebird, a wireless version—particularly useful given the default controller's relatively short cord. Compared to the Nintendo 64's controller, these models were safe bets, even if they lacked the sort of exciting, radical innovations that would play such a huge role in the Wii's success.

The Wavebird was a wireless GameCube controller. To extend its battery life, Nintendo omitted the rumble feedback feature of the wired version. Image courtesy of Evan-Amos, Vanamo Media.

One of the best GameCube accessories is actually the Game Boy Advance, which can be attached via a special cable. Developers who chose to integrate support for the GBA could do so in a number of ways, including using it as a secondary display—quite useful for multiplayer

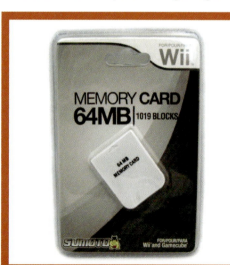

games. Probably the best such games are *The Legend of Zelda: Four Swords Adventures*, *The Legend of Zelda: The Wind Waker*, and *Final Fantasy Crystal Chronicles.* The setup is also useful for *Pokémon* games, which use the link to transfer creatures between games and fight with them using the GBA.[7]

Another extremely handy accessory was a memory card, used for saving games and transferring data between systems. Nintendo officially released memory cards with 59, 251, and 1019 save blocks (512 KB, 2 MB, and 8 MB, respectively), and larger ones were made by third parties. A few older games had compatibility issues with the larger cards.

While Nintendo's official memory cards went up 8 MB, third-party cards often went as high as 64 MB, like the one pictured here, or even 256 MB.

---

7   A large list of GameCube games that use the GBA link is available at Wikipedia, http://en.wikipedia.org/wiki/Nintendo_Game-Cube%E2%80%93Game_Boy_Advance_link_cable.

Another intriguing add-on was the Mobile Monitor, a 5.4-inch LCD screen with built-in speakers and a car adapter that also powered the GameCube. The unit was attached to the top of the GameCube and could be folded down when not in use. While not as portable as a GBA, a GameCube equipped with this Mobile Monitor (or equivalent) was a great solution for frequent travelers.

By far the most unusual GameCube accessory is the DK Bongos. Patterned after the barrels in the classic *Donkey Kong* arcade game, the bongos sported rubber drumskins and an internal microphone for detecting handclaps. The drums are used in *Donkey Kong Jungle Beat* and the *Donkey Konga* games.

These Maynard G. Krebs-approved DK Bongos are an attractive accessory for one of the system's most innovative games, **Donkey Kong Jungle Beat**.

Star Fox: Assault.

Star Fox: Assault
(2005, Namco/Nintendo)

The Super NES introduced us to *Star Fox*, a brilliant 3D space-shooter that was a showpiece of the console's graphical effects technology. For its GameCube line, Nintendo commissioned *Star Fox Adventures* from the UK-based Rare studio. *Star Fox Adventures* was an action-adventure inspired by the later *Zelda* games, and while most critics praised it, some felt it wasn't really a *Star Fox* game— and, indeed, it had begun life as an original property only to have the *Star Fox* license grafted on at the last hour. For *Assault*, Nintendo brought in Namco, who attempted to blend the earlier games' aerial combat with the latter's grounded action. Critics blasted the bland storyline and rigid on-rails structure, but most were at least initially intrigued by the ability to switch between the Arwing for flight and the Landmaster tank for ground missions. It's definitely not the best *Star Fox* game, but worth a look if for no other reason than to witness the boldness of the design team.

The Nintendo GameCube Community Then and Now

Nintendo tried a variety of tactics to build fan communities around its GameCube, including "Cube Clubs" established in major cities. As the name implies, the idea was to try to associate the GameCube platform with the dance club scene, complete with alcoholic beverages and sexy clothing. Unfortunately, for most of the gaming public, the GameCube was perceived as the system for gamers who were either too young or too poor for Sony and Microsoft's offerings. In short, most GameCube fans were stereotyped as children who spent their time playing adorably cute games such as *Animal Crossing*, *Super Mario Sunshine*, and the various *Pokémon* titles.

Of course, Nintendo still enjoyed a large number of dedicated older fans, many of whom had grown up playing its first-party franchises and were more than eager to see the latest incarnation of their beloved Mario and Zelda titles. These "platform faithful" were quick to point out the system's selling points on online forums, even if few Xbox and PS2 fans were listening.

The arrival of the Wii quickly overshadowed the GameCube, and since the early versions of the new console were backward-compatible, there seemed little reason to most fans to cling to the older unit. Still, it's not hard to find online message boards dedicated to the GameCube and nostalgia for the more straightforward console versus its more exotic successor will likely continue to grow over time.

There is a growing community of GameCube homebrew developers forming, though getting these programs will likely mean modding your console. This procedure can quickly get technical, but for those interested, detailed guides and videos are easily found online. Once your system is ready for homebrew, you can play a selection of original games as well as emulate other systems—including everything form the Atari 2600 all the way up to the Nintendo 64. What nerd could resist a hacked GameCube running a Sega Genesis or PlayStation emulator?

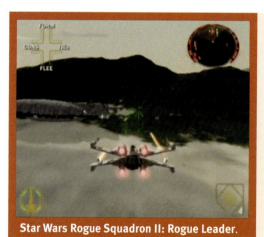

Star Wars Rogue Squadron II: Rogue Leader.

Star Wars Rogue Squadron II: Rogue Leader
(2001, Factor 5)

There have been many games based on the *Star Wars* license over the years, but arguably this one is the first that managed to perfectly capture the unique essence of the original films. The design team expertly applied the GameCube's graphics technology, depicting the space battles and imaginative alien planets of George Lucas' universe in convincing detail. Players take on the role of either Luke Skywalker or Wedge Antilles, and fight their way through glorious space battles in X-Wings, B-Wings, Y-Wings, and even Snowspeeders. If you've ever dreamed of flying through the trenches of the Death Star, this game will bring you there. Indeed, the only real complaint anyone had about this marvel was its relative brevity—always a good sign when you're looking for a fun and compelling experience.

Collecting Nintendo GameCube Systems

As with any Nintendo system, GameCube collectors have many unique and exclusive games and other items to search for. As an additional perk, the small size of the console and game discs makes them easy to store.

GameCubes are also available in a variety of colors. The purple or "Indigo" model is probably the most famous, but there are also black, silver, and even an orange model available. If you're a beer fan, you might try seeking out a limited-edition Heineken-branded model, but good luck— only 50 are rumored to exist. There were more limited edition models produced exclusively for the Japanese market, such as *Final Fantasy Crystal Chronicles* and *Mobile Suit Gundam* limited editions.

Probably the most useful version of the GameCube is the Panasonic Q, which is the only model that can play DVDs. Low sales scuttled production soon after its Japanese-only release in December of 2001. You probably won't find one of these in the wild, so be prepared to spend $300 or more acquiring one on an online auction site. As with other Japanese GameCube systems, the Q can only play region-specific games.

Super Monkey Ball.

Super Monkey Ball (2001, Sega)

This superb action-puzzle game is another definitive GameCube title that's about as far from the mainstream as you can get. Originally an arcade game, *Super Monkey Ball* lets players control a monkey encased in a transparent ball, which rolls about hair-raising courses comparable to Atari's 1984 arcade classic *Marble Madness*. However, instead of controlling the ball itself, players control the tilt of the board. The simple, tight, and intuitive controls, combined with the imaginative and well-designed courses, show off the skill and creativity of its design team. It was widely praised and is certainly a must-have title for any GameCube fan for its clever mini-games alone. Its 2002 sequel added a story-line and even more mini-games.

If you're new to collecting videogame systems, the GameCube would be a great place to start. Systems, games, and accessories are still more likely found in bargain bins than behind glass. Furthermore, there is still a healthy supply of third-party accessories and replacement parts available if you intend to actively play games on the system.

The Legend of Zelda: The Wind Waker.

The Legend of Zelda: The Wind Waker
(2003, Nintendo)

Nintendo fans look forward to the latest incarnation of their beloved *Zelda* franchise with the same passion and fervor of… well, nobody else compares, really. However, *The Wind Waker* arrived amidst some unusual controversy, brought about mostly by a misleading technical demonstration at a major industry event described earlier in this chapter. That demo had shown a realistic aesthetic, but *The Wind Waker* was something entirely different—a cartoon-like style that seemed to reinforce everything the cynics were saying about Nintendo's myopic focus on its youngest fans. Fans of the original games had grown up, so why was Nintendo still treating them like kids? Fortunately, gamers willing to put their inhibitions aside found much to enjoy about the new title. It was immaculately polished, and left intact or improved upon many of the gameplay elements that had made *Ocarina of Time* such a hit on the Nintendo 64. Many fans of the system consider it the best game ever made for the GameCube. It's no wonder that Nintendo made few changes when updating the game for the Wii U in 2013 as *The Legend of Zelda: The Wind Waker HD*.

Emulating the Nintendo GameCube

Unlike the PlayStation 2 and Xbox, there are several viable options for emulating the GameCube on modern PCs. The best known of these is *Dolphin*, which also (and less ethically) emulates the Wii. Available for Windows, Macintosh, and Linux, *Dolphin* requires a powerful computer for optimum performance. There are other programs such as *Dolwin*, *WhineCube*, and *GCEmu* available, but *Dolphin* is the most accurate and full-featured. If you want to use a real GameCube controller, you'll need a PC controller adapter, which can be found online.

The original Wii model is backward-compatible with GameCube games and controllers, but not the newer ones such as the Wii Family, Wii Mini, or the new generation Wii U console. For maximum compatibility, the most practical solution is still to simply pick up a secondhand GameCube.

Emulation for the GameCube is surprisingly robust thanks to the **Dolphin** emulator. Shown here is the emulator running **Luigi's Mansion**.

Index

St. Louis Community College
at Meramec
LIBRARY